Luke–Acts contains two short formal prefaces unlike anything else in the New Testament, and this is a study of the literary background of these prefaces. After surveying the different types of preface in ancient Greek literature, Dr Alexander concludes that the closest parallels to Luke's are to be found in Greek scientific and technical manuals of the hellenistic and Roman periods. This has important consequences for our understanding of the literary genre of Luke's Gospel and Acts, and casts new light on the social context of the author and the book's first readers.

SOCIETY FOR NEW TESTAMENT STUDIES

MONOGRAPH SERIES

General Editor: Margaret E. Thrall

78

THE PREFACE TO LUKE'S GOSPEL

The preface to Luke's Gospel

Literary convention and social context in
Luke 1.1–4 and Acts 1.1

LOVEDAY ALEXANDER

Department of Biblical Studies,
University of Sheffield

CAMBRIDGE
UNIVERSITY PRESS

Published by the Press Syndicate of the University of Cambridge
The Pitt Building, Trumpington Street, Cambridge CB2 1RP
40 West 20th Street, New York, NY 10011–4211, USA
10 Stamford Road, Oakleigh, Melbourne 3166, Australia

First published 1993

Printed in Great Britain at the University Press, Cambridge

A catalogue record for this book is available from the British Library

Library of Congress cataloguing in publication data

Alexander, Loveday.
  The preface to Luke's Gospel: literary convention and social
context in Luke 1.1–4 and Acts 1.1/Loveday Alexander.
      p.   cm. – (Society for New Testament Studies Monograph Series;
78)
  Revision of the author's thesis (Ph.D.) – University of Oxford,
1978.
  Includes bibliographical references and index.
  ISBN 0 521 43444 0 (hardback).
  1. Bible. N. T. Luke I, 1–4 – Criticism, interpretation, etc.
2. Bible. N. T. Acts I, 1 – Criticism, interpretation, etc.
I. Title. II. Series: Monograph Series (Society for New Testament Studies);
78.
BS2589.A44 1993
226.4′066–dc20   92–19062 CIP

ISBN 0 521 43444 0 hardback

CE

The refinement of our historical sense chiefly means that we keep it properly complicated. History, like science and art, involves abstraction: we abstract certain events from others and we make this particular abstraction with an end in view, we make it to serve some purpose of our will. Try as we may, we cannot, as we write history, escape our purposiveness. Nor, indeed, should we try to escape, for purpose and meaning are the same thing. But in pursuing our purpose, in making our abstractions, we must be aware of what we are doing; we ought to have it fully in mind that our abstraction is not perfectly equivalent to the infinite complication of events from which we have abstracted. I should like to suggest a few ways in which those of us who are literary scholars can give our notion of history an appropriate complication.

Lionel Trilling, *The Sense of the Past* (1970), p. 194

CONTENTS

ACKNOWLEDGEMENTS

This book originated in a thesis which was awarded the degree of Doctor of Philosophy in the University of Oxford in February 1978 (Alexander, 1978); a brief summary of its findings appeared in *Novum Testamentum* in 1986. The reasons for the delay in publishing the thesis were partly practical, partly personal: practical, in that the original thesis relied on the presentation of a substantial proportion of the evidence in the original Greek, which raised problems for publication; and personal, in that I was pre-occupied with personal and family concerns for a number of years after the thesis was finished. Revision has been proceeding at intervals during most of the intervening years; adepts of redaction criticism will no doubt be able to spot some of the redactional seams, but I trust that the finished text nevertheless has its own coherence. The chief difficulty in this prolonged gestation lies in the area of bibliography. The study of the social world of the New Testament, and particularly of Luke–Acts, has developed out of all recognition since I began my research in 1971; the production of a thesis naturally entails a complete bibliographical search in its preliminary stages, but I have made no attempt at a corresponding completeness during the later process of revision.[1] Nevertheless the encouragement of colleagues in the field, and my own reading, have satisfied me that there is a gap in Lucan studies which this monograph may hope to fill: seventy years after Cadbury, there is still no substantial study of the literary conventions employed in the Lucan preface and their social significance. This is the area I have attempted to explore in this book.

---

[1] One recent publication should, however, be mentioned here. Stanley Porter's *The Language of the New Testament: Classic Essays* (*JSNT* Supplement Series 60; Sheffield Academic Press, Sheffield, 1991) includes, alongside a number of important essays, a new translation of a section of Rydbeck's *Fachprosa* (Rydbeck, 1967), previously unavailable in English.

I shall argue in the study which follows that the fact that a statement is conventional does not necessarily entail that it is untrue. Whether those arguments are accepted or not, my readers are asked to take it on trust here that my prefatorial thanks, however conventional, are sincerely meant. Professor Dennis Nineham, as supervisor and mentor, has been unfailingly patient and encouraging, as were my two examiners, Professor G. B. Caird and Dr. Oswyn Murray. Friends and colleagues in Oxford, Manchester and Sheffield (and elsewhere) have listened, argued, threatened and cajoled over the years on the many occasions when it seemed that the work would never see the light of day: I am grateful to them all and especially, for patience above and beyond the call of duty, to Professor Graham Stanton. Philip, Anne and Thomas Alexander have put up with the pains of revision with remarkable forbearance and will be as pleased as I am to see 'Theophilus' finally brought to birth. My thanks are due to Dr Margaret Thrall and to all the staff at Cambridge University Press who have helped me reduce a complicated manuscript to some sort of order. But my dedication (following English rather than Greek convention) symbolically discharges a debt of even longer standing. This book is dedicated to those who first encouraged my fascination with the classical world – to my parents, Anne and Jack Earl, and to the memory of Eric Cumbers, classics master extraordinary at the Herbert Strutt School, Belper.

ABBREVIATIONS

References to scientific prefaces follow the forms set out in Appendix B. Other references to classical authors use the abbreviations found in LSJ. Papyri are listed according to the standard forms as given in E. G. Turner, 1968, pp. 157–71.

ABD   *The Anchor Bible Dictionary* (Doubleday, New York, 1992)

ANRW   *Aufstieg und Niedergang der römischen Welt*, eds. H. Temporini and W. Haase (de Gruyter, Berlin, 1972–92)

BAG   *A Greek–English Lexicon of the New Testament and Other Early Christian Literature*, 4th edn, translated and adapted W. F. Arndt and F. W. Gingrich (University of Chicago Press and Cambridge University Press, 1957)

BC   *The Beginnings of Christianity*, Part I, vols. I–V, eds. F. J. Foakes-Jackson and Kirsopp Lake (Macmillan, London, 1920–33)

BDF   *A Greek Grammar of the New Testament*, F. Blass and A. Debrunner, translated and revised R. W. Funk (University of Chicago Press and Cambridge University Press, 1961)

CBQ   *Catholic Biblical Quarterly*

CIL   *Corpus Inscriptionum Latinarum*

CMG   *Corpus Medicorum Graecorum* (Deutsche Akademie der Wissenschaften zu Berlin)

CPJ   *Corpus Papyrorum Judaicarum*, 3 vols., eds. V. A. Tcherikover, A. Fuks and M. Stern (Cambridge, Mass., 1957–64)

CQ   *Classical Quarterly*

DK   *Die Fragmente der Vorsokratiker*, ed. H. Diels, 9th edn W. Kranz, 3 vols. (Weidmann, Berlin, 1959)

FGH	*Die Fragmente der griechischen Historiker*, ed. F. Jacoby, 3 vols. (Brill, Leiden & Weidmann, Berlin, 1923–58)
GCS	*Die griechischer Christlicher Schriftsteller der ersten drei Jahrhunderte* (Preussischen Akademie der Wissenschaften, Kirchenväter-commission)
GGA	*Göttingische gelehrte Anzeigen* (Göttingen, Akademie der Wissenschaften)
GGM	*Geographi Graeci Minores*, ed. C. W. L. Müller (Didot, Paris, 1855–61)
GRBS	*Greek, Roman & Byzantine Studies*
HTR	*Harvard Theological Review*
JBL	*Journal of Biblical Literature*
JSNT	*Journal for the Study of the New Testament*
JTS	*Journal of Theological Studies*
KP	*Der Kleine Pauly*, eds. K. Ziegler and W. Sontheimer, 5 vols. (Druckenmüller Verlag, Stuttgart, 1964)
LCL	Loeb Classical Library
LSJ	*A Greek–English Lexicon*, H. G. Liddell and R. Scott, 9th edn revised H. S. Jones (Clarendon Press, Oxford, 1940)
MM	*The Vocabulary of the Greek Testament Illustrated from the Papyri and other Non-literary Sources*, eds. J. H. Moulton and G. Milligan (Hodder & Stoughton, London, 1914–29)
NTS	*New Testament Studies*
OCD^2	*The Oxford Classical Dictionary*, 2nd edn, eds. N. G. L. Hammond and H. H. Scullard (Clarendon Press, Oxford, 1970)
PG	*Patrologia Graeca*, ed. J. P. Migne
PGM	*Papyri Graecae Magicae*, ed. K. Preisendanz and others, 2 vols. (Teubner, Stuttgart, 1973–4); English version ed. H.-D. Betz, *The Greek Magical Papyri in Translation*, vol. I (University of Chicago Press, Chicago and London, 1986)
PIR^2	*Prosopographia Imperii Romani saec. I. II. III.*, eds. E. Groag, A. Stein, L. Petersen, 2nd edn
PLRE	*Prospography of the Later Roman Empire*, eds. A. H. M. Jones, J. R. Martindale, J. Morris, 2 vols. (Cambridge, 1971–80)

RE	Pauly–Wissowa–Kroll, *Realenzyklopädie*
SBLDS	Society of Biblical Literature, Dissertation Series
SBLMS	Society of Biblical Literature, Monograph Series
SBLSBS	Society of Biblical Literature, Sources for Biblical Study
SNTSMS	Society for New Testament Studies, Monograph Series
TWNT	*Theologisches Wörterbuch zum Neuen Testament*, ed. G. Kittel and others (Kohlhammer, Stuttgart, 1933–72)
ZNTW	*Zeitschrift für die neutestamentliche Wissenschaft*
ZWTh	*Zeitschrift für wissenschaftliche Theologie*

1

THE LUCAN PREFACE: QUESTIONS AND ASSUMPTIONS

One of the things that make research exciting – or dispiriting, depending on mood and temperament – is the way the questions keep changing. In particular, for a researcher with any sensitivity to the ancient world, the questions we pose as twentieth-century readers often seem to be the wrong tools for understanding first-century texts. Thus research becomes, as those engaged in it know only too well, not so much a quest for answers as a constant struggle to redefine the questions.

The thesis on which this book is based (Alexander, 1978) began with what appeared to be a question about literary genre. It took its starting-point from within a debate which has been going on since the beginning of the century: in what sense (if at all) is it proper to talk of the evangelists as 'historians'? To many New Testament critics, this is really a theological question (Haenchen, 1971, pp. 94–103); but to a student coming to the New Testament from the classical world, it seemed a question worth reframing in terms of ancient literary genre, i.e. by setting up a comparison between the Gospel writers and the historians of the Greco-Roman world. Granted that ancient expectations of history-writing may have been rather different from our own, it seemed natural to ask how the evangelists and their contemporaries would have seen their work. Did the Gospels look like histories of the same kind as those of Thucydides or Polybius, Josephus or Livy? If so, this might tell us what expectations the similarity would arouse in their readers. And if not, the differences might tell us something important about the nature of the Gospel account of Jesus.

Thus the question with which we started out became more narrowly defined: is it proper to describe the Gospels as 'histories' in terms of *ancient* literary genre? For Luke's Gospel at least, and by implication for Acts,[1] the question seems to have a clear answer. Here at least, critical orthodoxy maintains, is a New Testament writer who composes his work with an eye to the standards of contemporary literature; by his carefully chosen words, and even more by his deliberate choice of a formal preface-style, Luke[2] – or so it is claimed – announces unequivocally that his aim is to write up the story of Jesus and his followers in a manner worthy of the great tradition of classical historiography. The widespread assumption that we may justifiably set Luke's work alongside those of the great classical historians (Meyer, 1921; Toynbee, 1924; van Unnik, 1955; Barrett, 1961) is based to a surprisingly large degree on messages read off the preface, both direct and indirect. At the surface level, the vocabulary of the preface seems to speak the language of critical historiography: accuracy, research, investigation. Alone among the evangelists, Luke alludes to 'sources' and 'predecessors', those invisible entities so dear to the heart of the nineteenth-century critic. Despite its long-recognized linguistic ambiguities,[3] the preface has been widely accepted as an indication that Luke's ideals at least approximated to those of ancient and modern historians alike.[4]

The almost complete critical consensus on this point is bolstered by the observation, made by a number of critics around the beginning of the twentieth century, that the style and construction of the preface, as well as its vocabulary, are reminiscent of prefaces found among the ancient historians. On this view, not only is Luke making an explicit claim to high standards of historical accuracy, but the

---

[1] I have worked throughout with the critical assumption that Luke's two works should be regarded as two parts of a single whole – although, as we shall find in due course, the preface itself suggests some reasons to doubt that assumption: cf. also Conzelmann, 1987, p. 4; Haenchen, 1971, p. 136 n. 3.

[2] I use the name 'Luke' throughout to refer to the author of *The Gospel according to Luke* and *The Acts of the Apostles*, without implying necessarily any identification with the 'beloved physician' of Colossians 4.14. I have, however, made the assumption that the author of the two works is more likely to have been male than female, and have used the masculine pronoun throughout. If this assumption is wrong, I beg her pardon.

[3] As early as 1863, Aberle could say that the only sure conclusion from research on the preface up to his time (already a considerable body) was 'die Mehrdeutigkeit aller entscheidener Wörte und Wendungen in denselben' (F. Aberle, 'Exegetische Studien 2: Über den Prolog des Lucasevangeliums', *Theologische Quartalschrift*, 45 (1863), p. 99.) For a bibliography and summary of research up to 1870 see W. Grimm, 'Das Proömium des Lucas-evangeliums', *Jahrbücher für deutsche Theologie*, 16 (1871), pp. 33–78; up to 1922, Cadbury, 1922a, p. 489 n. 2.

[4] See W. M. Ramsay, *Was Christ Born at Bethlehem? A Study on the Credibility of St. Luke* (Hodder & Stoughton, London, 1898), pp. 10–19 for a good expression of this viewpoint.

preface-convention itself makes an implicit claim to informed contemporary readers that the work which follows is 'history'.[5] This
widely held view reached its definitive expression in 1922, with the
publication of Cadbury's detailed exegesis of the preface as an
appendix to Jackson-Lake's *Beginnings of Christianity*, vol. II
(pp. 489–510). This major study, to which all subsequent commentators have referred, has never been seriously challenged; it remains
the cornerstone of twentieth-century interpretation of the preface,[6]
and formed the starting-point for my own investigation in 1971.

As the investigation progressed, however, it soon became clear
that even within the terms of the genre question, a range of radically
different issues was being addressed. For many scholars, to describe
Luke as a 'historian' is to say something about the reliability of his
work: a statement about literary genre is essentially taken as a
statement about historicity.[7] Thus if, for example, Luke altered
Mark's account of an incident in the life of Jesus, this must be
because he had superior information from his own researches or
from another source. Against this others have emphasized the

---

[5] E.g. Plummer, 1922, p. 1; Dibelius, 1956, pp. 123–37; van Unnik, 1955; Trocmé,
1957, pp. 41, 78; Klein, 1964; p. 193; Conzelmann, 1966, p. 218; 1987, p. 4; Plümacher, 1972. Most recently, Aune, 1987, has a chapter entitled 'Luke–Acts and
Ancient Historiography' (pp. 120–210), and says of the preface: 'Conforming to the
conventions of Hellenistic historiography, Luke begins his work with a primary
preface describing the entire work (Luke 1: 1–4), and he prefixes a secondary preface
to Acts ... Historical prefaces allowed an author to display his rhetorical skill, and
this carefully crafted sentence does that for Luke. In fact, the phrase, 'the *events*
completed among us' ... indicates a *historical* rather than biographical focus ...
Prefaces had long been conventional features of Greco-Roman historiography with a
distinctive constellation of traditional *topoi* or motifs ... The *topoi* which Luke uses
include the dedication ...'

[6] Cadbury's exegesis in this Appendix was scrupulously uncommitted; his own
views on the positive interpretation of the preface are more clearly expressed in a
series of articles (1921; 1922b; 1956), and his views on Luke as historian in 1922a,
p. 15; 1927. The other major study of the literary affinities of the preface dates from
around the same period: Klostermann, 1929. Bibliography on the preface up to 1962:
Rengstorf, 1962, p. 12; to 1971, A. Vögtle, *Das Evangelium und die Evangelien:
Beiträge zun Evangelienforschung* (Patmos, Düsseldorf, 1971), pp. 31–42. For later
research, see J. A. Fitzmyer, *The Gospel According to Luke I–XI* (Anchor Bible
Commentary, Doubleday, New York, 1981) pp. 287–302; R. J. Dillon, 'Previewing
Luke's project from his prologue (Luke 1: 1–4)', *CBQ*, 43 (1981), pp. 205–27; V. K.
Robbins, 'Prefaces in Greco–Roman biography and Luke–Acts', in *Perspectives in
Religious Studies*, 6; SBL Seminar papers II, ed. P. J. Achtemeier (Scholars Press,
Missoula, 1979) p. 193–207; J. Wijingaards, 'Saint Luke's prologue in the light of
modern research I & II', *Clergy Monthly* 31 (1967) pp. 172–9, 251–8.

[7] E.g. W. M. Ramsay, *St Paul the Traveller and the Roman Citizen* (Hodder &
Stoughton, London, 1895), pp. 1–10. Similarly Barrett (1961, p. 9) and Marshall
(1970, p. 21) both focus on the ability to distinguish fact from fiction.

literary preoccupations of Greek historiography. As far back as 1918, Karl Ludwig Schmidt (1918, p. 280) had pointed out that if Luke was writing 'history' on the Greek model we should be careful not to attach too much significance to his alterations of Mark, since his motive was likely to be purely stylistic; Cadbury (1927, chs. 12 and 13) pursued this insight into the essentially rhetorical nature of Greek historiography with an extended study of the attitudes to source material in Josephus and other Greek historians. Thus the assimilation of Luke's work to that of the major Greek and Roman historians could be a double-edged tool with regard to historicity. The problem is particularly acute in the reporting of speeches, which ancient historians regarded not so much as 'data' to be transmitted accurately (even where there was an exact record of the original), but as occasions for displaying their own rhetorical skills.[8] Even the otherwise admirable Thucydides allowed himself quite a wide degree of latitude in the reporting of speeches made by his characters (I 22.1): and since Christian readers tend to attach particular importance to the recording of the *ipsissima verba* of Jesus and the apostles, the application of 'Thucydidean' standards to the dominical and apostolic speeches could have a devastating effect on Luke's reputation for accuracy in this central area of his work (Dibelius, 1956, pp. 70–3; 122–37; 138–85; Conzelmann, 1966, p. 218).

Moreover it had to be recognized that the very impressiveness of Thucydides' methodological claims poses problems for the student of historiographical convention. We cannot be certain whether Thucydides actually did achieve the accuracy and objectivity he claims, but it is clear that his preface itself created an atmosphere in which the making of such claims came to be expected in a historical preface: in other words, the claims themselves became 'conventional'. Thus the recognition that many later historians made similar claims has led, paradoxically, to the easy dismissal of just those elements in Luke's preface which had seemed most impressive to an earlier generation: 'convention' has become 'mere convention',[9] at worst a way of casting doubt on the claim to eyewitness testimony or

[8] Compare e.g. Tacitus' version of a speech by Claudius (*Ann* XI 24) with the official version which survives on an inscription (*CIL* XIII 1668): Tacitus would have had no difficulty in finding an accurate record of this speech. Further, Cadbury, 1927, ch. 12. In fact, as Cadbury demonstrates, Luke's practice with regard to the words of Jesus is precisely the opposite of the attitude of classical historiography (1927, p. 188).

[9] 'Mere convention': cf. Cadbury, 1922a, pp. 489, 490; 1921, p. 439 n. 12; Dibelius, 1966, p. 11; Kümmel, 1966, p. 91; Aune, 1987, p. 121.

the existence of 'many' predecessors,[10] at best little more than a way of exonerating Luke from the charge of outright deception. Either way, the idea that the preface is 'conventional' appears to imply a damaging recognition that its pretensions do not match the reality of Luke's literary achievement.[11] Thus, far from answering the question of Luke's value as an historian, the parallel with Greco-Roman historiography suggested by Luke's preface actually raised another set of questions, which could only be answered by means of detailed investigation into the actual practice of the historians.[12]

Meanwhile, however, other commentators had been drawing a different set of inferences from the literary character of the preface. Right from the start it had been obvious to many that Luke's use of this culture-specific literary convention had social implications, so that what appeared to be a literary question was also (as we might put it today) a sociohistorical one. According to this line of reasoning, Luke's preface does not only imply that his work is 'history': it also implies that it is 'literature'.[13] Haenchen's words (1971, p. 136) express well what many commentators have argued one way or another: 'Christianity is adopting the literary forms. It is therefore on the point of leaving the milieu of "ordinary folk" and entering the world of literature, the cultural world of antiquity. Thus its

[10] E.g. Norden, 1913, p. 316, n. 1; Nineham, 1958a, p. 18; 1960, p. 254; Lightfoot, 1962, pp. 103–5; Kümmel, 1966, p. 91.

[11] Cf. Dibelius, 1956, *passim*, e.g. pp. 1–2; 123ff.; Schmidt, 1918, p. 291; van Unnik, 1955, p. 324; Trocmé, 1957, p. 78. Overbeck, 1919, p. 79 denies that there is any inner relationship between preface and text (cf. ch. 2 n. 3, below). In the case of Acts, the mismatch is observed, but differently assessed, by Haenchen, 1971, p. 103: 'The elegant exordium of the third gospel has left many scholars with the impression that Luke would have been capable of writing the history of the dawn of Christianity in the style of a Xenophon, if not a Thucydides. However, he lacked at least two requisites for such an undertaking: an adequate historical foundation – and the right readers.'

[12] Since van Unnik, 1955, there have been a number of attempts to define more closely what kind of 'history' Luke was writing. Conzelmann, *Die Mitte der Zeit*, 3rd edn, ET G. Buswell, *The Theology of St. Luke* (Faber & Faber, London, 1960), p. 7 n. 1 (cf. also 1987, p. 4) argues that the use of a preface marks a development from history to 'monograph', but he does not pursue this line of thought beyond the preface. Plümacher, 1972, attempts a detailed analysis of hellenistic, as opposed to classical, historiography, without questioning the standard view of the preface or considering the sociohistorical plausibility of his comparisons: Luke is far more likely to have read Thucydides than Livy.

[13] Luke's claim to be writing 'Literature': Schmidt, 1918, p. 280; Meyer, 1921–3, pp. 1–8; van Unnik, 1955, p. 324; Schmid, 1955, p. 14; Trocmé, 1957, p. 41; Grundmann, 1961, p. 43; Rengstorf, 1962, p. 13; Schürmann, 1962, p. 48; Conzelmann, 1987, p. 5. Kümmel, 1966, p. 91 sums up this position: 'Luke claims, with this information, to create a work which can lay claim to literary quality, and he gives expression to this claim by means of the prologue and dedication.'

aloofness from the "world" in which it grew up, expecting the end of this aeon, is diminishing.' Thus the literary claim implied by the preface leads inevitably to questions about the audience which Luke envisaged for his work. As far back as 1899, Corssen had argued that the 'refinement' of the preface was intended for 'a wider public': 'with the Gospel of Luke, the Gospel stepped out from the darkness of the conventicle and into the book-market' (Corssen, 1899, pp. 305ff.). In other words, the audience implied by Luke's preface was clearly different from, and wider than, that of the other Gospels. Dibelius made a similar point in his 1941 article, 'The text of Acts':

> Luke wrote two books. He wrote them for a reading public which was not the public of Mark and Matthew. When an author writes a dedication like Luke 1.1–4 – a dedication whose style and choice of words are closely akin to the opening of many literary, secular writings – he has in mind readers who will appreciate such a prologue.
>
> (Dibelius, 1956, p. 88)

Such readers, Dibelius goes on to argue, would not be found in the church, and thus Luke's literary pretensions mark a new and decisive step in the progress of the Gospel towards a wider public. Whether or not a non-Christian audience would actually have understood Luke's work,[14] the very fact that Luke addresses such an audience has potentially enormous consequences for its theological content, as Haenchen has observed (1971, p. 136).

Both Corssen and Dibelius also made another suggestion which has had a long run in Lucan scholarship, the suggestion that the preface (and particularly the dedication) have specific implications for the means of production of Luke–Acts. Corssen had simply raised the possibility of Luke's work being intended for 'the book-market'; Dibelius linked this idea specifically with the textual problems of Acts, arguing that while the Gospel was preserved within the church because of its similarities with Matthew and Mark, Acts circulated for some time only 'in the book-trade', and thus lost both its author's name and its textual reliability (Dibelius, 1956, pp. 88–90; cf. also pp. 135–6). Nock's review (Nock, 1953) pointed out that Dibelius had been working with a mistaken conception of

---

[14] Some have expressed doubt as to whether a non-Christian reader would actually understand Luke's work: Meyer, 1921, p. 9; Nock, 1953, p. 501 = Nock, 1972, II p. 825; Haenchen, 1971, p. 136 n. 4.

the conditions of ancient book production, but the question of the production and dissemination of Luke's work has refused to go away. Goodspeed's 1954 article 'Was Theophilus Luke's publisher?' expressed in apparently naive form what has become an accepted *datum* of Lucan scholarship, the idea that the dedication presupposes some kind of obligation on the part of Theophilus to 'publish' Luke's work. At its simplest, this is little more than an extension of the widely recognized fact that a dedicated work is not a private letter, but Dibelius had assigned a more active role to Theophilus in the process of dissemination (Nock, 1953, 498): 'The author addressed himself to cultivated people in general (including pagans), and could depend on Theophilus to see to it that his two volumes found their way into circulation'. Haenchen's influential commentary is more specific: dedication 'honours [the dedicatee] as a patron (who in certain cases undertook to finance or disseminate the book)'; 'the person to whom the book was dedicated would give permission for copies to be made and see to its dissemination' (1971, p. 136 nn. 3, 4).

As Nock recognized, the question of 'publication' in the ancient world is a minefield, negotiable only for those equipped with a wide knowledge of ancient literature (further, ch. 9 below). But it would be too facile to dismiss the questions raised by Goodspeed and Dibelius as inappropriate to conditions in the ancient world. Both saw correctly that Luke's preface, and particularly the dedication to Theophilus, force us to think in specific and concrete terms about the social context in which the Gospels and Acts were written down and disseminated. How were Gospel writings copied and distributed? Does the preface make Luke's different from the other Gospels? What was the role of Theophilus? Did Christian texts ever circulate, commercially or otherwise, outside the churches? What means of distribution were used inside the churches? Did the Gospels or Acts ever have an existence as 'private' copies for personal reading? How many Christians could afford to own such a copy? And what effect did the conditions of writing, copying and dissemination have on the manuscript tradition? Was a text regarded as 'fixed' as soon as it was committed to paper? Were these Christian texts subjected to the same process of critical correction as literary texts of the period?[15]

---

[15] The critical labour of establishing a correct text against which future copies could be checked was only undertaken for literary classics, not for new compositions or for those of a factual nature (including the critics' own *commentarii*): E. G. Turner,

Whether or not we can easily find answers to them, these are all proper questions to ask: they direct our attention, rightly, to the social group in which our texts were produced, to the attitudes of that group toward texts, and to what Malherbe has called 'the sociological functions of the different types of literature with which we are concerned' (Malherbe, 1983, p. 16).

And finally, broader questions of social context are raised by the perception of the preface as literary convention. In Dibelius' words, the choice of such a convention presupposes the existence of readers who will appreciate it: and that in itself, as we now are increasingly aware, has social implications. Deissmann, propounding his thesis on the 'non-literary' (and therefore lower-class) nature of primitive Christianity 'was fully aware that Luke and the author of Hebrews were purposely edging 'toward producing literary works for higher circles' (Malherbe, 1983, pp. 32–3). The production of 'literature' and especially of 'history', implies a level of education and rhetorical culture which was never widely available in the Greco-Roman world. This is presumably why Dibelius assumed that the appreciative audience which Luke's work demanded could not be found within the confines of the church (1956, pp. 88, 146–8). Changes in our estimation of the social composition of the early church (further, below ch. 8), however, mean that more recent critics are happy to locate this educated audience within the church. Wengst (1987, p. 101) neatly summarizes this whole complex of sociohistorical assumptions based on the preface:

> It is significant that each of Luke's two volumes has a preface and dedication. This means that they lay claim to be literature. The address 'most excellent Theophilus' characterizes the recipient of the dedication as a person in a high position. The function of the dedication is to ensure that the person whom it honours sees to the public circulation of the work. It follows from this that Luke 'intended his work for a wider public'. Beyond the church, he is addressing 'sympathizers and interested non-Christians'. He therefore seeks – as this course implies – an educated public, which in antiquity was also socially privileged. It is in keeping with this that he has in view as an audience above all well-to-do Christians in groups within the church.

1968, pp. 112–13, 119–20. Even for a literary text, an 'edition' could mean just one correct copy.

Once again it should be noted that this observation, for Wengst, is not just a matter of historical detail but has an integral connection with the political message of Luke's work:

> By 'seeking to achieve the heights of ancient historiography', Luke has to adapt to the norms of the great world from which he is not too far removed as a result of his social status. So he comes to occupy a standpoint which makes him consider reality more from a perspective 'from above'. This quite evidently leads him to suppress violence which originated from the centre and to see only the 'sunny side' of the reality of Rome. (1987, p. 102)

Thus the apparently straightforward question about literary genre with which we began is only the launching-pad for a whole series of more profound questions about Luke and his work: questions about the reliability of his narrative, his attitudes to sources and the preservation of reported speech; questions about the 'fit' between the preface and the work as a whole; questions about social context and the functions of the text within that context. But none of these questions can be answered until the primary question of genre is rightly understood, and it is there that we must begin. Even on a preliminary overview, there seem to be good reasons for a fresh examination of the evidence. Despite Cadbury's twenty-page exegesis (1922a), there has never been a concerted attempt to find the right context for Luke's preface within the whole range of Greek literature. At a formal level, the comparison with historical prefaces seems to ignore some obvious and substantial divergences from classical historiographical convention. Thus, for example, the classical historians avoid the use of the first person: Thucydides uses the third person when he names himself as author.[16] Similarly, neither Thucydides nor any other classical historian prefaces his work with a second-person address.[17] Only a thorough examination of historical prefaces in Greek literature will show whether the conventions Luke adopts can be convincingly located within that tradition. In fact, on examination many of the most frequently cited parallels to Luke's 'conventional' language prove not to be found among the historians at all: they come from a wide range of texts,

---

[16] This point was observed by Schmid, 1955, p. 14.
[17] These points will be developed at greater length below, ch. 3.

many of them far from the rhetorical literature which Luke is assumed to be aping.[18]

If we are to have any chance of exploring the full implications of Luke's preface, then, we must first re-examine the foundations: that is, the literary judgement on which so much has been built. Is it true that Luke's preface follows Greek literary convention? If so, does he follow Greek *historiographical* convention? If not, what choices are there? This is the chief object of the study here presented. A preliminary survey of preface-writing in Greek and Jewish literature (chapter 2) enables us to narrow down the possibilities: apart from the historical prefaces, with which there is a *prima facie* case for comparison (chapter 3), the most likely candidates are the prefaces of the 'scientific tradition' (a term which will be explained in due course). Chapter 4 and 5 contain a detailed study of these prefaces, and in chapter 6 we shall present a detailed exegesis of Luke 1.1–4 and Acts 1.1 as 'scientific' prefaces. In chapter 7 we shall look back briefly at the prefaces found in hellenistic Jewish literature in the light of this broader study of Greek prefaces. In the concluding chapters we shall come back to consider the sociohistorical and literary implications of our analysis of the preface. Chapter 8 considers afresh how Luke's preface, on this new reading, fits into the broader social matrix of the early church; and in chapter 9 we conclude by asking what we can learn from the preface about Luke's readers and the immediate social situation of his work.

---

[18] Cadbury, 1922a, pp. 489ff. cites a wide variety of parallels without making a specific identification with historical convention; but the connection with history is made in 1922a, p. 15. For other parallels, cf. Lagarde, 1874, p. 165 (Dioscorides); Plummer, 1922, p. 5 (Josephus ('superficial'), Dioscorides, Hippocrates); Norden, 1913, p. 316 n. 1 (Ecclesiasticus, Dioscorides); J. Moffatt, *An Introduction to the Literature of the New Testament*, 3rd edn (T. & T. Clark, Edinburgh, 1918), p. 263 (medical treatises, e.g. Dioscorides, Galen); Cadbury, 1920b, p. 439 ('technical scientific treatises'; Vitruvius, Polybius); Klostermann, 1929, pp. 1–2 (Hippocrates, 'Aristeas', Dioscorides, Thessalos, Josephus, Polybius, Eusebius, Vettius Valens, Demosthenes, Galen, Philo); Schlatter, 1931, *passim* (Josephus); van Unnik, 1955, pp. 329f. (Josephus); Schmid, 1955, p. 28 (II Maccabees, Ecclesiasticus); Trocmé, 1957, p. 42 (Josephus, Galen); Rengstorf, 1962, p. 13 (Josephus). Cadbury, 1933, p. 57 quotes a late veterinary treatise, but treats the whole idea of parallels as a joke.

2

ON THE BEGINNINGS OF BOOKS

The task

The task of establishing the literary affinities of Luke's preface may be seen as an exercise in mapping. The outer limits of the field can be drawn without much difficulty. We need to look at prose prefaces from the fourth century BC (by which time the classic genres of Greek literature were already established) down to the second century AD, the latest possible date for the composition of Luke–Acts. Within that period only extant prefaces will be considered as primary data: notices and *testimonia* ('X wrote a book and dedicated it to Y') are interesting but only of use to us at a secondary level, since it is essential to our study to examine the actual *formalia* of prefaces and dedications, the author's *ipsissima verba*.

It is not easy, however, to select a narrower area of relevance within this large field. Faced with a bewildering amount of potential comparative material, the critic tends to opt for one of three ways of narrowing the field: (i) to find parallels in a single author and posit him as Luke's direct model; (ii) to point to parallels in an area with which Luke's literary links are already well established, e.g. hellenistic Jewish literature; or (iii) to pick out a likely looking area on the basis of *content* (history, biography) and look there for preface-topics (e.g. discussion of sources, purpose of the work) similar to those found in Luke. All three of these approaches are vitiated by a failure to establish a wider frame of reference against which the significance and extent of such 'parallels' can be assessed. Parallels in content or topic can mask obvious and crucial differences in form; and parallels with individual authors[1] are meaningless

---

[1] Except in the rare cases where the parallels are so overwhelming as to make the case for direct literary dependence unassailable. There are no such parallels for Luke's preface.

without the wider database which will enable us to say, 'Yes, Luke is like X but he is *more like* Y.'

This does not mean that the only course left to us is to examine every single Greek preface in turn within the allotted time span – although as a matter of fact this investigation did begin with just such an examination. The problem is not that prefaces are difficult to find: it is relatively easy, given a well-stocked library of classical texts, to move systematically round the shelves examining the beginning of every extant Greek prose text.[2] The problem lies partly with the presentation of information gained in this way: the results of a full survey would be cumbersome and virtually impossible to assimilate. Even more problematic, however, is the heuristic logic implicit in such a programme. Bluntly, there is little use in starting out on a search of ancient literature unless we have a fairly precise idea at the outset of what we are looking for. As Robert Jewett has observed in a different context (Jewett, 1986, 113–14), 'a process of selective perception is involved in the sifting of cultural details from archaeology, ancient history, literature … A listing of random details would not advance our quest.'

Before surveying the 'background', then, it is vital to have in mind a clear and serviceable description of Luke's preface. We need to draw up a list of its characteristics and to agree on the relative importance of these characteristics for the purposes of establishing significant parallels. Since a preface is a *formal* literary convention, formal and syntactical characteristics should take precedence over content. Style perforce comes last in the list, not because it is least important but because we still lack an objective descriptive language for the nuances of Greek style observable in such a short text as the preface (although that does not mean that such nuances are any the less real). Terms like 'literary' and 'rhetorical' are insufficiently precise, and it is difficult to proceed securely beyond them except by piecemeal comparison with other writers. However, style provides an essential fourth component once we have located points of contact in form, syntax and content. Following this line of approach we can set out a hierarchical checklist of possible points of comparison, and thence proceed to draw up some kind of diachronic guide to the field under review, on the basis of which we can build up a picture of the generic and other relationships within the broader

---

[2] My debt to the Lower Reading Room of the Bodleian Library, Oxford, will be apparent in everything that follows.

area, and so locate Luke's true position in a methodologically sound manner.

Luke's preface: an objective description

FORM
1. Short (one sentence)
2. First person
3. Second-person address: name (inserted vocative)
   pronoun (σοι)
   additional clause ('so that you may know')
4. Detachable: no connection with following narrative
5. Second volume: name repeated in vocative with brief résumé of first volume

SYNTACTICAL STRUCTURE
6. Periodic
7. Main verb = author's decision to write
8. Causal clause preceding main verb = reason for writing
9. Adverbial clause dependent on first subordinate clause = nature of material
10. Participial clause dependent on indirect object of main verb = information about author
11. Final clause after main verb = purpose in writing

TOPICS
12. Other writers (= 8)
13. Nature of material (= 9)
14. Author's qualifications (= 10)
15. Benefit for addressee (= 11)

STYLE
16. Traces of rhetorical style (periodic, feel for sonorous diction, impressive vocabulary), but rhetorical effectiveness limited
17. Contrast with following text in style, vocabulary, subject-matter ('secular' character)
18. Cumbersome vocabulary: multiple compound verbs, many *hapax legomena*, lack of clarity
19. Compression: large number of topics compressed into a single sentence

How may such a preface be characterized? Perhaps its most obvious formal trait (apart from its brevity) is its detachability, its lack of connection with the rest of the book. Franz Overbeck's rather overheated observation of 1919 was not in essence incorrect: 'This preface is alien to the very book to which it is attached, and looks in this position like no more than a beauty spot plastered on [*sc.* to a lady's face] ...'[3] This is not merely a matter of style; equally remarkable is the appearance and immediate disappearance of the first person.[4] It might most simply be described as a kind of label, stuck on at the beginning to explain what the author is doing, why, and for whom (how far the preface really does explain all this is another matter, which we shall discuss in due course). And it is a label with an address: a name is attached to the opening of the book, although this name is never explained or referred to again in the succeeding narrrative. So what we are looking for in the surrounding literature is an explanatory label, easily detachable[5] from the book itself, placed at the beginning of a text and incorporating a first-person speaker and a second-person address. Whether we shall find parallel phenomena with *all* these features in contemporary literature remains to be seen, but clearly we shall be looking for the parallels which exhibit the maximum number of correspondences.

Prefaces in biblical and Jewish literature

The Bible, Luke's chief source of inspiration in so many respects, contains very little preface-material of the type we are looking for. Most of the prophetic books of the Old Testament begin with the simplest of introductions, effectively a title: 'The words of Amos' or 'Vision of Obadiah'. Biblical narrative on the whole seems to need no introduction outside itself: 'And it came to pass ...' (Judges 1.1); 'And the Lord called to Moses ...' (Lev. 1.1); 'There was a man ...' (Job 1.1). Sometimes there is a simple chronology, enabling the story to be placed correctly in sequence: 'After the death of Moses

---

[3] Overbeck, 1919, p. 80: 'Es ist aber dieses Vorwort auch dem Buche selbst fremd, dem es vorgesetzt ist, und erscheint an seiner Stelle nur wie ein aufgeheftetes Schönheitspflästerchen ...' More soberly, Cadbury, 1920b, pp. 439; Sparks, 1943, p. 129; E. Haenchen, *Der Weg Jesu* (Töppelmann, Berlin, 1966), p. 1.

[4] A spasmodic first-person plural reappears in the second half of Acts, but this does not alter the fact that the narrator of the whole of the Gospel and of the bulk of Acts, unlike the speaker in the preface, is impersonal, omniscient and invisible.

[5] 'Detachable' in literary terms, that is. These explanatory prefaces should not be confused with the projecting tags (σίλλυβοι, *tituli*) on which the title of a book or its author's name could be described; see on these Kenyon, 1951, p. 62.

...' (Josh. 1.1); 'In the second year of Darius the king ...' (Hagg. 1.1). Apocryphal and intertestamental literature tends to be written after the biblical pattern and to use the same forms. There is perhaps a little more awareness of the written text as a physical object (cf. Tobit 1.1 'The *book* of the words of Tobit'),[6] but the basic forms are the same as in the older works. The narrative books of the New Testament, apart from Luke–Acts, follow this same biblical pattern of giving a short descriptive title, for this seems the best way to regard the opening words of Matthew, Mark and Revelation. John's Gospel, in conscious literary allusion, echoes the opening of Genesis; and the other books of the New Testament are in the form of letters, and so use the formal opening and closing devices of epistolary convention.[7]

A brief survey of rabbinic literature reveals no more scope for authorly introductions (Strack-Billerbeck cites no parallels to Luke 1.1–4). The classic texts (Mishnah, Tosefta, the two Talmuds and the tannaitic Midrashim) grew up over many generations, but the authors of the different collections which they embody, and the final editors who brought together the works as we know them, remain anonymous and invisible behind their productions. Much of the material was transmitted orally for generations, and the texts grew up in the academies and were intended for use there: they were written by the initiated for the initiated and required no external explanation. There is one preface-like form in the rabbinic corpus, namely the *petiḥah* of which Gen. R. 1.1 is a classic example. This device is found at the beginning of a sermon and shows an evident awareness of the dynamics of public address. It is rhetorically motivated and can be compared with the *prooimion* of Greek rhetoric, but bears no relation to the kind of explanatory preface we are looking for (further, J. Heinemann, 'The proem in the Aggadic Midrashim', *Scripta Hierosolymitana* 22 (1971), pp. 100–22).

It is where the biblical tradition intersects with the Greek that we begin to find prefatory material which looks more comparable to Luke's: see, for example, II Maccabees 2.9–32; Ecclesiasticus; the *Letter of Aristeas*; and the prefaces found in Philo and Josephus. It

[6] Cf. also Jubilees, prol.; Test.Reub.1.1; I. Baruch 1.1; III Baruch 1.1–2; Ep.Jer. 1. Several of the Dead Sea Scrolls begin with an indication of their contents (e.g. 1QSa, 1QM). CD begins with an exhortation.
[7] Current 'rhetorical criticism' is happy to talk of the 'exordium' of a letter; but this is simply a transference from the sphere of rhetoric. Formally speaking, the conventional opening of the letter is quite distinct from that of the speech; and all the NT epistles, apart from Hebrews and I John, follow the former.

might seem logical therefore to begin with a detailed comparison with these prefaces, but we shall defer their examination until we have presented a full discussion of explanatory prefaces in Greek literature. It is clear even from a superficial examination that Luke's preface cannot be derived solely and directly from any one of the extant hellenistic Jewish prefaces, or even from any combination of them: it has too many differences from them, and too many affinities with comparable prefaces in secular literature. Conversely, the hellenistic Jewish prefaces themselves belong to the most 'Greek' side of this literature. They are all original Greek compositions, not translations, and all show clearly the influence of Greek writing convention; the depth of that influence will become more evident from the study which follows. Our primary object at this stage is to make a study of preface-conventions in Greek literature, that literature being the common parent both of Luke's preface and of the prefaces found in hellenistic Jewish texts; having done that, we shall be in a better position to chart the relationship between the two 'gemelli'. We shall therefore defer a detailed analysis of the hellenistic Jewish prefaces to chapter 7.

Greek prefaces in rhetorical theory

When we turn to Greek literature, things look immediately very different. Not only do Greek writers use a wide variety of introductory devices, but there is an extensive critical literature on the *prooimion* or preface, both ancient and modern. Already Plato (*Phaedrus* 266d) mentions the *prooimion* as an essential part of a speech, and he makes it clear that earlier rhetorical treatises had dealt with the subject (Fuhrmann, 1960, p. 124 n. 2). Aristotle devotes two chapters of the *Rhetorica* to the preface (III 14–15; cf. also 13), in terms which presuppose that the theoretical treatment of the subject was well developed in his day. Subsequent writers reduced this theoretical analysis to ever more abbreviated rules; probably the most famous of these is the dictum that the aim of the preface is 'to make the audience well-disposed, attentive and teachable' – 'benevolos, attentos, dociles facere auditores'.[8]

[8] Cf. Cicero, *De inventione* I xvi 22; *De oratore* II 323; on which especially A. D. Leeman, *Orationis Ratio* (Hakkert, Amsterdam, 1963) I, pp. 120–1. For further discussion of the maxim, see the rhetorical handbooks: R. Volkmann, 1963, pp. 126ff.; H. Lausberg, 1960, sect. 263. There is an excellent brief summary in H. Hunger, *Prooimion*, (Wiener Byzant. Stud. I, Wien, 1964) I, 2, pp. 19–26; otherwise, cf. Janson, 1964, p. 25; Herkommer, 1968, pp. 13ff.

It is, however, difficult to feel that this kind of theorizing has much to do with our particular quest. Tore Janson experienced a similar difficulty in his work on Latin prefaces, and he suggested one reason, namely that the rhetorical precepts are 'too general' (Janson, 1964, pp. 24–6). But there is more to it than that. The precepts of the rhetors were never intended to function as a tool for literary analysis in the modern critical sense: they originated rather as rules-of-thumb to assist in the *composition* of effective prefaces (cf. Marrou, 1964, pp. 84–5). And the fundamental problem is that Greek literary theory is 'a by-product of rhetoric' (Russell, *OCD²*, s.v.). It is originally and essentially a part of the activity of training orators; and it looks back particularly to the great classical period of rhetoric, its flowering in Athens in the late fifth and early fourth centuries BC, when it had its proper place as an organ of persuasion in the lawcourts and the deliberative assemblies of the city (cf. Plato, *Phaedrus* 261b).

In ancient literary theory, therefore, the *prooimion* means primarily the preface to a speech, forensic, political or epideictic (and even the last two did not really need one, if Aristotle's suggestion is to be adopted: *Rhet.* III 13.3, 14.12). In this oral context it has a precise function. The speaker must give a brief account of his case, and thus a brief explanation of his 'subject' (but the full statement follows in the next section of the speech, the *narratio*/διήγησις). He does not usually need to identify either himself or his audience, nor in general terms does he need to explain what kind of activity he is engaged in: all these are defined externally to the text, in the actual or imagined oral *Sitz im Leben*. His most important task in his opening section is to capture his hearers' attention, to promise them enough to keep them interested, and to win them over to his side. It was this psychological aspect of the preface that really engaged the attention of the ancient theorists, and it is this interest which determines the particular slant of the *technai*. Thus although the influence of rhetoric was widely extended in time, both through its application to other branches of literature and through its controlling interest in education, the fact remains that the rules devised for prefaces in rhetoric were devised for a very specific situation and are of limited usefulness outside that situation.[9]

[9] Thus to call dedication a *captatio benevolentiae*, as does Ruch (1958, p. 98) is either a metaphor or a patent distortion. The difficulty of applying rhetorical theory with any precision to another genre is well illustrated by Lucian's *How to Write History*, on which see particularly Avenarius, 1956.

Explanatory prefaces in Greek literature

We have to look outside the range of the rhetorical discussion to find prefaces of the sort we are looking for. The fourth century BC was a period of transition in Greek culture in many respects, of which one is of particular significance for our quest. Writing, though widespread by the fifth century BC, was still essentially secondary to oral expression: the function of a written text was to act as *hypomnēma* or *aide-mémoire*, 'a reminder to one who knows what the writing is about' (Plato, *Phaedrus* 275d), and the classic literary forms were still those of oral literature: epic and lyric verse, drama, rhetoric. By the fourth century writing had become a primary means of expression in its own right;[10] the classic forms had begun to take on new life as texts written with readers as well as hearers in mind (as for example with the controversial 'written speeches' of Isocrates[11]), and new forms were emerging to meet the new situation. It was a transition which aroused theoretical interest among the thinkers of the day. Plato was particularly alert to the change and its potential hazards:

> Once a thing is put in writing, the composition, whatever it may be, drifts all over the place, getting into the hands not only of those who understand it, but equally of those who have no business with it; it does not know how to address the right people and not to address the wrong. And when it has been ill-treated and unfairly abused it always needs its parent to come to its help, being unable to defend or help itself.   (*Phaedrus* 275d–e, tr. Hackforth)

Among the side-effects of the change from oral to written expression, in other words, are an increased need for *explanation* and a feeling that it may be desirable to name a specific *audience*.

Reponses to these needs, conscious or unconscious, were many and varied. Plato's own answer to the problem of defining the right audience was a characteristically subtle one. He wrote no philosophical handbooks or treatises to match the rhetorical handbooks so scorned in the *Phaedrus*; instead, Platonic philosophy was

[10] Kenyon, 1951, pp. 20–6, esp. 24–5; Friedländer, 1958, vol. I ch. 5. See now also Thomas, 1989, ch. 1.1; Harris, 1989, ch. 4.

[11] Friedländer, 1958, pp. 112ff.; on 'written speeches', pp. 110–11, and see note 6 p. 357. Cf. also C. Eucken, *Isokrates* (Berlin/New York, 1983), ch. 3, 'Das Problem von Schriftlichkeit und Mündlichkeit', and pp. 272f.; R. L. Howland, 'The attack on Isocrates in the *Phaedrus*', *CQ* 31 (1937), pp. 151–9, esp. p. 158.

brought to the general public in a series of dramatic dialogues, intended, it has been plausibly argued, to provide an inbuilt dialectic and so simulate the living master–pupil interaction which Plato saw as essential to real philosophy.[12] The *Dialogues* themselves still required some sort of explanatory scene-setting, but in Plato this is provided by an introductory scene or framework dialogue so that the dramatic mould of the whole is not broken.[13]

Another (and simpler) solution to the need to define an audience was to adopt a literary form which allowed one to name a specific reader. The fourth century sees the beginning in Greek prose of a long tradition of protreptic and moral discourses and of substantial open letters addressed to named, real individuals. Both forms contain a personal address, not tacked on as an extra but integral to the genre: in other words, 'personalization' is achieved here not by attaching a personal 'label' to an impersonal form, but by choosing a form which itself demands a personal address. These addressed discourses and letters, as I shall argue, are not themselves examples of 'dedication' of the type we are looking for, but they do provide an important clue as to its development: see further below, chapter 4, pp. 54–6.

The need for explanation, similarly, is met in a variety of ways in fifth- and fourth-century prose. Isocrates exhibits a particularly artless response in the *Antidosis*:

> If this discourse which is about to be read had been like the speeches which are produced either for the law-courts or for oratorical display, I should not, I suppose, have prefaced it by any explanation. Since, however, it is novel and different in character, it is necessary to begin by setting forth the reasons why I choose to write a discourse so unlike any other.   (Isocrates XV 1, tr. Norlin, LCL)

In rhetoric, however, this is an isolated literary phenomenon; few rhetorical writers are as happy as Isocrates apparently was to step outside the generic fiction and speak *in propria persona* in this fashion.

[12] This is the position argued by Friedländer, 1958, I p. 113. Cf. Harris, 1989, p. 92 on Plato's ambivalent stance towards writing.
[13] On prefaces to dialogues, see Ruch, 1958. Aristotle appears to have adopted an 'explanatory' type of preface for his (now lost) dialogues (Ruch, 1958, pp. 41–3, 325ff.). Cicero, as Ruch argues, moves back more closely to the dramatic form (approached now with the eye of the historian, p. 332); however, in his addition of dedication Cicero breaks completely with dramatic convention (330ff.).

Among the historians, on the other hand, the habit of using a preface for personal explanation was already established by the fifth century, and extensive prefaces were characteristic of Greek historiography from Thucydides onwards. These prefaces merit a chapter on their own account, and will be discussed in chapter 3. Even at this stage, however, it is worth observing that there is a perceivable reluctance to break out of the mould of impersonal narration which the historians inherited from the epic tradition. There is no second-person address, and both Herodotus and Thucydides use the third person, not the first, when speaking of themselves.

It is perhaps significant that classical literature shows this reluctance to step outside the bounds of a given literary form to add the simple kind of explanatory 'label' that we find in Luke 1.1–4. Certainly it is on the fringes of that literature, and in minor works falling less readily into the classic forms, that we begin to find explanatory prefaces closer to what we are looking for. Thus in his non-historical works, Xenophon has a number of explanatory prefaces, as individual as their author. The *Agesilaus* begins with a personal confession which also serves to introduce the subject. In the *Constitution of the Lacedaemonians*, the preface explains, perhaps rather artificially, the train of thought which led the author to his subject ('It occurred to me one day ...'). Both these prefaces are of a length comparable to Luke's, but they have little else in common with his apart from the use of the first person. The closest parallel comes in the *Art of Horsemanship*, where Xenophon makes clear his own experience of horsemanship, describes the subject and the readership he has in mind, and explains the relationship between his own work and that of his predecessors. By itself, however, this preface provides few detailed parallels with Luke's at the level of formal structure, vocabulary and style, and in terms of Xenophon's work it is an isolated literary phenomenon.[14]

The military writer Aeneas Tacticus, by contrast, favours a more philosophical opening gambit. The short preface to his book on siegecraft is entirely theoretical and generalizing, and makes no mention of either author or reader. Like Xenophon, the author writes in a literary style, with the difference that, where Xenophon's

[14] Since the work is in some sense a technical manual, written for the country gentlemen all over Greece for whom matters concerning horses and dogs were an integral aspect of *paideia* (*Cynegeticus* I 5), it is perhaps not surprising that this should have much in common with the prefaces to other technical works which we shall discuss in chs. 4 and 5.

language is simple and its effectiveness natural, Aeneas produces 'careful', 'studied' effects in a 'conspicuous ... effort to achieve literary style'.[15] This rather pretentious approach to the preface, and the style that goes with it, were inherited by later writers on warfare such as Onasander (first century AD): the preface to his *Strategeticus* betrays an equally clear literary effort, as indeed does the whole text.[16]

The major *locus* for explanatory prefaces, however, is really outside the normal canon of classical literature altogether, in the long and multiform tradition of technical or professional prose (*Fachprosa*) which began to proliferate in the fourth century. I have called this, for want of a better word, the 'scientific' tradition – using 'scientific' not in the limited sense operating in the British educational system, where 'Science' is distinguished from 'Arts' or 'Humanities', but in a sense closer to that of the French, or of the German *wissenschaftlich*. Rydbeck (1967) uses *Fachprosa* for this class of literature, a term which is most obviously translated 'technical prose', though standard German dictionaries also suggest for *fach-*, 'professional', 'specialist', 'specialized' or 'expert'. But it is not possible to determine in advance whether these texts, in Greek society, belong to the area which we would call trade or professional manuals or to the academic sphere: each case must be decided individually. Given that all the choices pose their own problems, then, 'scientific' (understood in the sense described) seems as good a solution as any.

The important distinction in isolating this class of Greek literature is one of origin and form, not of subject-matter. It includes treatises on medicine, philosophy, mathematics, engineering, rhetoric and a wide variety of other subjects right down to the mantic and magical sciences of the second century AD, with treatises on

[15] L. W. Hunter, *Aeneas on Siegecraft* (Oxford, Clarendon Press, 1927), p. 102): 'This short paragraph has the appearance of having been composed with special care ... '

[16] Cf. Rydbeck, 1967, p. 23, where Rydbeck argues that the *Strategeticus* cannot really be described as *Fachprosa* in view of the author's obviously stylish intentions; despite the basically *Koine* character of his language, the style is 'blumenreich'. In content (dedication etc.) Onasander's preface owes much to developments that had taken place in scientific preface-convention over the intervening years, but the whole tone and approach are significantly more literary. This must have something to do with the book's audience: the art of warfare was not 'banausic' but on the contrary close to the heart of aristocratic Roman (and earlier Greek) society. It is noticeable that Hero's treatise on siege-engines (*Belopoeica*, discussed below in chs. 4 and 5) stands out from his other mathematical works in having a similarly pretentious philosophical introduction.

astrology and the interpretation of dreams. Not unexpectedly, this is precisely where Plato had identified the problems caused by writing in their most acute form;[17] but Plato, himself a writer, was mounting a rearguard action against the inevitable. His doubts did not affect the appearance, from the fourth century onwards, of a vast output of technical writing in all subjects which was *not* conceived as 'Literature', *not* initially for public consumption: in Aristotelian terms, the 'esoteric' as opposed to the 'exoteric' works. It is here that the explanatory preface as 'label', with or without address, comes into its own; and these prefaces will form the subject of an extensive study in chapters 4 and 5.

[17] Plato begins with the topical problem of 'written speeches', but it is clear that his particular interest in this passage was the nature and use of technical handbooks ('school texts') as a mode of instruction. On the surface the discussion deals with rhetorical *technai* (cf. esp. 268a–269d), but Plato's real concern was with the relationship between writing and teaching in philosophy – a subject touched on again in the Seventh Letter. See Friedländer, 1958, ch. 5 and esp. pp. 112ff.; Alexander, 1990, pp. 237–42. On the growth and importance of technical literature in the fourth century, see now Harris, 1989, p. 82.

3

HISTORICAL PREFACES

The information available to us about Greek historical prefaces, as about so much else in the Greek historical tradition, is incomplete.[1] Of a rich tradition, comparatively few works have survived whole, and while the content of a history is often preserved through the work of epitomators and anthologists, formal elements like prefaces tend to disappear in the process. The surviving examples, however, can be supplemented by a few passages of theoretical discussion in rhetorical works. Especially important here is Lucian, *De hist. conscr.* 52–5, and the commentary on it in Avenarius, 1956, pp. 113–18. There is a full discussion in Herkommer, 1968, ch. 2.

General features

We may consider historical prefaces under three aspects: the pattern set by the fifth-century classics, Herodotus and Thucycides; the influence of rhetoric from the fourth century onwards; and the intrusion, at a later date, of some of the practical considerations of book production.

The insistence of later writers that the writing of history was an *opus oratorium* (Cicero, *De leg.* I 5), and their subsuming of historical prefaces under the general rhetorical rules for prefaces, should not blind us to the fact that Greek historiography, as one of the oldest genres of prose writing, had its independent origins in the fifth century BC: in practice, the essential pattern for historical prefaces was established then. Thus history always retained the impersonality of the relationship between author and audience,

---

[1] The starting-point for any study of these prefaces is still the fundamental work of Engel, 1910, and Lieberich, 1899. Of modern studies, the most useful I have found overall is that of Herkommer, 1968, which discusses the Greek background to each Roman convention. There is a useful collection of translated prefaces in Toynbee, 1924, which I have quoted in places.

characteristic of ancient narrative art: right through from the fifth
century, historians followed epic rather than didactic tradition in
eschewing any address to an audience, individual or collective.
Similarly the third-person *sphragis* or author's seal, a feature of
many kinds of literature in the early period (Herkommer, 1968,
pp. 46–7), was adopted by Herodotus and Thucydides and
remained a recognizable characteristic of historical writing long
after it had disappeared in other genres (further, pp. 26–7 below).

In a similar way, the range of subjects discussed by Thucydides in
his preface became hallowed. Lucian's list (*De hist.conscr*. 53)
reflects it, and elsewhere Lucian notes the first appearance of the
theme of 'utility' in Thucydides (*De hist.conscr*. 42): despite the
considerable differences between Thucydides' passing remark and
the fully developed *topos* of the hellenistic historians, the simple fact
that Thucydides made the remark was sufficient to justify the later
development. Most important of all, Thucydides sets the tone for
the succeeding tradition: on the one hand, with his high-minded
insistence on truth, accuracy (so far as either was possible) and
careful investigation; and, on the other, with his view of the work as
'a possession for all time' (I 22.4), a view which implicitly condemns
mere rhetorical display and yet shows itself aware of rhetorical
standards and professes to aim not below but above them. It was
this view, again showing the kinship of history to epic,[2] which
ensured the characteristic bent of Greek historical writing, its constant awareness of being 'literature' rather than mere record or
research, its effective severance from the philosophical–scientific
tradition which, like history, had its roots in Ionian *historia*. Unlike
scientific prose, history was and remained one of the ancient
'literary' genres in a narrow sense, akin to poetry and rhetoric and
judged by their standards.[3]

The effective annexation of historiography by rhetoric in the
fourth century thus merely emphasized the continuity of one aspect
of the fifth-century tradition. As regards prefaces, it gave the theor-

[2] On the 'epic' nature of Thucydides' conception, see F. Wehrli, 'Die Geschichtsschreibung im Lichte der antiken Theorie', *Theoria und Humanitas: gesammelte
Schriften* (1972), p. 133. Compare Dionysius of Halicarnassus, *Ant.Rom*. I 1.2
(monuments to posterity), I 6.3–4 (immortality through history); Diodorus I 1.5,
2.3–5 (immortality); Josephus, *BJ* I 15 (record for posterity); Procopius, *De bellis* I
1.1; Agathias, *Hist*. I pref. 1–3. Cf. also Alexander's famous lament over Achilles,
and Arrian's reaction to it (Arrian, *Anab*. I 12.2–5), and Pliny, *Ep*. V. 8.1.

[3] Compare e.g. Vitruvius V pref. 1, Diodorus I 2.55–8, Pliny, *Ep*. V 8, Agathias,
Hist. I pref. 12.

ists a licence to analyse historical prefaces under the heads used for
the preface of a speech, but it is doubtful if this analysis had much
effect on practice.[4] The main practical effect of rhetoric seems to
have been Ephorus' innovation of composing prefaces to each
separate book. If we accept Laqueur's convincing hypothesis that
the Ephoran prefaces were of the type represented in the prefaces to
Diodorus Siculus' Books IV–XX (Laqueur, 1911), Ephorus
departed radically from the Thucydidean model. Each book is
treated as a literary unit, and the prefaces, in place of the factual
approach of Thucydides, employ a rhetorically varied opening with
a saying, or a proposition on some topic of general interest, which
introduces the subject of the book in an indirect fashion reminiscent
of epideictic oratory.

The third point which stands out in the development of historical
prefaces is the eventual adoption, by a few hellenistic writers, of the
more mundane devices of summary and recapitulation. This development did not affect the tradition deeply (Laqueur, 1911) , but it
did introduce a new element which cannot be traced back either to
rhetoric or to the fifth-century classics. Summaries of the kind
found, for example, in Diodorus I–III were more common in the
scientific tradition, in works whose main purpose was informative,
and they seem more at home in a scholastic than in a literary milieu.
Laqueur (1911), suggests certain specific reasons for their appearance; but in general we may note that their use may be due to the
newly encyclopedic nature of works like Diodorus' *Library*.[5] It also
seems to be related, at least in the case of Diodorus, to a new
consciousness of the practical problems of book production (I 5.2):
Herodotus and Thucydides apparently did not think of their work
in terms of 'books' at all. The device of summary and recapitulation
is so obviously useful for the historian that it seems strange that it
should not have been adopted more widely; perhaps the constant
literary preoccupation of the historians deterred them from using a
conventional formula which it was difficult to render into elegant
and varied prose.

[4] Herkommer notes that the more specifically rhetorical *topoi* do not appear in
Greek historical prefaces, though they were popular with Roman writers (1968,
p. 180). But see Dionysius of Halicarnassus, *De Thuc.* 19 for some objections to the
content and structure of Thucydides' prefaces; Dionysius' own conforms much more
closely to rhetorical precepts.

[5] Note also that some of the other examples cited by Laqueur (Josephus, *Ant.*,
Eusebius, *HE*) are closer to the antiquarian tradition than to history proper (for the
distinction, see Momigliano, 1969, pp. 3–5).

A consideration of these diverse roots, then, may enable us to understand various aspects of the prefaces of the Greek historians. It is easier, however, to analyse origins than to describe in general terms the form and content of the historical preface. To seek such a description, indeed, is to fail to appreciate one essential feature of Greek historiography. Its literary ambition entails, among other things, that originality of expression is a thing to be valued in itself. Thus while we do find that certain subjects are regularly discussed, and that certain conventions are observed, we find also a wide variety – which is quite deliberate – in order and in methods of expression (Herkommer, 1968, pp. 181–82). It is not possible, there-fore, to draw up a *schema* for historical prefaces, to define a clear form and pattern; equally, it is wrong to try to force such a *schema* on to the extant examples, or to assume that they are all deviations from a lost pattern. Nevertheless it is possible to pick out certain salient features, which may be grouped under two heads: formal characteristics (pp. 26–31) and recurrent topics (pp. 31–4). Under both heads, other examples could have been cited: for further material, see Avenarius, 1956, and Herkommer, 1968. Those which we have picked, however, will give a good idea of the scope and style of the historical preface in Greek literature. In pp. 34–41 we shall discuss in greater detail one convention which has a particular bearing on Luke's preface, the convention of *autopsia*.

Formal characteristics

Author's name

See Herkommer, 1968, pp. 46–9. Hecataeus, Herodotus, Thucydides and Antiochus all begin their works with an announcement of the author's name and place of origin (or lineage) in the third person (Herkommer, 1968, p. 47 n. 5). This form of self-identification seems to have been widespread in early prose and verse. It gradually disappeared in the differing circumstances of later literature, but continued to be regarded as a distinguishing mark of historical writing: cf. Agathias, *Hist.* I pref. 14 (tr. Toynbee), 'I have first to follow the usual practice of historical writers and to explain my identity'. The archaic third-person form and the position in the opening words were not, however, generally retained: Lucian regards it as an affectation when one of his contemporaries copies the wording of Thucydides (*De hist.conscr.* 15). For examples and further comment on the practice, see: Dion. Halic., *Ant.Rom.* I 8.4; Appian, *Hist.Rom.* I pref. 15; Josephus, *BJ* I 3; and compare Arrian, *Anabasis* I 12.5 (Herkommer, 1968, p. 46 n. 6). (Diodorus I 4.4 gives place of origin, but no name.) This practice was not adopted by Roman historians.

Dedication

Dedication was not normal practice among the classical historians. The apostrophe of the second person, whether in direct address (vocative) or in epistolary form, does not fit with the impersonal third-person narrative style of history, and was generally avoided: in Herkommer's words (my translation), 'the dedication of historical works was not customary among the Greeks ... Further, dedication does not belong by nature to Roman historical writing.'[6]

The first extant example we have of a dedicated historical work is Josephus' *Antiquities*, which was dedicated to Epaphroditus, as we learn from *Vita* 430 (originally the epilogue to the whole *Antiquities*). Since the subject-matter of the *Antiquities* is one that may properly be distinguished from that of 'history' proper as conceived by the classical tradition (Momigliano, 1969, pp. 3–5), it is possible that Josephus did not feel constrained in this work, as he did in the *Bellum*, to follow exactly the conventions of classical historiography. But it must also be pointed out that even here there is no *formal* transgression of the convention: the preface to the *Antiquities* contains an eulogy of Epaphroditus, which employs language customary in dedications (I 8),[7] but it bears no address or salutation, and if it were not for *Vita* 430 we should not know that the *Antiquities* was dedicated at all.[8]

Otherwise evidence for the few Greek histories thought to be

---

[6] Herkommer, 1968, p. 25: 'Die widmung von Geschichtswerken war bei den Griechen nicht üblich ... Auch zum Wesen der römischen Geschichtsschreibung gehört keine Widmung.' Cf. also ibid. p. 48 n. 1. On dedication generally, see also Ruppert, 1911, ch. 2 sect. 2; Janson, 1964, pp. 66–7; Graefenhain, 1892.

[7] E.g. the themes of the author's reluctant yielding to persuasion (a Roman convention, cf. Janson, 1964, pp. 116ff.), and of the patron's general culture and supoort for the arts (note the characteristic dedication-courtesy of συμφιλο-καλοῦντι: ch. 5, p. 100.

[8] It might be objected that the dedication could have been expressed in a letter attached to the outside of the work and subsequently lost; but in view of the unusual third-person reference to the patron in I 8, and in view of the infrequency of dedication in historical works, it seems more likely that Josephus has deliberately avoided the form of the second-person address in his preface.

dedicated is indirect. Diogenes Laertius II 83 and Dionysius of Halicarnassus, *Ant.Rom.* I 4.3 speak of histories 'sent to' or 'written to please' hellenistic monarchs, like the *Chronica* of Apollodorus, a compilation in iambic verse said to have been 'composed for' the Attalid dynasty (Ps.-Scymnus 1ff.; Jacoby, 1902, p. 4). Later *testimonia* suggest that the works of the Egyptian Manetho and the Chaldean Berossus may fall into this class. The evidence for these dedications is not strong,[9] and in the absence of direct textual support, we cannot be certain that the works were actually formally addressed to their patrons. As Ruppert correctly insists (1911, pp. 29–30), the statement in a later text that an author wrote 'for' another person does not necessarily imply a formal dedication. Both writers were non-Greeks, presenting an account of their national antiquities to the Greek-speaking world, and thus perhaps more dependent than many on the patronage of the hellenistic courts (Ruppert, 1911, pp. 29–30), which might account for the break with tradition; but, as we shall see in chapter 4, it is a mistake to assume that the need for, or even the acceptance of, the support of a hellenistic monarch automatically resulted in dedication. If there was formal dedication here, it was an innovation; but it should be noted that the works of Manetho and Berossus, like Josephus' *Antiquities* and the Libyan *historia* recorded in Diogenes Laertius II 83, belong to the antiquarian and ethnographic side of Greek history rather than to the Thucydidean. The example, if it is one, was not widely imitated. Josephus knew both works (cf. e.g. *C.Ap.* I 73ff., 129ff.); and Callinicus of Petra (*FGH* T1) may have been influenced by them.

Among Roman writers the dedication of histories is a little more common (Herkommer, 1968, pp. 25–6). But even here it remains exceptional, and the major Roman historians follow the Greek convention. Herkommer suggests that Roman influence may lie behind the dedications in one of two Greek writers of the Roman

---

[9] Berossus: the evidence for dedication lies in Tatian's statement that Berossus 'drew up the history of the Chaldeans in three books for Antiochus' (*FGH* 680 T2). No hint of a dedication comes through in Josephus and Eusebius, our major sources for Berossus' work. On the other hand, where could Tatian have obtained such information, if not from an address in the text which he or his source was using? (P. Schnabel, *Berossus und die babylonisch-hellenistische Literatur* (Leipzig/Berlin, 1923), p. 6.) Manetho: Syncellus informs us that the *Egyptian History* was addressed to Ptolemy Philadelphus (*FGH* 257 T11c). The two surviving dedications, however, are forgeries. See further, O. Murray, 'Herodotus and hellenistic culture', *CQ* 22 pp. 200–13, p. 209 n. 2.

period.[10] In general, however, it must be regarded as a testimony to the strength of convention in the classical tradition, that, despite the increasingly widespread use of dedication in Roman literary circles,[11] very few histories of any kind, either Latin or Greek, were dedicated before the Byzantine period.

The subject of the book

See Herkommer, 1968, pp. 64–6. The earliest historians, like early writers in other fields, use the opening words of the first sentence to indicate the subject of their work, whether generally, as in Herodotus ('the results of his researches') or more precisely, as in Thucydides ('the history of the war between the Peloponnesians and the Athenians'). The same kind of 'titular' opening is found later in Josephus (*BJ* I 1), Appian (*Hist.Rom.* I pref. 1), Cassius Dio (LXXII 23) and Procopius (*De bellis* I 1). Most later writers, able to rely on the transmission of a separate title with their works, preferred to dispense with this kind of opening.[12] It remained customary, however, to use the preface to indicate the subject covered by the work, if in a more oblique fashion (Polybius I 1.5: Herkommer, 1968 p. 65 n. 1). Several writers adopted the method favoured by rhetoricians (Dion.Halic., *De Thuc.* 19 pp. 855–6) of giving a detailed account of the scope and plan of the work at the end of the preface: cf. Diodorus I 4.6–5.3; Josephus, *BJ* I 19–30; Dion. Halic., *Ant.Rom.* I ref. 13–15. Polybius reserves this account for the preface to Book III, the point where his main narrative begins (III 2.1–5.6). The same purpose could be served, as in biblical history, by mentioning simply the chronological starting-point of the work (Herkommer, 1968, 65 n. 5).

Length of the preface

Lucian advises that the preface to a history should be proportionate to the size of the whole work, neither too long nor too short (*De hist.conscr.* 55). This is standard rhetorical theory (Avenarius, 1956,

---

[10] Herkommer, 1968, p. 26 and n. 2, referring to Josephus, *Ant.*, Callinicus of Petra, Phlegon of Tralles (a chronicle rather than a history proper) and Luke–Acts.

[11] Roman dedication properly falls outside the scope of this study: see further Ruppert, 1911; Janson 1964; Graefenhain, 1892.

[12] Wilamowitz, *Euripides Herakles* (1889), pp. 123ff. Polybius, Diodorus and Dionysius of Halicarnassus all open with a reference to 'other historians', which also serves to alert the reader to the genre of the work in front of him or her.

p. 115). What he would have considered 'too short' Lucian does not
tell us in so many words, though he did reckon it a fault to have no
preface at all;[13] but we may gain a more concrete idea on this from
Quintilian, who expresses the opinion that while prefaces must be
brief, it would be ridiculous to follow the extreme example of those
who restrict themselves to four sentences (*Inst.or.* IV 1.62). Quintilian is thinking of speeches, which were naturally shorter (and
more concerned with brevity) than histories (Herkommer, 1968,
pp. 152–4); historians tended to err in the opposite direction. Thucydides' twenty-three-chapter introduction is too long for the
rhetorically formed taste of Dionysius of Halicarnassus (*De Thuc.*
19–20, pp. 855–61; Avenarius, 1956, p. 115); Dionysius' 'improved'
version takes about three pages.

In practice, we may gain a rough idea of the relative lengths of
historical prefaces from a comparison of the texts in a uniform
edition. Thus, in the Teubner text, Herodotus' preface covers three
pages; Thucydides: 14; Polybius Book I: 6½; Diodorus: 8; Dion.
Halic., *Ant.Rom.*: 13; Josephus, *BJ* 6; *Ant.*: 5; Arrian, *Anab.*: 1;
Appian, *Hist.Rom.*: 9; Herodian: 1½; Procopius: 3. Agathias covers
seven pages of a comparable size. Arrian's preface, which is the
shortest in the list (and which is in many other respects untypical of
historical prefaces), still contains about six sentences. These figures
should be borne in mind when reading passages like II Maccabees
2.32 ('It is a foolish thing to make a long prologue to the history,
and to abridge the history itself'), or *Letter of Aristeas* 8 ('that I may
not weary you by too lengthy an introduction, I will proceed to the
substance of my narrative'). These are highly conventional tran-
sition-formulae, both alluding to 'brevity' as a rhetorical ideal (see
further, ch. 5, n. 50.) Both the prefaces in question are, in fact,
several sentences long. Moreover, II Maccabees is formally speaking not a history but an epitome, and this is the point of the author's
remarks.

Transition

The end of the preface, Lucian teaches, should provide an apt and
easy transition to the narrative (*De hist.conscr.* 55). This too was a
standard piece of advice from the rhetorical theorists (Avenarius,
1956, pp. 117–18; Herkommer, 1968, p. 122 and n. 4), but it is

---

[13] Lucian, *De hist.conscr.*23. On the meaning of the 'virtual prefaces' which Lucian
did allow, see Avenarius, 1956, p. 114.

doubtful if it was really necessary in the case of the historians, who were from the beginning conversant with this basic aspect of literary craftsmanship. For example of transitions in the historians, see Herkommer, 1968, p. 123 nn. 2–4.

Recurrent topics

The magnitude of the subject

See Herkommer, 1968, p. 167 nn. 4 and 5. The historian, according to Dionysius of Halicarnassus, 'is under an obligation in the first place to choose a good subject of lofty character which will be truly profitable to the reader' (*Ant.Rom.* I 1.2, tr. Toynbee). Lucian makes a similar point: 'They will pay attention to him if he shows that the subject on which is he to to speak is great, or necessary, or relevant, or useful ...' (*De hist.conscr.* 53). The importance of choosing a lofty subject for a history seems to have been recognized by most of the surviving Greek historians, and the magnitude of the particular war or series of events they are going to record is a constant theme in their prefaces. The tone was established by Thucydides: 'in the belief that this war would eclipse all its predecessors in importance' (I 1.1, tr. Toynbee). Similar statements can be found in Polybius I 1.4–2.8; Dion. Halic., *Ant.Rom.* 2.1–3.6; Josephus, *BJ* I 1.4–5; Appian, *Hist.Rom.* I pref. 8–11; Herodian, *Hist.* I 1.3; Procopius, *De bellis* I 1.6–17; Agathias, *Hist.* I pref. 10. Where the peculiarity of the work lies not in the choice of a particular subject but in a novel method of presentation, it is the latter which is defended in the same terms: cf. Diodorus I 3.5–8 and Theopompus (Herkommer, 1968, pp. 165–6).

The aims and value of history

Besides the importance of the particular subject chosen, historians frequently discuss the aims and the value of history in general, its powers to amuse and instruct, and the question which of these should be its primary aim. Polybius informs us that this was a standard topic among his (now lost) predecessors (I 1.1–3). Polybius himself ostensibly forbears to discuss the topic at this point, though his preface does contain an eulogy of universal as against local history (I 4.1–11); points from the general discussion appear elsewhere in his work (e.g. in the attack on Timaeus in Book XII:

Avenarius, 1956, pp. 17 n. 7, 23–4). There is a classic exposition of the usefulness of history as against other branches of literature in Diodorus I 1.1–2.8.

In the generalized form described by Polybius and exemplified by Diodorus, this a post-Thucydidean theme; Thucydides mentions by the way one specific advantage to be gained from the perusal of such works as his (I 22.4), but he does not (*pace* Lucian, *De hist.conscr.* 42) speak of 'history' in general. The generalized form probably came into history from the Isocratean school: Ephorus apparently discussed it in his general preface (*FGH* 70 F7–9, with Commentary). It echoes a debate on the relative values of the different branches of literature which goes back at least to Gorgias and by the mid-fourth century had given rise to a set of well-defined theoretical positions.[14] The catchwords and themes of the debate reappear frequently in the surviving historical prefaces. Agathias, like Diodorus, presents a fully fledged *laudatio historiae*; Dionysius of Halicarnassus and Procopius refer to the 'lessons' of history; and Dionysius, Josephus, Herodian, Procopius and Agathias all discuss the object of history and its concern with truth.[15]

The author's sources of information

Dionysius of Halicarnassus' second requirement for the historian is that he should 'devote the utmost care and industry to the task of providing himself with proper sources for his own composition' (I 1.2, tr. Toynbee). The importance of having proper sources of information, and of verifying and testing the information received from tradition or from hearsay, was recognized in Greek historiography at least from the time of Herodotus. Herodotus, however, does not discuss his sources in general terms *in his preface*: his much quoted remarks on the value of eyewitnesses occur not in the preface but as *obiter dicta* attached to specific items of information (e.g. IV 16.1): Verdin, 1970, pp. 224–6. It was Thucydides who introduced the topic into the preface with a generalized discussion on the

[14] K. Ziegler, art. 'Tragoedia', *RE* II 6 cols. 1899–2075 (sect. xxx, 2053ff.). Full discussion in Avenarius, 1956, pp. 16ff., sects. B.b–d.
[15] Agathias, *Hist.*. I pref. 4–5, 16–20; Dion. Halic., *Ant.Rom.* I 1.2 (utility), I 6.4–5 (*exempla*; aims of history); Procopius, *De bellis* I 1–2 (lessons); I 1.4–5 (proper object of history); Josephus, *BJ* I 13–16; Herodian, *Hist.* I 1.1 Cf. also Strabo, *Geog.* I 1.2 (p. 2), 12–23, especially 22–3. On truth as the object of history, see further Avenarius, 156, pp. 40ff., sect. D.b.

reliability of hearsay evidence, and from his time onwards it becomes a regular – though not an inevitable – preface-topic.[16]

The example of Herodotus and Thucydides was also an influential factor in the decision as to what constituted 'proper' sources. Certain themes can be traced throughout the literature. The value of care, trouble, expense and travel in the collection of material is exemplified in Herodotus and Thucydides, and frequently stated by later writers: cf. e.g. Diodorus I 4.1; Dion. Halic., *Ant.Rom.* I 1.2; Josephus, *BJ* I 16 (Avenarius, 1956, p. 78). From Herodotus onwards, the importance of not being credulous was emphasized: it was recognized that one must have some way of assessing the reliability of informants, if only by recognizing and discounting any bias they might have (Avenarius, 1956, pp. 77; 46–54). A prime value was placed on 'seeing for oneself', or failing that on finding and questioning eyewitnesses. This is already evident in Herodotus (e.g. II 29.1)[17] but was elevated into a fetish by the tradition following Thucydides, who had expressed a radical scepticism about the reliability of tradition, even local tradition (I 20–1), and had laid stress on his own opportunities for direct observation of the course of events and for the cross-examination of witnesses (I 22; V 26.5). One result of this was, as Momigliano has demonstrated (1969, pp. 130–1), a recurrent belief that contemporary history was the only proper subject for a real historian. More generally, however, Thucydides' stress on his own participation in the events he describes (I 22.2, V 26.5) was probably responsible for a lasting tendency in an historical preface to lay stress on one's own experience, regardless of the kind of history involved. This 'experience' could take various forms, according to the circumstances. If possible, the historian liked to point out that he had participated in the events of his history (e.g. Polybius III 4.13; Josephus, *BJ* I 3; Cassius Dio

[16] Polybius III 4.13; Diodorus I 4.1–4; Dion. Halic., *Ant.Rom.* I 7.1–3; Josephus, *BJ* I 3, 18; Arrian, *Anab.* I pref.; Herodian, *Hist.* I 1.3; Procopius, *De bellis* I 1.3. Ctesias, Theopompus, Ephorus and Timaeus all discussed the topic in one way or another (Avenarius, 1956, p. 76 and n. 14; Herkommer, 1968, pp. 88–9 and notes; G. Schepens, 'Éphore sur la valeur de l'autopsie', *Ancient Society* I (1970), pp. 163–82); it is a reasonable assumption that these discussions were located in their prefaces, but it is impossible to be certain. Many later historians also maintained the Herodotean habit (which was contrary to Thucydides' practice) of adverting to their sources of information at intervals throughout the work, in relation to specific items: e.g. Polybius X 11.4; Diodorus III 38.1; Cassius Dio LXXII 4.2.
[17] But the proverbial 'Eyes are more reliable than ears' is not put forward by Herodotus as a methodological principle: it appears during the narrative, as a passing remark on the lips of Candaules (I 8.2).

LXXII 7.1). Where such personal participation could not be claimed, however, it was just as valuable to have visited the sites of the events described (e.g. Diodorus, I 4.1; Appian, *Hist.Rom.* I pref. 12) or, failing even that, a general experience of political and military affairs was claimed to give the historian a superior ability to understand the contents of his narrative.[18]

Written sources, by contrast, were not mentioned by either of the fifth-century giants, and, probably for that reason, are rarely named in the prefaces of the Greek historians, even though most later historians in fact relied heavily on written sources. Timaeus appears to have broken with this convention,[19] only to be exposed to the scorn of Polybius. Roman historians generally had a rather different attitude to written sources (Herkommer, 1968, pp. 96ff.), and it may be their example that has influenced Diodorus and Dionysius of Halicarnassus.[20]

The convention of *autopsia*

As we have noted, an important feature of Greek historiography from the fifth century onwards was the claim that the best history was written on the basis of personal experience. It is customary to speak in this connection of 'the convention of *autopsia*',[21] using the abstract noun αὐτοψία which is formed from the personal noun αὐτόπτης. The name is a useful one; but it should not be taken to mean that the Greek word lies behind every instance of the convention. In Avenarius' list, for example (1956, pp. 78–9), none of the six

[18] Cf. Lucian, *De hist.conscr.* 37; Avenarius, 1956, pp. 35–40. With Lucian's remarks in mind, we may perhaps regard the biographical allusions of some later historians (e.g. Appian, *Hist.Rom.* I pref. 15) as a kind of 'author's qualifications': cf. F. G. B. Millar, *A Study of Cassius Dio* (Oxford, Clarendon Press, 1964), pp. 5–7. Dionysius of Halicarnassus' emphasis on 'consorting with leading men' (*Ad Pomp.* VI 3) may reflect the same concern; cf. Polybius XII 28.2–5.

[19] Herkommer, 1968, p. 89 and n. 5; Momigliano, 1969, pp. 215–16. Cf. Millar, *Cassius Dio*, (see n. 18) p. 35.

[20] Diodorus I 4.4 on the use of Roman archives; Dion. Halic., *Ant.Rom.* I 7.3. Dionysius actually names some of the authors he has used, as one might expect in a work which is an inheritor as much of the 'antiquarian' as of the strictly 'historical' side of Greek historiography (Momigliano, 1969, pp. 4, 217). But even so Dionysius' list falls short of being a satisfactory bibliography in modern terms, or even in comparison with the exhaustive lists supplied in the prefaces to Varro's *Antiquities* or Pliny's *Natural History*.

[21] E.g. Herkommer, 1968, p. 90; Avenarius, 1956, p. 80; G. Nenci, 'Il motivo dell'autopsia nella storiografia graeca' *Studi Classici e Orientali* 3 (1955), pp. 14–46; Schepens, *Ephore* (see n. 16); Norden, 1913, p. 316; F. H. Colson, 'Notes on St. Luke's preface', *JTS* 14 (1923), pp. 307ff.

Greek passages cited contains this particular word; and the one historian who stressed the importance of 'seeing for oneself' above all others, Thucydides, never uses the word αὐτόπτης at all, either in the preface or anywhere else.

In fact, as we shall demonstrate in this section, αὐτόπτης and its derivatives[22] were not as common in Greek historiography as is often supposed: there *is* a 'convention of *autopsia*', but it occurs in a rather specialized sphere, almost always in connection with the verification of pieces of information from or about distant *places*. This specialized usage is not limited to the historians, but is shared with a number of scientific writers, and has links with a related usage in the Empiricist school of medicine.

Autoptēs is not a particularly common word.[23] Leaving aside the papyri, and late Christian and magical or theurgical texts, our survey found about 90 instances in Greek literature. Of these, 30 are from Galen and 22 from Polybius, which leaves a mere 38 scattered over the whole *corpus* from Herodotus to Cassius Dio. These divide about half-and-half between 'general' and 'methodological' uses. The 'general' uses (11 in Polybius and 18 in other writers) cover a wide range of contexts and meanings. Here the objects of the *autopsia* do not fall into any readily discernible pattern: they range from the misdeeds of a tyrant (Dinarchus III 15; Lucian, *Phalaris* II 6) to the education of one's children (Plutarch, *Mor.* 9d), from a sea-battle (Cassius Dio XLVIII 18.4) to a woman's beauty (Josephus, *Ant.* XVIII 342).[24] The remainder (11 instances in Poly-

[22] In what follows 'the word αὐτόπτης' may be taken to include the whole word-group: αὐτόπτης, αὐτοψία, αὐτοπτικός, αὔτοπτος, αὐτοπτέω. It seems clear that all these are derived at a relatively late stage from the first, which is cited from Herodotus onwards. αὐτοπτικός first appears in Ps.-Scymnus (c. 120 BC), and the verb αὐτοπτέω in Pausanias (c. AD 150). Our earliest recorded αὐτοψία is in Dioscorides (c. AD 70); cf. Galen's observation that αὐτόπτης is the only form used by 'the ancients', whereas αὐτοψία is used by 'the more recent writers' (*Subfig.Emp.* p. 47; Deichgräber, 1930, p. 47).

[23] The following analysis is based on a detailed study set out in Alexander, 1978, pp. 31–8 and Appendix C, pp. 234–50, where all known instances of the word-group are displayed. This study was carried out before the advent of computers had revolutionized the potential for exhaustive word-searches in ancient literature, and full publication of the results must be delayed until a computer-assisted check is possible. But in fact most central classical texts already had an exhaustive *Index Verborum*, and it is not anticipated that major changes to these conclusions will be necessary.

[24] Where a crime or a death is in view, the *autoptēs* is not necessarily an 'eyewitness' (in our sense) of the crime itself: the status can equally be acquired by inspecting the corpse for subsequent verification of the fact, as in Josephus, *Ant.* XIX 125; Cassius Dio LXII 14.2. This echoes the technical legal use of the word in the papyri,

bius, 20 in other texts, plus all the Galen passages) occur in what we might call 'methodological' contexts – i.e. in a passage where the writer speaks in his own person, whether in a preface or in the text itself, on sources or on methods of verifying information. Thus 'methodological' usages account for a high proportion of the total incidence of the word – a fact which appears to justify the common belief that the *autoptēs*-group was particularly associated with the conventional language used in methodological discussion of sources.[25]

The question is, what kind of information is particularly associated with *autopsia*? Closer analysis of the objects of the *autopsia* claimed reveals that the word occurs most frequently in connection with two kinds of information, medical and geographical. The evidence for the former rests on Dioscorides (*Mat.Med.* I pref. 5) and Galen, who in this respect may be reckoned as good as a class in himself, for he states explicitly that the word-group was character-istic of writers of the Empiricist sect, both 'ancient' and 'more recent'.[26] It appears that *autopsia* was something of a watchword for this sect: it was for them the most fundamental of the three essential parts of the art of medicine. Galen himself, an eclectic as regards the sects, constantly urges on his students the value and indeed indis-pensability of *autopsia*, especially (and here he differs from the Empiricists) that gained by watching anatomical dissections.[27]

The majority of the remaining examples concern what we might broadly call 'geographical' information. Thus Ps.-Scymnus and Pausanias are writers of geographical descriptions, and Lucian's *De Dea Syria* is a pseudo-Herodotean ethnography.[28] Aristotle is speaking of such writers when he says that the authors of *Periodoi* of

where an *autoptēs* is not an eyewitness to a crime but an official sent down after the event to make a personal inspection of the scene, or to survey disputed property (refs. see below ch. 6 p. 121 s.v. αὐτόπται). Two senatorial decrees quoted by Polybius (XXV 6.5; XXXIII 8.3: note the future tense) also reflect this usage, and may indicate that it is older than any of our surviving documentary evidence.

[25] The evidence of the papyri points in the same direction: the one clearly non-technical use of the word, in a private letter home from a traveller visiting Alexandria (P.Oxy. VIII 1154) echoes the literary convention (see below ch. 6 p. 122 s.v. αὐτόπται).

[26] Galen, *De sectis* 2 = K I 67; *Subfig.Emp.* (Deichgräber, 1930) pp. 47, 49. Deichgräber's Index gives 13 instances of the *autoptēs*-group from this text.

[27] Galen, K II 12, II 832, III 117, III 420, III 508, IV 158, IV 195, XI 796–7, XIII 570, XIII 609.

[28] Ps.-Scymnus, *Periegesis* 129; Pausanias IV *Messeniaca* 31.5; Lucian, *De Dea Syria*, pref. Cf. also Galen, *De optima secta* 14 = K I 148, which concerns geo-graphical rather than medical information.

the earth write on the basis of their enquiries, where they do not happen to be *autoptai* (*Meteor.* I 13/350a17). So is Aelius Aristides when, in his encomium of Rome, he compliments the Romans on their achievement of opening up the world for travel: 'There is no need now to write a *Periegesis* of the earth, but you have become *Periegetae* for all ... providing the possibility for any who wish to become *autoptai* of everything' (*Or.* XIV = I 226.7 (395) Dindorf, my trans.). Among the historians, too, the overwhelming majority of instances concerns the verification of information from and about distant lands. Herodotus uses it three times in speaking of points at the fringes of the known world (II 29.1; III 115.1; IV 16.1). Diodorus, when he speaks of *autopsia* in his general preface (I 4.1) is speaking of his travels in Asia and Europe; the word occurs again at II 38.1 in a geographical digression on the Arabian Gulf.[29] Similarly, Cassius Dio uses the word at XXXIX 50.3 in an excursus on Britain, speaking disparagingly of the work of earlier geographers. The same pattern is repeated in Polybius: in six of his 'methodological' instances of the word, the reference is clearly to *autopsia* of places, especially of strange and distant places.[30] Even Ctesias and Theopompus, lost historians whose claim to *autopsia* is frequently derided, are arguably making the claim in regard to geographical rather than historical information.[31]

The thread running through all these passages is the tradition of *historia* as it was conceived by Herodotus and the Ionians, that is an investigation of the world in general, of which the narrating of past events, 'history' in our sense, formed only a part. Thus the three instances of *autoptēs* from Aristotle's *Historia animalium* all fall into the same pattern.[32] Interestingly, these examples already bring us back round to Dioscorides, whose claim to *autopsia* is linked with his opportunities for travel, and his questioning of the 'locals' (*epichōrioi*), a word which itself provides a link with the geographical investigations of the historians (Verdin, 1970, esp. p. 186 n. 10). The link with Ionian *historia* may indeed explain the simul-

[29] Diodorus' information is based partly on extracts from the royal records in Alexandria, partly on the examination of *autoptai*. The words may be taken from Diodorus' source for this section, the *Periplus* of Agatharchides of Cnidus: W. Peremans, 'Diodore de Sicile et Agatharchide de Cnide', *Historia* 16, (1967), pp. 432–55.

[30] Polybius III 58.8; IV 38.12; X 11.4; XII 2.1; XII 4c.4; XII 28a.4.

[31] Ctesias: *FGH* 688 T8 = Photius, *Bibl.* 72 p. 36. Theopompus: *FGH* 115 T20a = Dion. Halic., *Ad Pomp.* VI 3 (783). In both cases the reference is arguably to the geographical/ethnographical aspect of the work, not to the historical facts related (further, Alexander, 1978, p. 35).

[32] Aristotle, *Historia animalium* IX 29 (618a18); IX 37 (620b23); IX 41 (628b8).

taneous, and apparently independent, use of *autoptēs/autopsia* by the Empiricists, and their uncertainty about its relationship with *historia*.[33] In less academic circles, *historia* itself seems to have meant primarily a geographical account: see Plautus, *Menaechmi* 234ff., where the slave, listening to his master's account of six years' wandering around the Mediterranean, sardonically comments, 'I suppose we've come home to write a *historia*'. Compare the odd vernacular use of *autoptēs* in P. Oxy. VIII 1154 (see below, ch. 6 s.v. αὐτόπται).

Thus it is the Herodotean side of Greek historiography, not the Thucydidean, which uses the word *autoptēs* in this conventional way. Herodotus did not lay any particular stress on presence at the events described as a qualification for writing history; it was Thucydides who was responsible for that convention, and Thucydides did not use the word *autoptēs*. We would suggest that this simple fact (perhaps accidental, since there is no obvious reason why Thucydides should not have used the word) accounts for its distribution among the historians. Almost without exception, the later historians reserve it for the 'Herodotean', geographical portion of their work; the 'Thucydidean', convention, that of claiming to have witnessed the events of the narrative oneself, does not employ it.[34]

There are only two certain exceptions to this pattern, in the well-known passages in Polybius (III 4.13) and Josephus (*Contra Apionem* I 55).[35] In both there is a clear reference to the author's *autopsia* of the *events* described in the history (or part of it). Thus Polybius claims that, for the events covered in his later books, 'I was not only an eyewitness (αὐτόπτης) of most, but in some cases a participant (συνεργός) and even a director (χειριστής) of others'. Josephus' claim is expressed in strikingly similar terms: 'My qualification as a historian of the war was that I had been an actor (αὐτουργός) in many and an eyewitness (αὐτόπτης) of most of the events; in short, nothing whatever was said or done of which I was

[33] Cf. Galen, *De sectis* 2 (K I 67) and *De optima secta* 14 (K I 148), plus the whole of *Subfig.Emp.* III (Deichgräber, 1930).

[34] Particularly striking is the case of Cassius Dio, who makes frequent use of his own personal testimony to the events he describes, but does not use *autoptēs* in any of these passages (e.g. LXXII 4.2; LXXII 18): cf. Millar, *Cassius Dio* (see n. 18), ch. 1 and App. III. Compare also, besides the passages cited by Avenarius, 1956, pp. 78–9, *Ep.Aristeas* 10.91; Dion. Halic., *Ant.Rom.* I 6.2; Diodorus I 83.9. The same pattern is seen clearly in Polybius XII 4c.4: 'presence at' events (παρεῖναι), 'being an *autoptēs*' of places.

[35] Polybius XII 4d.2; XXIX 21.8 are also possible examples.

ignorant.' (Josephus *C.Ap.* I 55, tr. Thackeray LCL). There is good reason to believe that Josephus is actually dependent on Polybius at this point,[36] and if this is the case, we are left with a single question: why did Polybius use *autoptēs* in this unusual fashion?

It is immediately obvious that Polybius has an unusual predilection for the word. His figure of eleven 'general' uses is startling over against the total of eighteen for the rest of Greek literature, and he uses it in 'methodological' contexts more liberally than any other historian. But within this class, as we have seen, the majority of references fit the 'Herodotean' pattern of geographical reference; and one factor behind Polybius' fondness for the word may be his particular interest in geography.[37] In rejecting the 'mathematical' geography of Eratosthenes and others like him, Polybius naturally aligned himself with the more discursive *historia*-tradition, which concentrated on describing the world as it actually appeared, so as to enable the reader almost to be an *autoptēs* him/himself.[38] This subjective approach, together with his interest in the periphery of the world (van Paassen, 1957, p. 307) suggests at least a partial explanation for Polybius' use of the word *autoptēs*: it was a vital weapon in his constant campaign to vilify mathematical geography and justify his own approach (van Paassen, 1957, p. 308), and from that point of concern may have spilled over into his general vocabulary.

There is another factor to be taken into account. Polybius clearly knew of the medical debate between the Empiricists and the Dogmatists, and his use of *autoptēs* may also have been influenced by its use in that debate. The attack on Timaeus in XII 25d–e contains an elaborate comparison between history and medicine:

[36] Josephus creates the unusual contrast 'not only *autoptēs* ... but also *autourgos* (cf. Polyb. XII 25h.6), whereas the usual pair is '*autoptēs*, or where this is not possible, *autēkoos*'. This involves using *autourgos* in an uncommon sense to mean 'personally involved'. The word is not a common one, in any sense, but Polybius uses it, together with the abstract *autourgia*, five times, and is the only authority cited for the latter in the sense 'experience' in LSJ. Thus although Polybius uses συνεργός at III 4.13, the language of Josephus at *C.AP.* I 55 is distinctively Polybian and suggests that he has the Polybius passage in mind, if not actually before him. Avenarius, (1956, p. 79 n. 22) also believes that Josephus, *C.Ap.* I 55 is dependent on Polybius.

[37] F. Walbank, 'the geography of Polybius', *Classica et Mediaevalia* 9 (1948), pp. 155–82); C. van Paassen, 1957, pp. 290ff.; P. Pédech, *La méthode historique de Polybe* (Paris, 1964), ch. 12.

[38] Cf. Polyb. IV 38.12 and van Paassen, 1957, p. 299. Polybius' attitude to the mathematical geographers may be compared with that of Herodotus (IV 36.2ff.). Cf. also Aristotle, *Meteor.* 362b12.

the 'bookworm' is compared to the Dogmatists, οἱ λογικοὶ τῶν ἰατρῶν, and these are described in some detail. There is no doubt which side Polybius favours: he repeats all the Empiricist polemic and turns it against Timaeus, and his portrait of the Dogmatist (XII 25d.4ff.) is so vivid and so venomous that it is tempting to imagine that it is lifted direct from an Empiricist pamphlet.[39] We already know that *autopsia* was an important catchword in Empiricist polemic; this could well be another reason why Polybius attached particular significance to the word.[40]

We would suggest, then, that Polybius' use of *autoptēs* may have been influenced by these two theoretical concerns. In the first place, its importance both in medicine and in geography may simply have enhanced its importance for Polybius, to such an extent that he uses it both more frequently and more widely than any other historian. Secondly, its use in the Empiricist debate brings it closer to the more general sense of 'experience' (πεῖρα or ἐμπειρία) than to the 'seeing for oneself' of any specific object.[41] This sense would be the most appropriate for XX 12.8, and III 4.13 is also understood by Avenarius in this sense (1956, p. 38). Whatever the case, Polybius III 4.13 should not be cited as a typical example of the *autopsia-*

[39] F. W. Walbank, *Historical Commentary on Polybius* (Oxford, Clarendon Press, 1957/67) *ad loc.*, speaks of a 'handbook of medicine', but it seems reasonable to suggest that Polybius might actually have come across a polemical pamphlet of the sort we know the early Empiricists wrote (Deichgräber, 1930, pp. 163ff., 253ff.). Elsewhere (*Polybius*, (Berkeley/London, University of California Press, 1972), pp. 71–4), Walbank points out the awkwardness of the whole passage: the medical theory does not really fit Polybius' argument about the nature of history. Certain turns of phrase in this passage can in fact be paralleled elsewhere in Empiricist literature:

τὴν ἐν λόγῳ δύναμιν, τῆς τοῦ λόγου πιθανότητος: Dioscorides, *Mat.Med.* I pref. 5; Blum, 1936, p. 89.

τοῖς ἐκ βυβλίου κυβερνῶσιν: Blum, 1936, pp. 86–8; Galen, *Temp.Med.* VI pref. (K XI 796–7); *De libr.propr.* 5 (K XIX 33 = SM II 110.25–7); *On Medical Experience* IX 2 (Walzer, 1944, p. 98 and notes). C. Wunderer, *Polybios-forschungen: Beiträge zum Sprache- und Kulturgeschichte, 3 Teile in einem Band.* (repr. of edn of Leipzig, Scientia Verlag, Aalen, 1969) I 65 misunderstands the comparison; but in III 10.4 he notes that the 'picturesque language' employed in this passage is untypical of Polybius.

[40] *Autoptēs* in 1 4.7 may also be best explained by the medical parallel: the figure suggests an anatomical dissection.

[41] Cf. Galen, *De sectis* 2 (K I 67 = SM III 3): 'This collection [of primary observations] is called by the Empiricists *autopsia*. They call the same thing *empeiria*, and the recounting of it *historia*; for the same thing is *autopsia* to the observer, and *historia* to the one who hears about the observation.' *Idem*, *De optima secta* 14 (K I 148): 'The Empiricists say that there is no need to judge *historia* by *peira*: for they say that just as you believe that Crete is an island on the basis of the *historia* of others, although you are not *autoptai* of Crete yourselves . . .'

convention among the Greek historians. It is actually a highly untypical passage, influenced probably by Polybius' knowledge of the convention in two other spheres, and does not appear to have influenced subsequent historians with the exception of Josephus.

4

SCIENTIFIC PREFACES: ORIGINS AND DEVELOPMENT

The place of prefaces in the scientific tradition as a whole

Prefaces, we shall argue, are neither integral nor necessary to the scientific tradition as a whole. But first, what can be said about the tradition as a body of literature?

We have already indicated (above p. 21) the rough area covered by the word 'scientific' in this study.[1] It includes for the purposes of literary analysis the 'esoteric' treatises of the philosophers as well as the technical treatises of the mathematicians or engineers; it includes astrological herbals and books on dream-interpretation as well as what we would call 'scientific' medicine; and it includes even rhetorical schools. It must be clear, then, that we are not talking about a homogeneous collection of writings: the texts belong to different, independent traditions and come into being in diverse ways. Thus there is no equivalance of *form* between (say) the Hippocratic *Epidemics*, the Euclidean *Elements* and the *Eudemian Ethics* of Aristotle: each scholastic tradition tends to develop and preserve its own favoured means of expression, and has to be understood in its own terms.

In terms of *function*, however, it is possible to make broader generalizations encompassing the tradition as a whole. Thus the majority of scientific texts fall into one of two broad categories:

(a)   Those which reflect more or less directly the oral situation of the lecture hall: such are most of the surviving works of Aristotle, and the musical treatises of Aristoxenus of Tarentum. (Even when the mode of presentation has passed from primarily oral (pupils' or teacher's notes of actual

---

[1] Cf. above pp. 21–2. For a general account of Greek science and more specialized bibliography, see Lloyd, 1970 and 1973. Fraser, 1972, vol. I ch. 7 gives a full survey of Alexandrian science. On rhetorical and other *technai*, see Furhmann, 1960. See further Appendix B.

lectures) to primarily written, the natural conservatism of the form itself tends to preserve references to 'speaking' and 'hearing'.)[2]

(b)   Those which reflect a primarily written schematization of the *technē*, systematized into memorable form for use as school handbooks. This category is represented in many of the writings of the Hippocratic corpus (e.g. *Epidemics, Aphorisms*) and in mathematical textbooks of the Euclidean type, which from the third century BC onwards developed their classic format of presentation as a series of theorems (Fraser, 1972, I pp. 390ff.) Within this class we may also include 'systematic handbooks' like Anaximenes' *Ars Rhetorica* (Fuhrmann, 1960), which proceeds by means of definitions and divisions of the subject.[3]

The scientific writers also share an approach to composition which sets them apart from the rest of Greek literature. Theophrastus pinpoints the distinction between the two approaches rather neatly: 'Of the (two) forms of discourse, one concerns itself with the audience (*tous akroatas*), the other with the facts (*ta pragmata*): the former is [the one] pursued by poets and orators, the latter by philosophers (Fr. 64 Wimmer).' 'Poets and orators' covers everything that we should call 'literary composition', 'philosophy' to Theophrastus includes the whole Aristotelian study of physics, biology etc. and can legitimately be extended to other scientific texts. An analogous distinction is made by G. E. R. Lloyd, writing in 1975 on the Hippocratic Corpus:

> Many of the Hippocratic treatises are practical manuals, and those who used them in the fifth and fourth centuries were, no doubt, less concerned with such questions as the exact original text or the identity of the author or authors, than with the substance of their contents, the useful medical knowledge they conveyed.   (Lloyd, 1975, p. 181).

[2] E.g. Aristoxenus, *El.Harm.* III 59.6. See further Steinmetz, 1964, pp. 14ff.

[3] The Hippocratic *Corpus*, like the Aristotelian, also contains a small number of 'exoteric' works, the *epideixeis* or public lectures written in a more rhetorical style, apparently by a non-specialist (Lloyd, 1978, p. 10; cf. Jones, LCL *Hippocrates*, vol. II pp. 185–6, 221–5). There are also signs of the beginnings of a tendency to polemical writing (i.e. the basing of one's presentation on the refutation of others) which came into its own in the Alexandrian medical schools (Fraser, 1972, vol. I pp. 352–9), but which is not so prominent in other disciplines.

This is fundamental to the whole scientific tradition. Lloyd's characterization of the Hippocratic Corpus, indeed, is worth quoting in full since so much of it applies (*mutatis mutandis*) across the whole tradition (Lloyd, 1975, p. 189):

(1)   With the exception of some rhetorical ἐπιδείξεις, they are not polished literary works.

(2)   In many cases the treatises do not form clearly defined unities, but are composite works, compilations consisting of several more or less disparate parts.

(3)   Additions, interpolations, and borrowings ... can be established on many occasions and may be suspected on many others.

(4)   There is some evidence of joint authorship and of later revisions ... it would be wrong to attribute our own concern for establishing an original text and preserving it intact to those who used and transmitted practical medical manuals in this period.

The growth of prefaces – or of the various degrees of prefatory material which may be found at the beginning of a text – is very much bound to this pragmatic approach to composition. There is little overt concern for presentation beyond what is necessary to make the subject clear, and there is very little explanation of the book *qua* book: it is clearly assumed that the reader will know what to expect before he or she picks it up. This is especially true in the second of our two broad categories (above p. 43), where there is often no introductory material at all. Many of the medical texts simply open with a statement of fact, sometimes in note form (*Epid., V.C., Mochl., Aph.*), while others have the most rudimentary of titles: 'This is how one should diagnose ...' (*Vict.* II cf. *Salubr., Exsect., Gland.*) Similarly the mathematical texts begin either with a list of definitions or hypotheses (Aristarchus of Samos, Autolycus of Pitane, Euclid, *El.* I–VI) or with a proposition or a problem (Euclid, *El.* VIII, IX, XII, XIII, *Phaen.*). Category (a) produces rather more in the way of introductory material, related apparently to a need for orientation, either vis-à-vis the subject itself or vis-à-vis other practitioners. Aristotle's constant desire to relate one part of the field of human knowledge to another produces good examples of orientation vis-à-vis the subject: cf. *Met.A, Eth.Nic.* I and Aristoxenus of

Tarentum, *El.Harm.* I. 1. Orientation vis-à-vis others is more common among the medical writers (Hippocrates, *VM, Vict.*; cf. also Aristoxenus of Tarentum, *El.Harm.* I 2–9).

All of this, however, is almost completely impersonal. Generally speaking, there is nothing in these introductions to identify either author or readership. If the author is concerned with the facts rather than the audience, in Theophrastus' words, he assumes equally that his readers will be concerned with the subject-matter and not with himself. Even in the most polemical writings of the *Corpus Hippocraticum*, there is a minimum of information about the author himself. He is content to assert, 'My predecessors are wrong and I am right,' without explaining in autobiographical terms how he came to his conclusions. And the fourth-century scientific tradition seems to have equally little room for a second-person address. There is nothing in these prose texts to suggest a formal link with the conventional second-person address which links Greek didactic verse with oriental wisdom-literature (Hesiod, *Op.* 10, 27; Empedocles fr. 1.1 = DK I 31 fr. B1.1). The technical and philosophical prose of the fourth and third centuries BC is conducted almost exclusively in the third person. If the first person is used in argument, it is normally in the plural. A second-person singular imperative does appear occasionally in the mathematical theorems ('Drop a perpendicular ... '), but neither individual pupil nor composite audience is ever addressed as such.[4]

The pattern thus established at the beginning of the Greek scientific tradition runs strongly throughout its long history. Towards the end of the fourth century BC we notice some minor changes in the manner of introductions, reflecting the fact that the book is coming to be taken for granted as a means of communication in its own right. A comparison of Aristotle with Theophrastus shows the later writer more conscious of the problem of organizing his own writings than his master was; each book begins with a transitional phrase summarizing the contents of the previous one and the intended subject of the present work. These lists of contents are a simple development of the internal transitional phrases found already in a wide range of technical literature in the fourth century (Fuhrmann, 1960, p. 142); they are neatly rendered into prose and cleverly varied. Another useful stylistic trick, and one to which the Greek

---

[4] The dedicated prefaces to Anaximenes' *Ars rhetorica* (= Ps.-Aristotle, *Rhetorica ad Alexandrum*) and Theophrastus' *Characters* are not fourth-century products: both are agreed to be later additions, possibly Byzantine. See further Jaeger, 1948, p. 230.

language lends itself particularly well, is that whereby the subject of the book is placed at the beginning of the opening sentence, but in an oblique case. This distortion of the natural word order provides an invaluable aid to identification in an age when the 'title' was a small label attached to the outside of a roll which could all too easily be lost. It remained popular throughout the tradition.[5]

But beyond such minor adaptations, there was no necessity for any further development. Scientific texts continued to be produced in situations essentially the same as those of the fourth century BC, and therefore needed no more elaborate prefaces than the earlier works: moreover, the tradition itself in course of time came to provide its own context, in which the work of succeeding generations could be understood. Thus many later works, like those of Asclepiodotus, Cleonides, Dionysius Thrax, Demetrius, Hephaestion, Rufus of Ephesus, Apollonius Dyscolus or Albinus,[6] have no introductory material beyond the kind of rudimentary practical aids already seen. Others, like the Aristotelian commentator Aspasius, prefer a philosophical introduction, obviously modelled on Aristotle.[7] But neither group takes us outside the range of introductory material employed in the fourth century BC.

It is therefore something of a surprise to find, right through from the beginning of the third century BC to the third century AD, a number of scientific texts from different subject areas within the tradition which introduce a strong personal element. These are the prefaces which form the basis of our study.

Personal prefaces: the texts studied

The first known text with a preface of the new type is a medical one, the *Letter to Antigonus* of Diocles of Carystus[8] (end of the fourth

[5] West notes a similar phenomenon in early poetry: M. L. West, *Hesiod's Theogony* (Oxford, Clarendon Press, 1966), p. 151. For 'titles', see Kenyon, 1951, p. 62.

[6] Asclepiodotus, *Tactica* (before II AD, perhaps I BC); Cleonides, *Introductio harmonica* (II AD); Dionysius Thrax, *Ars grammatica* (II BC); Demetrius, *De elocutione* (possibly I AD); Hephaestion, *Encheiridion* and other metrical works (probably II AD); Rufus of Ephesus, medical writings (I–II AD); Apollonius Dyscolus, grammatical works (II AD); Albinus, *Introduction* and *Epitome* of Platonic philosophy (II AD).

[7] Aspasius, *Comm.in Eth.Nic.* D. Earl, 1972, suggests the influence of this 'Aristotelian' opening device (characterized by sweeping generalization) on the prefaces of Sallust.

[8] The authors covered in this analysis are listed, with dates and bibliographical information, in Appendix B.

century BC), a short treatise on hygiene addressed to Antigonus I, one of the 'Successors' of Alexander, probably between 305 and 301 BC.[9] After Diocles there are no surviving dedicated prefaces in medical literature until Apollonius of Citium in the first century BC; our evidence for the hellenistic period comes chiefly from the fields of mathematics and engineering. Of primary importance are the letters preserved along with several of the treatises of Archimedes, together with those which serve to preface the eight books of the *Conica* of Apollonius of Perge; both these third-century BC mathematicians sent their treatises across the Mediterranean to fellow-mathematicians in other centres of learning, and dispatched letters of explanation to accompany them. From Archimedes we also have a second-person address of a rather different kind in the *Psammites*, addressed to the young prince Gelon in Archimedes' home court of Syracuse. From the second century BC we may add the mathematician Diocles, whose short treatise *On Burning Mirrors* (Toomer, 1976) begins with a short 'story' about the genesis of the problem very like those found in Archimedes and Apollonius of Perge. Although the treatise uses both first and second person fairly freely, no epistolary address survives; however, Diocles' introduction refers to both letters and visits between mathematicians, and thus provides valuable confirmation of the picture gleaned from Archimedes and Apollonius. From the same period comes Hypsicles, whose treatise on the dodecahedron and the eicosahedron (known to the tradition as the fourteenth book of Euclid) is dedicated in a rather formal preface to an unknown Protarchus; and finally the astronomer Hipparchus, whose *Commentary on the 'Phaenomena' of Aratus and Eudoxus* has lengthy prefaces addressed to 'Aischrion'.

Contemporary with these mathematicians is a series of mechanical writers. Around the end of the third century BC, Bito's *Kataskeuai*, 'On the Construction of War-engines and Catapults', was dedicated to one of the Attalid kings of Pergamum; and Philo of

[9] There are no dedications in the *Corpus Hippocraticum*. Diocles apparently dedicated another work to the Macedonian prince, Pleistarchus: Wellmann, 1901, nos. 102–46, pp. 162–88; cf. Jaeger, 1938, pp. 62ff.; 1948, p. 410. From the Empiricist medical writers the only possible dedicated works are those said to have been composed by Heraclides of Tarentum (I BC) to Antiochis and to Astydamas (Deichgräber, 1930, pp. 259–60, fr. 203ff., 208ff., pp. 188–93). Fraser, 1972, vol. II p. 535 n. 212 and p. 653 n. 38 suggests that these are more likely to have been polemical works. Heraclides' *Nicolaus* (Deichgräber, 1930, p. 180.2 and p. 260) was probably, like Diocles' *Archidamus* (Wellmann, 1901, nos. 147–8, pp. 188–90), a dialogue.

Byzantium addressed the various books of his 'Mechanical Compendium', including our surviving *Belopoeica* and *Pneumatica*, to his friend Ariston. In the first century BC we find comparable preface-patterns, translated into Latin but very obviously dependent on Greek tradition, in Vitruvius' *De architectura*, dedicated to Octavian; and the tradition continues in the first century AD with Hero of Alexandria, whose prefaces, broadly similar to those of his predecessors, are unusual only in having (apart from one exception) no dedications.[10]

At the end of the hellenistic period (in all probability) we have an isolated representative of the grammatical-rhetorical side of education in the little treatise of 'Demetrius' on letter-writing, addressed to a friend or pupil, possibly a minor official, Heracleides. One at least of the two geographical texts also belongs to this period: Ps.-Scymnus certainly wrote around the end of the second century BC; the date of Dionysius Calliphontis is less certain. These two writers belong to a rather different category from the other scientific writers, since both composed in verse; but their prefaces, while constrained by the requirements of the metre (and in the case of Dionysius, by an acrostic as well), in fact show a marked similarity to the basic style and structure of the scientific preface. They are not highly literary works, being composed in iambic trimeters rather than in the affected epic manner of didactic poetry like that of Nicander of Colophon; and the essential mode of expression of the prefaces is closer to the scientific than to the poetic. Dionysius' poem is dedicated to an unknown Theophrastus; Ps.-Scymnus' to a king Nicomedes of Bithynia.

With Apollonius of Citium (mid-first century BC) we return to medicine. This Cypriot writer addressed the three volumes of his illustrated commentary on the *De articulis* of Hippocrates to a 'King Ptolemy', probably the younger brother of Ptolemy XII Auletes. From the first century AD we have dedicated prefaces in Dioscorides, *De materia medica* and in Erotian, *Glossary to Hippocrates*, both addressed to highly placed fellow-doctors. Galen in the second century AD exhibits a whole spectrum of preface-types, shading from the very few works with no preface at all (e.g. K V 911), through those which begin with a question (e.g. K VII 666), up

---

[10] Vitruvius' contemporary Athenaeus Mechanicus also has some interesting material in his preface and epilogue, but this preface is so rhetorical in style and content that it effectively breaks with scientific convention, and we have not included it in our detailed analysis.

through the more common amplified introduction, describing the mistaken views of others (e.g. K V 104), to the unexpected story as in K XIV 1ff. or K VI 755ff. Out of the whole Galenic corpus, about twenty works are dedicated, most commonly to the author's 'friends' or to enthusiastic amateurs of medicine, *philiatroi*: it is in these dedicated prefaces that Galen, normally an independent stylist, approaches most closely to the stereotyped style and manner of dedicated prefaces elsewhere in the scientific tradition.

Contemporary with Galen is our one further rhetorical writer, Hermogenes of Tarsus. Like Galen, Hermogenes is relatively independent of convention, but his prefaces show some significant affinities with those of scientific writers elsewhere. Only one of them bears a dedication, to a certain Julius Marcus. From the first and second centuries AD came also a group of texts from the sciences of magic and divination: Thessalus' astrological herbal, ostensibly dedicated to the emperor Claudius; Artemidorus Daldianus' five books on the interpretation of dreams, dedicated successively to the rhetor Cassius Maximus and to the author's son; and Vettius Valens' *Anthology* of horoscopes, addressed to a pupil. Finally, we have included in our survey the mathematician Serenus to exemplify the persistence of convention right through to the third century AD: other third-century texts could have been included (e.g. Diophantus and Marcianus[11]), were they not rather far from our immediate centre of interest. Serenus' two treatises both bear short prefaces addressed to an otherwise unknown Cyrus.

Much of the content of these prefaces is severely practical, and can be explained as a direct development of the kind of explanatory material found in non-personal introductions (above, p. 44–6).Thus we find regularly a certain amount of information about the subject-matter, the relationship of the author to his predecessors, and the relationship of the book to others by the same author. Such material arises directly out of the circumstances and needs of composition; the only difference may be that in a separate dedicated preface or letter the author can express himself more fully than was either possible or necessary for a man like Theophrastus, lecturing in the closed world of the school. So, for example, the wealth of bibliographical information contained in some of Archimedes'

[11] Diophantus, *Arith.* I 1, addressed to 'the most honourable Dionysius'; Pappus, e.g. *Coll.* VII 1, addressed to Hermodorus; Marcianus, *Epitome peripli Menippei* (*GGM* I 594) begins with an epistolary saluation to his friend Amphithalius.

letters[12] clearly reflects both the increasing geographical distance between author and reader in the hellenistic world, and the increasing size and complexity of the world of books itself. Similarly the introductory and transitional phrases already seen in embryo in the fourth-century texts have a constant place in the more elaborate later prefaces, and for the same reasons. In particular, the increasingly stylized summaries of contents which often appear at the beginnings of books (and sometimes at the ends as well) have obvious practical advantages in a period when books could easily go astray or lose their titles.[13]

The explanatory content of these prefaces, then, is not radically new; if there is more of it than there used to be, this could be seen as a natural response to changing circumstances. But what are we to say about the personal element? This is certainly new: as we have seen above, fourth-century scientific prose, and much of the later tradition, had little room for the first-person singular and none for the second. What circumstances lie behind this (apparently) sudden change of direction?

The roots of dedication

The scientific tradition employs two forms of address, the epistolary ('X to Y, greeting') and the rhetorical (recipient's name inserted in the vocative into the opening sentence). These two forms correspond to two originally distinct categories of dedication: on the one hand, the letter to a friend or colleague (in effect a covering letter sent to accompany a new manuscript text), as exemplified in the letters of Archimedes (*Sph. Cyl.* I–II, *Con.Sph., Spir., Quadr., Eratosth.*) and of Apollonius of Perge; and, on the other, the address to a monarch, as exemplified in Diocles of Carystus and in Archimedes' *Psammites*. With the exception of Diocles, writers dedicating a text to a monarch invariably use the rhetorical form of address;[14]

---

[12] E.g. *Sph.Cyl.* I, vol. I p. 2.2–4.13; *Sph.Cyl.* II, vol. I p. 168.5–19; *Eratosth.*, vol. II p. 426.2–428.15. It was presumably because o˙ the value of this material that the letters were preserved.

[13] Cf. also ch. 3 above p. 29. For examples of summaries, see the opening and closing lines of Hipparchus, Books I and II; Philo, *Belopoeica*; and Apollonius of Citium, Books II and III.

[14] Diocles' *Letter to Antigonus* is anomalous: it bears a separate address in the manner of a letter, but lacks the normal epistolary salutation. This is not a letter formula found in the papyrus letters (Kim, 1972, ch. 1A); but of course Diocles predates most of the papyri. The Attalus of Apollonius of Perge, *Conica* Books IV–VIII is not likely to be one of the royal Attalids: Fraser, 1972, vol. I p. 417f.

thus in Archimedes we can see a clear formal distinction between the letters to friends and the dedication to Gelon:

> 'Archimedes to Dositheus, greeting. Previously I sent you ... *Sph.Cyl.* I

> 'There are those who think, King Gelon, that the number of the sand is infinite in amount ...' *Psamm.* 1

In the latter the vocative address is simply inserted into the opening statement of the argument: there is not, strictly speaking, any separate preface, such few personal remarks as Archimedes makes to Gelon being confined to the epilogue (vol. II p.258.5–12). In formal terms, then, the whole of the *Psammites* is addressed to Gelon. With the earliest letters the opposite is the case: the letter is an external addition to the text, complete with its own opening and closing formulae,[15] and it can concern itself with matters quite extraneous to the treatise itself.

This clear distinction soon becomes blurred. Even in Archimedes and Apollonius of Perge the closing letter formula is sometimes missing,[16] so that letter and text are no longer clearly demarcated. Conversely, in Bito's dedicated treatise on siege-engines, the address to Attalus is inserted into an opening sentence of a general, introductory nature, more like a true preface than the opening of the *Psammites*. Eventually the two forms coalesce: Hipparchus uses rhetorical and epistolary address indiscriminately in different volumes of the same work (contrast Books I and II), and in later texts it becomes difficult if not impossible to differentiate between the two forms. It appears that the address to a friend ceased to have the purely practical function of the early letters and assumed much of the style, and presumably also the functions, of dedication to a monarch. An early example is the mathematical treatise of Hypsicles, apparently dedicated to a friend, which has a rhetorical address (p.2.1: 'Basileides the Tyrian, O Protarchus ...'), uses the only Greek word which might be described as a technical term for literary dedication (προσφωνῆσαι p.2.16–17), and speaks of itself as a προοίμιον (p.4.5); the very phrasing of the closing sentence (p.4.4–5) suggests a degree of attention to the niceties of composition which one would expect rather in a dedication to a

[15] Archimedes, *Sph.Cyl.* I, vol. I p.2.1., p. 4.21; *Con.Sph.*, vol. I p.246.1, p.258.17; *Quadr.*, vol. II p. 262.1, p.266.4. Apollonius of Perge, *Con.* I, p.2.1, p.4.28; *Con.* II, p.192.1, 10.
[16] Archimedes, *Sph.Cyl.* II, *Spir.*, *Eratosth.*; Apollonius of Perge, *Con.* IV.

monarch. We shall return below to the question of the social situation implied in these non-royal dedications.

In view of this fusion of forms, dedication in the scientific tradition can be considered as a single phenomenon. The two forms serve, however, as a valuable clue to two originally distinct social situations, both characteristic of the new circumstances of Greek scholarship in the third century BC: its dispersal over a wide area of the Mediterranean basin, and its dependence on the patronage of the hellenistic courts. The letters of Archimedes and Apollonius of Perge (and the preface of Diocles, *On Burning Mirrors*) give a very clear picture of the physical and social circumstances of the men who wrote them: 'Mathematics during the Hellenistic period was pursued, not in "schools" established in "cultural centres", but by individuals all over the Greek world, who were in lively communication with each other both by correspondence and in their travels' (Toomer, 1976, p. 2). Dedication to a monarch is apparently equally easy to explain as a natural response to the patronage of the courts, 'an automatic recognition of the dependence of writers on the ruler' (Fraser, 1972, I p. 311). But in fact in this case the relationship between social context and literary convention is rather more complex than these words imply, and will repay closer scrutiny.

First of all, it must be stated clearly that dedication as a response to royal patronage is by no means 'automatic'. There were many hellenistic writers who did not dedicate their works to kings. Philo of Byzantium, for example, speaks warmly of the support (*chorēgia*) afforded to the technicians in Alexandria διὰ τὸ φιλοδόξων καὶ φιλοτέχνων ἐπειλῆφθαι βασιλέων (Philo, *Bel.* Th. 50.25–6); but he says nothing about dedication, and his own works are dedicated to an unknown Ariston. Diogenes Laertius' much quoted passage (VII 185) tells us only that Chrysippus did not dedicate any of his writings to any of the kings (τοσαῦτα γοῦν συγγράψας οὐδενὶ βασιλέων προσπεφώνηκεν). The fact that Diogenes cites this as an example of 'arrogance' may tell us something about Diogenes himself, but it is doubtful if it constitutes good evidence for hellenistic social convention. Certainly Chrysippus (who, Diogenes tells us more pertinently, also refused an invitation to go to Alexandria to the court of Ptolemy Philopator) was not the only hellenistic philosopher to dedicate nothing to the kings, as Diogenes should have known: look for example at his lists of works attributed to Sphaerus, who did accept Philopator's invitation (VII

177–8), and Strato, who 'taught Ptolemy Philadelphus and received, so it is said, 80 talents from him' (V 58–9).

Secondly, the dedication of a technical treatise, as found in the scientific tradition, was not the only polite way to show one's gratitude. As we have shown above, the second-person address was neither integral nor necessary to the scientific tradition (above p. 45). Similarly with the historians and antiquarians (ch. 3, p. 28): if there are antiquarian writers who, contrary to normal historical convention, dedicate their works, the dedication is 'tacked on' to a pre-existing form, an addition reflecting outward circumstances (perhaps, in the case of Manetho, Berossus and the hellenistic Jewish writers, the circumstance of being cultural 'outsiders') rather than the inner logic of the genre itself. But there were other writers who chose to make a literary gesture to the kings more directly by adopting a genre specifically adapted to that purpose. This is most clearly seen in verse: cf. Theocritus' encomium of Ptolemy Philadelphus (*Idyll* XVII), Arcesilaus' epigram for Attalus (Diogenes Laertius IV 30) or Nicander's *Hymn to Attalus*.[17] In prose, the equivalent will be a moral treatise like Theophrastus' *On Kingship* (addressed to Cassander),[18] or a protreptic discourse urging the advantages of a philosophical way of life, like Aristotle's *Protrepticus*, addressed to the Cypriot prince Themison.[19] It is arguably wrong (or at least unhelpful) to call works like these 'dedicated': to quote Werner Jaeger: 'In Aristotle's day the dediction of treatises was unknown.' 'With Aristotle, the address to a particular person is still the living expression of the mood of earnest ethical exhortation. It is organic to the protreptic style as such' (Jaeger, 1948, pp. 230, 56). Whether or not we accept Jaeger's terminology, his distinction is a vital one. Addressing a monarch in a genre already adapted to the personal is one possible response to patronage; dedicating to him an impersonal scientific treatise is another.

[17] Nicander, fr. 104: see Gow and Scholfield, *Nicander* (Cambridge University Press, 1953), Introd. p. 6.

[18] Athenaeus, *Deipnos.* IV 144e (the author may be Sosibius rather than Theophrastus). Herkommer fails to draw the distinction advocated here, and cites this work without qualification as an example of dedication (Herkommer, 1968, p. 24). Similarly Janson, 1964, p. 102, cites Seneca's *De clementia ad Neronem* simply as a dedication. See further in next note.

[19] This work is fully discussed by Jaeger, 1948, pp. 54ff. (cf. also p. 230). Testimonia and fragments in Ross, *Aristotle: Fragments* (Oxford, Clarendon Press, 1955), pp. 26–7. The reference in Isocrates, *Ad Demon.* 4 to '*protreptikoi logoi*' may well be to this work of Aristotle's.

There are in fact remarkably few real parallels to the scientific practice of dedicating a technical treatise to a monarch, and there are certainly none earlier than the first scientific examples. Arcesilaus may have dedicated a philosophical treatise to the Attalid Eumenes I.[20] Colotes' treatise on the Epicurean philosophy, addressed to Ptolemy Philadelphus, may have been a work of the protreptic type (Plut., *Adv.Col.* 1107e). Archelaus of Cappadocia may have dedicated some of his *paradoxographa* to a Ptolemy, probably Euergetes I.[21] Outside the world of science and philosophy, there are the antiquarian writers, Manetho and Berossus (see above, ch. 3 p. 28), Apollodorus' *Chronica*,[22] and the two Jewish writers, Aristobulus and 'Aristeas' (below ch. 7). Other examples could perhaps be added, but in any event the list will not be a long one.

It is natural to ask at this point: where did the idea come from? Here I think we need to distinguish the practice of dedication from the literary convention in which it is expressed. For the intrusion of the practice of dedication into the essentially impersonal world of scientific literature, I would suggest that there is an obvious analogue in the ancient religious practice of dedicating an invention, an artefact or a discovery in a temple. Herodotus (IV 87–8) tells us of Mandrocles of Samos, who set up 'in the temple of Hera at Samos ... a representation of the bridge which he built for Darius across the Bosphorus'. It is only a logical extension of this idea, in the new context of Ptolemaic patronage, when Eratosthenes sets up a monument in bronze of his new instrument for the duplication of the cube, with a dedicatory epigram to Euergetes I, or when Ctesibius dedicates an automatic drinking-cup in the temple where Arsinoe Philadelphus is worshipped as Arsinoe Zephyritis, or when a sundial in Miletus carries a dedication to Ptolemy Philadelphus.[23] It is not difficult to see how a scientific treatise, a sample of the scholar's work, could be treated in the same way.

This religious analogy does not, however, explain the particular

---

[20] Diogenes Laertius IV 38. This reference is puzzling, since Diogenes has already said that Arcesilaus 'according to some' did not publish anything (IV 32); but cf. the epithet *philogrammatos*, IV 30. The confusion in Diogenes' sources seems to have found its way into the article on dedication in *OCD*.

[21] Fraser, 1972, vol. I pp. 778–9; vol. II p. 841 n. 305, p. 1086 n. 443; p. 1090 n. 459. There is some doubt about this dedication, which is conjectural.

[22] See Ps.-Scymnus lines 16–49 and Jacoby, 1902.

[23] These 'dedicated inventions' are described by Fraser, 1972, vol. I pp. 410–13, q.v. for references.

literary form adopted by the scientific writers. As we have observed, dedication to monarchs, in contrast to correspondence with friends or colleagues, almost always uses the rhetorical form of address; the language of religious dedication occurs only in Dioscorides (ἀνατίθεμεν *Mat.Med.* I pref. p. 2.20, *Simpl.* I pref. p. 151.13).[24] Classical rhetoric belonged in the public domain and was normally addressed to a plural audience: 'Men of Athens', 'Gentlemen of the jury'. Towards the end of the fourth century, however, there were two simultaneous developments both of which issued in a class of speeches addressed to individuals rather than groups. Both are exemplified in the Isocratean corpus, the first in the *Ad Philippum* (*Or.* V), the result of Isocrates' realization that political speeches must in future be made to individuals if they were to be of any effect (*Or* V 12–14); and the second in the moral-philosophical protreptics addressed to the Cypriots Nicocles and Demonicus (*Or.*I and II).[25] This latter form of prose parenesis probably goes back to the sophists, who used their new tool of rhetorical prose to replace the ancient wisdom-literature of the poets (Jaeger, 1948, pp. 55–6). In Isocrates, the difference between the *Ad Demonicum* and the *Ad Philippum* is chiefly one of content: the first deals with general issues of moral and political philosophy, the second with a particular point of policy. The opportunity for the latter disappeared in time with the autonomy of the Greek city-states; but the more universal genre of advice remained popular. It is exemplified both in the treatises 'On Kingship' which became popular in the hellenistic era (Aristotle to Alexander, Theophrastus to Cassander etc.), and in the protreptic discourses which urged the advantages of a philosophical way of life, such as Aristotle's *Protrepticus*.

It is not a long step from here to our earliest examples of dedication in the scientific tradition. Diocles of Carystus' *Letter to Antigonus* urges on the king the (purely theoretical) advantages of addressing himself to the 'philosophy' of hygiene and medical prognostication (p. 75.3–5), and in other ways the philosophical protreptic seems to have provided a ready model for the scientific writer looking for a form of words with which to dedicate his work. Such a model would explain the rhetorical form of address, which is constant after Diocles, and could also account for certain verbal links. Thus both Diocles and Aristotle insist on the 'suitability' of the

---

[24] But compare Pliny, *NH* pref. 11 and 19.

[25] The *Ad Demonicum* is probably not by Isocrates himself, but is the work of a contemporary: Jaeger, 1948, pp. 58ff.

monarch for the subject addressed to him.[26] Something similar has occurred already in the two Isocratean speeches (*Ad Demon.* 3; *Ad Nic.* 2), and later on the laconic remarks of Archimedes at the end of the *Psammites* (vol. II p. 258.11–12) and of Bito at the end of the *Kataskeuai* (W 67.5) look like echoes of the same theme:

> ... which is why I thought that it was not unfitting (οὐκ ἀνάρμοστον) for you too to contemplate these things.
>
> (Archimedes)

> We have written up as much as we thought most suitable (ἁρμόζειν) for you ...   (Bito)

In more general terms, it is customary for the hellenistic scientists, whether dedicating their work to kings or addressing them to friends, to lay stress on the disposition of the dedicatee towards the subject as a factor in their own decision to write (see below ch. 5, pp. 74–5). We may note too that the word *philomathēs*, a favourite in scientific dedications (see below ch. 5, p. 100), appears already in Isocrates, *Ad Demon.* 18; and that Hypsicles' allusion to a long-standing family link with his dedicatee (p. 4.2–3) recalls the similar (though opposite) relationship in *Ad Demonicum* 2.

Functions and development of dedication

We have noted a gradual fusion of the two originally distinct forms of personal address in the scientific tradition, the epistolary (letters to friends or colleagues) and the rhetorical (dedication to monarchs). The former category includes the letters of Archimedes and Apollonius of Perge, and probably Diocles *On Burning Mirrors*; the latter covers Archimedes' *Psammites*, Bito's *Kataskeuai*, Vitruvius' *De architectura*, Ps.-Scymnus, Apollonius of Citium, and (if the dedication is authentic) Thessalus. We have yet to consider whether this fusion of form also entails a fusion of function, and if so how that fusion balances out: does the 'private' address to a friend come to assume more of the functions of 'public' dedication to a monarch, or is it the friendly relationship between peers which predominates in the later development of the convention? What can we say about the social setting of the address in Hypsicles, Hippar-

---

[26] Diocles of Carystus, lines 2–4. 'Suitability' is the whole point of Stobaeus' anecdote about Aristotle's *Protrepticus ad Themisonem* (fr. 50, Ross (cited in n. 19 above) p. 26), and it seems reasonable to assume that the passage in question occurred at the beginning of the book.

chus, Philo of Byzantium, Hero of Alexandria, 'Demetrius', Dionysius Calliphontis, Dioscorides, Erotian, Galen, Hermogenes of
Tarsus and Serenus?

It must be acknowledged clearly in the first place that we actually
know comparatively little about the function and social setting
even of demonstrably royal dedications. The general description 'a
response to patronage' actually tells us very little about the precise
relationship of any individual writer to the monarch he addresses.
Thanks for tangible support and solicitations for future support are
probable but conjectural motives: none of our authors actually
mentions either in so many words. The closest we get to it is in Ps.-
Scymnus' long and rambling account of his own arrival at the Bithynian court of Nicomedes: inspired, he says, by the example of
Apollodorus (who had dedicated his *Chronica* to Attalus II cf. lines
16–49), he had resolved to experience royal kindness for himself
and 'to see what a king is, so that I myself could pass the message
on to others' (50–4). So, persuaded by Apollo, he came to the
hearth of Nicomedes – a hearth (*hestia*) which, he says, is more or
less common property to 'those who love learning' (τοῖς φιλομαθοῦσιν 61–3). What the writer obviously values here is not so
much the provision of a pension to an isolated scholar as the creation of favourable circumstances for mutual scholarly communication; and in these circumstances the dedication of a book to the
monarch, besides having an honorific function (45–9, 106–8), is
also an integral part of that scholarly communication process: 'I
have resolved', Ps.-Scymnus says in the initial description of his
project, 'to offer you this useful compilation so as to provide
through you a common service to all those who wish to pursue
learning' (5–10).

It is clear from this passage (as we might have suspected anyway)
that the monarch addressed is not by any means the only or even
the primary audience envisaged in the composition of a dedicated
work. The same distinction between the dedicatee and the wider
audience is made explicitly by Vitruvius (I 1.18 'peto, Caesar, et a
te et ab iis, qui ea volumina sunt lecturi . . .') and by Pliny the Elder
in the preface to the *Natural History*: 'Why do you read that stuff,
Imperator [sc. Titus]? It was written for the common crowd, for the
mob of farmers and craftsmen, and then for those with leisure for
study . . .' (*NH* pref. 6). And it is easy enough to infer this disparity
of audience from many of our texts: despite the author's frequent
profession to be writing *for* the addressee, these texts are not com-

posed for his private use.[27] Archimedes' *Psammites*, for example, is presumably outside the comprehension of any save the best mathematical minds of his time; it is really written for Archimedes' own peers, not for the prince of Syracuse to whom it is addressed. Bito's *Kataskeuai* 'transports us straight back into the workshop of an ancient artificer, his condensed lists of instructions and measurements being clearly intended for experienced mechanics' (Marsden, 1969, p. 3 cf. 1961, p. 62): it is full of peremptory and wholly practical commands which are surely not meant to be followed in person by the royal dedicatee.[28] And Cassius Maximus, the rhetor to whom Artemidorus Daldianus dedicated the first three books of the *Oneirocritica*, is clearly much less close to the audience really envisaged by Artemidorus than is the author's son, the recipient of the last two books.[29]

So what is the audience envisaged by these writers? Vitruvius and Pliny both name two groups:

> not only to builders but also to all the wise [omnibus sapientibus].   Vitruv. I 1.18

> for the mob of farmers and craftsmen, and then for those with leisure for study [studiorum otiosis].
>
> Pliny, *NH* pref. 6

The identity of one of these groups is obvious: they are the professionals, those actively engaged in the craft in question (we need not concern ourselves here with the question how many craftsmen would actually have engaged in reading books like these; but presumably neither Vitruvius nor Pliny found the thought implausible).

[27] Nevertheless there does seem to be some attempt to find a 'suitable' subject for a dedicated work. The *Psammites* presents material easier to render into flowing prose than Archimedes' geometrical works. Bito's war-machines were potentially of real practical interest to the hellenistic monarchs (Plutarch, *Vita Marcelli* XIV 4ff.). Hipparchus' *Commentary on Aratus* is on a topic of literary interest, even if his treatment of it is strictly scientific; and Apollonius of Citium deals with one of the topics most calculated to appeal to the public at large (for the publicity value of machinery in bone-setting operations, see Hippocrates, *Art.* 42/Apollonius of Citium, pp. 50.19–22, 8.30–84.9, and Galen, *Subfig.Emp.* in Deichgräber, 1930, p. 83.3ff.). Space precludes the pursual of this important topic here.

[28] E.g. W 44.3–4, 5–6; 45.1; 55.1–2; 66.3. Even Vitruvius, generally more conscious of a non-technical audience, still retains many practical instructions not strictly appropriate for Octavian: e.g. X 10–11; VI 6.7 'ut sint aedificatoribus non obscurae'.

[29] As may be seen from the newly detailed and personal note that appears in the prefaces to books IV and V. Artemidorus may even have been a little embarrassed in his choice of Maximus as a dedicatee, in view of his own inclination towards Empiricist progaganda against 'mere *logoi*': C. Blum, 1936, ch. 5.

Naturally enough, this group does not appear in Ps.-Scymnus, whose subject, geography, is not a *technē* but a subsection of *historia*. Ps.-Scymnus does, however, mention the other group, 'those who wish to pursue learning' (τοῖς θέλουσι φιλομαθεῖν line 10, cf. τοῖς φιλομαθοῦσιν line 63). *Philomathia* appears frequently in scientific prefaces and is a regular element in the vocabulary of dedication. Hipparchus' addressee Aischrion is *philomathēs* (I pref. p.2.7, p.4.16), and the book's purpose is 'so that neither you nor the rest of the learned (τοὺς λοιποὺς τῶν φιλομαθούντων) should be in error' (p.4.23–5).[30] The *philiatros* of Apollonius of Citium (I pref. p.10.3, II pref. p.38.11) is simply a specialized version of the *philomathēs*. From the parallel *philotechnos* in Philo of Byzantium, *Bel.* pref. Th. 50.26 it seems clear that the *philo* element is to be linked with patronage and connoisseurship rather than with amateur practice: the *philiatroi* are not so much 'amateur doctors' (LSJ s.v.) as 'amateurs in medicine' like George Eliot's Mrs. Cadwallader, who was 'much too well-born not to be an amateur in medicine'.[31] The *philiatroi* appear again in Dioscorides (V 19.3) and Galen (K XIII 636ff., K VI 269ff.); here we are evidently talking not of royal patrons but of enthusiastic adherents of medical theory from the leisured classes. Unlike the professional practitioner (a socially inferior breed obliged to earn a living from practice), these amateur scientists have a vigorous interest in the minutiae of medical theory. Galen makes it clear that he writes for both groups.

It is in this context that we must assess the characteristically detached manner in which the scientific writers recommend their subjects, and their constant predilection for words like *theoria* (intellectual study pursued for its own sake) and *poikilos* (a value word designed to appeal to the connoisseur).[32] Their tone is not that of instruction as of master to pupil. They speak to intellectual curiosity, to academic appreciation of the niceties of an abstruse subject, not to the novice nor layman eager for a few do-it-yourself

[30] Further on *philomathēs* in dedications, below ch. 5, p. 100. The whole subject of the *philomatheis* and the *philiatroi*, and in general that of the audiences for which these technical writings were conceived, deserves much fuller treatment than is possible here; Galen, in particular, drops many informative hints, which could well form the basis of a separate study.

[31] Only the privileged few were actually in a position to practise their hobby on their dependants (Galen, K XIII 636–7) or courtiers (Plutarch, *How to Tell a Flatterer*, *Moralia* II 58a).

[32] See below, ch. 5, pp. 97–8 for references. Note especially the use of *poikilos* in Philo, *Bel.* Th. 73.21–3 and similar passages: siege-engines and catapults are commended not for their practical usefulness but for their ingenuity.

tips. This tone corresponds to the actual relative situations of author and dedicatee: the author is not in the normal didactic position of a superior giving instruction to a child or pupil (note the almost complete absence from our prefaces of the characteristic Roman practice of dedication to a son, corresponding to the traditional Roman pattern of father-to-son education).[33] Nor in most cases is he writing an 'Introduction' to the subject, but rather presenting a sample of his art at its highest for the appreciation of his peers and of the educated public at large.

All this means that there is a smaller gap than might at first be supposed between 'public' and 'private' dedication, since both envisage behind the dedicatee the same wider audience of *philomatheis*, plus the appropriate group of professionals. But it is still worth asking what more we can infer about the role of the 'private' dedicatee. Was he necessarily a patron in some sense? Was dedication automatically linked with place-seeking? Or can we also assume the survival of friendly dedication between peers as in the letter of Archimedes?

The problem here is lack of outside evidence: private individuals tend *ipso facto* to be unknown, and frequently the prefaces themselves give us no more than a name. Sometimes the preface may contain indirect hints: thus Hypsicles' Protarchus is described as a friend of the author's father (p.4.2–3), and therefore was presumably to be treated with the respect due to a member of the older generation. If Hipparchus' *Commentary on Aratus* was, as has been suggested, a youthful work, then his dedicatee too may have been in a position of seniority.[34] But these are little more than conjectures.

When we reach the Roman period we are on slightly firmer ground. After the demise of the hellenistic courts the centre of power in the Mediterranean world – political, economic, social, cultural – was Rome. We should therefore expect a predominance of Roman names in dedications if the commonest object of dedication was to introduce the writer or his subject to the Establishment, to

[33] On the Roman pattern of instruction, cf. Marrou, 1964, part III ch. 1, pp. 314–15. Father-to-son dedication in our texts does not appear until Artemidorus Daldianus IV and V (second century AD). In the earlier texts, Archimedes' choice of Gelon, rather than his father, as his dedicatee for the *Psammites*, may reflect the traditional didactic posture. For a genuine piece of hellenistic didactic literature, see the papyrus school-book on astronomy, *Eudoxou technē* (P. Letronne I, *Notices et extraits des mss.* XVIII/2 (Paris, 1865), pp. 25–76.).

[34] Neugebauer, 1969, p. 69: but a caution in Manitius' edition of Hipparchus, p. 287.

the charmed circle of those who mattered.[35] In fact purely Roman
dedications are rare in our group: Vitruvius to Octavian, Thessalus
to Claudius or Nero (if genuine) and Hermogenes to the unknown
Julius Marcus. Alongside these are the Greeks linked in some way
with Roman society: Dioscorides' Areius, a compatriot of Dioscorides but clearly linked with the consular C. Laecanius Bassus;
Erotian's Andromachus, a Greek serving as court physician to
Nero; and Artemidorus' Cassius Maximus, possibly to be identified
with the sophist Maximus of Tyre and if so a Greek prominent in
Roman society. All these, interestingly, confirm Bowersock's
picture of the position of the Greek sophists in the second century
AD: 'Roman intimates of (Greek) Sophists were largely cultivated
men from their own part of the empire' (Bowersock, 1969, p. 88).
Then there are the purely Greek names with no known affiliation:
Hero's Dionysius and Serenus' Cyrus.[36] The data are particularly
striking in the case of Galen, who himself held a prominent position
in Roman society (Bowersock, 1969, ch. 5). Despite his own obvious
pride in the imperial patronage he enjoyed (*De libr.propr.* 2, K XIX
18ff = SM II 98ff.) and in the attentions of the consular Boethus (*De
libr.propr.* 1, K XIX 13 = SM II 94), there is a preponderance of
Greek names among his many dedications.[37]

[35] Cf. the Alexandrian philosopher Aenesidemus (fl. 50–40 BC), who dedicated
the eight books of his *Pyrrhoneian Arguments* to L. Aelius Tubero: see Fraser, 1972,
vol. I p. 491 and nn. 123–5, vol. II pp. 712–13. Note, however, that Photius describes
Tubero as a *sunairesiōtēs*, presumably here 'a member of the same (philosophical)
sect', and in that sense not strictly an 'outsider' to the subject. The dedication at any
rate seems to have had little effect on Roman society: Fraser, 1972, vol. I p. 493 and
n. 133, vol. II p. 714.

[36] Vitruvius: I pref. i, etc.; Hermogenes, *Inv.* III pref., p.126.2 (Julius Marcus could
even be of Greek extraction); Thessalus I.1ff., see Friedrich *ad loc.*: either Claudius or
Nero, but may not be authentic (App. A). Dioscorides, *Mat.Med.* I pref., esp. p.1.3,
3.1–4. The Andromachus of the *De simplicibus*, if the work is genuine, may be the
same as Erotian's addressee. Erotian, pref. p.3.1 (Nachmanson p. vii). Artemidorus
Daldianus I pref. etc.: Cassius Maximus, a rhetor, possibly to be identified with the
sophist Maximus of Tyre (cf. Pack pp. xxvf.), on whom see Bowersock, 1969, *passim*,
Hero of Alexandria, *Definitiones* pref. (vol. IV p.14.3); Serenus, *Sect.Cyl.* pref. p.2.2,
Sect.Con. pref. p.120.2.

[37] *Roman names*: Bassus (K XIX 8 = SM II 91); Caecilianus (K XI 356); Piso (K
XIV 210, probably spurious). Boethus also received some now lost works (SM II
94.18–26). *Greek names*: Patrophilus (K I 224); Thrasybulus (K I 106 and V 806);
Antisthenes (K II 799); Epigenes (= ?Postumus? K V 899 and XIV 599); Teuthras (K
VIII 453 and XIX 62); Theuthras (K XIX 346, probably spurious); Hieron (K X 1);
Glaucon (K XI 1); Solon (K XIV, 390, probably spurious). *Hybrid names*: (Latin
-*ianus* formation on a Greek name, possibly indicating servile origins: see R. P. C.
Weaver, *Familia Caesaris* (Cambridge University Press, 1972), p. 213): Eugenianus
(K X 456 and XIX 49); Pamphilianus (K XIV 295); Diogenianus (K XIX 721, pos-
sibly spurious).

It seems, then, that the relationship between dedication and social setting remains complex throughout the Roman period. Dedication must in some cases be linked directly or indirectly with patronage, imperial or otherwise; but there are others where no such link can be assumed. It is significant that we do have evidence in Rome of mutual dedication among a group of 'friends', viz. among Cicero's circle in the first century BC.[38] Something very similar seems to be happening in the second century AD with Galen and his 'friends'. It is also worth noting that the latent didactic force in dedication apparently becomes more prominent at about the same time: Arte-midorus Daldianus dedicates his last two books to his son, Vettius Valens addresses his *Collection of Horoscopes* to anonymous *threp-toi*, apparently pupils,[39] and two at least of Galen's dedicated works are of a didactic nature, the *De constitutione artis medicae ad Patrophilum* (K I 224) and the *De pulsibus libellus ad tirones* (K VII 453) – although not all Galen's eisagogic works bear a dedication. None of these addresses have any obvious honorific or place-seeking motivation.

This is really as far as our evidence will take us in reconstructing the social setting of dedication among scientific writers in general. In the case of Galen, however, we have a unique opportunity to build up a more concrete *Sitz im Leben*. The preface to *De methodo medendi* VII (K X 456–8) is particularly interesting: 'Since you and many others of my friends have been begging me for a written reminder of the treatments which you have often seen me perform in practice on the sick, I shall add what still remains to this study' (K X 485.5–8) (compare K I 224.3–5, K II 651.1–5, K II 779.1–4, K V 1.1–5). In these and other similar cases the book is described as a 'reminder' (*hypomnēma*)[40] of something which the addressee has already heard delivered orally or else seen in practice. A more circumstantial account of one such case is given in *De libris propriis* II (K XIX 20ff. = S, II 100ff.), where Galen describes the original setting of the lectures he gave on 'Anatomical Procedures' and

[38] J. S. Reid, *M. Tulli Ciceronis Academica* (MacMillan, London, 1885), intro-duction sect. 4, pp. 28–51. But cf. Gold, 1987, on the use of 'friendship' language in the context of patronage.

[39] *Threptoi*: Book III epilogue, Kroll p. 157.28–34, esp. 29, 33f. The use of this word (which LSJ cite only from this passage) probably reflects the motif common in the occult sciences of passing on esoteric knowledge from father to son: Festugière, 1944–9, I pp. 332ff.

[40] *Hypomnēma* is used here concretely of a written text (hence the plural), but with a strong feeling for the root sense of the word: Galen certainly has in mind Plato, *Phaedrus* 276d, cf. K X 456.8ff. and K XIII 656.

explains how Boethus subsequently encouraged him to write up his notes as a permanent 'reminder' of the lectures.[41] It seems clear from these passages that in some cases at least the text presented to the dedicatee is a written version of something already familiar to him as oral teaching or practical demonstration; the text itself is merely a 'reminder', not a new subject to which he is being introduced for the first time. Galen was undoubtedly a rather unusual doctor; but there is no reason to suppose that in this respect his practice was unique – see Hermogenes, *Inv.*III p.126.2–4, which apparently alludes to a similar situation.

It would be inadequate to describe this situation simply as 'didactic': these addressees are probably not pupils in the normal sense. Galen speaks of Eugenianus as a 'friend', not as a pupil, and there is no suggestion of youth (K X 456.1–2). Galen's anatomical demonstrations were not given in a medical school, but by way of cultured entertainment for the leisured classes in Rome, a sort of scientific rival to the rhetorical and philosophical public 'demonstrations' which anyone could attend. Many of the dedicatees, therefore, may be *philiatroi* rather than professional colleagues, and some of them were probably eminent members of society whom Galen wished to impress. But there is no evidence to suggest that they *all* were, and no reason to discount Galen's own abundant testimony as to the way in which he wrote, on request and almost at random, for a wide circle of 'friends'. The very fact that the consular Boethus is the only one of these friends singled out for individual mention in *De libris propriis* may well suggest that Boethus was the only one of any significant rank in Roman society.[42]

The influence of rhetoric

The typical form of address in dedicated scientific prefaces from the third century BC onwards is that which we have called the 'rhetorical', and we have suggested that this form derives ultimately

---

[41] See also *Anat.Admin.* I 1 and XI 12 (Singer, 1956, pp. 1–2; Duckworth, 1962, pp. 107–8 = K II 215ff.). *Pace* Duckworth (1962 p. xi), there seems no real reason to doubt Galen's account of the genesis of these works, even if we take the picture of the 'reluctant author' with a pinch of salt.

[42] Contrast SM II 94.10ff. and 95.22 (K XI X 12–13, 14) with SM II 94.19ff. For a wider view of Galen's position in Roman society, see Bowersock, 1969, ch. 5. But Jutta Kollesch (Nutton, 1981, pp. 1–11, esp. 7ff.) issues a caution. Galen's resemblance to the sophists should not be overplayed: he was always more than just a 'lion of society'.

from the prose protreptics of fourth-century philosophy and rhetoric. The fourth century BC was a period of considerable cross-
fertilization between the philosophical and rhetorical schools of
Athens (Fuhrmann, 1960, pp. 138–44), and we know of some interaction between rhetoric and medicine, too (above p. 43 and
n. 3). So it is quite reasonable to assume that the formation of
scientific preface-convention owes something to fourth-century rhetoric. Rhetorical influence on its subsequent development, however,
is slight and easily detected. Already at the end of the fourth century
there is a marked contrast between the flowing, varied style of the
Isocratean protreptics and the curt, formulaic preface of Diocles of
Carystus; it is the latter which is typical of the scientific tradition.

Preface-writing for the orator – and for any prose writer who took
rhetoric seriously – was an art, an exercise in variety and invent-
iveness. It is instructive to look at the Demosthenic collection of
prefaces for various occasions (Demosthenes 1418–62), marked
precisely by their variety and by the lack of formal similarity
between them, despite the limited number of topics envisaged and
their unavoidably general nature. The scientific prefaces, by contrast, show a slavish devotion to a limited number of forms and
topics (described below in chapter 5), together with a style that
leaves much to be desired by rhetorical standards. The difference is
all the more marked when we come across the rare scientific author
who does compose prefaces more acceptable to literary taste:
compare Vitruvius, whose prefaces show a deliberate concern for
originality, deal with topics of general interest, and make great use
of variety (especially in the opening words) and of entertaining
anecdotes; and 'Demetrius', where the second paragraph of the
preface (pp. 1.14–2.8) may allude to some rhetorical *topos*.[43] Otherwise, rhetorical influence can be seen in the intrusion of the occasionally literary cliché, as in Hypsicles (p. 2.21–2): 'It may be time to finish
the preface and begin the treatise.'[44] This is not to deny the truth of
the common observation[45] that scientific writers seem to aim at a
more elevated style and a more sophisticated presentation in their
prefaces. This is certainly (though not invariably) the case, as is
evidenced by the frequently marked difference in style between

[43] Some of Vitruvius' prefaces recall the 'Isocratean' preface-style apparently
favoured by Ephorus: see R. Laqueur, 'Ephoros: 1. Die Proömien', Hermes 46
(1911), pp. 200ff. and Fraser, 1970, pp. 115–22, esp. p. 118 and n. 4.
[44] Cf. Ps.-Scymnus 13–15. On 'brevity' as a rhetorical ideal, see below ch. 5 n. 50.
[45] Cf. e.g. Norden, 1909, I p. 432, quoted by Cadbury, 1920b p. 439 and n.

preface and text. Writers whose normal style is simple, paratactic and clear, in their prefaces get involved in overweight periods, and sometimes find it difficult to extricate themselves.[46] Certain sentence structures, recognizably effective from the literary point of view, are repeated again and again (see below p. 91f.). The direct statement of fact is avoided, and grammatical subordination is pursued sometimes to extremes (cf. especially Diocles of Carystus and 'Demetrius'). There is some recourse to such well-worn stylistic devices as litotes and alliteration (see below p. 92f.).

That all these devices originated in rhetoric – albeit in its practice rather than its theory[47] – is undeniable; but to call the prefaces in general 'rhetorical' would be misleading, or at least unhelpful.[48] Rhetoric provided the basic education of Greek society, and thus had some influence on anyone with any degree of literacy. But when we meet with rhetorical influence in this diluted form, it is more helpful to speak simply of 'style'. The same attachment to clichés and to certain well-worn patterns of expression, which distinguishes these from the really rhetorical prefaces, paradoxically at the same time witnesses to an attempt at 'style'. Up to a point, the use of literary formulae might simply be a matter of convenience for a writer not accustomed to write freely except on technical subjects, and faced with the necessity of composing transitional and introductory passages. But it does also seem expressive of a feeling that a more formal style than usual was appropriate in the preface, particularly in a work dedicated to an eminent patron. Interestingly, the second-person singular pronoun tends to reappear (if at all) precisely at those 'editorial' points in the body of the work where the formal language-patterns of the preface come to the surface again (summary and transition, mention of illustrations etc.).[49] In such

[46] Cf. Warren, 1960, p. v., on Vitruvius: 'When he does attempt a periodic sentence, he becomes involved, and finds it difficult to extricate himself.' The observation could be applied with equal justice to Apollonius of Citium, some of whose periods have defeated scribes and editors alike.

[47] Cf. e.g. Fraenkel, 1961: further, below p. 109.

[48] It will be clear that we are using the term 'rhetoric' here in a more limited sense than that current in contemporary literary criticism (e.g. in Burke's *Rhetoric of Religion* (Boston, 1961) and *Rhetoric of Motives* (University of California Press, 1969)). We use 'rhetoric' here in the more traditional fashion to cover approaches to composition derived specifically from a Greek rhetorical education at an advanced level (Marrou, 1964, Pt. II ch. 10 pp. 267ff.).

[49] E.g. Hipparchus p. 184.22–6; Philo, *Belopoeica* Th. 56.8, 16; 59.1–2; 61.21–4; 67.2–8; 70.35; 72.5; 73.21–3; 78.34; Bito, *Kataskeuai* W 48.3f.; 52.1f.; 57.1ff.; 61.2; 65.1. In Apollonius of Citium the second-person pronoun likewise reappears intermittently, generally in a phrase drawing attention to the illustrations (e.g. p.12.28).

circumstances, the existence of a pattern of appropriate language could be welcome to a writer who was not himself a literary craftsman.

It remains to ask whether the scientific writers show any conscious awareness of rhetorical standards. Tore Janson, in his study of Latin prose prefaces, has traced the development of a number of 'approaches to rhetoric' ranging from an apology for defective style to a renunciation of rhetoric as incompatible with factual accuracy (Janson, 1964, pp. 98–100 and 124–41). There is little evidence in our prefaces of this (in itself a rather rhetorical pose), or indeed of any conscious awareness of rhetoric: it may be seen in Vitruvius (I 1.18), in Artemidorus Daldianus (II pref., p.100.13–19) and in Vettius Valens (VI 9 p. 260.26–9), and perhaps in a more allusive form in Galen's apologies for the length of some of his books.[50] Otherwise, the negative attitude towards *logos* which appears in Greek scientific prefaces seems to be rather an epistemological than a stylistic question, a reflection of the Empiricist debate, or of the attitudes of craftsmen towards book-learning, rather than an attitude towards rhetoric as such.[51]

[50] Cf. K V 586–7; *De Hipp.Plat.Decret.* IV pref. (K V 360ff.), VII pref. (K V 586ff.), *Meth.Med.* VI pref. (K X 384.).
[51] See further, below pp. 88–91.

5

SCIENTIFIC PREFACES: STRUCTURE, CONTENT AND STYLE

General characteristics

For our immediate purposes it is less important to discover the origins of the prefaces found in the scientific tradition than to determine whether it is possible to discern in them any kind of overall pattern. There is always a danger in this kind of analysis of imposing a false uniformity on the material; but in fact there are remarkable similarities in structure, in content and in style between the prefaces we are considering. Some display interests which in the nature of the case are limited to a particular subject,[1] while others, especially the earlier ones, contain personal material which is necessarily unique;[2] but overall it is not the differences which strike the reader so much as the similarities.

Three general tendencies are evident in the development of these prefaces. First, there is a marked tendency towards *combination*. We have already shown how elements pertaining to presentation (introduction, epilogue, summary and transition) appeared originally independently of, and prior to, dedication, but were taken up into dedicatory prefaces and combined with elements belonging properly to dedication. Similarly elements belonging properly to the beginning of the 'systematic handbook' (definition and division of the subject), which again had an independent and prior origin, came to be used among other preface-material in books whose organization is only vaguely 'systematic'.[3] So too with material reflecting the

[1] E.g. Bito W 44.4–6; Philo, *Bel.* Th. 49.12–51.7; Dioscorides, *Mat.Med.* I p.1.9–2.15; Erotian p.4.20ff.

[2] Cf. Archimedes, *Sph.Cyl.* I p.4.14ff. *Spir.* p.2.2–21, *Quadr.* p.262.3–9; Apollonius of Perge, *Con.* II p.192.2–11; Hypsicles p.4.2–3.

[3] On the form of the systematic handbook, see Fuhrmann, 1960, *passim*. The definition of the aim of artillery construction, which appears in similar form but in different positions in the prefaces to the *Belopoeica* of both Philo (Th. 51.8–10) and Hero (W 74.10–12), looks like one of these elements; cf. also the definition of 'missile'

methodological discussion: our prefaces contain a number of allusions inteligible only as part of a wider and pre-existent debate (see below pp. 88–91). It appears that certain elements came in time to be regarded as obligatory 'preface-material', although they had initially had a more specific *locus* and function.

The obverse of this tendency towards combination is a movement towards *compression*. The trend is to combine more and more material into one or two sentences, with the inevitable result that *topoi* are introduced in allusive rather than in fully developed form. This is particularly marked in the prefaces of Demetrius and Hero.[4] And, finally, phrases tend by the same token to become *formulaic*, and often seem to be little more than clichés or catchwords. This is true, surprisingly, not only of the merely presentational (such as the phrase στοχαζόμενος τῆς συμμετρίας, on which see below p. 96), but equally of topics which we would expect to be of more pressing concern to the scientist, like the methodological discussion (see below pp. 88–91). The similarities in this discussion between the words used by Vitruvius and Hero, and those of Apollonius of Citium, are striking if, as we are led to suppose, Apollonius was actually an Empiricist, that is a follower of a school passionately propagandist about one side of the debate. And it is perhaps even more surprising to find how certain words and phrases seem to be used formulaically even when they have no readily discernible ideological importance (see below pp. 94–101).

All this adds up to a conspicuous lack of individuality across the tradition as a whole. We can observe a common stock of ideas to be expressed in prefaces, and of words and phrases in which to express them, as well as a remarkably unified approach to the structuring and composition of the preface, to the language of dedication, and (where they are used) in summary and transitional passages throughout the work. This phenomenon is vaguer than the 'systematic' structure investigated by Fuhrmann (1960), but it is also more widely distributed. His analysis deals with a particular type of book in a fairly rigid form; ours, rather, with a community of modes of expression over a wide range of forms and subjects. Thus there is

and the divisions into euthytone and palintone instruments in Hero, *Bel.* W 75.1–2, 74.5–9. The 'systematic' elements are more noticeable in Vitruvius, and Fuhrmann (1960), ch. 7) analyses the *De architectura* along these lines; but it is clear that Vitruvius' organization, while more thoroughgoing than Philo's or Hero's, is nowhere near as schematic as that of the rhetorical handbooks.

[4] Engel observes a similar phenomenon of compression in historical prefaces (1910, pp. 99f.).

much in common between Apollonius of Citium, a medical writer, Philo of Byzantium, an engineer, and Hipparchus, an astronomer – despite the fact that each is working in a distinct and unrelated field of study.

Structure and content

The topics most common in the prefaces may be summarized under seven heads:

(1)   the author's decision to write
(2)   the subject and contents of the book, with explanation where necessary of particular aspects of the presentation (e.g. illustrations)
(3)   dedication: the second-person address, and topics related to the dedicatee
(4)   the nature of the subject-matter
(5)   others who have written on the subject or who have opinions on it, whether predecessors or rivals
(6)   the author's qualifications
(7)   general remarks on methodology

The last two were the least common, and their development and relatively late arrival on the scene will be discussed in detail below. The others (with a certain amount of qualification with regard to no. 5) could be described as the stock-in-trade of the scientific preface from our earliest examples; other topics reflecting particular circumstances or the peculiar interests of the writer may occur, but these five recur with remarkable consistency throughout the tradition.

But it is possible to observe much more than a common stock of topics – all general enough, after all, to occasion little surprise. There is also a strikingly constant pattern of expression, of binding these elements together, which results in a much greater uniformity than the list itself would suggest. Even when other elements are introduced, this pattern appears in one position or another: it is so persistent, and is used so mechanically, that it seems legitimate to speak of a 'scheme'. The scheme is not only a topical one, but also (and to a slightly lesser extent) a syntactical one: that is, the topics tend to recur not merely in the same pattern/patterns within the preface, but in the same relative positions of subordination within a single periodic sentence. Two particularly comprehensive examples may be seen in the prefaces of Diocles of Carystus and Demetrius. The syntactical structure is, however, not a rigid one: sometimes the same pattern of expression can be recognized in a syntactical structure involving, say, two separate sentences rather than a single period.[5] In what follows, minor syntactical variations will not always be noted individually where they do not detract from the basic pattern.

1   The author's decision

First, logically, comes the statement of the author's decision to write. Unnecessary as this may seem, it is almost universal, at least in the first preface to a series of books, and usually forms the grammatical centre of the first or major sentence of the preface. The commonest form is 'I (have) decided' or 'I think it necessary/better', the latter sometimes in impersonal form, 'it is necessary/better'. We meet less often the factual 'I have written', the deprecating 'I have tried/shall try', or the more consciously dedicatory 'I present'.[6] We

---

[5] E.g. Galen K V 899 = SM I 93.1ff., K VI 453: the first topic of the preface, 'other writers have dealt with this subject', is stated in an independent sentence, whereas in many other cases it is introduced in a subordinate clause, 'since others have dealt with this subject . . .' (e.g. Demetrius p.1.4–7; Hero, *Spir.* I p.2.4ff., *Aut.* p.338.3ff., *Dipotr.* p.188 .4–6, *Bel.* W 73.6–9; Vitruvius IV pref.; Dioscorides, *Mat.Med.* I p.1.4ff.; Galen K VI 554, K VI 816, K VII 463, K VII 584). This fluidity is especially characteristic of Galen, perhaps because his linguistic sensibilities revolted against the overweighted periods of less fastidious writers.

[6] '*I (have) decided*': Archimedes, *Eratosth.* p.428.20f.; Hypsicles p.2.16; Hipparchus pp.2.15, 4.16; Bito W 43 end; Vitruvius I 6.12, I 7.2; Hero, *Metr.* I p.4.5f.; Galen K V 587.4, K VI 554, K VI 816, K XIV 390; Vettius Valens 331.8; Serenus, *Sect. Cyl.* p.2.5.

'*I think it necessary/better*': Archimedes, *Stom.* p.416.3f.; Vitruvius IV pref.; Apollonius of Citium I pref. p.10.6; Hero, *Spir.* I p.2.7f., *Catoptr.* p.320.6, *Dioptr.* p.188.5, *Bel.* W 73.9; Erotian p.3.10; Galen K VII 463.2, K X 1.7; Hermogenes, *Stat.* 28.7.

'*It is necessary/better*': Philo, *Bel.* Th. 49.2.9; Galen K II 651.7, K VI 454.8; Hermogenes, *Inv.* p.171.1.

'*I have written*': Diocles p.75.5; Hipparchus p.6.16; Demetrius p.1.8 ('I have treated'); Ps.-Scymnus 66; Dionysius 4 ('I now relate'); Galen K II 779.4, K V 1.4 ('I shall now do this'), K VI 755.10 (' shall discuss'), K X 458.7f. ('I shall add'), K XIV 210.5.

'*I have tried/shall try*': Dioscorides, *Mat.Med.* I p.16; Hermogenes, *Inv.* III 4 p.133.17.

'*I present*': Dioscorides, *Eup.* I p.151.13, cf. *Mat.Med.* I p.2.20. Cf. also the more dedicatory 'I wish to respond to your desire' of Philo, *Pneum.* p.458.8f.; Galen K I 224.3.

Further variations within the same basic pattern: Galen K XII 895.4f., 'I have begun this work', and Serenus, *Sect.Con.* p.120.6, 'It seemed to me that it was not good . . .'

should probably reckon as deliberate such exaggerated variation as Erotian's 'I have dared' (p.6.3) or Thessalus' 'I think I alone have succeeded' (I p.45.5–6). 'I am sending' does not occur except in the earliest letters (Archimedes and Apollonius of Perge). The conservative approach of these writers to preface-composition may be seen in the fact that the 'decision' is almost invariably the main verb of the sentence, however long and complicated.[7]

2   Subject and contents

The 'decision' sentence normally (and naturally) doubles as a statement of the subject and contents of the book. The subject may appear either as object of the main verb or as subject or object of a subordinate clause preceding it or both:

> 'I have decided to write about x ...'
> 'Since x is worthy of attention, I have decided ...'
> 'Since you are interested in x, I have decided ...'
> 'Since others have written about x, I too have decided ...'

There is a tendency to bring the first mention of the book's contents as far forward as possible in the sentence and in the preface, so that when the opening sentence is a simple one the book's subject-matter will be placed (in the accusative) ahead of its verb right at the beginning of the text (e.g. Bito W 43 end, Galen K X 456.1). More often, however, the opening sentence is complex, and in this case the forward position of the subject-matter is retained by placing it in one of the subordinate clauses preceding the main verb. Here too it tends to occupy the very first words of the preface,[8] but where this is not possible, there will usually be some indication of the book's contents in the first few lines of the preface.[9]

---

[7] The only exception in the earlier prefaces is in Hero, *Def.* Of the later writers, Hermogenes and Galen do not always conform to the pattern and Artemidorus has what seems to be a wilful variation, I pref. p.1.8ff.

[8] As in Archimedes, *Stom.*; Demetrius; Hero, *Spir.* I, *Aut., Dioptr., Def.*; Dioscorides, *Eup.* II; Erotian; Galen K II 779.1ff. (object of both main and subordinate verbs), K V 899 = SM I 93, K VI 453; Serenus, *Sect.Con.*

[9] Subject in first few lines of text:
(a) *as object of main verb*: Hipparchus I; Philo, *Bel.*; Dionysius; Dioscorides, *Eup.* I; Galen K II 651.1f., K IV 767, K XIV 106.2ff.; Hermogenes, *Inv.* III pref. *Id.* I pref.
(b) *as subject/object of subordinate clause*: Diocles; Philo, *Pneum.*; Vitruvius IV pref.; Apollonius of Citium I pref. (reading θεωρῶν see App. B); Demetrius; Dioscorides, *Mat.Med.* I; Galen K V 1.3f. K VI 816.2ff., K VII 463.1f., K VII 584.3ff., K X 1.2f., K XIV 210.3f., K XIV 390.1f.; Hermogenes, *Stat.*; Artemidorus IV; Serenus, *Sect.Cyl.*

This position has obvious practical advantages for the immediate identification of the book (cf. above ch. 4 p. 46), but it will not always give sufficient scope for the author to explain exactly what he is doing. Thus in many cases we find a second statement of the contents *after* the main verb, sometimes in a separate sentence or paragraph.[10] Where the initial statement has indicated only the general area of study, the second will be more precise;[11] where the first is reasonably specific, the second may expand on the particular method or angle followed by the author.[12] A third way of including the contents is seen in Ps.-Scymnus 73ff., where a final clause dependent on the main verb, 'so that you may learn ...' is given a precise object in the form of a long list of contents. (Ps.-Scymnus' insistence on listing the entire contents of the book under this clause, which thus extends over some twenty lines, is an exaggerated example of the tendency to compress as much as possible into the minimum number of sentences.) Apollonius of Citium uses this theme in the same way, only he devotes a separate sentence to it (I p.10.15ff., II p.38.8–10, III p.64.10–12).

Two general points may be noted about the practice of the scientific writers here. First, it is perhaps significant of their predominantly practical concern that their prefaces are so informative about the subject-matter of their books; we may contrast the deliberate 'variety', inevitably obscuring the subject-matter, of the rhetorical type of preface seen in Vitruvius II, III, VI etc. (above ch. 4 n. 43). Very few of the scientific writers fail to give this information in their prefaces one way or another: Ps-Scymnus and Hero, *Belopoeica*, keep the statement of the subject until rather late in the preface, and Galen, K V 806.1ff. and K XII 894–5 are singularly uninformative, but these are unusual. Most obscure are the prefaces of Artemidorus and Thessalus, both of whom specify their subject-matter only obliquely, Thessalus through the story of his 'conversion' and Artemidorus through the allusions to *mantikē*

Note that even the earliest letters, composed along less formal lines, tend to give some indication of the book's subject in the first few lines: Archimedes, *Sph.Cyl.* I and II, *Psamm.*; Apollonius of Perge, *Con.* I, II, IV; the same is true of Hypsicles, despite his unconventional opening.

[10] E.g. Hero, *Bel.* W 73.11ff.; Galen K VII 585.2ff.; Serenus, *Sect.Cyl.* 2.11ff.

[11] Compare Diocles 2 φιλοσοφίας with 4–5 τὴν περὶ τῶν ὑγιεινῶν ...; 5ff. πόθεν etc. Similarly Apollonius of Citium I pref. p.10.4ff. with 7ff.; Demetrius p.1.2 with p.1.8ff.; Dioscorides, *Eup.* II p.242.3 with p.242.7f.; Erotian p.3.3 with p.3.9ff.

[12] Vitruvius IV pref. 1, 'de architectura'/14–15. 'ad perfectam ordinationem perducere'. Similarly Hero, *Spir.* p.2.4/8ff., *Dioptr.* p.188.3/5ff., *Bel.* W 73.6/10ff.; Galen K Vi 816.2–7/8ff., again 817.2ff., K VII 463.1/2–3, K VII 584.3ff./6ff.

(I p.1.6, 15). Secondly, it is characteristic of these prefaces that the subject of the book is almost always in an oblique case. On the rare occasions where it forms the subject of a sentence and stands in the nominative case, this sentence is related indirectly rather than directly to the book itself (Hero, *Bel.*; *Metr.* I; Dioscorides, *Simpl.* I), and may be contrasted with the four-square opening typified by Ptolemy's *Geographia* (and by the systematic handbooks), which launches directly into an analysis of the subject.

3 Dedication

The author's relationship with the dedicatee is expressed by means of the insertion of a direct address after the first few words, or by an epistolary salutation, and is furthered by the introduction of the second-person pronoun wherever possible in the preface and in summary and transitional passages throughout the work. Thus 'I have decided to write about x' becomes 'I have decided to write *for you* about x'.[13] For most writers, however, this is not enough: courtesy, or convention, demands that a closer link be forged between the dedicatee and the subject of the book. There are three ways in which this may be achieved. The least common in our prefaces, though it is popular elsewhere, is that whereby the author asks the dedicatee to pardon or to correct any mistakes he may have made: see Janson 1964, pp. 106ff. 141ff. This convention seems to have been popular among Latin writers, especially in the later Empire as modesty came to be regarded as a virtue; it is probably to be related to the rhetorical *topos* of asking pardon as a means of ensuring *benevolentia*. Among the scientific writers it is found only in Vitruvius (I 1.18), Erotian (p.116.16ff), Artemidorus (II p.202.22f) and Serenus (*Sect.Con.* p.120.13ff); cf. also Galen K V 899.7ff. = SM I 93.7ff. These are all later writers, and all more likely to be influenced by Roman convention.

---

[13] Diocles p.75.5; Archimedes, *Eratosth.* p. 428.21; Apollonius of Perge, *Con.* IV p.2.6; Hypsicles p.2.17; Hipparchus p.2.15, p.6.16; Philo, *Bel.* Th. 51.10, 78.23 (also 49.1,3): Vitruvius IV pref. 1; Apollonius of Citium pp.10.8, 36.9, 62.1,3,6, 64.3,6,16; Ps.-Scymnus 66; Hero, *Def.* p.14.2; Dioscorides, *Mat.Med.* I p.1.6, *Eup.* I p.151.13, *Eup.* II pp.242.4, 317.10; Galen K I 224.5, K II 779.2, K XIV 210.3, K IV 390.2; Hermogenes, *Inv.* III p.126.3; Thessalus p.195.1; Artemidorus pp.202.23, 204.4, 237.26, 300.26, 302.7. The fuller form σοι χαριζόμενος is also found occasionally, especially in Galen: cf. Galen K V 587.4, K X 1.3f., K X 456.2, K XIV 390.2; Artemidorus p.236.4. The same thought underlies Demetrius p.1.11–12, and possibly also Philo, *Pneum.* p.458.7–9.

The two standard ways of involving the dedicatee in the Greek scientific preface are found already in embryo in Diocles of Carystus; they probably go back to the earlier protreptics. First, Diocles' decision to write is preceded by a subordinate clause in which the decision is made partly dependent on the character, or favourable disposition, of the recipient: '*Since* it happens that *you* are the most cultured of kings ... I have written up *for you* ...' (Diocles of Carystus, p.75.1/5). This form of courtesy is very common, especially in the hellenistic period; often it is placed, as in Diocles, before the main verb, sometimes after it ('I have decided to write ... *because of your philomathia* ...').[14] In some cases it takes the form of a reply to a request for enlightenment, though this is not as common as it seems to have been in Roman prefaces (Janson, 1964, pp. 116ff.): see Apollonius of Citium I p.10.4, 8; Philo, *Pneum.* p.458.6ff.; Hipparchus I p.2.6ff.; and, for the 'request' theme in Galen, see above chapter 4 pp. 62–3. It is tempting to relate this theme not only to the protreptic background (above ch. 4 pp. 55–6.) but also to the conventions of letter-writing: Hipparchus' preface, for example, is very close to a letter at this point. Indeed, the use of standard epistolary conventions in Apollonius of Perge, *Con.* I and II shows how it was customary to begin with remarks about the addressee before turning to oneself and the real subject of the letter. Conversely, among the earlier writers, Bito's *Kataskeuai* and Archimedes' *Psammites*, which are closer to the rhetorical than to the epistolary side of the tradition, do not begin with this kind of personal allusion to the dedicatee: instead, both express the hope at the end of the work that its subject was 'suitable' (Archimedes, *Psammites* p.258.11ff.; Bito W 67.5).

Secondly, Diocles ends his preface with the words, 'But you, if you believe what I say, will (be able to) follow them (sc. the signs of approaching disease) accurately' (p.75.11.12). This looks rather like a didactic exhortation: in later prefaces such exhortations are found in Dionysius Calliphontis (11.21–3) and in Artemidorus (IV p.238.2ff.), but they may be due to the influence of a different tradition.[15] The great majority of scientific prefaces stress not the

[14] Diocles p.75.1–3; Archimedes, *Eratosth.* p.428.18ff.; Apollonius of Perge, *Con.* I p.2.6f., *Con.* IV p.2.6–8; Hypsicles p.2.17–4.4; Hipparchus I p.2.7–8, 4.16; Philo, *Pneum.* p.458.6–7; Apollonius of Citium I p.10.3; Demetrius p.1.7–8; Dioscorides, *Mat.Med.* I p.2.19ff., *Eup.* I p.151.13ff., Artemidorus Book III p.204.1–2, IV p.236.1–2 (third-person form).

[15] The remote origins of this type of address in parenetic literature may be reflected in Diocles' faintly didactic tone (p.75.11–12). There may also be some

effort to be made by the dedicatee but the results he can expect: 'I have decided to write ... *so that you* may learn ...'[16] This theme tends to follow the main decision sentence, sometimes as a separate sentence, frequently as a final clause dependent on the main verb. It is found even in non-dedicated works eventually in an impersonal, generalized form: 'so that anyone who wishes may learn ...', 'so that the reader may learn ...'[17]

4   The nature of the subject-matter

This theme too is found from Diocles onwards. Its characteristic form is that seen in Archimedes' *Stomachion*: '*Since* the so-called *stomachion* has a *poikilan theorian* ... I felt it necessary to set out ...' (Archimedes, *Stom.* p.416.2–3). In Diocles it appears alongside the theme of the dedicatee, in a parallel subordinate clause before the main verb:

> *Since you* ...
> *and since* I feel that *hygiene is* a royal and suitable philo-
> sophy both to hear and to contemplate,
> *I have written for you* ...'   (Diocles, p.75.1–5)

The same combination of the two themes, in reverse order, is found in Demetrius (p.1.2–7/7–8). It makes for a remarkably cumbersome sentence; most of our writers base their decision to write *either* on the disposition of the dedicatee *or* on the nature of the subject, not both. In fact this theme, in combination with (5), becomes increasingly favoured from the first century AD onwards, and seems partially to have displaced the theme of the disposition of the dedicatee. Note that although Hero is particularly fond of this *topos* (cf. *Spir.* I p.2.4ff., *Aut.* p.338.3ff., *Catoptr.* p.318.9–11, *Dioptr.* p.188.3ff.), it does not appear in *Definitiones*, the only dedicated work in the corpus. For further examples of the *topos*, see Diosco-rides, *Simpl.* I p.152.3ff., Galen K VI 453.1–8, K VII 463.1–2,

influence from didactic verse convention in the versifier Dionysius: cf. e.g. Vergil, *Georg.* II 39ff., III 40f. Artemidorus seems to have been affected both by Roman didactic convention, which he follows in dedicating books IV and V to his son, and by religious convention: cf. above pp. 73–4.

[16] Archimedes, *Eratosth.* p.428.22ff.; Hipparchus I p.2.17f., cf. also p.4.23ff. and 6.19ff.; Bito W 44.1–3; Philo, *Pneum.* p.458.10ff.; Apollonius of Citium I p.10.15ff., II p.38.ff., 62.6ff., III p.64.10ff., 16ff; Ps.-Scymnus 73ff.; Dionysius 17; Hero, *Def.* p.14.6ff.; Artemidorus IV p.236.3–4 (third-person form).

[17] Hero, *Spir.* I p.2.10ff., *Mech.* III p.200.13f., *Bel.* W 73.11f. Cf. also Vitruvius VI 6.7; Galen K VI 817.1, K VII 463.3ff.; and Vettius Valens IX pref. p.331.12ff.

Serenus, *Sect.Con.* p.120.2–5, and, more remotely, in Hermogenes, *Stat.* p.28.3–7. Hero's *Belopoeica*, with its rather pretentious opening remarks on philosophy (W 71.end-73.5), may be a development of the theme.

5   Other writers

Orientation vis-à-vis other writers in the field is one of the natural ways in to any subject (see above, ch. 4 p. 44f.). The letters of Archimedes and of Apollonius of Perge, and the prefaces of Diocles *On Burning Mirrors* and of Hypsicles, all provide examples of this kind of explanation, aimed simply at clarifying the precise nature of the author's task; while Hipparchus and Philo, *Pneumatica*, show a more particular concern to define their own position vis-à-vis others whom they think mistaken. In Hipparchus, in Philo and in Archimedes' *Eratosthenes*, the topic of 'predecessors' is raised regularly as the second major topic of the preface, to be discussed after the preliminaries of subject and dedicatee; cf. also Artemidorus Book I, where it is the third major topic.[18] But in later writers the theme is very often found at the head of the main 'decision' sentence, and thus at the very beginning of the preface: '*Since others* have written ..., *I have decided* to write ...' Examples of this structure may be seen already in Philo, *Belopoeica* Th. 49.7–9, and in Hipparchus I pref. p.4.12ff., but it is a particular feature of the post-hellenistic prefaces regularly to place this theme at the beginning of their work and to make the work of others the explicit basis of the author's own decision to write.[19] This basis is by no means always polemical, and in many cases it is virtually impossible to distinguish this theme from (4). Hero's prefaces show this particularly well:

> *Since the subject* has been thought worthy of treatment *by others, I too* ...   (*Spir.* I p.2.4ff., *Aut.* p.338.3ff./342.4ff.)

> *Since the subject* is useful *and others have written* on it, *I think it necessary* ...   (*Dioptr.* p.188–3ff.)

[18] Hipparchus I p.4.1ff.; Philo, *Bel.* Th. 49.1ff., *Pneum.* p.458.12ff.; Archimedes, *Eratosth.* p.430.1ff.; Artemidorus I p.2.1ff.

[19] Hero, *Bel.* W 73.6ff.; Dioscorides, *Mat.Med.* I p.1.4ff.; Erotian p.3.3ff.; Galen K V 899.1ff = SM I 93.1ff., K VI 453.1–454.8, K VI 816.1ff., K VII 584.1–6; Hermogenes, *Inv.* III 4 p.133.15ff.; Thessalus I pref. p.45.2ff.; Serenus, *Sect.Cyl.* p.2.ff., *Sect.Con.* p.120.5–6. Note that this kind of opening does not preclude a fuller discussion of the author's predecessors elsewhere: cf. Dioscorides, *Mat.Med.* I p.1.9–2.15; Erotian p.3.16ff. and p.4.21ff.

(See also Erotian p.3.3ff.; Galen K VI 453.1ff., K VII 463.1–2.)

It is clear that in many cases the work of others is mentioned solely to demonstrate that the subject is worth spending time on, and thus fulfils exactly the same function as theme (4). One or other of these two themes tends in the post-hellenistic prefaces to displace the disposition of the dedicatee as the opening gambit.

There are of course those who employ the theme of 'other writers' to criticize the deficiencies or to attack the views of their predecessors.[20] Since our analysis is structural rather than logical or thematic, there is no need to make a distinction between critical and non-critical approaches to the topic: what is important for our purposes is the form of its introduction, and that remains constant. Thus we can say that earlier writers regularly (but not invariably) introduce the theme of other writers as the second major topic in their prefaces, whether by 'others' we mean rivals or predecessors, literary documents or oral tradition, those whom they criticize or those whom they follow. Even more clearly can it be seen in the later writers that the scheme beginning 'Seeing that many have written . . . I have decided . . .' is a favourite whether the relationship is causal or concessive: in fact the form, 'Seeing that . . .', or the convenient ambiguity of the genitive absolute, ensure that in some cases only the content will make it clear whether the 'others' are being followed or criticized. There is no *formal* distinction between:

> Many have tried . . . I alone have succeeded . . .
> (Thessalus I p.45.2–6)

and

> Since many have discussed . . . I too decided . . .
> (Galen K VII 463.1ff.)

or

> Seeing that many think . . . I have decided . . .
> (Serenus *Sect.Cyl.* p.2.2ff.)

where the 'many' are the ignorant public at large. And while a thematic analysis of this theme might prove interesting, it is the constancy of form which is striking.

These five topics make up the most universally found themes in scientific prefaces. It will be clear from our analysis how they are not only favourites as individual themes, but are regularly found in a

---

[20] E.g. Hero, Dioscorides, Galen (K VI 816–17), Thessalus.

certain order, linked, with a small amount of variation, in a favourite scheme. Naturally not all writers use it all the time: a writer like Galen, for example, has too much literary resource to be bound slavishly to any scheme, and there is always scope for the introduction of new themes (e.g. Hero, *Catoptr.*, *Metr.* I, *Bel.*), or for individual variation (e.g. the idiosyncrasies of Erotian and Thessalus, which look like wilful variation on an already well-worn theme). Yet overall the recurrence of sentences of the form, 'Since you are inclined to be *philomathēs* ..., I have decided to write to you about ... so that you may learn ...', or 'Since many have written about x, I have decided to ... so that any who wish may learn ...' is too frequent to admit of dismissal. The distribution of the scheme illustrates the growing tendency to combine as much as possible into a single sentence (although one of the most unwieldy examples is found as early as Diocles), and confirms an impression that in individual cases the topics are simply mentioned because it is the right thing to do so, not out of personal conviction. More than anything else, however, the steady recurrence of the pattern reveals the relatively low literary level of most of these writers, their lack of invention and literary resource. It is worth noting, for example, how Philo uses essentially the same scheme at other transitional/editorial points in this book (compare *Bel.* Th. 49.7–11 with Th. 56.8ff. and Th. 67.29ff.): faced with the necessity of free composition, this seems to be all he can think of. The same kind of repetitiousness is found in Hipparchus: cf. I p.4.12–18, p.6.14–21. This sort of formality is not imposed from outside: it is not a matter of rhetorical theory, but can be accounted for sufficiently by a conservative tradition and a low level of literary ability. We shall meet a similar uniformity, arising from the same causes, when we turn to consider style and vocabulary (see below pp. 91–101).

6   The author's qualifications

The earliest writers in the scientific tradition show no interest at all in the question of authority. If a writer's work has a polemical slant, like Hipparchus', he is content to assert, 'I am right and they are wrong' without giving any explanation of his authority for making this statement (Hipparchus I p.4.1–11, 4.18–6.3). If his work is simply new and original as against others', like Archimedes', he will say that this is the case without making any attempt to bolster the statement by explaining his credentials (Archimedes, *Spir.* p.2.18–4.1, *Quadr.* p.262.10f., 13ff.). For Archimedes, indeed, such validation might well seem unnecessary: his name would be sufficient warrant in itself, certainly among the mathematicians to whom he was writing. But there seems to be a more general principle here as well; in the climate in which these works were being produced, scientific work was apparently expected to provide its own validation. It would stand or fall on its own merits, and these would be recognized by those who had the ability to judge the matter correctly.[21] Such, at any rate, seems to be the case with Diocles of Carystus, Archimedes, Apollonius of Perge, Diocles', *On Burning Mirrors*, Hypsicles, Hipparchus, Bito, Demetrius and Dionysius Calliphontis. For whatever reasons, the topic of the author's qualifications does not figure in their prefaces.

The subject is discussed, however, by four hellenistic writers (Philo, Vitruvius, Apollonius of Citium and Ps.-Scymnus), and in post-hellenistic prefaces it plays an increasingly important role. It may be said to have become one of the stock preface-themes, used even where it is not immediately appropriate to the subject-matter, although it was never regarded as obligatory (Hermogenes and Serenus do not mention the topic).

The writer may base his claim to authority, or that of his material, on one of three things: (i) written sources; (ii) personal experience; (iii) tradition: or on a combination of these.

(i)   Written sources

The least common of the three. Ps.-Scymnus gives a list of sources as the first part of his two-fold *pistis* (110–27): Vitruvius presents a similar list of authorities in the preface to Book VII, and again at VIII 3.27; and Artemidorus bases his own claim to authority partly on the possession of a large library (I p.2.11ff.), though he does not actually mention names. The lists of names in Dioscorides (*Mat.Med.* I p.1.9ff.) and Erotian (p.4.21ff.) fall under the category 'other writers' rather than that of 'authorities', though they do lend a certain weight, an impression of scholarship, and so indirectly fulfil the same function. Apart from these, there is no other refer-

[21] Cf. Archimedes, *Sph. Cyl.* I p.4.13f./20f., *Spir.* p.2.8–10, *Psamm.* p.258.7–10; Apollonius of Perge, *Con.* I p.4.26–8; Hypsicles p.4.1–2; Ps.-Scymnus 4; Dionysius 7–8.

ence to written sources in the prefaces under discussion,[22] and since
the elder Pliny complains of precisely this point, we may take it that
the omission was normal (Pliny, *NH* pref. 22). It is an omission all
the more striking in cases where it is clear that the writer is actually
heavily dependent on one or more written sources, as is the case
with Philo, Vitruvius and Hero.[23] The naming of written authorities
seems to be a convention associated primarily with writers of the
encyclopedic type of which Pliny is a prime example (cf. Varro, *De
re rustica*).[24] Artemidorus' claim, however, does possibly suggest
that at a later date the mere mention of a large library was enough to
create the impression of a comprehensive erudition.

(ii)   Personal experience

The authority claimed by Ps.-Scymnus rests not only on written
sources but also on *autoptikē pistis* (1.129): he has personally visited
the places he describes. This kind of claim, and the use of the word
autoptikē, belong properly to the tradition of geographical *historia*
in which Ps.-Scymnus is writing (above, pp. 34–41): cf. Vitruvius
VIII 3.27, where the same combination occurs, again in a geographical context: 'Ex his autem rebus sunt nonnulla, *quae ego per*

[22] The references to sacred books in Thessalus (I pref., *passim*) and in Vettius
Valens (Kroll 329ff. and see index svv. *Nechepso, Petosiris*) belong to religious rather
than to scientific convention – although neither writer shows any reluctance to
criticize or to improve on his authorities.

[23] *Vitruvius*: see Marsden II, 1971 pp.3–5. A substantial portion of Book X
(chs. 13–15) is paralleled in the περὶ μηχανημάτων of Vitruvius' contemporary
Athenaeus Mechanicus, where the material is explicitly derived from the Greek
Agesistratus. The most acceptable explanation is that Vitruvius too based his account
on Agesistratus (whom he names in VII pref. 14). See also Drachmann, 1963, p. 196
for another possible case of dependence on a written source.

Philo and *Hero* are both heavily indebted to the great Alexandrian mechanician
Ctesibius. Carra de Vaux has suggested, indeed, that Philo may be 'little more than
the principal redactor of the school of Ctesibius' (Philo, *Pneum.* p. 39) and cf. Tittel,
art. 'Heron', *RE* VII/1 col.1037. There are significant correspondences between the
texts of the *Belopoeica* and the *Pneumatica* of both writers; there is, however, no clear
case where Hero can be said to be dependent on Philo, and in many cases Hero's
version, although later, seems to be the longer and more original of the two. See on
this, Marsden II, 1971, pp. 1–2, 8–9; de Vaux, (Philo, *Pneum.*) pp. 28, 33–5, 39;
Fraser, 1972, I pp. 427–8/II p. 618 nn. 411–12. The most economical conclusion is
that the two represent independent recensions of the Ctesibian *Mechanics*. See
further, Alexander, 1978, ch. 2.3 n. 113.

[24] The naming of authorities is also connected, both in Vitruvius and in Pliny, with
a concern about literary plagiarism ('theft') which animated some literary circles in
the early Empire. Both show an awareness of the wider issue (cf. especially Pliny,
pref. 22); and both allude to the 'Homeromastix' Zoilus (Vitruv. III pref. 8–9, Pliny,
pref. 28). See further Momigliano, 1969, pp. 131–4, 141 n. 3.

me perspexi, cetera in libris graecis scripta inveni ...' However, the claim to personal experience becomes a central feature from the first century AD onwards in many scientific prefaces too. Dioscorides claims superiority over his predecessors precisely on the basis of the *autopsia, peira* and *empeiria* which he has won from his many travels and toils; Galen puts forward 'what I have learned through long experience'; Artemidorus not only has a library but has travelled to talk to seers all over the world – and both these are included under the term *peira.* Thessalus and Vettius Valens also insist on their travels in search of education; for Thessalus, this is a matter of 'many trials and dangers', and for Vettius Valens, once again, of 'experience' and *autopsia.*[25]

It is striking here how a nexus of words and ideas recurs constantly in different writers: *autopsia, peira* and *empeiria,* 'toils' and 'travels'. All are linked with the Ionian *historia*-tradition (above pp. 36–8), and the first three have also a special link with the Empiricist debate in medical circles (Deichgräber, 1930, Index s.vv.), so it is not surprising that the terminology of this debate should appear in the prefaces of the medical writers Dioscorides and Galen. But its use in Vettius Valens and Artemidorus[26] suggests that by the end of the second century AD at least, 'Empiricist' terminology has travelled outside the field of medicine and has lost some of its precise application in the process. It is hard to see how *autopsia,* in the root sense of the word, could be involved in the collection of horoscopes; but Valens' horoscopes are real ones,[27] and his claim can be justified if we take it to mean simply that he is 'using

---

[25] Dioscorides, *Mat.Med* I pp.2.3–3.11, especially 3.4ff.: contrast between τὴν ἐν λόγοις δύναμιν and τὴν ἐν τοῖς πράγμασι μετ' ἐμπειρίας ἐπιμέλειαν; claim to base bulk of his work on αὐτοψία, the rest on ἱστορία.
Galen K VI 755.10 τὰ διὰ μακρᾶς πείρας ... γνωσθέντα.
Artemidorus I pref. p.1.13 διὰ πείρας.
II epil. p.202.19 τὴν πεῖραν μάρτυρα καὶ κανόνα τῶν ἐμῶν λόγων ἐπιβοῶμαι.
IV pref. p.236.13ff. οὐχὶ ψιλῇ εἰκασίᾳ ἀλλὰ πείρᾳ ...
V pref. p.302.1f. τὴν ἀπὸ τῆς πείρας πίστιν.
Ps.-Thessalus I pref. p.45.8 μετὰ πολλῶν βασάνων καὶ κινδύνων etc.
Vettius Valens IV II p.172.26 τῆς τῶν παθῶν αὐτοψίας.
　　　　　VI 9 p.260.26ff. ἐγὼ δὲ οὐ λόγῳ καλῷ χρησάμενος, πολλὰ δὲ καμὼν καὶ παθῶν αὐτόπτης γενόμενος τῶν πραγμάτων ...
cf. also IX pref. p.330.14ff. πολυχρονίᾳ πείρᾳ καὶ πόνοις ...
[26] On Empiricism in Artemidorus, see Blum, 1936, ch. 5. The whole question of the use of *autoptēs* in the Ionian *historia*-tradition and in medicine, especially among the Empiricists, is explored at greater length in Alexander, 1978, pp. 31–3 and App. C; see also above ch. 3 pp. 36, 39–40.
[27] See Neugebauer and van Hoesen, 1959, p.176 n.1.

empirical material'. What we have here is a collection of value words, suitable for use in conventional passages to bolster one's 'scientific' credentials;[28] for these writers, Empiricism is no longer an 'idea' but an 'ideology', to borrow Lionel Trilling's distinction:

> Ideology is not ideas; ideology is not acquired by thought but by breathing the haunted air. [It is] the habit of the ritual of showing respect for certain formulas to which, for various reasons having to do with emotional safety, we have very strong ties of whose meaning and consequence in actuality we have no clear understanding.
>
> (Trilling, 1970, pp. 274, 285)

(iii)   Tradition

A very different type of validation is put forward by Philo of Byzantium and Apollonius of Citium. Philo (who is in fact the earliest of our writers to raise the topic of the author's credentials at all) promises at the end of the preface to the *Belopoeica* that he will give an account 'just as we received it' from the expert technicians in Alexandria and Rhodes (Th. 51.10ff.). Apollonius assures the reader that, of the treatments he describes, 'some I have performed myself, while others I have watched in Alexandria as a pupil of Zopyrus' (I pref. p.12.1ff.). In both it is the continuity of tradition that is important: Philo emphasizes that he had a personal introduction to the craftsmen concerned, and Apollonius cites the testimony of Posidonius (evidently known to Ptolemy) to the fact that Zopyrus was a faithful follower of Hippocrates. Both speak from

---

[28] Compare further the use of *autoptēs* in Valens' contemporary Theophilus of Antioch, *Ad Autol.* III 2. Theophilus asserts that 'writers (*or*: historians) ought to have had personal experience (αὐτοὺς αὐτόπτας γεγενῆσθαι) of the things on which they make statements, or to have acquired accurate information from those who have seen them'. This very general assertion is clearly a cliché: it has little relevance to the indictment of 'worthless' Greek writers which follows (ranging from Homer and Hesiod to 'Plato and the other philosophers'), and little connection with Theophilus' ultimate conclusion. A similar combination of themes (worthlessness of pagan literature; importance of *autopsia*; 'eyes more trustworthy than ears') is found in the prefaces of Mark the Deacon, *Vita Porphyri* and Theodoret, *Rel.Hist.* (*PG* LXXXII 1292C–1293A). Possibly the whole nexus of ideas has been taken over as a preface-topic by Christian writers from the late second century. Mark, like Vettius Valens and Dioscorides, also has some strictures on the virtues of the simple over the ornate style (see further, Janson, 1964, pp. 127ff.).

within a living tradition (in this case a tradition of *practice*), not as outside investigators.

While there are certain similarities between this kind of authentication and the insistence on personal experience described under (ii), there is a marked difference in tone and language. Even though Apollonius mentions that he has performed some of the treatments for dislocation himself, his statement lacks the self-consciously individualistic tone of Ps.-Scymnus and the later writers. What is stressed is not so much personal research as faithfulness to a living tradition. On the other hand, we are also a long way from (i), the naming of written sources, a fact all the more striking when we consider that Apollonius' work is actually a commentary on a written text, and that Philo probably reworked material from Ctesibius for his *Belopoeica* (cf. n. 23).

This insistence on the right background, on studying with the right teachers and being in touch with authentic tradition, probably reflects an attitude deeply rooted in the craft traditions, where oral instruction from a practitioner was seen not only as the normal method of acquiring information (Marrou, 1964, II ix.1, pp. 263–5), but also as the ideal. It is not easy to find written evidence for these attitudes, since our sources inevitably are written themselves; nevertheless, traces of it can be found, especially in medical literature – for Greek medicine, in spite of vigorous theoretical debate, remained essentially a craft rather than a science as regards practice (Temkin, 1953).

Galen begins one of his prefaces by quoting a 'saying' current among 'most craftsmen' to the effect that 'gathering information out of a book is not the same thing, nor even comparable to learning from the living voice'.[29] The same attitude is expressed in the 'proverb' quoted more than once about 'people who try to navigate out of a book' as opposed to those who 'gain personal experience by the side of the teacher himself'.[30] Galen's own attitude to these pieces of wisdom is ambiguous: the first he quotes only to disagree with it, but on other occasions he shows a distinct inclination to this view, and even applies the same principle to his philosophical works (*De libr.propr.* xi. K XIX 42 = SM II 118.22–4). It is clear, however,

[29] K XII 894.1–4. The similarity with Papias' famous phrase (Eusabius, *HE* III 39.4) is remarkable, and suggests that Papias too was alluding to a well-known proverb. See further Alexander, 1990.
[30] *Temp.Med.* VI pref. (K XI 796) and *De libr.propr.* 5 (K XIX 33 = SM II 110.25–7). Cf. also *On Medical Experience* IX 2 (Walzer p. 98), with Walzer's notes *ad loc.*; further, Blum, 1936, pp. 86–8.

that the opinion does not originate with him. The taunt about 'navigating out of a book' appears as early as Polybius (XII 25d 4ff.), and Polybius probably found it, along with much else in this polemical passage, in an Empiricist pamphlet.[31]

Thus when we find several passages in Apollonius of Citium and in Vitruvius expressing doubts as to whether it is possible to convey their material adequately in writing (or even 'in words'),[32] we may fairly cite in comparison the rather suspicious attitude to books as a means of passing on teaching which surfaces again later in Galen; and Galen's emphasis on the importance of learning one's craft by the side of a teacher will explain the preference of Philo and Apollonius for precisely this kind of 'tradition-based' validation. Galen again makes explicit what could well have been their thoughts in a passage on the difficulty of learning to identify herbs and their uses (K XIV 6): those who have not learned from a teacher giving a simultaneous demonstration of the subject, but have had to rely on reading a book, will need much more by way of *autopsia*. It is implied that the former case is to be preferred, even though the book may be a good one, and even if it is supplemented by *autopsia*. This kind of attitude could well explain why writers like Philo and Apollonius, though they use written sources, prefer to ground their authority on contact with the living tradition passed on from teacher to pupil (and why the Empiricist Apollonius makes no claim to *autopsia* himself). Another passage from Galen provides interesting confirmation:

> As for me, even if none of Erasistratus' books had been preserved, but they were all now lost as happened with Chrysippus', I would still rather trust what his disciples say about their teacher in the matter than (I would trust) people who have never seen Erasistratus himself or even one of his disciples. (*De venae sect.* 5, K XI 221)

In other words, what arouses respect in this field is the chain of tradition from master to disciple, even in a man as intellectually sophisticated as Galen.[33]

[31] Cf. ch. 3 above pp. 39–40.

[32] Apollonius of Citium II pref. p.38.11ff.; Vitruvius X 8.1 X 8.6, and cf. IV 8.7 and X 11.9, 'quantum comprehendere scriptis potuero'. Cf. also Hippocrates, *De articulis* 33 (Littré IV 149–50), 'But it is not easy to explain the whole (*or*, every) mode of operation in writing ...'

[33] Contrast the rather ironical comment of Ammianus Marcellinus XXII 16.18, '... in place of any testimony it suffices to commend his art if he can say he was taught in Alexandria'.

Galen's own prefaces show a varying practice as regards his own authority. In some he insists on his own experience in the manner of (ii) above; but in one preface at least the tone is more reminiscent of Philo and Apollonius: see K IV 767.3ff., where the book's thesis is said to rest on trials made 'not alone by myself, but from the beginning in the company of my teachers'. The emphasis here, with its disavowal of originality, is interesting; as a rule, however, validation by tradition appears to be confined to earlier writers, and is gradually superseded by validation by personal experience among later writers. Vitruvius does not show much interest in the topic in his prefaces, but he does frequently introduce a piece of information in the text with the words, 'as I have received it from my teachers', or a similar formula.[34] The occasional allusion to his own experience is, as in Apollonius, subordinate beside this appeal to tradition (X 11.2), and in one place, like Galen, he explicitly rejects any claim to originality (IX 7.7). Significantly, Vitruvius provides clear examples of the appeal to tradition even where he is using written sources.[35] Hero of Alexandria in the following century likewise presents the contents of some of his treatises as 'the tradition received from the ancients', usually with the added weight of personal experience.[36] A similar claim seems to be implied in one of the prefaces of Hermogenes, though in a rather indirect fashion (*Stat.* pref. p.28.4–5).

The *manner of presentation* of element (6) does not show anything like the kind of regularity that we observed with elements (1)–(5). In many cases, and especially where some weight is laid on the question of the author's credentials, it forms a separate section of the preface, and one or more sentences may be devoted to it. Sometimes the author's own qualifications are placed in contrast with those of his

[34] Cf. Vitruvius II pref. 5, IV 3.3, IV 8.7, IX 1.16, IX 7.7 X 11.2, X 13.8.
The wording in these passages suggests oral transmission (cf. also the metaphor of 'following', almost of discipleship, in the phrase 'quorum secutus ingressus', VIII 3.27 and II pref. 5); but Vitruvius uses words like these in at least one subject where he was expert, and where we should expect his information to come from a book: see IX 1.16, where the subject is astronomy.

[35] This is quite clearly the case in X 13.8, on which see Marsden II, 1971, p. 4; the information which Vitruvius claims to have received from his 'teachers' is paralleled in Athenaeus Mechanicus, and must have come from the common source of the two writers, Agesistratus – as indeed does the material which Vitruvius quotes from Diades. Thus, in Marsden's words, '(Vitruvius') reference to *praeceptores* conceals his complete indebtedness to one instructor, that is to one source.' Such references to a chain of tradition seem to have been widespread among engineers – cf. Vitruvius X 13.3.

[36] Hero, *Spir.* I p.2.8–10, *Catoptr.* p.320.6f., *Metr.* I p.4.6–7, *Dioptr.* p.188.5ff.

predecessors or rivals. One particular pattern, however, may be detected, providing a further example of the tendency already noted towards combination and compression. In Vitruvius the topic usually occurs in transitional sentences of the form: 'We shall now relate/have related *as we received from our teachers* ...' Both Philo and Apollonius use a similar formula, in the last sentence of the preface forming a transition to the beginning of the book. But Hero, whose prefaces are generally much more compressed, tends to place this kind of phrase directly in the opening sentence of the preface as the object of the main 'decision' verb. And in Dioscorides, Artemidorus Daldianus and Galen the brief phrase 'what I have learned through experience' (or the equivalent) may be inserted in this position, even though the author's experience is also discussed more fully elsewhere.[37]

The question of *origins* is a little more complicated. The language of (ii), the appeal to personal experience, clearly owes quite a lot to the Empiricist debate (above pp. 36–40). The appeal to tradition (iii) also appears to have some links with Empiricist propaganda, but we seem to be dealing here with a feeling already deep-rooted among craftsmen which was simply picked up and used by the more intellectual Empiricists to support their position, a piece of folk-wisdom like that of Caleb Garth in *Middlemarch*: 'A good deal of what I know can only come from experience: you can't learn it off as you learn things out of a book.' It is explicitly so used in the Empiricist argument described by Galen in K VIII 141.3ff. (Deichgräber, 1930, p.96.31ff.); and of course the Empiricists themselves were not really averse to books (cf. the definition of *historia* as 'what is contained in books'). It is significant that though both Philo and Apollonius apparently use Empiricist language in their prefaces, they do so in connection with 'Methodology' (below), not in discussing their own credentials. We may suggest, then, that the appeal to tradition arose independently among writers related to the craft traditions, where it appears first as a transitional phrase qualifying the writer's information, and that the Empiricist debate influenced its later development and expression in terms of personal experience.

The question still remains, however, whether there is any external *literary* influence governing the adoption of 'the author's quali-

[37] Dioscorides, *Eup.* II epil. p.317.9; Galen K VI 755.10f., K XIV 390,3; Artemidorus I pref. p.1.12f. Note the formal equivalent in Serenus, *Sect.Con.* p.120.8; but this phrase lacks the specific reference to 'experience'. Cf. n. 25 above.

fications' as a preface-topic. Was the scientific tradition influenced here by classical historiography, where the theme figures prominently from Thucydides onwards (above pp. 32–4)? The listing of written authorities as in (i) is not typical of Greek historiography. The historians, like the scientific writers, adopted it relatively late, and it was never accepted by historians concerned to preserve classical convention. And the appeal to a living teaching tradition (iii) has clearly little place among the historians. What is characteristic of historical prefaces is (ii), the vaunting of personal experience. Thucydides' views on the nature of historical evidence largely dictated the choice of contemporary events as the preferred subject-matter for later historians, since it was only here that personal experience was possible. More importantly, Thucydides' preface laid down the lines of expression for subsequent prefaces: whether or not the writer had restricted himself to contemporary history, his preface would emphasise his 'personal experience' in one form or another, if only in the claim to have travelled widely in search of information.

But there are two factors which should warn us against a hasty conclusion that this historiographical convention must have influenced scientific prefaces here. First, the Empiricist language which is often used in this connection clearly belongs to the world of the scientific writers in a way that it does not to the historians; and in the case of one historian, Polybius, there are clear indications that the influence worked the other way round (above n. 31). And, secondly, the closest link between the two traditions is at the point where personal experience takes the form of travel, and this goes right back to the common parent of both historical and scientific research, Ionian *historia*. Indeed we have argued elsewhere[38] that one particular conventional word, *autoptēs*, actually belongs here on the 'geographical' side of history, and was only later (and only partially) adopted by Polybius for the 'Thucydidean' claim to personal experience of events. We must beware of the unconscious snobbism that leads us always to assume the influence of the 'higher' literary forms on the 'lower'. What the evidence seems to suggest here is rather a cross-fertilization of preface-topics between one tradition and another than a one-sided literary influence either way. It is clear, at any rate, that the topic of the 'author's qualifications' was well established in the scientific tradition by the first century AD.

[38] See above, ch. 3 pp. 34–41.

7   Methodological issues

The earliest writers do not usually raise questions in their prefaces about the methodology of the subject they are dealing with. If they do so, it is only in relation to very particular problems, as when Archimedes gives a brief sketch of the problem and of his own method of arriving at a solution. This may be a way of placing the particular problem on the map, as it were, of contemporary geometrical knowledge, or it may be a question of defining the type of method adopted, as in the preface to *Eratosthenes* (p.428.23ff.).[39] In striking contrast stands the lengthy passage in Philo's *Belopoeica* (Th. 49.12–51.7), where the author discusses the methodology of his subject in such a way as to raise fundamental questions of epistemology, and concludes by enunciating the general principle that 'not everything can be conceived by reason (*logos*) or by mechanical methods, but that many things are also discovered by experience (*peira*)' (Th. 50.26ff.). Even more general is the opening of Vitruvius Book I, which begins by defining the architect's art as a combination of practice and theory, *fabrica* and *ratiocinatio*. Less direct, but equally remarkable, is the beginning of Hero's *Belopoeica*, which asserts the value of this branch of mechanics in producing *ataraxia*, the chief object of philosophical speculation, in a way never achieved by research διὰ τῶν λόγων. Hero is known also to have divided mechanics into τὸ λογικόν and τὸ χειρουργικόν, possibly in a lost preface,[40] and a distinction between *logos* and the direct perception of the facts appears in the classification of his predecessors in *Spir.* I (p.2.5–7); cf. also the closely parallel sequence of ideas in Galen K VI p.453.8–454.3.

It is evident that these passages must be related to a wider debate on epistemological issues. In particular the allusions to the roles of *logos* and *peira*, of *tuchē* and *technē*, can be filled out by reference to

[39] Cf. Archimedes, *Sph.Cyl.* I for an example of the former type, and *Quadr.* for both. Of the other hellenistic writers, Apollonius of Perge (*Con.* I) and Hypsicles only touch on this sort of information in the sense that the 'story' they both give about the origins of the problem indicates what kind of problem it is (cf. also Diocles, *On Burning Mirrors*). Bito has a practical note on the importance of preserving the correct proportions in constructing his machines (W 44.4ff). Diocles of Carystus, Ps.-Scymnus and Dionysius Calliphontis are not concerned with methodology at all in their prefaces.

[40] Pappus VIII 1 (1022, 13ff. Hultsch): cited and discussed by Fuhrmann, 1960, p. 171. The passage may well have formed part of a lost preface to Book I of Hero's *Mechanics*, composed on similar lines to Vitruvius I 1.1.

the Empiricist debate, which was preoccupied with these issues.[41] But we may also suggest a rather more precise location within the context of the late hellenistic/early Roman debate about the nature and status of the crafts, traces of which can be seen, for example, in Varro (*De re rustica* I 18.7) and in Posidonius (Seneca, Ep. 90). The theme of the origins of the crafts which appears here is not necessarily a philosophical one: it could be simply archaeological, or it could be connected with poetic 'Golden Age' speculation (Vergil, *Georg.* I 118–59), or it could be used for a rather different philosophical purpose as in Lucretius V 925ff. It is not necessary for our purposes to enter into the tortuous question of the relationship between these texts.[42] The simplest explanation for both their similarities and their differences is that there was an independent account of the discovery of fire and the origins of the crafts (cf. Vitruv. II pref. 5) which each writer used for his own purposes. Posidonius used the theme, apparently, to demonstrate the all-embracing utility of philosophy; Philo, who most probably antedates Posidonius, uses it to throw light on the epistemological status of mechanical know-how.[43] The same theme appears in Hero's *Metrica* and at the beginning of Vitruvius Book II, a book which Vitruvius admits could well have been placed first (II 1.8).

But is there any particular reason why this very general methodological debate should have become a regular preface-topic? One rather convincing suggestion has been made by Manfred Fuhrmann

[41] See on this debate in general Deichgräber, 1930. A comparison of the Philonian discussion (*Bel.* pref. Th. 50.14–51.7) with the wider debate is particularly instructive: cf. e.g. Deichgräber, 1930, nos. 95, 97, 102: further examples cited in Alexander, 1978, ch. II 3 n.132. Marsden's notes here (II, 1971, pp. 157 n. 6 and p. 44 n. 2) are hardly adequate: Philo is engaged in something rather more abstruse than 'scarcely veiled criticism of the normal Greek attitude towards the practical'. He reduces the issue to abstractions, and shows himself aware of the finer dimensions of the problem: 'experience' is not simply one observation set against the deductions of theory, but is based on life-long observation and comparison. This methodological interest evidently reflects the actual position of Philo, and of the Ctesibian school in general, at a point of intersection between the long-established craft tradition in artillery construction, working mainly by empirical methods, and the mathematics and natural philosophy of Alexandria.

[42] It is tempting to assign a large role to the relatively unknown Posidonius, but the differences between his account of the origins of the crafts, as we have it in Seneca, and those of Lucretius and Vitruvius, must not be underestimated. Lucretius' ultimate source was presumably Democritus: see Bailey, 1949, III p. 1520.

[43] A similar though much briefer passage in Hero's *Belopoeica* on the role of *peira* in the discovery of one of the fundamentals of artillery construction (W 112.7–113.4) may indicate that this goes back at least in part to Ctesibus and/or Strato. For further discussion, see Spoerri, 1959, ch. 2; Walbank, 1972, pp. 138f. and notes.

(1960, p. 160 n. 5, cf. pp. 171–2), referring to the work of H. Dahlmann (1953). Dahlmann has documented discussions on 'the nature of the art' regularly found at the beginning of manuals on literary subjects such as poetry, and he sees this not as a peculiarly literary phenomenon, but simply as an instance of a tendency to begin *technai* of all kinds with a definition of the *ars* and the *artifex* (ch. 3 pp. 99(13)–111(25)). It is not hard to see how the customary definition could lead naturally to the raising of epistemological questions: was the art in question a *technē*, an *epistēmē* or an *empeiria*?[44] One way to approach this question was to discuss how the art came to be discovered in the first place: cf. a classic example in the *Introductio sive medicus* ascribed to Galen (K XIV 674ff.). Quintilian, *Inst.or.* III 5.1 provides a briefer, more allusive discussion similar to Vitruvius'; cf. also *Rhet. ad Herennium* I 3, Cicero, *De oratore* I 14. Vitruvius X 1 provides a further example of the approach to a subject by means of a discussion of its origins.

The pattern described by Dahlmann thus seems to provide a plausible explanation for the emergence of the methodological discussion as a regular feature of prefaces: from being a topic to be discussed at the beginning of a systematic treatise, it became something to be discussed at the beginning of any treatise, i.e. a preface-topic. The fact that it features so prominently in Philo, Vitruvius and Hero may indicate that it had a particular importance in the mechanical tradition; but there are allusions to the debate elsewhere in the later scientific tradition. Thus Apollonius of Citium alludes to the conflict between *cheirourgia* and *logos* while making conventional remarks about the difficulty of the subject and the benefit of his illustrations (II pref., p.38.11ff.). Erotian's criticisms of his Empiricist predecessors lead him to a general remark on the purpose for which *logos* was given to man (p.3.4ff., p.4.1ff.). Hermogenes begins one book with a long section on the importance of learning the subject as an *epistēmē*, and not relying on mere experience (*Id.* p.213.14ff.). In a not dissimilar vein, Serenus insists on the necessity for geometrical proof while attacking mere *pithanologia* (*Sect.Cyl.* p.2.9): this is noticeably more generalized than the methodological remarks of Archimedes. And the disavowal of *pithanologia* is linked with the insistence on *peira* in Dioscorides (*Mat.Med.* I p.3.5f.), in Artemidorus (Bk. II epil., p.202.16ff.) and in Vettius Valens (VI

<hr />

[44] Cf. the opening definition in the *Ars Grammatica* of Dionysius Thrax, 'Γραμματική ἐστιν ἐμπειρία ...', which sparked off a long scholastic debate on whether grammar was an *empeiria* or a *technē*: see Deichgräber, 1930, nos. 52–6.

p.260.26ff.).[45] What is striking in these texts is the tendency to generalize, to revert, if only momentarily, to abstract issues, even where these are incidental to the problems of the book itself. And once again we may note how many of these allusions seem to reflect the ideology of Empiricism: the debate between the medical sects, so graphically described by Galen,[46] and evidently known to the general public, at least in outline, seems to have had the effect of polarizing the issues for many outside the field of medicine. It certainly provided the less original with an arsenal of propaganda words, ready to hand when the occasion arose to discuss (or at least to show themselves familiar with) some of the basic issues of epistemology.

Style

Our analysis of form and content has already shown how much there is in common between the prefaces of the different writers in the scientific tradition. The impression is reinforced when we turn to consider more general aspects of their style and language.

Periodic construction

Quite apart from the fondness for the particular schemata already described, there is a general predilection for periodic construction, especially at the beginning of a preface. This is particularly noticeable in authors who do not normally write long periods (e.g. Vitruvius and Apollonius of Citium) and who seem slightly unhappy when they do. It is sometimes carried to ridiculous lengths – as seen, for example, in the artificial subordinating of one part of a list of contents or *anakephalaiōsis* to another.[47]

[45] It is impossible to trace here all the parallels to these phrases in Empiricist writing and elsewhere; a good sample is discussed in Blum, 1936, ch. 5.

[46] Galen's *Subfiguratio empeirica* and *On Medical Experience* are both essays in defence of the Empiricist position. The works *On the Sects* and *On the Best Sect* discuss the problem in a more detached fashion; cf. also the polemical passage in *De Comp.med.sed.loc.* VIII pref., K XIII p.116.

[47] Cf. e.g. Hipparchus II pref.; Ps.-Scymnus 69–97; Dioscorides, *Mat.med.* II pref., *Eup.* II pref; Demetrius p.1.2–15 (see Appendix A. no. 3) and Erotian p.3.3–4.1 provide examples of exceptionally long sentences. On the style of Vitruvius, see above ch. 4 n. 46; on Erotian, Wilamowitz, 1890, pp. 17, 19: '... ingentibus periodorum flexuris ...', '... hic deficio. qui enim halitus tanta periodo non defatigatur, in qua una particula εἰ per duodecim versus regnat, neque luculentiore exemplo Erotiani artem illustrare possum ... Scribit autem quantum potest ornate et copiose, et periodorum labyrinthos extruit e quibus ne ipse quidem feliciter se exolvit.'

Certain forms of periodic construction are particularly favoured: sentences begin frequently with ἐπεί (or ἐπειδή), with a genitive absolute or (especially in earlier writers) with the participle, 'seeing that ...', agreeing with the subject of the sentence.[48] These are all constructions which in Greek give an impression of sonority and weight, and their use (especially in the opening sentence of a preface) accords with the heightened, formal style which these writers seem to aim for.

The subject of the work frequently appears in an oblique case in the opening words of the first sentence: conversely, it is very unusual to find it at the beginning in the nominative (above p. 71f.). As we have noted elsewhere, there was a certain practical advantage in this device; but the avoidance of the obvious and direct approach may be seen itself as a stylistic cliché.

Rhetorical devices

Some stylistic devices of a more rhetorical nature contribute to the sonorous effect:

> Litotes: e.g. Archimedes, *Psamm.* p.258.11; Philo, *Bel.* Th. 50.12,28, 78.24,7, 6.22,77.8 and *Pneum.* p.458.11; Apollonius of Citium II pref. p.38.10,11 and Vitruvius X pref. 4, X 2.11.
> Alliteration on the favourite p-sound, especially using forms or derivatives of the word πολύς (πολλοί, πολλά- κις etc.).[49] The Greek language seems to have found this form of alliteration particularly effective (further below, p. 109)

[48] Ἐπεί/ἐπειδή: Diocles p.75.1; Philo, *Bel.* Th. 49.7 and 56.8ff.; *Pneum.* p.458.6 'Quia'; Vitruvius I 6.12, IV pref. 1; Apollonius of Citium I pref. p.10.8, III pref. p.64.12; Hero, *Bel.* W 73.6; Galen K 224.1, K V 1.1, K V 587.1, K VI 454.6.11, K VI 554.1, K VI 816.1, K VII 584.1, K X 1.1, K X 458.5, K XIV 390.1; Hermogenes, *Inv.* IV p.170.21; Artemidorus p.204.1, 236.2.
Genitive absolute: Archimedes, *Stom.* p.416.1; Demetrius p.1.1; Hero, *Spir.* I p.2.4, *Aut.* p.338.3, *Catoptr.* p.320.5 (abl. absol.), *Metr.* I p.4.4, *Dioptr.* p.188.3, *Bel.* W 71 end; Dioscorides, *Mat.med.* I pref. p.1.4; Galen K VII 463.1; Hermogenes, *Stat.* p. 28.2, *Inv.* III p.133.15; Thessalus I p.45.2; II p.195.1.
'Seeing that ...': Archimedes, *Eratosth.* p.428.18; Hipparchus I pref. p.4.12; Philo, *Bel.* Th. 59.23, 60.18; Apollonius of Citium I pref. p.10.3 (see textual note, p. 217f.); Demetrius p.1.7; Hero, *Catoptr.* p.318.9; Erotian p.3.4.
[49] Alliteration on p-sound, especially with πολύς: Apollonius of Perge, *Con.* IV pref. p.4.2–3 (cf. also vol. I p.4.10–11 πολλὰ καὶ παράδοξα θεωρήματα). Philo has a

Occasionally we find a rhetorical transition-formula at the
end of a preface, in a phrase to the effect that a preface
must not go on too long – or, more briefly, that 'it is time
to finish the preface . . .'[50]

All this adds up to the fact that there will often be a certain
difference in style between the preface and the body of the work,
apparently due to a striving for sonority and weight in the opening
sentences. It is fair to ask what is the relation between this apparent
desire to impress and the circumstances of the publication of the
book – in particular, its relation to the dedication of the book: some
discussion of this point has been reserved for our final chapter (see
below, pp. 193–200). Nevertheless, in view of the continuity of the
style over different authors within the scientific tradition, it is clearly
important not to overvalue the individual, conscious element in the
adoption of this type of preface by any one author. Once the style
was established within the scientific tradition, it could well provide
its own impetus: the composition of a preface in this style may have
come to be accepted as the proper thing, irrespective of the particular circumstances which originally gave rise to the practice.
(This would explain, for example, why a type of preface which is
earlier associated with dedication is found in some later writers
without it.) Certainly the appearance of a 'rhetorical' convention in
one writer need not be taken as evidence for that writer's connection
with rhetorical literature, if it can be shown that the convention was
already established in the scientific tradition. What is striking as a

propensity for a repeated p-sound at moments of excitement, cf. *Bel.* Th. 59.1f.,
68.14–17. Add: Apollonius of Citium I pref. p.10.15; Hero, *Spir.* I p.2.4.f., *Aut.*
p.338.3–6, *Metr.* I p.2.3f., *Dioptr.* p.188.3ff., *Bel.* W 73.6; Dioscorides, *Mat.med.* I
p.1.4–7, *Eup.* I p.151.3–7; Erotian p.3.3–5; Galen K I 224.1–3, K IV 767.2–3. K V
806.1–4 = SM III 333.1–4), K VII 463.1–2; Hermogenes, *Inv.* III 4 p.133.15–17;
Thessalus I p.45.2, 6; Artemidorus Daldianus pp.1.1ff., 203.6–8, 204.1–3, 238.7;
Vettius Valens pp.172.21–2, 260.29–31. See further below, ch. 6 s.v. πολλοί.
    [50] Hypsicles p.4.4–5; Artemidorus Daldianus p.3.1ff.; cf. also p.100.19–20. Cf:
Lausberg, 1960, sect. 271. In rhetorical theory, the ideal of *brevitas* properly belonged
to one particular section of the speech, the *narratio*; but it seems to have been
transferred to the preface, as it was transferred, less appropriately, to other forms of
literature – see Curtius, 1953, Excursus XIII (pp. 487ff.). Cf. also Herkommer, 1968,
pp.152f., 161f. for the 'brevity-formula' in the historians. It seems to have been used
commonly for *excursus* – i.e. for any digression from the main narrative – a use
clearly analogous to its appearance at the end of a preface (Herkommer, 1968, p. 153
and n. 5). The use of the formula is 'rhetorical' only in that it implies awareness of the
existence of rhetorical precepts. The rhetorical theorists would not themselves have
approved of such a naïve expression of the ideal. For examples of rhetorical tran-
sition-formulae, cf. Herkommer, 1968, p. 124 n. 2.

sign of individuality is a departure from the common 'scientific' style, such as Vitruvius' attempts at prefaces adapted to a more elevated literary taste (cf. above, p. 64 n. 43).

Phraseology and vocabulary

While each writer has his own favourite turns of expression, there are phrases and words which are found distributed throughout the scientific tradition. Some of these have their ultimate origins elsewhere – 'brevity', for example, where it has not the obvious significance which it has for an epitomator (such as Ps.-Scymnus or Dionysius Calliphontis), but is put forward as a self-evident ideal, seems to come from rhetoric (see note 50). Others may be taken to express, perhaps unconsciously, the values of the scientific tradition, while others again seem to be popular for no particular reason. The more striking may be listed as follows, roughly (and to some extent arbitrarily) classified according to their use.

The vocabulary of presentation

'*briefly*': Philo, *Bel.* Th. 60.12, 72.5; Dionysius 1.10; Ps.-Scymnus 3, 7, 14ff.; Vitruvius I 6.12, Hermogenes, *Inv.* III p.126.15. 'As briefly as possible': Vitruvius X 8.1; Hero, *Def.* p.14.3.

Cf. also the disavowal of prolixity in Philo, *Pneum.* 458.19ff.; Apollonius of Citium pp.80.18, 88.6; Vitruvius V pref. 3, IX 7.7; and Galen K V p.586, K VI p.305 and K X p. 384.[51]

'*clearly*', or 'as clearly as possible': Hipparchus p.2.17; Apollonius of Citium p.38.13.16; Ps.-Scymnus 3, 11; Vitruvius VI 6.7, IX 8.15, X 8.6; Hero, *Mech.* III p.200.11; Galen K II 652.1; Hermogenes, *Stat.* p.28.5, *Inv.* III p.133.17; Artemidorus p.2.26; Vettius Valens p.157.30; Serenus p.120.16.

---

[51] For 'brevity' as an ideal, see previous note. For the phrase 'as briefly as possible' first found in the Attic orators, see Herkommer, 1968, p. 152 n. 5.

The choice of verbs often reflects the same interest: cf. the popular διασαφεῖν (e.g. Hipparchus pp. 2.13–14, 6.21, 8.3; Apollonius of Citium pp. 64–3, 112.7–8). Cf. also Erotian p.9.23 διδασκαλίας εὐσήμου ἕνεκεν.

'*accurately*', or 'as accurately as possible', using ἀκριβῶς, ἀκριβεία, or a form of the verb ἀκριβοῦν. Philo, *Bel.* Th. 67.27, 73.23; Apollonius of Citium p.36.9; Ps.-Scymnus 72; Dioscorides, *Mat.Med.* I p.3.7, 9; Galen K VI 817. 13f.; Artemidorus p.100.14; Vettius Valens pp. 271.10f., 272.31, 359.15.

Cf. also Diocles p.75.12 (used generally) and Dioscorides, *Mat.Med.* I pp. 1.17, 2.1; Galen K VI 7; Artemidorus p.1.20f. (used of others).

'*complete*': Philo, *Bel.* Th. 78.24; Vitruvius X 11.2, 'finita'; Apollonius of Citium pp.38.10, 62.6, 64.11f., 16f.; Hero, *Mech.* p.200.8, *Catoptr.* p.320.8f.; Dioscorides, *Mat.Med.* I p.3.17f. and p.1.8. Artemidorus has a particular concern with 'completeness': cf. pp. 100.7f., 202.8, 204.6, 235.13, and 99.14–16, which expresses the desire that the book should contain neither too much nor too little. The epilogue to Vitruvius Book X (X 16.12) voices the same thought.

'*in order*': a concern for correct organization of the material is common: Vitruvius IV pref.1; Hero, *Spir.* p.2.9; Dioscorides, *Mat.Med.* I p.3.9; Artemidorus pp.3.11ff., 100.13ff., 204.4, 236.9. Cf. also Dioscorides' criticisms of his predecessors in *Mat.Med.* I p.2.11–15.

The same concern has probably influenced the choice of words for 'next' (describing either a sequence of thought, or the order of books): not only the neutral ἑξῆς, but the rather more expressive ἀκολούθως are found: cf. Apollonius of Citium p.64.18; Vettius Valens p.55.7; Hero, *Spir.* p.2.12 ἀκόλουθον ... τῇ ... ἕξει. Vitruvius is presumably translating some such phrases in his odd 'insequatur ordo' (e.g. II pref. 5, II 7.1); cf. also II 10.3, 'uti ordo postulat'.

A concern for '*symmetry*' is less common: both Apollonius of Citium (p.66,24f.) and Hipparchus (p.216.14) use the

phrase στοχαζόμενος τῆς συμμετρίας, which is also found
in Diodorus Siculus and elsewhere.[52]

'*easy to remember*'/'*easy to grasp*'. Concern for ease of
memorization is expressed in various forms: generally,
see Apollonius of Citium p.64.16f., p.10.14f.; Dionysius
11.17f.; Serenus p.120.22f.

Particularly favoured are the various compound adjectives of the εὐμνημόνευτος type:

εὐμνημόνευτος: Ps.-Scymnus 35.

εὐκατάληπτος: Erotian p.3.15; Artemidorus p.2.25;
Vettius Valens p.157.30.

εὐεπίγνωστος: Artemidorus p.300.20.

εὐπαρακολούθητος: Apollonius of Citium pp.10.15,
38.9; Hero, *Bel.* W 73.11; Dioscorides, *Eup.* p.151.5.

εὐκατανόητος: Hipparchus p.8.7.

εὐσύνοπτος: Hero, *Def.* p.14.7.

εὐκαταρίθμητον καί εὐκαταμάθητον: Galen K VII
436.

ἀσυμμνημόνευτα: Dioscorides, *Mat.Med.* I p.2.14.

Vitruvius I 6.12, 'ut facilius intellegatur', V pref. 5, 'quo
facilius ad sensus legentium pervenire possint . . . ita enim
expedita erunt ad intellegendum' etc. seem to be trying to
express the same idea in Latin. In the phrase 'uti non sint
ignota' (VI 6.7, cf. II 10.3), the same thought seems to
have been reduced to an almost meaningless formula.

Vocabulary used of the contents

πραγματεία and its verbal form *πραγματεύεσθαι* are almost
universal in the scientific prefaces. Although the words
are used in other contexts too (LSJ s.vv.), they may have
seemed particularly suitable for the scientific writers with
their connotations of 'factuality' and 'seriousness'. For
examples, see: Archimedes, *Sph.Cyl.* p.2.7f., *Spir.* p.2.10;

[52] Cf. also Diodorus Siculus I 41.10; Diogenes Laertius VII 160; Josephus, *C.Ap.* I
320; *Ant.* I 7. The phrase may have originated as a rhetorical precept (cf. Avenarius,
1956, pp. 105–113 and p. 115: Isocrates XII 33 speaks of συμμετρία συντεταγμένη
τοῖς προοιμίοις), but if so its rhetorical origins are by now rather remote. Birt, 1882,
pp. 147ff. connects it with practical considerations of the proper length for a book-
roll, and this would fit many of the above examples, including Hipparchus. In
Apollonius, however, as in Diogenes Laertius, it seems to mean simply 'brevity'.

Apollonius of Perge, *Con.* I p.2.13, IV p.2.7f., Philo, *Bel.*
Th. 49.5, *Pneum.* p.458.20 ('negotio'); Demetrius p.1.7;
Ps.-Scymnus 49; Hero, *Spir.* I p.2.4, *Aut.* p.338.3,
Catoptr. pp.318.3, 5, 9, and 320.6, *Metr.* I pp.2.13, 4.5,
Dioptr. p.188.3, 14, *Def.*, p.14.7; Dioscorides, *Mat.Med.* I
pp.1.7, 10, 2.19; Erotian p.3.3; Galen K VII 469, VII 585,
X 1, C 456–8; Hermogenes, *Id.* I p.214.16; Artemidorus
pp.99.13, 203.7f., 204.2–3, 235.16, 237.5; Serenus
p.120.6.

ἀξιόλογος or the equivalent: Archimedes *Sph.Cyl.* I p.2.7;
Vitruvius IV pref. 1 (? 'dignam'); Hero, *Spir.* I p.2.4, *Aut.*
p.338.4, *Catoptr.* p.318.10 ('dignum studio'); Galen K VI
453; Artemidorus p.237.10.

ποικίλος (see above p. 59 and n. 32 on the implications of this word): Archimedes, *Stom.* p.416.2; Apollonius of Perge, *Con.* IV p.4.3; Philo, *Bel.* Th. 73.21–3,
Pneum. p.458.7 ('subtilia'); Hero, *Spir..* I p.2.18, *Aut.*
pp.338.4, 342.6, *Catoptr.* p.316.7 ('multa et varia ratiocinatio'); Vettius Valens p.132.5; Serenus p.120.4. Cf. also
Vitruvius X 8.6, 'curiose et subtiliter', and I 1.1, 'pluribus
disciplinis et variis eruditionibus'.

'useful' or *'helpful'*: Apollonius of Perge, *Con.* IV p.4–7;
Hipparchus pp.4.10, 17, 22, 8.6; Philo, *Bel.* Th. 59.1;
Vitruvius IV pref. 1, IX 8.15, X 13.8; Apollonius of
Citium pp.38.10, 62.7; Ps.-Scymnus 93; Hero, *Spir,* I
p.2.11f., 18ff., *Mech.* p.200.12f., 16, 20, *Catoptr.*
p.318.18, *Metr.* pp.2.5, 4.6, *Dioptr.* p.188.4.6, *Bel. ad init*;
Dioscorides, *Mat.Med.* I p.3.11ff.; Galen K IV 767, K V
899, K VI 453, K X 1, K XVII 895; Hermogenes, *Stat.*
p.28.5ff., *Id.* I p.213.5ff.; Artemidorus p.235.12ff.
Compare also the frequent expression of the 'decision
to write' in terms of *'necessity'*: Archimedes, *Stom.*
p.416.3f.; Philo, *Bel.* Th. 49.2; Apollonius of Citium
pp.36.5, 64.14; Hero, *Spir.* I p.2.7f., *Catoptr.* p.320.6,
Metr. I p.4.4, *Dioptr.* p.188.5; Galen K II 651, K VI 454,
K VII 463; Hermogenes, *Inv.* IV p.171.1; Thessalus
p.198.1–2; Artemidorus pp.1.9, 3, 7, 237.21; cf. Vitruvius
IV 3.10, 'necesse est', X 3.1, 'necessaria'.

θεωρία (see above ch. 4, p. 59): Diocles p.75.5; Archimedes,

Stom. p.416.3, Eratosth. p.428.20; Hipparchus p.4.25;
Apollonius of Citium pp.38.10, 62.7; Demetrius p.1.2.f.;
Hero, Aut. p.338.5f., 342.4, Catoptr. pp. 316.3 ('specu-
latio'), 6, 318.10f., 17f., Def., p.14.6; Galen K VI 453, VII
463; Vettius Valens p.172.27; Serenus p.120.4.13.

'tradition': παράδοσις and its cognate verbs are common:
Philo, Bel. Th. 49.10, 51.10, 59.1, Vitruvius IX 1.16, X
11.2, 13.8 ('accepi'); Apollonius of Citium p.38.11; Hero,
Spir. I p.2.8, Catoptr. p.320.6 ('accepta'), Dioptr. p.188.6,
Bel. W 73.11; Dioscorides, Mat.Med. I pp.1.11, 17, 2.3, II
p.121.3, Eup. I p.151.3; Thessalus p.195.3; Artemidorus
p.236.4; Vettius Valens pp.132.5, 172.2.

See further above pp. 82–5 on 'tradition'.

Related to this is the question of the writer's attitude
towards those sources or predecessors whom he calls οἱ
ἀρχαῖοι or οἱ παλαιοί. The earlier writers (cf. Philo, Bel.
Th. 50.14ff.; Hero, Spir. p.2.5, 9, Aut. p.342.3, Metr. I
p.2.3ff.; Dioscorides, Mat.Med. I p.1.14, 16) tend to have
an ambivalent attitude, combining respect with criticism;
but in the late first and second centuries AD there is a
perceptible increase in reverence towards 'the ancients',
tending to preclude criticism: cf. Erotian pp.3.6, 6.1ff.;
Galen K V 899; Hermogenes, Stat. p.28.4, Inv. III
p.126.12, Artemidorus pp.23.5ff., 100.8ff., 237.1ff.

Words more openly laudatory of the material are rare:
'wonderful', 'surprising' (Apollonius of Perge, Con. I
p.4.10f.; Hero, Spir. I p.2.19, Aut. pp.338.5, 342.4,
Catoptr. 318.10; Thessalus p.45.3, 6) or 'giving pleasure'
(Ps.-Scymnus lines 4, 92; Dionysius 7; Vitruvius X 9.7).
Equally rare is the more obvious (and expected) 'true'
(Galen K IV 767, V 587; Artemidorus p.237.19). The
scientific writers do not set out directly to give a laudatio
generis of the type found in historical prefaces: the
impression created by such words as those listed is
indirect.

Vocabulary used of the author

Unlike the historians, scientific writers rarely give much direct
information about themselves, except on the matter of their 'quali-

fications' (above pp. 78–87). A certain personal impression is, however, created indirectly by the first-person 'decision to write' (see above n. 6) and especially by the use of 'modest' terminology:

> '*I have tried/will try*': Archimedes, *Sph.Cyl.* II p.170.2, *Psamm.* p.216.16; Philo, *Bel.* Th. 62.23; Dioscorides, *Mat.Med.* pp.1.6, 3.9; Erotian p.116.15; Artemidorus p.300.25; Hermogenes, *Inv.* III 4 p.133.17.

> '*as far as possible*': Vitruvius VI 6.7, X 8.6; Apollonius of Citium pp.38.16, 60.27, 62.5, 64.9, 17; Hero, *Mech.* III p.200.7f.; Galen K X 1.5; Artemidorus pp.202.7f., 236.5.

> This type of modesty is on the whole more characteristic of the later prefaces. Self-deprecation may also be a motive behind the occasional description of an author's own work as 'notes' or 'a sketch'.[53]

> *Self-commendation*, by contrast, is not common; Thessalus' boastfulness (p.45.1–6), and Artemidorus' more restrained allusion to his own 'wisdom' (p.236.4–5), stand out as exceptional. Both Galen (K IV 767) and Dioscorides (*Mat.Med.* I p.2.16) incidentally mention an involvement in the subject from youth, perhaps a further aspect of the 'author's qualifications'.

The vocabulary of dedication

Certain words tend to recur, reflecting not so much the technicalities of the relationship as a particular style of courtesy:

> *verbs* are generally neutral. προσφωνεῖν, which became something of a technical term for dedication in other contexts,[54] occurs only three times in our texts: Hypsicles p.2.16f.; Artemidorus p.237.26f., Vettius Valens p.157.29f. The religious term ἀνατιθέναι occurs in our texts only in Dioscorides (*Mat.Med.* I p.2.20, *Eup.* I p.151.13, II p.242.4). The scientific writers prefer the

---

[53] Hypsicles p.2.16, ὑπομνηματισάμενος; Hero, *Def.* p.14.2, ὑπογράφων σοι καὶ ὑποτυπούμενος; Dioscorides, *Mat.Med.* I p.3.4f. Galen's frequent description of his works as ὑπομνήματα (e.g. K I 224.4f., K X 456.9, 458.3,7) should, however, probably be given a more precise significance: see above, pp. 62–3.

[54] See Cicero, *Ad Att.* XVI 11.4 and H. J. Rose, 1921, p. 108 s.v.

plainer 'to write for you', 'to explain to you', 'to give you', 'to show you', etc.: cf. above p. 70 and n. 6.

the *suitability* of the subject for the dedicatee is a common theme in earlier prefaces: see above p. 74.

the dedicatee is sometimes said to be, or urged to be, σπουδαῖος: Archimedes, *Eratosth.* p.428.18; Apollonius of Perge, *Con.* I p.2.6; Philo, *Pneum.* p.458.6f., 10 ('diligencie tue'); Dionysius 22; Artemidorus p.236.2; cf. also Vitruvius V 4.1, 'qui diligentius attendent'.

the most striking feature of hellenistic dedication-courtesy is the popularity *of adjectives and verbs compounded with philo-* (especially, but not only, *philomathēs*) applied to patrons or readers: Hipparchus I pp.2.7, 10, 4.16, 24 (φιλομαθίαν, φιλοτεχνίαν); Philo, *Bel.* Th. 50. 25–6 (φιλοδόξων καὶ φιλοτέχνων ... βασιλέων); Apollonius of Citium pp.10.3, 38.11 (φιλιατρῶς, φιλιατροῦντι); Demetrius p.1.6–7 (φιλοτίμως ἔχοντα πρὸς φιλομάθειαν); Ps.-Scymnus 10, 63, 104 (φιλομαθεῖν, φιλάγαθον); Dionysius 23 (συμφιλομάθησον). Cf. also Galen K XII 894 (φιλοπόνοις) and Vettius Valens pp.172.22, 272.22 (φιλομαθοῦς).

General linguistic characteristics

Finally, some more general characteristics may be noted. We cannot attempt here a thoroughgoing stylistic analysis, but even a cursory reading will show that our authors betray a remarkable fondness in their prefaces and transitional passages for verbal periphrasis and for multiple compound verbs. To a certain extent this is a feature characteristic of hellenistic prose in general,[55] and particularly of that non-literary, non-vulgar *Koine* which is sometimes described as 'office prose' ('Kanzleistil') and which has been isolated and more precisely described in such studies as those of Jonas Palm (1955) and Lars Rydbeck (1967).[56] But it is a characteristic that adds directly to

[55] Cf. Jaeger, 1938, pp. 22f.: 'Ein Charakteristikum der hellenistischen Prosa sind die zahlreichen Verbalkomposita mit zwei oder drei Präpositionen, deren Neubildung teils durch die Abschwächung der Kraft der einfachen Präpositionen erklärt, teils dem Bedürfnis nach feinerer Differenzierung entspricht.'

[56] Cf. also Warren's remarks on the style of Vitruvius: V. 'not infrequently adopts a formal language closely akin to that of specifications and contracts, the style with

the impression of pomposity. At first sight, these long words and periphrastic constructions seem merely unnecessary, but on closer examination they can be seen to serve two interests: first, they are used to achieve subordination in the construction of periods – particularly compounds in *hupo-* and *pro-*;[57] and, second, they are used for the sake of variety. This trait is most evident in the vocabulary used for elements which recur frequently, such as the 'decision to write', and in words for 'composition'. The variation attained by some writers in their vocabulary for these essential phrases is astonishing,[58] and not infrequently the words they use are found nowhere else. Yet they are not drawing on a recondite vocabulary: these are not really unusual words. They are immediately comprehensible, if not necessarily in the normal sense: it is simply a question of unpicking the various elements of the compound. So in so far as the style of the scientific writers is generally clear and direct in technical exposition, this tendency to use long words and contorted constructions in prefaces and transitional passages marks a difference in style between preface and text. It should be emphasized once again, however, that the style of the prefaces is not in any full sense of the words 'literary' or 'rhetorical'. If the authors are aiming at a more formal and elevated style than normal, their resources and vocabulary in this respect are limited. They give little evidence of direct acquaintance with the resources of hellenistic literary education.

which he was, naturally, most familiar' (from the introduction to Morgan's translation, 1914, p.v.).

[57] See for example Hipparchus II pref. p.212.24ff.; Apollonius of Citium III pref. p.64.17ff.; Demetrius p.1.10f.; Hero, *Metr.* I p.4.8ff.; Dioscorides, *Mat.Med.* II p.121.67ff.; *idem, Eup.* I p.151.15ff., II p.242.3ff.

[58] Cf. the passages cited in the previous note, and the adjectives cited above (p. 96). It is instructive to note the variety achieved by Apollonius of Citium in expressing the idea, 'Hippocrates says': p.12.6, ἐνῆρκται; 12.9f., διελθών ... διασαφεῖ; 12.20, ἐκτέθειται; 12.23, δηλοῖ; 14.13f., ὑπογέγραφεν ... κατακεχώρικεν ...; 14.28, ἐπήνεγκεν; 18.6, φῆσιν; 20.8, ἐπεφώνησεν; 22.7, ὑποτέταχεν; 28.20, προσεπιλέγει; 30.15, σεσήμαγκεν; 32.14, τοῖς προδιηριθμηένοις ... ἐπέζευξεν; 40.5, παρακελεύεται; 40.26, μέμνηται; 46.12, ἀπεφήνατο; 48.10, παρέστακεν; 52.9f., ὑφέσταται.

6

LUKE'S PREFACE

Introduction

We are now in a position to return to the classification of Luke's preface. As our discussion of historical prefaces in chapter 3 has demonstrated, there are difficulties with the long-standing academic assumption that Luke's opening verses are to be classified with the prefaces of the Greek historians. Luke's single-sentence preface is far shorter than even the briefest historical preface. Historical prefaces are expansive in their discussions of methodology and sources, and in their treatment of such standard *topoi* as the importance of the subject-matter and the usefulness of history: Luke's brief and allusive introduction is scarcely comparable. Luke does not present his own name, as was normal with the Greek historians. The address to Theophilus runs counter to the conventions of historiography, which eschewed dedication: historians liked to think of their work, in Thucydides' phrase, as 'a possession for all time' (Thuc. I 22.4), not as a time-bound communication to an individual. And Luke's style, though unusual by New Testament standards, hardly reaches the rhetorical heights of hellenistic historiography, where stylistic and topical *variatio* were central concerns.

None of these factors, taken individually is decisive. It would be absurd to pretend that we could prove that Luke was not at least trying to write a preface in the manner of the historians: if he failed, he would not be the only one, as Lucian's *How to Write History* shows. But the negative points are not without weight; and their force is increased when it becomes clear, on the positive side, that Luke 1.1–4 does have clear affinities with another type of Greek preface. In fact, as we observed above, many of the parallels cited by the commentators are not from historians but from scientific writers.[1] As our study has shown, scientific prefaces and historical prefaces are not derivatives from a common archetype, but evolved separately in response to the distinct needs of different types of literature.

It is our intention to argue in this chapter that Luke, far from trying, and failing, to compose a 'historical' preface, was actually composing within a different literary tradition which had its own preface-conventions, and that this tradition, which we have called the 'scientific', provides significantly better parallels to Luke's preface, both in general and in detail, than the conventions of Greek historiography. Such details of the preface as are not paralleled in the scientific tradition are no better accounted for by the 'historical' parallel: rather, as we shall argue, they belong to no Greek literary tradition as such but are idiosyncrasies reflecting Christian or biblical modes of speech.

First, some general points of comparison.

(a) Length. Few prefaces anywhere are as short as Luke's, but the scientific tradition contains a number of single-sentence prefaces (e.g. Hero, *Def*; Galen K VII 463 and K XIV 390). More important, the overall space allotted to prefaces is less among scientific writers than among historians. There is an observable tendency to shorten prefaces and to compress into one sentence as many separate topics as possible (see above p. 68): both Demetrius and Hero may profitably be compared with Luke in this respect. On the length of historical prefaces, see above ch. 3 pp. 29–30.

(b) Transition. The abruptness of the transition from preface to narrative has often been remarked: not only does Luke's third-person narrative (Luke 1.5) begin without any lead-in from the first-person preface, but the style changes abruptly from classical period to 'septuagintal' paratactic narrative. Both these features can be paralleled in scientific texts, where the change is from an elevated, formal and elaborate mode of composition to a plain and factual exposition. The change from a periodic to a paratactic style is often marked, as is the shift from first to third person. This change in style

---

[1] Cf ch. 1 n. 18. There seems to be an underlying assumption here that all Greek writers were aiming at the same sort of thing in their prefaces. It is true that the distinctions between one type of preface and another are not rigid, and that all Greek prose prefaces have certain things in common. Nevertheless, as we have demonstrated above, it is quite possible to distinguish between different traditions; and in so far as there is 'mixing' this seems to be a late phenomenon, not the result of a common origin.

is observable in the majority of the texts studied, although it is less evident in the more competent writers like Galen and Hermogenes; it may be seen particularly clearly in the mathematical texts and in those which follow a schematic mode of presentation (Demetrius; Galen K VII 463, K VII 584–5, Artemidorus Daldianus V). The abrupt change of subject-matter is also a feature of scientific texts. Some writers soften the transition with 'let us begin . . . ' or similar phrases (e.g. Galen K VII 463.7, 585.7; Philo, *Bel.* Th. 51.14), and very occasionally there is a rhetorical transition-formula (e.g. Hypsicles). The majority, like Luke, have no lead-in at all from preface to text. Such an abrupt break was intolerable to the rhetorical canons of historiography (above, ch. 3 pp. 30–1).

(c)   The language and style of the preface fit better with the scientific than with the historical tradition. There are rhetorical clichés behind Luke's opening words (see below); but precisely the same touches of rhetoric are found in the scientific writers. Luke's language is elevated and formal in the preface; there is a certain literary flavour, and the long words sound impressive. But, again, these are exactly the marks of formal style which appear in scientific prefaces, and the scientific writers also share Luke's limitations as a writer of classical literary prose. Alongside the classical form παρέδοσαν is a word condemned by the Atticists (καθώς). The long words which give such a ponderous effect are precisely those which the burgeoning classicism of the first century was trying to eliminate from the written language: empty compounds, used not for greater precision but merely to give weight, where a simple word would have done instead (further below). The influence of this newer, 'purer' vocabulary ideal may be seen already in Josephus (Cadbury, 1927, p. 174; Pelletier, 1962, esp. pp. 254–9); contemporary scientific writers were more or less bypassed by the movement, at least until the third and fourth centuries AD (Rydbeck, 1967, *passim*). Like Luke, they tend to avoid the more flowery hellenistic vocabulary, but the use of multiple compounds for verbs of writing and composing is typical of their prefaces (above ch. 5 pp. 100–1).

Luke's limitations as a stylist become clearer as we try to work out the precise significance of his words. It was Cadbury himself who voiced the suspicion that 'in some of his longer words the writer has overshot the mark and sacrificed clearness to sonorous style' (1927, p. 198). In fact the effect of the long words is to obscure the thought Luke is trying to convey. Obscurity is deepened by the amphibolous position of several words: in general it is not a good sign that so much effort has been expended in trying to understand a text whose informational content is essentially simple.[2] It is a mistake to use words like 'pregnant' or 'lapidary' in this context,[3] as if Luke were deliberately exploiting ambiguity and trying to cram as much meaning as possible into a small compass. The obscurity of the preface may be ascribed to two factors: (i) its allusiveness is convincingly explained if we accept that, like the prefaces of the later scientific writers, it comes at the end of a long period of development, during which the expression of stock ideas has become compressed through familiarity; and (ii) like many scientific writers, Luke gives the impression that he is not fully in control of this formal style, particularly of the demands of periodic composition.[4] The period is nicely balanced to the ear, and its general structure is clear enough ('Since ... I decided ... so that ... '), but Luke cannot take us much further: his καθώς-clause (verse 2) hangs uneasily between the opening subordinate clause and the main clause. Unlike the author of Hebrews, Luke does not write periods often; it is worth noting that the only other example of a full-blown period in his writings, in the Apostolic Decree (Acts 15.24ff.) uses broadly the same structure as this one. We begin to suspect that Luke's powers of original composition in this style were limited, and our suspicion is only confirmed by the discovery that the same structure was not only widespread in official decrees in the eastern Empire but was also a favourite with scientific writers.

(d)   Finally, the content of Luke's preface is classic for the scientific tradition. A single sentence announces in its main verb the author's decision to write; this decision is related to the dedicatee by means of an address in the vocative and the insertion of the personal pronoun, and reinforced by the final clause ('so that you ... '). The basis of the decision is given in the opening clause ('Since

---

[2] Cf. E. Haenchen, *Der Weg Jesu* (Töppelmann, Berlin, 1966), pp. 1f: 'If [Luke] had been willing to write the first verse in a simpler fashion, it would have read something like, "many have told the story of the things that have happened among us"' (my trans.). Similarly van Unnik, 1963, p. 9: 'Had he spared himself the trouble of writing such a master-sentence, he would have saved his later readers a nightmare of exegetical puzzles.' It is instructive to compare the preface to Xenophon's *De equitandi ratione*, which covers much the same ground as Luke's but in a clear and simple fashion.

[3] 'Pregnant': Schürmann, 1962, p. 50; 'lapidary': van Unnik, 1955, p. 329.

[4] Cf. the curt but refreshingly hard-headed judgement of Lagarde: 'the very ineptitude (*ineptia*) of the Lucan preface compels me to believe that I am reading a tedious imitator (*otiosum imitatorem*)' (1874, p. 168, my trans.).

many ... '), and information about the author and his method of working is subjoined in a participial phrase attached to the main clause. The author does not give his name, as is normal where the address is of this 'rhetorical' type.[5] The 'decision' itself, although it is the grammatical centre of the sentence, is effectively over-shadowed by the opening subordinate clause, and it is this clause which introduces the subject of the book in a grammatically indirect fashion typical of scientific prefaces. The subject appears again, equally obliquely, in the final clause, but on neither occasion is our author very informative: Luke carries the obliquity of the scientific preface to extremes.

These points and others will be discussed in the detailed commentary which follows. This is not intended to replace Cadbury's word-by-word commentary in *The Beginnings of Christianity*, vol. II (1922a pp. 489–510). That scrupulous piece of work, which remains fundamental, aimed to cover exhaustively all the possibilities open to the exegete. It did not attempt to draw positive conclusions; Cadbury's own choice of exegesis (in some cases different from his apparent conclusions in *Beginnings*) appeared in a series of separate articles (see bibliography). Our aim here is to argue a consistent line of interpretation of the preface as a whole seen within the matrix of the Greek scientific tradition, while pointing out any elements which do not fit with that framework. The commentary on each verse is divided into three sections: (i) Structure: comments on the verse within the general structure of the preface and its scientific parallels; (ii) Vocabulary and style: detailed comments on individual words; (iii) Interpretation: what does the verse mean?

Verse one

Ἐπειδήπερ πολλοὶ ἐπεχείρησαν ἀνατάξασθαι διήγησιν περὶ τῶν πεπληροφορημένων ἐν ἡμῖν πραγμάτων ...

[5] Probably in the original setting of these works there was no need for identification, since the author was known to the readers. Once the book passed out of that immediate circle, however, the author's name could easily be lost. Compare Galen's story (*De libr. propr.* pref. K XIX 8f. SM II 91) of finding a book on sale in Rome with his own name (mistakenly) inscribed on the *titulus*; the situation had arisen because his books were 'given to friends of pupils without a *titulus* [χωρὶς ἐπιγραφῆς] not being for publication' (K XIX 10). Cf. also Galen, *De meth.med.* VII pref., K X 457 15ff. In the case of other scientific writers less forthcoming than Galen, we simply do not know how their books were labelled; but it is obvious in many cases from the state of the MS tradition that their authorship was early in doubt (cf. the confused state of the traditions of Hero and Hermogenes, and especially the Arabic Philo tradition).

Inasmuch as many have undertaken the task of compiling
an account of the matters which have come to fruition in
our midst . . .

Structure

The preface opens with a causal clause giving the reason for the
author's 'decision to write'. Parallels in the scientific tradition are
numerous: it is normal to begin a new text with a subordinate clause,
and the causal clause ('Since . . . ' or 'Seeing that . . . ') is one of the
commonest types encountered.[6] The topic covered in this opening
clause varies according to period. In the hellenistic period (IV–I
BC), it most often refers to the disposition of the dedicatee ('Since
you . . . '), or to the intrinsic interest of the subject ('Since the *theoria*
of the subject is *poikilē* . . . '); in these cases, the topic of 'predecessors' is allotted to a separate sentence. But from the first century AD
onwards 'predecessors' comes regularly to be the topic of the
opening clause (above, ch. 5 p. 76). See for example the prefaces
to Hero, *Pneumatica*. I and Galen, *De typis* quoted in Appendix A.
From the rhetorical point of view there is little difference in essential
function between the three opening gambits: both the hellenistic
topics (the subject and the dedicatee's interest) serve to establish
that the subject is worth attention, and, as we have argued above,
the topic of 'predecessors' often works in essentially the same way
(above, ch. 5 pp. 76–7).

In the nature of the case, this grammatically subordinate clause
also gives Luke his first chance to tell the readers what his book is
about. It is normal in Greek prefaces of all kinds to introduce the
subject-matter of the book in an oblique case in the opening clause
(above ch. 5 pp. 71–3; ch. 4 pp. 45–6), and thus inevitable that
the author's own subject will often first be described as that of his
predecessors.[7] Cadbury is thus quite correct to observe (1922a,
p. 494) that Luke's words here apply to his predecessors, but this
does not mean that they may not be describing his own project as

[6] E.g. Diocles; Archimedes, *Stom.* p.416.2ff.; Philo, *Pneum.* p.458.6ff.; Vitruvius
IV pref.1; Apollonius of Citium I pref. p.10.3ff. (see Appendix B); Demetrius p.1.2ff.;
Hero, *Aut.* p.338.3–6; *Catoptr.* p.318.9–11; *Dioptr.* p.188.3ff.; *Bel.* W 73.6ff.; Diosco-
rides, *Mat.Med.* I p.1.4–9; Erotian p.3.3ff.; Hermogenes, *Stat.* p.28.3ff.; Artemidorus
IV pref. p.236.2ff.; Serenus, *Sect.Cyl.* p.2.2ff. For Galen, see n. 9 below.
[7] For parallels in scientific prefaces, cf. Hero, *Spir.* I, *Aut., Dioptr.;* Dioscorides,
Mat.Med. I; Galen, K VI 453ff., K VI 816f., K VII 463, K VII 584f.; Vettius Valens
p.132.4–9.

well: in fact they would almost certainly have been understood that way by contemporary readers. Luke has two other chances to explain what he is writing about in verse 3 ('I decided to write < what? > ') and in verse 4 ('so that you might know < what? > '). He tells us very little at either point, so it is fair to assume that what we have in verses 1–2 is the closest we shall get to a description of his own work as he saw it.

Vocabulary and style

The composition of this clause is weighty and impressive. Long words and multiple compounds are used where a more classical stylist might have preferred simplicity. Note the number of p-sounds: Greek formal style at all levels seems to have found this effective.[8] I have tried to reflect this rather pompous style in my translation.

'Επειδήπερ: **'Inasmuch as'**. The conjunction here is purely causal, unusually for the NT (N. Turner, 1963, p. 315). The strengthened ἐπειδή is also classical and literary (ibid.). In earlier classical prose the causal sense is more frequently expressed by the shorter form, except in official decrees: 'ἐπειδή *whereas* is used in the preambles of decrees' (LSJ s.v.). The reason for the preference is presumably aural, the longer form having more weight. Both were popular for the opening of a formal composition: Galen uses them more than any other subordinating conjunction as a first word,[9] and they are common in other scientific prefaces (ch. 5 n. 48). The formality of an official pronouncement is perhaps never very far away: Galen three times pairs ἐπει(δή) with ἔδοξε(v), the verb used in decrees, just as Luke does here and at Acts 15.24–5.[10]

The addition of -περ merely adds weight and emphasis. The triple combination is attested occasionally in classical writers (LSJ s.v.) but not as the first word of a text.[11] Nigel Turner's observation is pertinent here: 'the

---

[8] P-alliteration: see above ch. 5 n. 49 for examples in scientific prefaces, and compare also Acts 1.1, 24.2f. Further examples in Demosthenes, *Prooem.* VI; the second sentence of *Prooem.* IX; and the openings of Or. II, LVII, LIX. Weichert, 1910, p. xxxiii; Rabe, 1931, nos. 2, 6A, 13. Alliteration in Josephus and 'Aristeas': Pelletier, 1962, pp. 237–40, esp. p. 239.

[9] ἐπειδή: Galen K II 532; K V 1; K V 587.1ff.; K VI 554–5; K VI 816–17; K VII 584–5; K X 1; KX 458.5ff.; K X 944; K XIV 106–7; K XIV 390.

[10] ἐπειδή ... ἔδοξε(v): Galen K V 587; K VI 816–17; K VII 584–5.

[11] Initial ἐπειδήπερ: only two examples are known to me in non-Christian Greek texts, both in Galen, K I 124.9; K XVIIA 794. end. [Dem.] *Erot.* is not a true parallel, since this opening is meant to look like a fragment of a continuing conversation. Rabe, 1931, no. 10 is medieval (Rabe, 1907, 262ff.); Hermippus, *De astrologia dialogus* (Teubner, p. 3.11) is a Christian author.

Koine and NT are more careless than the older Greek regarding the position of particles and display the popular love of over-emphasis' (1963, p. 329).

Luke's first word thus strikes a formal note (although the occurrence of ἐπηδή in one of the bar Kochba letters, 5/6 Hev. 3, shows that it was a widespread cliché). But the use of the unnuanced compound is more typical of late hellenistic and literary *Koine* than of Attic prose. The word is popular with Luke's contemporary Hero of Alexandria (Reinhardt, 1930, pp. 153–5).

πολλοί: 'many'. Greek rhetoric of all periods shows a fondness for πολύς and its derivatives at the beginning of a speech or composition. E. Fraenkel, 'Eine Anfangsformel attischer Reden', *Glotta* 29 (1961), pp. 1–5 gives a full list of classical parallels, which can easily be supplemented: see Alexander, 1978, ch. 3.2 n. 11 for further examples. But the cliché was by no means limited to rhetorical and literary writers: it is found in New Comedy, in ben Sira (*Prol. v. 1*), in Heb. 1.1 and in the speeches of Acts 24.2 and 10. *Corpus Hermeticum* XI 1 provides a splendid example:

> Ἐπεὶ πολλὰ πολλῶν καὶ ταῦτα διάφορα περὶ τοῦ παντὸς καὶ τοῦ θεοῦ εἰπόντων ἐγὼ τὸ ἀληθὲς οὐκ ἔμαθον, σύ μοι περὶ τούτου, δέσποτα, διασάφησον (cf. Festugière, 1944–9, *ad loc.* and 1939 p. 56 n. 3).

The formula πολλάκις σοι ἔγραψα, which is common in papyrus letters, may also reflect its influence (Koskenniemi, 1956, pp. 65–7). For examples in scientific prefaces, see Demetrius p. 1.2; Hero, *Dioptr.* p. 188.3; *Bel.* W 72.1; Dioscorides, *Mat.Med.* I p. 1.4; Galen K VI 453.2, K VII 463, K X 1, K XII 894; Hermogenes, *Stat.* p. 28.3; Thessalus p. 45.2ff.; Artemidorus p. 1.1; Vettius Valens p. 132.5; Serenus p. 2.1. Luke's use of this convention therefore attests the formality of his opening sentence, but does not necessarily entail a direct acquaintance with high classical rhetoric.

ἐπεχείρησαν: 'have undertaken the task'. The word is classical, but common enough in later literary writers. It occurs 11 times in LXX (4 in II Macc.), but in the NT only here and at Acts 9.29, 19.13. The weighty combination ἐπεχείρησαν ἀνατάξασθαι διήγησιν makes an important contribution to the rhetorical balance of the sentence, and, as Casaubon observed long ago, was probably put together largely or wholly to achieve a sonorous effect (Cadbury, 1922a, p. 494).

Periphrases involving ἐπιχειρεῖν or πειρᾶσθαι are common in prefaces, scientific and other. In the first person, they imply no more than a becoming modesty: cf. Dion. Halic., *Ant. Rom.* XI.1; Polybius I 15.13, II 37.4, III 1.4; Aristoxenus, *El. Harm.* II p. 32.19; II Macc. 2.23; 'Aristeas' 1, 297, 322, and see above ch. 5 p. 99 for examples in the prefaces studied. For examples in the third person, cf. Aristoxenus, *El. Harm.* I 6.23; Hippocrates, *VM* I 1; Polybius XII 28.3; Diodorus Siculus I 3.2, IV 1.2; Josephus,

C. Ap. I 13; Archimedes, *Quadr.* p. 262.14; Thessalus p. 45.2; and others cited by Cadbury *ad loc.* and BAG s.v. Logically speaking it is impossible to escape the derogatory implications when the phrase is used in the third person: one can hardly be modest about someone else.[12] But the phrase is such a stylistic commonplace (cf. especially Diod. Sic. I 3.2 ἐπεχείρησαν ἀναγράφειν and Galen K VI 269 ἐπεχείρησα διηγεῖσθαι) that it is tempting to believe that Luke might have used it without taking much note of its precise meaning. (See further below, Interpretation.)

ἀνατάξασθαι: 'of compiling'. Not a common word, and not classical.[13] The few examples, all from late Greek, were exhaustively analysed by earlier commentators in a fruitless endeavour to discover the precise significance of the compound and of its middle voice. In view of the practice of scientific writers of Luke's period, I would have little hesitation in reading it as equivalent to συντάξασθαι or ἀναγράψαι/ἀναγράψασθαι. The compound formation and the middle voice both serve to give sonority and fullness. The rarity of this particular compound presents no difficulty: scientific writers show a marked fondness for creating variation by changing the compound elements in verbs of composition (above, ch. 5 pp. 100–1 and nn. 57–8). Greek speakers never entirely lost sight of the root meanings of a word and its several elements, so that it was continually possible to endow a compound with a new meaning:[14] this creativity is particularly characteristic of the hellenistic period, and gradually decreases with the growth of classicism from the first century AD onward. So ἀνατάξασθαι is not so much a choice or a recondite word as a newly coined variant on the standard συντάξασθαι. The choice of compounds of -τάσσειν, stressing the ordering of pre-existent material rather than creation *de novo*, is characteristic of the scientific tradition. Historians tend to prefer συγγράφειν.[15]

[12] Cadbury cites as exceptions Josephus, *C.Ap.* I 13 and Polybius XII 28.3, but it is disingenuous to say that Josephus uses the phrase 'without any criticism' (the whole passage is critical), and Polybius, writing about the ideal historian, is in a position to be modest since he is treating of his own aspirations. See also van Unnik, 1963, p. 15: but again a critical stance seems to be implied by Diodorus in the passages cited.

[13] Cadbury *ad loc.* cites Plutarch, *De sollertia animalium* 968cd; Irenaeus III 21.2; *Ep.Aristeas* 144; Marcus Aurelius III 5.2; Cassius Dio LXXVIII 18.5 (on one reading); and a possible reading in LXX Eccles. 2.20.

[14] Observable for example in the use of ὑποτάσσειν in the sense, 'subjoin', which is common in official documents (LSJ s.v.III 1) and in scientific writers (e.g. Apollonius of Citium pp.10.17; 38.8; 64.19); this use retains the separate force of both elements in the compound, completely bypassing the developed sense 'subject', 'subdue', which is common in the NT. For 'rare' compounds of this type, cf. Apollonius' προκαταχωρίζων (Ap. Cit. p.64.17) or Dioscorides' προσπαραλημψόμεθα (*Mat.Med.* I p.3.16). In all these cases, the force of the different parts of the compound is perfectly clear. On this phenomenon in Greek generally, see Nock, 1972, I pp. 345–6.

[15] E.g. Dion.Halic., *Ant.Rom.* I 6.1; Herodian II 15.7; Millar, 1964, pp. 32–3 and p. 183 n. 3; Herkommer, 1968, p. 80 and n. 2. Full list of the terms used by historians to describe their work, Herkommer, 1968, p. 81. For 'order' in the scientific writers,

διήγησιν: 'an account'. Found in late classical prose, but not common (LSJ s.v.); only here in NT, but common in biblical Greek (Ecclus., II Macc., 'Aristeas', Philo, Josephus). While the verb is fairly widespread and general in meaning, the noun in ancient rhetorical theory had a limited, technical use, and many of the later instances reflect that usage. In forensic rhetoric, the διήγησις (Lat. *narratio*) was the statement of the facts of the case which followed the preface: this often (but not necessarily) involved telling a story (cf. esp. Plato, Rep. 392d). Lucian, *De hist. conscr.* 55 applies it by trans-ference to historical narrative, but the word is not particularly favoured by historians. Where it does occur, it is frequently used in a semi-technical way to distinguish the body of the text from preface or excursus: cf. e.g. Polybius III 36.1, 38.4, 39.1; II Macc. 2.32, 6.17; Jos., *Vita* 336; Ep. Aristeas 8. But the usage in Ep. Aristeas 1 and 322, like Luke's here, is more general. The papyri do not suggest widespread colloquial use,[16] but in Ecclus. (which accounts for 7 out of the 11 LXX occurrences) the word is used to translate a wide range of concepts: 'talk', 'discourse', even 'proverb'.

Luke's choice of word is thus exact but not technical: 'narrative' is appropriate for a Gospel, but the more general 'account' is well attested. The word is not found in the scientific prefaces studied, but is used elsewhere by Galen of his own medical works and others' (e.g. K XIII 718, XIV 51). Hobart (1882 p. 87) cites these and other examples, and notes that 'in his commentary on the *Epidemics* of Hippocrates alone, [Galen] uses it at least 73 times of some one or other of the treatises of Hippocrates'. The underlying sense of Luke's words here is essentially the same as that of Galen's ἐπεχείρησα διηγεῖσθαι (K VI 269).

πεπληροφορημένων: 'which have come to fruition'. A 'heavy' word used without precise regard to its force. It is now abundantly clear from the papyri and other non-literary texts that πληροφορέω had come to be used in spoken *Koine* simply as an equivalent for πληρόω (which occurs as a variant at II Tim. 4.17). In his definitive article, ('Le Sens de Luc. 1.1 d'après les papyrus', *Bulletin d'ancienne littérature et d'archéologie chrétiennes*, 2 (1912), pp. 96–100) M.-J. Lagrange shows that it is the versions, rather than the learned patristic tradition, which preserve the correct understanding of this word in daily usage. Lagrange describes the word as 'one of those preferred by the more decadent epochs' because its size 'seems to give more intensity to the sense', and compares a similar progression in French from 'règle' to 'règlement' to 'règlementation' (p. 97); cf. J. Lyons, *Introduction*

---

see above, ch. 5 p. 95; below s.v. καθεξῆς. But the distinction should not be pressed too firmly: historians sometimes talk of 'ordering' material in their prefaces (Polybius I 3.8; III 1.2; Jos. *BJ* I 1.3), and scientific writers sometimes use συγγράφειν (Apollonius of Citium, p.10.5, 7; Galen K X 458.1).

[16] MM cite one papyrus text, PSI I 85, a third-century AD rhetorical treatise: Preisigke cites four late examples, of which P.Oxy. 1468.11 may show a colloquial use not unlike Luke's here: τὰ δὲ τοῦ πράγματος τοιαύτην ἔχει τὴν διήγησιν.

to Theoretical Linguistics (Cambridge University Press, 1968), p. 90 for a more neutral description of this well-known linguistic phenomenon. This preference for the longest possible form of the word is consistent with Luke's own habits, especially in the preface, and also with the habits of most of the scientific writers (cf. Vettius Valens, Kroll p. 226.20); the word is not favoured by hellenistic literary language (much less by the classicizers), but reflects the popular and official usage of the papyri.[17]

ἐν ἡμῖν: **'in our midst'.** To whom does this pronoun refer? The phraseology of verses 1 and 2 clearly implies two groups of people, those among whom the events were 'accomplished' and those to whom the tradition was handed down, and the same pronoun is used of both. There must therefore be a general reference to the *corpus christianorum* (A. Hilgenfeld, 'Prolegomena zum Lukas-Evangelium', *ZWTh*, 40 (1897), pp. 412ff., 423), much as in Justin's παρ' ἡμῖν ἀνήρ τις, ᾧ ὄνομα Ἰωάννης (*Dial.* 81). Compare Josephus' use of the pronoun 'we' to refer to the Jewish nation in general, its past state as well as its present, in (e.g.) *Ant.* I 5, *C. Ap.* I 4, 5, 74, 132. A similarly vague use of the pronoun can be found among scientific writers: see below on ἡμῖν, verse 2.

πραγμάτων: **'the matters'.** Common in Greek of all periods: 11 times in the NT. There are no grounds for saying, with Klein, that 'the concept of the πράγματα is current in secular historiography' (1964, p. 199; cf. also Grundmann, 1961, p. 43; van Unnik, 1963, p. 12; du Plessis, 1974, p. 263). The word is of course used by historians (e.g. Dion. Halic. I 7.4), but is not characteristically used of the stuff of history. Much more characteristic is the active πράξεις or 'deeds', *res gestae* (Herkommer, 1968, pp. 67ff.). For the Greek and Roman historians, history was primarily an account of great deeds and the men who performed them (cf. Herod., *Proem.*), rather than of 'events'. The word can be used in a religious context (e.g. II Macc. 1.33, 34), but is essentially a neutral word. If it has any special connotations it is along the lines of the English 'the facts': cf. the almost invariable use of πραγματεία, πραγματεύειν in scientific prefaces (above, ch. 5 pp. 96–7). In the NT, however, the latter only occur in their more colloquial sense of 'doing business affairs' (Luke 19.13, II Tim. 2.4).

Interpretation

It is a common fallacy to assume that the identification of literary convention in a text is the same thing as the elucidation of its

[17] Lagrange also gives conclusive reasons for discarding the old interpretation 'believed', which is favoured by many of the oldest commentators. The application of the passive to πράγματα was never very convincing, and should be abandoned entirely (Schlatter (1931) and Grundmann (1961) try to retain it in addition to Lagrange's interpretation).

meaning. We have established that the structure of verse 1 in relation to the preface as a whole is one of the typical structures found in scientific prefaces, and that the topic of 'predecessors' is a common one. We have observed that Luke's vocabulary is picked to achieve a certain effect, with the result that an essentially simple clause of the form, 'Since many have tried to put together an account of the business that has happened among us', becomes the more pretentious, 'Inasmuch as many have undertaken the task of compiling an account of the matters which have come to fruition in our midst'. But in saying this we still have not determined quite what Luke is trying to *say*.

First, what is he saying about his subject-matter? If this point in the preface represents, as we have argued above, Luke's chief opportunity for explaining to prospective readers what the book is about, it cannot be described as a successful piece of communication. The crucial words are περὶ τῶν πεπληροφορημένων ἐν ἡμῖν πραγμάτων, and Cadbury aptly cites in comparison Luke 2.15 τὸ ῥῆμα τοῦτο τὸ γεγονὸς ὃ ὁ Κύριος ἐγνώρισεν ἡμῖν. The preface takes the palm for style (in Greek literary terms), with its alliteration and sandwiching of noun and article. Instead of the Semitism ῥῆμα we have the neutral and secular πραγμάτων (the plural is also more idiomatic than the singular). But in terms of information-load Luke 1.2 is remarkably barren: we are not told what the 'business' actually was.

The only clue to its character is in the rather mysterious passive participle πεπληροφορημένων, 'fulfilled' or 'accomplished'. This word, if it is anything more than a roundabout way of saying 'has happened', seems to point back to something behind the author's immediate subject: it is a contract, a promise or an intention that is 'fulfilled'. The reader in the know, that is the Christian reader, might well see in this a covert allusion to the fulfilment of prophecy, but it is unlikely that anyone less privileged would have grasped the allusion. Similarly the passive participle, to any reader of the New Testament, points upward to divine intervention, and it is possible that this was as near as Luke wanted to go, in this *prima facie* secular preface, to hinting at the divine authorship of the events he describes. This is certainly not the way a Greek historian would have depicted his subject-matter; but it contrasts equally with the explicitly religious language of the hellenistic Jewish writers (see below ch. 7) and of the narrative which follows in Luke 1–2. Quite *why* Luke is so reluctant to lay his cards on the table here in the preface is a matter for debate; but this allusiveness must in itself cast doubt on the theory that the preface is a proof that the book was designed for 'publication' on the open book-market (further, below ch. 9).

Secondly, what is Luke saying about his predecessors? How 'many' were they, and is he implying that they have failed? Luke's words here have always held out the hope of supplying much-needed information about the earliest stages in the history of the Gospel tradition, and indeed about his own date (Bauer, 1960, pp. 263–6). Does the verse imply a number of previous written texts which perhaps also functioned as sources? Does it imply a late date for Luke? If Mark and Matthew (or Q) were his only sources, could 'many' be a parabolic exaggeration for 'two'? If not, what happened to the others and why does Luke not use them? The discovery of the 'conventional' nature of the *topos* seemed to many commentators to provide a valuable tool for cutting through a great deal of unwarranted speculation: compare Cadbury's warning (1922a, p. 493), 'one must not press πολλοί here to mean *very many* predecessors in Gospel authorship'. Kümmel goes so far as to claim (1966, p. 91), 'The likewise traditional πολλοί reveals *nothing* about the number of predecessors known to Luke' (my italics).[18] Does our study of parallels throw any light on the interpretation of this conventional phrase?

Scientific writers certainly show a propensity to describe their predecessors as 'many': cf. Hipparchus p. 4.1–2; Vitruvius IV pref. 1; Hero, *Dioptr.* p. 188.4f.; Dioscorides, *Mat.Med.* I p. 1.4ff.; Erotian p. 3.4ff., cf. p. 4.3ff.; Galen K VI 453.1f. In some cases, the word is substantiated by a long list of names (Erotian, Dioscorides); in others, we simply do not know whether there really were 'many'. But ancient writers were probably no more inclined than their modern counterparts to write unnecessary falsehoods: convention was served by finding something to say within the accepted range, rather than by conforming to a rigid pattern. If Luke had wished simply to introduce the conventional πολύς, there were many other ways to do it: compare the variations in Acts 24.2 and 10, or, in the scientific tradition, Hero, *Dioptr.* p. 188.3f. πολλὰς καὶ ἀναγκαίας παρεχομένης χρείας, or Galen K VI p. 453.1f. ἐν πολλῇ σπουδῇ

[18] Though he cannot have it both ways: on p. 105 he asserts equally confidently, 'Lk.1:1ff is hardly compatible with this dating, for according to the Lukan prologue there must have existed in this case already about the year 60 *many* Gospel writings' (my italics).

θέμενοι τὴν θεωρίαν (cf. also Hermogenes, *Stat.* p. 28.1ff.; Thessalus p. 45.2ff.). There was no convention which could *compel* Luke to mention 'many' predecessors unless he wanted to do so.

It is simplest, then, to conclude, short of positive indications to the contrary, that Luke meant what he said. If this causes problems for our views on Gospel sources or chronology, perhaps we need to look more closely at those views and their assumptions. Part of the problem, I suspect, is the tendency of critics to think exclusively in terms of the documents we know: Mark and Matthew/Q are two, not 'many', and it seems unwarranted to hypothesize a number of other written Gospels, now lost without trace. But Luke never says that his predecessors had produced *written* documents: using the conventional language of any school treatise, he says merely that they had tried to 'put together an account' – a splendidly ambiguous phrase which could be interpreted in a number of historically plausible ways.

This brings us to the last question. Does Luke intend us to understand that his predecessors have failed in some way? The verse was certainly understood in this way by ancient commentators (cf. e.g. Origen, *Hom. in Luc.* I; Jerome, *Prol. quatt. evang.*); and, as we have seen, in terms of strict logic it is hard to escape the implication of criticism when the verb ἐπεχείρησαν is used in the third person. The real difficulty with this reading lies not in the parallels or in the verb itself, but in its relation with the text as a whole, for in succeeding verses Luke (a) by implication enlists these same predecessors alongside himself as recipients of authentic tradition (verse 2), and (b) ranges himself beside them, not against them, with the words 'it seemed good *to me also* ... ' (verse 3). In terms of preface-convention, this is by no means unusual. A Thessalus may claim to have succeeded where all others have failed, while Dioscorides and Erotian list their predecessors only to disparage them; but Hero and Galen are content to say, 'Since the subject has been thought worthy of treatment by others, *I too* have taken it up ... ' (above, ch. 5 pp. 76–7).

But in that case, why ἐπεχείρησαν? One solution is to translate, as we have suggested, 'have undertaken the task of' rather than 'have tried to'. If there is a failure, it could just as well be a failure to complete the task undertaken: how many would-be evangelists simply failed to achieve the success of Mark, Matthew and Luke in reducing the multiplex and varied Gospel tradition into a coherent written narrative? It is certainly not necessary to assume that those who did complete it are included in Luke's mild and ambiguous deprecation, much less that there was anything improper about the enterprise itself. Alternatively, we would have to fall back on the stereotyped nature of the phrase and argue that Luke has used it without paying much attention to its precise meaning.

One final point emerges from our analysis of scientific prefaces. In terms of rhetorical function, making a statement about the author's predecessors is probably the least important aspect of an opening clause of this type. Essentially these 'predecessors' are only there to reassure the reader that the subject is worth spending time on. The informational value of the clause lies much more in the apparently incidental opportunity it gives the author to identify his subject-matter. The allusive manner in which Luke chooses to do this may tell us as much about his audience as it does about himself.

Verse two

... καθὼς παρέδοσαν ἡμῖν οἱ ἀπ᾽ ἀρχῆς αὐτόπται καὶ ὑπηρέται γενόμενοι τοῦ λόγου, ...

... just as the tradition was handed down to us by the original eyewitnesses and ministers of the world, ...

Structure

This additional clause, loosely subjoined to the opening clause, gives a further description of the work of Luke's predecessors: it is based on tradition handed down by a group called 'the original eyewitnesses and ministers of the word'. The expansion of the basic period by the insertion of extra clauses is typical of the later stages of the scientific tradition; it is also very common in these prefaces to find an important new topic introduced in this unemphatic and allusive fashion.[19]

For the form of the clause, compare:

---

[19] As noted by Kollesch and Kudlien, 1961, p. 328f., Apollonius of Citium often composes in this way: see e.g. p. 38.8ff., with oblique references to the usefulness and completeness of the subject all loosely attached to ὑποτάξω; cf. 64.9–10. Similarly Demetrius p.1.1ff. where six verbal clauses and sub-clauses are dependent on the single finite verb ἐπραγματευσάμην, followed by three participial clauses dependent on ὑποδέδειχα; or Hero, *Pneumatica*. I, where there are three clauses and sub-clauses dependent on the main verb (see Appenix A).

ἱστορήσομεν οὖν σοι, καθότι καὶ αὐτοὶ παρειλήφαμεν.
Philo, *Bel.* Th. 51.10

De zona XII signorum et septem astrorum (etc.), uti a
praeceptoribus accepi, exposui; nunc de crescenti lumine
lunae deminutioneque, uti traditum est nobis a maioribus,
dicam.   Vitruvius IX 1.16

In terms of structure, however, Luke is closer to his contemporary
Hero, who combined this element into the single 'decision' sentence
as the object of the main verb, than to earlier writers like Philo who
treated it separately (above, ch. 5 pp. 85–6). It may be objected
that in all these parallels the relevant words refer to the writer
himself and not, as in Luke, to his predecessors. But the divergence
is neither very important nor very profound. The formal structure is
the same whatever the subject of the verb; and in any case Luke's use
of ἡμῖν here and the καί of verse 3 clearly show that, like Hero, he
has no wish to dissociate himself from the 'many'. The loose position of the clause, grammatically dependent on verse 1 but inevitably read in conjunction with verse 3, reinforces the impression that
it is Luke's own contact with the tradition, not that of his predecessors, which he really wants us to appreciate.

The form of authority named here should therefore be seen
against the background of the authorities named by the scientific
writers: see above ch. 5 pp. 82–5. Philo and Apollonius of Citium
lay great stress on personal contact with the bearers of the tradition:

> We shall recount to you, then, just as we received the
> tradition both in Alexandria, having been introduced to
> most of the craftsmen who concern themselves with this
> subject, and in Rhodes, having been introduced to not a few
> master-carpenters and having learnt from them.
> (Philo, *Bel.* Th. 51.10ff.)

> Some operations I have performed myself, others I
> observed while in the school of Zopyrus in Alexandria. And
> Posidonius, who studied with the same doctor, will testify
> with us that this man practised medicine ... with the highest
> degree of fidelity to [*lit. 'following'*] Hippocrates.
> (Apollonius of Citium I p. 12.1ff.)

Hero, in shorter and more formulaic passages, professes to be
passing on 'the tradition received from the ancients' (*Spir.* I p. 2.9
τὰ παραδοθέντα ὑπὸ τῶν ἀρχαίων); compare Vitruvius IX 1.16, X

11.2, X 13.8 'as I received it from my teachers', 'as the tradition was handed down to us by our forbears'.

Vocabulary and style

It is almost impossible to reproduce the tight, classical interlocking of words in this verse while remaining faithful to nuances of meaning. Only by using 'eyewitnesses' can we come close in style to the Greek. 'The people with personal experience' gives more attention to the 'feel' of αὐτόπται (see below), but fails to convey the neatness of the Greek.

καθώς: 'as'. Not a mark of good literary Greek: the word is explicitly condemned by the Atticist Phrynichus (N. Turner, 1963, p. 320; and compare Weichert, 1910, p. xxxii, where the occurrence of this word in a preface is seen as a 'vulgar' characteristic). Eusebius and D correct it to the more correct καθά (Cadbury, 1922a, p. 496).[20] Commentators have found it difficult to work out what precisely in verse 1 is qualified by this connective (Grimm, 1871, s.v.). In the passages from Philo and Vitruvius quoted above, the analogous conjunctions (καθότι, *uti*) depend on a single verb of narration/exposition (ἱστορήσομεν, *exposui, dicam*). If we take Luke's ἐπεχείρησαν ἀνατάξασθαι διήγησιν as a composite equivalent for this single verb, we have an exact parallel. Luke's περί-clause is not paralleled in Philo, where the verb is absolute, but in Vitruvius its equivalent is the list of contents '*de zona* ... ' etc.

παρέδοσαν: '[they] handed down [the tradition]'. The form of the aorist used here is classical, uniquely in the NT; elsewhere Luke uses the hellenistic παρέδωκαν (e.g. Luke 23.25, Acts 3.13); cf. Blass–Debrunner, 1961, sect. 95 and n. 1. A similar variation is found in Dioscorides, *Mat.Med.* I p. 2.3/II p. 121.3. The verb and its cognate noun are found frequently in scientific prefaces, together with the correlative παραλαμβάνω (Lat. *tradere, accipere*): cf. the passages quoted above and further, ch. 5 p. 98. Their popularity is a testimony to the reverence for tradition which the hellenistic schools shared with the Jewish and Christian academies.[21] In scientific

[20] BDF sect.453 suggest that D and Eusebius are right, but it is a mistake to make a prior assumption that the language of the preface is 'literary' and then to iron out the non-Atticisms which conflict with that assumption, especially in view of the known Atticizing tendency of later scribes including D (J. K. Elliot, 'Moeris and the textual tradition of the Greek NT', in J. K. Eliott (ed.), *Studies in NT Language and Text: Essays in honour of G. D. Kilpatrick* (Supplement to *Novum Testamentum* XLIV, Brill, Leiden, 1976), pp. 144–52, p. 145).

[21] Compare the use of the verbs in I Cor. 15.1–3. On *paradosis* in early Christianity, cf. Dibelius, 1966, p. 20 n. 1; O. Cullmann, 'The tradition', in A. J. B. Higgins (ed.), *The Early Church* (SCM, London, 1959, pp. 56–99) pp. 59ff.;

prefaces, a common form of guarantee for the author or his material is the assertion that he has been in personal contact with authentic tradition. Originality is positively eschewed, and even where the author is following written sources, he uses the language of 'tradition'. See on this further above ch. 5 pp. 82–5.

ἡμῖν: 'to us'. Luke ranges himself alongside his predecessors as a recipient of authentic tradition. Compare Vitruvius IX 1.16 *uti traditum est nobis a maioribus*, and perhaps Hero, *Catoptr.* p. 320.7 *accepta ab hiis qui ante nos.* Compare also the anonymous and unexplained ἡμῖν in Philo, *Bel.* Th. 77.29f., 'Ctesibius used to demonstrate to us': the sudden appearance of the personal pronoun is strange, both because Philo's text is otherwise impersonal and because it is unlikely that Philo actually sat at Ctesibius' feet himself: this 'we' looks like a fossil element already in the tradition (or text) which Philo was using.

οἱ ... γενόμενοι: 'those who were ... ' The sandwiching of words between article and participle is classical, and the phrase, with its single article, must be taken as a unity: there is no justification for the view that the αὐτόπται and the ὑπηρέται τοῦ λόγου are different groups of people, or that the participle denotes a different point in time when the αὐτόπται 'became' ministers of the word (*contra* Klein, 1964, pp. 204f.; Michaelis, *TWNT* V 347f.). Redundant γενόμενος is a feature of hellenistic style (Palm, 1955, p. 176f.). Further, as Cadbury observes ad loc., γίνεσθαι is very common with αὐτόπτης.

ἀπ' ἀρχῆς: 'from the beginning'. The precise point of reference of this phrase is far from clear. Does it qualify both 'eyewitnesses' and 'ministers', and if so does it refer to a different 'beginning' in each case? This depends partly on the sense we give to αὐτόπται (see below), but Luke's own usage of the concept of the 'beginning' is also to be taken into account.[22] Acts 1.22 and 10.37 suggest that Luke regarded 'John's baptism' as the proper 'beginning' of the apostolic proclamation, but in 21.16 ἀρχαῖος can hardly refer to a particular point in Jesus' ministry (Mnason, a Cypriot with a Greek name,

C. K. Barrett, 'The Bible in the New Testament Period', in D. E. Nineham (ed.), The Church's Use of The Bible (SPCK, London, 1963, pp. 1–24), p. 6; E. H. Riesenfeld, *The Gospel Tradition*, tr. E. M. Rowley and R. A. Kraft (Basil Blackwell, Oxford, 1970), pp. 17ff., 20; Gerhardsson, 1961, esp. pp. 282ff., 288ff. Further, Alexander, 1990.
[22] See, besides Cadbury's discussion, H. Conzelmann, *Die Mitte der Zeit*, 3rd edn, ET G. Buswell, *The Theology of St. Luke* (Faber & Faber, London, 1960), *passim*, esp. p. 22 n. 3; p. 38; p. 147; *idem*, 'Was vom Anfang war', in *Neutestamentliche Studien für R. Bultmann* (ZNTW Beiheft 21, 1959), pp. 194ff.; Klein, 1964, pp. 201ff.; G. W. H. Lampe, *St. Luke and the Church of Jerusalem* (Athlone Press, University of London, 1969), p. 16; van Unnik, 1963, n. 67; and especially Samain, 1973, pp. 299–328.

is not likely to have been a disciple during Jesus' lifetime) and must be
simply a vague term of approbation. The apostolic preaching in Acts gives
us no precedent for the inclusion of the narratives about Jesus' infancy with
which Luke actually begins his Gospel: are these also part of the 'eyewitness' tradition which both he and his predecessors are drawing on?

It is important here to realise that, whatever its Christian significance, the
notion of the ἀρχή had its own significance in the secular world. The value
of antiquity is a feature of antiquarian literature, and it figures in much
ethnic and religious propaganda: Josephus, *C. Ap.* I *passim*, Manetho,
Berossus, Philo of Byblos. Luke however refers not to ancient books or
archives but to anonymous oral tradition, and this brings him closer to
scientific writers like Vitruvius and Philo (above, ch. 5 pp. 82–5). Reference to 'the ancients' (οἱ ἀρχαῖοι) is common in scientific prefaces: in the
hellenistic period such reference can be neutral or even derogatory (e.g.
Archimedes, *Spir.* p. 2.11–12; Philo, *Bel.* Th. 49.9, 50.27), but in later
centuries reverence for the ancients becomes more normal, and the word
acquires commendatory overtones. This is particularly evident in reference
to one's authorities: ἀρχαῖος is used to emphasize valuable links with
authentic tradition, as in Hero's promise to pass on τὰ παραδοθέντα ὑπὸ
τῶν ἀρχαίων (*Spir.* I p. 2.9). Luke's phrase may be compared also with
Hermogenes' description of the precepts of rhetoric as καταληφθέντα ... ἐξ
ἀρχῆς (*Stat.* p. 28.4) (where the precise reference of the 'beginning' is even
more difficult to define than in Luke), and with Galen's reference to 'things
which I have learned ἀπ᾽ἀρχῆς ἅμα τοῖς διδασκάλοις' (K IV 767). These
rather vague uses suggest that the force of the phrase is emotive rather than
precisely descriptive,[23] and should warn us against trying too hard to find a
precise temporal reference in Luke's phrase here. The adman's favourite
'original' provides a good analogy.

αὐτόπται: 'eyewitnesses'. 'Eyewitnesses' is the neatest and most obvious
equivalent for αὐτόπται, but it has misleading associations for modern
readers. For us, the word has forensic links: an eyewitness is characteristically a witness who was present *at the time when an accident or a crime took
place*, very often a passer-by whose connection with the incident is accidental. The Greek word is hardly ever used in this way, and a better
translation might be, 'those with personal/first-hand experience: those who
know the facts at first hand'.[24]

---

[23] Cf. Vitruvius, who uses *antiqui* in general to refer to the ancients with respect,
prisci where he disagrees with them (IV 3.1–2/VII 3.3). Artemidorus uses the word in
a different sense, but is equally commendatory: see below on ἄνωθεν. Note Galen's
surprise that Serapion should venture to criticize the earlier medical authorities:
Deichgräber, 1930, pp. 86.1ff.

[24] The following is a summary of a detailed survey whose results are presented in
full in Alexander, 1978, pp. 32–8 and App. C, and in more summary form above,
ch. 3 pp. 34–41.

(i)   Αὐτόπτης is not normally used in forensic contexts (the oft-cited
      Dem. XXII 22 is an exception, not a typical instance). It occurs
      only twice in the whole corpus of the Attic Orators, that great
      body of forensic speeches from the classical period.

(ii) The phrase ἐπὶ τὴν αὐτοψίαν in the papyri points to a rather
      different usage in forensic and official circles: an αὐτόπτης is a
      person called in *after* the event to inspect the scene of a crime or
      dispute, not a chance observer. Cf. e.g. P. Tebt. II 286.20, P. Oxy.
      X 1272.19, P. Oxy. XII 1557.5, plus an analogous usage in Polyb.
      XXV 6.5, XXXIII 8.3.

(iii) A concern for *autopsia* is often ascribed to the Greek historians
      (ch. 3 n. 21), but in fact the historian most closely identified with
      this concern, Thucydides, never uses the word, and it is rarely
      found in methodological discussion of the presence of the author
      or his sources at the *events* he describes. Its characteristic use by
      historians from Herodotus onwards in methodological passages is
      in connection with a piece of geographical or scientific infor-
      mation from or about distant *places*. The fact that the same usage
      turns up in a variety of scientific and other 'travel' contexts
      reminds us that history and science both spring from the same
      roots in Ionian *historia*; but it is the Herodotean side of Greek
      historiography, not the Thucydidean, which is so keen to lay claim
      to the testimony of the *autoptēs*. There are only two clear cases
      where a historian uses the word in a preface or other 'methodolo-
      gical' passage to claim his presence at the *events* of his narrative:
      Polybius III 4.3 and Josephus, *C. Ap.* I 55. As we have argued in
      detail elsewhere (above ch. 3 pp. 38–41), Polybius has a special
      fondness for the word and develops unusual uses of it, and
      Josephus appears to be directly dependent on Polybius in the
      relevant passage: these two instances should therefore be regarded
      as exceptional.

(iv) The use of the word in the scientific tradition reflects the same
      semantic pattern. Galen is the largest single user in the whole of
      Greek literature (at least 60 instances; Polybius is the second with
      22), and he reflects its widespread use in earlier medical literature
      (*Subfig.Emp.* p. 47). He uses it of the personal inspection of
      medical practice (*Meth.Med.* XIV 16/K X 1011), of medicinal
      herbs (*Temp.Med.* VI pref./K XI 796–7), of anatomy (*Nat.Fac.* I
      6/K II 12), or of the effects of wounds (*Comp.Med.Sec.Gen.* III
      21/K XIII 609): the modern medical 'autopsy' presumably devel-
      oped out of this usage. Dioscorides uses the word in the intro-
      duction to his *Herbal* (*Mat.Med.* I p. 3.7), in much the same way
      as Aristotle speaks of the gathering of biological information from
      distant places (*Hist.Anim.* 618a.18, 620b.23, 628b.8). All this is
      firmly within the Ionian *historia* tradition. A new development is

recorded by Galen in several general works on medical methodology, especially on the 'Empiricist' school which treated *autopsia*
as roughly equivalent to *empeiria* (see esp. *De sectis* 2, K I 67/SM
III 3).

(v)   This broader, less specific use is found again in Vettius Valens
pp. 172.25 and 260.30, where *autopsia* is linked with 'daily experience', with 'knowledge of humanity', and with 'many toils and
trials'. It is hard to define a precise object for this author's *autopsia*
(his subject is horoscopes), but it is clearly equivalent to 'personal
experience'; this usage may well have developed out of the diffu-
sion of Empiricist ideology (ch. 5 n. 26).

(vi)   Magical papyri from the third century AD onwards use the
adjective αὐτοπτική in two connections: (a) a spell for seeing
oneself (*PGM* VII 329) and (b) a spell for obtaining a vision of a
god (e.g. *PGM* III 699). The latter sense is also found in literary
texts, e.g. Iamblichus, *De mysteriis* 73.14, 76.14. Thessalus provides what may be the earliest example of this usage at I pref. 14.
(See Appendix B on this preface and its date.)

(vii)   The papyri show little evidence that the word had a popular
currency apart from the official and the magical uses. The one
clear example of a colloquial usage is in P. Oxy. VIII 1154 (late
first century AD), where a soldier writes to his sister from Alexandria, 'Don't worry about me being in a strange place, for I am an
autoptēs of the places (αὐτόπτης γὰρ εἰμὶ τῶν τόπων) and I am
no stranger here.' The only translation that makes sense here is
Hunt's, 'I am personally acquainted with these parts': in confirmation of the geographical connotations of the word, *autoptēs* to
this Egyptian soldier simply means 'well-travelled'.

It is thus too simple to say that Luke's use of this word reflects historiographical convention (Norden, 1913, p. 316; Cadbury, s.v.; van Unnik, 1963,
pp. 12–14; and many other commentators). Our study has confirmed the
earlier observation that the word is not common in everyday language, and
that it does have a strong link with methodological discussion in prefaces
and elsewhere. When used by historians, however, it is normally with
reference to information gathered from distant lands. It is theoretically
conceivable that Luke could have known Polybius, and even (if we date him
late enough) that he could have known Josephus' *Contra Apionem*; but to
suggest such direct dependence on one or two passages is to suggest a much
more limited, and inherently more improbable, thesis than the influence of
a widespread literary convention. In any case, there is no need to go to the
historians here at all. The word is equally if not more at home in the
scientific tradition, and appears in the preface of Dioscorides (*Mat.Med.* I
p. 3.7) and in two prefatorial passages in Vettius Valens (see (v) above). The
less precise usage of Vettius Valens seems on the face of it to provide the

best parallel to Luke's usage: in both the word lacks a direct object (πραγμάτων being the most likely), and its precise reference is a matter of debate. Hence a more accurate translation might be, 'those who have first-hand experience (of the facts)'.[25]

ὑπηρέται: **'ministers'**. The word and its cognates are used of medical assistants: cf. Apollonius of Citium I p. 12.1, Oribasius, *Collect.Med.* I, *CMG* VII/1 p. 4. It was not, however, a technical term; its use here should be compared with Acts 26.16, where it is paired with μάρτυς.

τοῦ λόγου: **'of the word'**. In itself a neutral word, λόγος is used freely of scientific and other discourse (see below on Acts 1.1). Here, however, in close conjunction with ὑπηρέται, it is hard to think of it as anything but a Christian term. On its significance, see B. T. Holmes, 'Luke's Description of John Mark', *JBL*, 54 (1935), pp. 63–72; Samain, 1973, pp. 318ff.

Interpretation

Once again we have to cope with a kind of double focus in assessing the significance of Luke's words. The informational function of the clause is to draw attention to the fact that, like his predecessors, Luke is presenting traditional material derived from a specific group. This group is described in terms of two roles: they are 'ministers of the word', that is they have a special responsibility for passing on this tradition;[26] and they have 'first-hand experience' of the facts they report.

Since Luke describes just such a group in the narrative of Acts, it seems reasonable to look there first for an explanation of his words

---

[25] We are not of course suggesting direct dependence on Vettius Valens (see Simpson, 1930, for other parallels). Galen attests to the wider currency of this general use. For the influence of the Empiricist ideology outside medical circles, cf. Blum, 1936, ch. 5; Polybius XII 25d–e.

The theurgical use provides another possible model for Luke's usage. Its relatively late attestation is no real barrier, given the fragmentary state of our knowledge, but it should be noted that for Justin, *Dial.* 115(343) being in a state of *autopsia* is the *opposite* of being 'in ecstasy'. But the 'geographical' use cannot be discounted out of hand. As is well known, Acts carries a significant amount of geographical information, and this may have been part of its appeal to a readership which enjoyed armchair travelling (Pervo, 1987, pp. 69–70).

[26] Among other things. We would not be justified in assuming that the 'ministry of the word' described in Acts (e.g. 6.4) consisted solely in Luke's view of the recitation of Gospel traditions. At the very least Luke clearly also envisages the exposition of Scripture as an essential element in the apostolic proclamation. But in the context of the preface it seems reasonable to assume that the primary reference of 'the word' is to the tradition incorporated (as Luke claims) in the book before us.

in the preface. The group of disciples led by Peter are described as having a particular responsibility for the 'service (διακονία) of the word' in Acts 6.4, and Luke repeatedly draws attention to their role as 'witnesses', primarily of the resurrection (1.22), but also of 'all that [Jesus] did both in the countryside of the Jews and in Jerusalem' (10.39) – that is more or less the scope of the Gospel narrative. Whether this group historically existed as Luke describes them, whether they exercized the functions he assigns to them, and whether his material actually derives from them, are questions outside the world of the text and our concern here. It is also not immediately clear if this description of his sources is also meant to apply to Acts (further, below on Acts 1.1). But it is worth noting that Paul is also described as μάρτυς καὶ ὑπηρέτης 'of the things in which you have seen me and of those in which I will appear to you' (Acts 26.16). Since Paul must be reckoned the ultimate source for the Pauline sections of the Acts narrative, it would seem quite fair to read this verse in the preface as a claim to be in contact not only with the apostolic Gospel tradition but also with authentic Pauline tradition – especially for the Pauline 'resurrection experience' (I Cor. 15.8) of which Acts contains no less than three accounts (Acts 9.1ff., 22.1ff., 26.2ff.).

Had Luke been willing to use the term μάρτυς in the preface his intentions might have been clearer, at least for the Christian reader (although we must be careful not to assume that the text of Acts was already written when he composed the preface); the double reference of μάρτυς (backwards to the event witnessed and forwards to the action of testifying) also makes it a better pair to ὑπηρέται τοῦ λόγου than αὐτόπται. But, as we saw in verse 1, Luke goes out of his way to avoid explicitly Christian language in the preface. The word he chooses to use here has a long and eminent pedigree in the Ionian *historia*-tradition. As the commentators have rightly observed, it is not a neutral word, but constitutes some sort of claim. The question is, what sort of claim?

If we are right to see Luke's usage in terms of the popular, diffuse Empiricism of Vettius Valens rather than the literary tradition of the historians, the claim may be quite a general one: the *autoptēs* is one who knows what s/he is talking about from personal experience. The writer with access to such sources may also be claiming implicitly to be following sound 'scientific' methods. But there is little evidence of 'investigation' in the modern sense, and no sign of the searching out and sifting of eyewitness testimony. The tradition is simply there, to be received at its own valuation; and this is well within the range of the attitude to sources we have identified as belonging particularly to the 'craft' side of the scientific tradition, with its stress on personal contact with living tradition (above ch. 5 pp. 82–85). Even for Galen, that most prolific of writers, the correct way to learn medicine is by *autopsia* at the side of a master, not by booklearning; and 'disciple-tradition', authenticated by a chain of personal contacts, is the best guide to a master's thought (above ch. 5 p. 84; Alexander, 1990).

Verse three

... ἔδοξε κἀμοὶ παρηκολουθηκότι ἄνωθεν πᾶσιν ἀκριβῶς καθεξῆς σοι γράψαι, κράτιστε Θεόφιλε ...

... it seemed good to me also, having followed everything carefully and thoroughly, to write it all up for you in an orderly fashion, most excellent Theophilus ...

Structure

An announcement of the 'decision to write' is central to almost all scientific prefaces (above ch. 5 pp. 70–71). Here the simple ἔδοξε ... γράψαι is linked with the dedicatee by the insertion of σοι and by the following vocative. This is also a typical feature of the prefaces studied (above ch. 5 pp. 73–75). The late position of the address in the sentence is post-classical. In classical rhetoric, the address normally follows the opening two or three words of the sentence. Scientific writers in the hellenistic period follow this convention: there are rarely more than six words before the address, and it is inserted into the opening subordinate clause, considerably in advance of the main verb. In later prefaces the average number of words before the address increases, and there is a greater tendency to place the address at a natural break after the first clause, sometimes considerably later.[27] Luke does not allude to Theophilus

---

[27] Hero, *Def.* p.14.3 (after 16 words and first clause); Dioscorides, *Mat.Med.* I p.1.6 (after 18 words and first clause); Artemidorus p.202.9 (after 19 words and first clause); Hermogenes, *Inv.* III p.126.2–3 (after 6 words including main verb); Galen, *De remed.par.*, K XIV p.390 (after 8 words and first clause), and compare the irregular position in K X pp.530, 663, where the address is not in the first sentence at all.

anywhere else apart from Acts 1.1, and this also is common in the scientific tradition.

Luke does not appear to avail himself of the opportunity which naturally arises here to tell us more about his subject-matter: his γράψαι has no direct object. Instead the clause is filled out with a participial phrase dependent on ἐμοί. The closest formal parallel to this in the prefaces studied is in Galen, *Ther. ad Pis.* pref. (K XIV p. 210): τοῦτόν σοι τὸν περὶ τῆς θηριακῆς λόγον ἀκριβῶς ἐξετάσας ἅπαντα, ἄριστε Πίσων, σπουδαίως ἐποίησα ..., where we find a similar participial clause referring to the author. But we may also compare the generalized descriptions of the subject-matter of the book which often appear at this point as object to the main 'decision' verb. Sometimes these give a detailed list of topics (Diocles p. 75.5ff., Demetrius p. 1.8ff.), sometimes they point out the particular aspect to be studied (Apollonius of Citium p. 10.7). In the post-hellenistic prefaces authors regularly use this point to highlight the *epistemological* status of the material: how did the author acquire his knowledge? Thus Hero gives us 'what has been handed down by the ancients and what I have discovered for myself' (*Spir.* I p. 2.8f., cf. *Catoptr.* p. 320.5f., *Metr.* I p. 4.6f., *Dipotr.* p. 188.5ff.). Others talk of 'such material as has come to my knowledge' (Artemidorus p. 1.12f., Serenus *Sect. Con.* p. 120.8) and of 'what I have discovered from experience' (Artemidorus p. 1.12f., Galen K VI p. 755.10f., K XIV p. 390.3, Dioscorides, *Eup.* II p. 317.9). Similar phrases occur in Vitruvius (and therefore presumably go further back in the Greek tradition than our extant sources would suggest), but in transitional passages rather than prefaces:

> participial phrase referring to the author: 'following in whose footsteps I have written in this book ... ' (VIII 3.27 cf. IV 2.6);
>
> object of main verb: 'what I myself have discovered to be true in practice and what I have in part received from my teachers' (X 11.2; cf. also the barely distinguishable phrases with *uti* or *quemadmodum* at IX 1.16, X 13.8).

If these parallels are valid, they will give us a useful yardstick for assessing the particular significance of Luke's words; we shall return to this point below.

Vocabulary and style

Once more, Luke's words are carefully interwoven to form a classical-sounding main clause, with a complex participial phrase intervening between ἔδοξε and its infinitive. Again, however, the net result is a lack of clarity which has caused problems to commentators, chiefly that of determining which adverb goes with which verb. Καθεξῆς clearly goes with γράψαι. Ἀκριβῶς in terms of sense could go with either γράψαι or παρηκολουθηκότι; but it would be clumsy to take both adverbs with γράψαι, and therefore it seems better to read παρηκολουθηκότι ἄνωθεν πᾶσιν ἀκριβῶς as a unitary phrase. This means that both ἄνωθεν and ἀκριβῶς modify παρηκολουθηκότι, but Luke has carefully cushioned them by placing πᾶσιν between them. We are therefore committed to finding a meaning for the participle which will make sense in conjunction with the adverb.

ἔδοξε κἀμοί: 'it seemed good to me also'. Luke's 'decision' is unusual in biblical literature (only paralleled in *Ecclus.* prol. and II Macc. 1.18). It evidently caused problems to some early readers, who felt that this purely human 'decision to write' lacked a spiritual dimension. Thus the Muratorian Canon emphasizes the humanistic nature of the decision: 'Lucas ... nomine suo ex opinione conscripsit', while two of the ancient prologues to the Gospel assert Luke's inspiration in spite of this: 'Lucas ... sancto instigante spiritu ... hoc scripsit evangelium' (Aland, 1968, pp. 538, 539, 547). The same motive may lie behind the interpolation in some Old Latin and Gothic MSS of *et spiritui sancto* in verse 3 – although the gloss in itself may simply have been triggered by an awareness of the verbal link between the preface and Acts 15.28, perhaps a sort of *masorah* linking two otherwise unparalleled constructions.

The verb is common in the NT but is almost always used personally. Impersonal δοκεῖ μοι, 'it seems to me' hence 'I think' is classical, and rare in the NT, while the more pregnant classical idiom 'it seems good to me' hence 'I have decided' is found only here and in Acts 15 (vv. 25, 28, 34). The idiom had clearly dropped out of everyday language but would still have been familiar through its survival in official documents and in the decrees which were displayed on inscriptions all over the Greek East. There is a good example at Jos., *Ant.* XVI 162–5; cf. further LSJ s.v. II 4b. The classical idiom also survived in formal prefaces. Absolute ἔδοξέ (μοι) is found in Galen (K V 587.4, K VI 816.8, K VII 584.6), in Hermogenes (*Inv.* III p. 126.15) and in Vettius Valens (pp. 258.4, 331.8). With a qualifying word or phrase it occurs in Galen (K II 532), in Serenus (p. 120.6) and in Vettius Valens (p. 172.16).

παρηκολουθηκότι: 'having followed'. The Greek verb ἀκολουθεῖν and its compounds have a range of literal and metaphorical uses very similar to those of the English 'follow'.

(a) of physical accompaniment, **'having followed [them] all'**, sc. the 'eyewitnesses and ministers of the word'. So, many early commentators, taking πᾶσιν as masculine (Cadbury s.v.). But this is not the normal sense of the compound form of the verb. When used of one person following another it has the sense of 'dogging one's footsteps', and in most of the cases cited by BAG and LSJ s.v. the subject is an impersonal entity like 'fate'. This sense would also be difficult to construe with ἀκριβῶς.

(b) of 'following' as a mental activity, **'being thoroughly familiar with the whole affair'** (taking πᾶσιν as neuter). This is the best-attested use of the compound in Greek sources and fits naturally with ἀκριβῶς, with which it is often combined. It is used of 'following' a course of events (Dem. XVIII 172), a narrative or an argument (Anaximenes, *Ars Rhet.* 29(30)1), a text or a subject (Jos, *C. Ap.* I 218); cf. also its frequent application to the understanding of the reader in prefaces.[28] The perfect participle is used (like εἰδώς) with present force: 'I have paid attention' hence 'I (now) understand': cf. Arrian, *Epictetus* I 9.4 ὁ τοίνυν τῇ διοικήσει τοῦ κόσμου παρηκολουθηκὼς καὶ μεμαθηκὼς ὅτι κτλ. This sense also infects other tenses, for we find the word used absolutely (as in the construction παρακολουθεῖν ὅτι) in contexts where it can only mean 'I understand': cf. Galen K V p. 14 = SM I 10.22 and LSJ s.v. Thus Hipparchus' τοῖς καὶ μετρίως παρηκολουθηκόσιν (I p. 4.7f.) must mean 'those who are only moderately well versed in the subject', and is a foil to his παρακολουθῶν ἑκάστοις ἀκριβῶς (p. 6.19–20). The manner in which this understanding is acquired is not specified in the verb. If the object is a written text, then the process of παρακολουθεῖν will naturally involve reading, but the verb does not *mean* 'to read'. Similarly it does not mean 'to do research' or 'to investigate', although both these activities might be required in the process.[29]

[28] Παρακολουθεῖν: e.g. Diocles p.75.11f.; Apollonius of Citium, pp.10.15, 38.9; Hero, *Bel.* W. 73.11; Dioscorides, *Eup.* p.151.5.; Hipparchus p.4.7f., p.6.19.
[29] So, rightly, Cadbury s.v. Kümmel (1966, p. 127) insists that the verb 'can by all means mean "to investigate a thing"', and Bauer's *Lexicon* gives the same meaning. But the examples cited from Demosthenes do not support this interpretation. In both, παρακολουθηκώς is parallel to εἰδώς, and is to be understood in much the same sense. The Vulgate's *assecuto* provides little assistance either way, since the verb *assequi* has much the same range of meanings as παρακολουθεῖν (although the physical sense is the commoner), and was probably chosen by the translator for that reason: cf. I Tim. 4.6, II Tim. 3.10. Jerome paraphrases the clause, '*quaedam altius repetens*' (*Comm.in Matt.*, proem 7).

(c)   **'having participated in [them] all'**, sc. the events. This was Cad-
        bury's own suggestion, argued with caution in 1922a p. 502, but
        with more commitment in 1922b and again in 1956. The verb is
        found fairly often with πράγματα as object, and Cadbury argued
        that in certain cases it meant to have first-hand experience by
        being a participant oneself. This verse was therefore an anticipa-
        tion of the 'we-passages' in Acts. Quite apart from the exegetical
        problems it poses,[30] this interpretation can be ruled out purely on
        semantic grounds. Cadbury cited Jos., *Vit.* 357, *C. Ap.* I 53,
        Lucian, *Symp.* I, Philo Judaeus, *De decalogo* 88; but in all these
        cases the verb can be sufficiently understood under category (b)
        above: 'being acquainted with the course of events' is an adequate
        translation, the manner of acquisition of this understanding being
        supplied by the context. When Josephus does claim to have
        participated in events he uses παρατυγχάνειν, as in *C. Ap.* I 56.
        As Cadbury perceives, there is a 'claim' inherent in the use of
        παρακολουθεῖν, but this is simply because it is, like 'know', an
        'achievement-word'.[31]

(d)   **'having followed [them] all'**, sc. as sources. Parallels with scientific
        prefaces suggest one further possibility, a variant on (a), in which
        πᾶσιν is masculine but refers to the 'eyewitnesses and ministers of
        the word' not as people Luke may have known but as the *sources*
        he is 'following'. This usage is found with ἐπακολουθείν in Jos.,
        C. Ap. I 130, and with ἀκολουθεῖν in Marcian, *Epitome peripli
        Menippei, GGM* I 565.12f.; both Hipparchus and Apollonius of
        Citium use κατακολουθεῖν in this way (Hipparchus I p.6.10, Ap.
        Cit. I p.12.4). Luke's phrase would then parallel Vitruvius'
        '*quorum secutus ingressus*' (VIII 3.27, cf. II pref. 5, IV 2.6) as a
        claim to be a faithful transmitter of his sources. There are no
        instances of this usage with παρακολουθεῖν in scientific or literary

---

[30] Cf. Kümmel, 1966, p. 127; E. Haenchen, 'Das "Wir" in der Apostelgeschichte
und das Itinerar', *Zeitschrift für Theologie und Kirche*, 58 (1961), pp. 329ff.;
J. Dupont, *Les Sources du livre des Actes – état de la question* (1960), ET K. Pond
(substantially rev.), *The Sources of Acts* (Darton, Longman & Todd, London, 1964),
pp. 99ff., esp. p. 102 n. 3; 1964, pp. 104–12, which contains some additional material;
Klein, 1964, p. 206 n. 77.

[31] 'Achievement-word': G. Ryle, *The Concept of Mind* (Hutchinson's University
Library, London, 1949), p. 149 and *passim*. The view argued in the text is confirmed
by the fact that Josephus says that his prerequisites for historical writing were
fulfilled not only for the *Bellum* but also for the *Antiquitates* (*C.Ap.* I 54). In the latter
it was not a question of personal experience but having sufficient familiarity with the
priestly tradition to interpret the sacred books. Compare *C.Ap.* I 218, where παρακολουθεῖν is used in precisely this context, and is contrasted (*pace* Cadbury) with
ἐνέτυχον (217) as 'understanding accurately' with merely 'reading'. Cf. also the
papyrus letters cited by Cadbury, where the process of παρακολουθεῖν τοῖς πράγμασιν is to be achieved by reading the letter (PSI 411.3ff.; P.Lond. 23.54ff.; P.Par.
46.19f.).

texts, but the NT knows such a use at I Tim. 4.6, II Tim. 3.10, and
Bauer (BAG s.v. 2) cites further examples from papyri and
inscriptions.

Of the four options explored here, sense (b) follows the best-attested use of
the compound and sits most easily with both its adverbs (see below). Senses
(a) and (c) are both against normal Greek usage, and neither sits well with
ἀκριβῶς; πᾶσιν is also a difficulty, especially on Cadbury's view, for Luke's
'participation' can only apply to limited sections of the Acts narrative, and
not at all to the Gospel events which must be primarily in view in the
preface. The use of the perfect tense may count somewhat against sense (d),
but it is an attractive possibility which cannot be ruled out. The translation
'having followed' is an attempt to cover both possibilities, (b) and (d).

ἄνωθεν: 'thoroughly'. In its temporal sense ἄνωθεν can mean 'from the
beginning', 'for some time back', 'from way back', or, more generally,
'thoroughly'. It is roughly equivalent to ἀπ' ἀρχῆς: cf. esp. Aelian, *De
natura animalium* XVII 40, where the οὐκ ἀπ' ἀρχῆς of Aelian's source is
replaced by οὐκ ἄνωθεν οὐδ' ἐξ ἀρχῆς (Palm, 1955, p. 53). The same pair
recur in Acts 26.4–5. Commentators have tried to work out the precise
reference of the word, whether to a 'beginning' in Luke's material (e.g. the
birth-stories) or to a point in his own experience,[32] but it is unnecessary to
look for a precise time-scheme here. Its use with verbs of knowing strongly
suggests the general sense 'thoroughly', especially when used of knowing a
person as in Acts 26.5 (cf. Aelius Aristides, *Or.* 50.78). It should be
compared with Demosthenes' παρηκολουθηκότα τοῖς πράγμασιν ἐξ
ἀρχῆς (XVIII 172) or Galen's παιδευόμενος ἐξ ἀρχῆς (K XIX 40 = SM II
116.24f.), where the words are intended to convey a general impression of
complete and thorough knowledge, not to raise questions as to its precise
scope. Note also Artemidorus p.238.10 ἀπ' ἀρχῆς ἀναγράφω, and p.2.11,
where a previous treatise is criticized as being ἄκοσμον καὶ ὥσπερ οὐκ ἀπ'
ἀρχῆς.[33]

πᾶσιν: 'everything' (or: 'them all'). The antecedent of this word depends on
the interpretation of 'following' adopted (see above). Cadbury remarks on
Luke's fondness for using the word in a general sense. It is common in such
claims, cf. Dem. XIX 257 ἀκριβέστατ' εἰδὼς ἐγὼ καὶ παρηκολουθηκὼς
ἅπασι, Galen K XIV 210 ἀκριβῶς ἐξετάσας ἅπαντα.

[32] Inclusion of the birth-stories: e.g. Plummer, 1922, *ad loc.*; Samain, 1973, p. 319f.
esp. n. 73. Reference to a period in Luke's own life: Cadbury, 1922b p. 409 and
1956/7 p. 130. The point is also argued by Klostermann, 1929, *ad loc.*, and by
F. Dibelius, 'Die Herkunft der Sonderstücke des Lukasevangeliums', *ZNTW*, 12
(1911), pp. 325–43, p. 338. Cf. also P. Schubert, 'The structure and significance of
Lk 24', in *Neutestamentliche Studien für R. Bultmann* (*ZNTW* Beiheft 21, 1954),
pp. 165–86, p. 171.
[33] Cf. also Agrippa's words in a letter quoted by Josephus, *Vit.* 366, μαθεῖν ...
ἀρχῆθεν. The Greek is obscure and not wholly competent. Ἀρχῆθεν, which I have
not found elsewhere, may be a conflation of ἄνωθεν and ἀπ' ἀρχῆς.

ἀκριβῶς: 'carefully', 'accurately'. Like the two previous words, ἀκριβῶς
tends to recur in the context of a claim to possess knowledge: Luke is rather
drawn to clichés in his choice of words. Besides the passages already cited,
cf. [Dem.] XLVIII 40 τοῖς εἰδόσιν ἀκριβῶς ἅπαντα ταῦτα τὰ πράγματα
ὡς ἔχει παρηκολουθηκόσιν ἐξ ἀρχῆς. It is found with παρακολουθεῖν in
Hipparchus p.6.19–20 (cited above) and in Galen (K XIV 216.15–16); cf.
also Diocles p.75.11f. παρακολουθήσεις τῇ ἀκριβείᾳ. It is very common with
verbs of knowing and perceiving; its meaning veers between 'carefully' and
'accurately', 'precisely', 'exactly' or 'in detail', and may perhaps embrace all
these at once.

Cadbury remarks that the word is common 'where the writing of history
is discussed', but it is equally if not more at home in the scientific tradition:
cf. Jaeger, 1938 p. 86 and 1954 III pp. 19, 33; Hobart, 1882 pp. 250–1;
above, ch. 5 p. 95. It seems in fact to have become something of a value
word, used not so much for any specific idea it conveyed as for its general
aura of 'scientific' respectability, as in phrases like ἀκριβῶς καὶ ἐμπειρῶς
(Hipparchus pp.176.11, 178.12) or ἀκριβῶς καὶ ἐπιστημονικῶς (Galen, K
XIV 312). While literary culture had its doubts about the value of
akribeia,[34] in scientific contexts to call a piece of work ἀκριβής was to say
something to its credit: cf. Porphyry, *De antro nymph.* 4 (ed. Nauck p.58.3),
ἄριστα καὶ ἀκριβέστατα or Oribasius, *Collect.Med.* I (*CMG* VI 1/1 p. 4, 14)
καὶ τῶν ἄριστα συγγραψάντων καὶ τῶν μὴ ὁμοίως τὸ ἀκριβὲς ἐξεργα-
σαμένων. This may explain its frequency in prefaces and methodological
discussions of all kinds. The short preface to pseudo-Galen, *Ther. ad Pis.* (K
XIV 210ff.) uses it no less than seven times.

καθεξῆς: 'in an orderly fashion'. A less common form of the adverbs ἑξῆς,
ἐφεξῆς; it is found in late literary texts (Aelian, Plutarch, Oppian: LSJ s.v.),
and in 'Aristeas', Test. XII, and I Clement (Cadbury s.v.). It is not
recorded in the papyri, but LSJ cite an inscription from Smyrna (*IG Rom.*
IV 1432.9). Only Luke uses it in the NT (five times). It is clear that καθεξῆς
covers much the same range as the other two forms: compare Luke 8.1 with
7.11, and Luke's καθεξῆς in Acts 18.23 with the parallel uses of ἑξῆς in
Ps.-Scymnus 133 and of ἐφεξῆς in Xen., *Hell.* IV 6.4. Cadbury rightly
remarks on the variation of prepositional elements in compounds as a
feature of hellenistic style; it is one that can often be observed among
scientific writers (above ch. 5 pp. 100–101). It would be wrong, therefore, to
think of the word as a 'choice' or 'rare' one. Its distribution in fact suggests
that it became popular first in sub-literary Greek, only later being adopted
by literary writers.

---

[34] Erotian, pref. p.7.10 speaks of τὸ ἄγαν ἀκριβές. Criticism of overmuch exact-
ness belonged particularly to the sphere of literary criticism, especially when *akribeia*
came to be a hallmark of the Atticizers (cf. Phrynichus, *Ecloga* pref.). The literary
side of Greek culture here stands apart from the scientific, which adopted *akribeia* as
a necessary watchword, despite some early doubts as to its ungentlemanly character
(Jaeger, 1954, III p. 15, referring to Aristotle, *Pol.* 1337b15, 1337b8).

132 *The preface to Luke's Gospel*

Cadbury suggested 'hereinafter' as a possible translation here, with an eye to the common use of the word in transitional passages in reference to 'what follows'. But in these contexts the reference is generally clear, and Luke's word here seems too far from the end of the preface for this sense.[35] More to the point is the common use of this group of adverbs to modify verbs of saying or recounting (e.g. Plato, *Plt.* 281d, Isoc. IV 26). Luke's own usage at Acts 11.4 confirms this pattern. Compare Galen K XIV 106.9f. σχεδὸν ἁπάσας τὰς ἀρίστας ἔγραψεν ἐφεξῆς ὁ ᾿Ανδρόμαχος. The link with ἁπάσας exemplifies a common pattern (cf. LSJ s.v.; F. Mussner, 'καθεξῆς im Lukasprolog', (*Jesus and Paulus*, Festschrift W. G. Kümmel, ed. E. E. Ellis and E. Gräber, Vandenhoeck & Ruprecht, Göttingen, 1975, pp. 253–5; Völkel, 1973, pp. 289–99), which may also underlie this passage, if (as seems likely) the πᾶσιν of the previous phrase is the unexpressed object of γράψαι. The meaning of the adverb in these contexts is variously defined as 'in order', 'successively', 'continuously', 'one after another': a regular, connected account is in view.

γράψαι: 'to write [it all] up'. The scientific writers hardly ever use the verb 'to send', which was characteristic of poetic dedication and of Roman writers (Herkommer, 1968, p. 27 and n. 4). The simple γράφειν is one of a range of verbs used in scientific prefaces: cf. Diocles p.75.5, Hipparchus p.2.15, Bito W 43. end, Ps.-Scymnus 66. The verb is used regularly without an object, especially with the dative (LSJ s.v. II 4), and the following purpose-clause might be reckoned to act as object. It would, however, be more natural to take the object(s) of the previous clauses as understood here, either 'the matters' or 'the tradition of the *autoptai*', both effectively subsumed under πᾶσιν: hence 'to write it all up for you'.

κράτιστε Θεόφιλε: 'most excellent Theophilus'. On the position of the address, see above under Structure. The address without ὦ is post-classical (N. Turner, 1963, p. 33; Blass-Debrunner, 1961, §146). In scientific prefaces, we find ὦ used in rhetorical addresses throughout the period studied (e.g. Hipparchus p.120.24; Serenus, *Sect. Cyl.* p.2.2), but there is an increase in addresses without ὦ after the hellenistic period (e.g. Hero, *Def.* p.14.3). A variety of superlatives appears along with the names of dedicatees: λαμπρό-τατε (Hero, *Def.* p.14.3); φίλτατε (e.g. Dioscorides, *Mat.Med.* I p.1.3); τιμιώτατε (Dioscorides, *Eup.* I p.151.3); θαυμαστότατε (Erotian fr. 60 p.116.15f.); ἄριστε (Galen K XIV p.210.4). For κράτιστε, compare Diosco-

35 J. Kürzinger, 'Luke 1, 3 ... ἀκριβῶς καθεξῆς σοι γράψαι ...', *Biblische Zeitschrift* 18/2 (1974), pp.249–55, (esp. pp. 252–3) attempts to prove that here and everywhere in Luke–Acts, ἑξῆς/καθεξῆς always means 'next' or 'as follows'. This is scarcely credible. Kürzinger places dubious reliance on what he calls the 'Grund-bedeutung' of the word, irrespective of context; he fails to distinguish between different forms of the adverb (the passage on which his argument is based has the more emphatic ἐν τῷ καθεξῆς); and he fails to distinguish the different verbs which may be modified by the adverb (verbs of motion, verbs of recounting, etc.).

rides, *Mat.Med.* I p.3.1f.; Hermogenes, *Inv.* III p.126.2f.; Artemidorus p.236.2f.; Galen K X p.78, K XIV p.295, K XIX p.8.

In certain official contexts and at certain periods κράτιστος was applied properly to officials of equestrian rank. But it is now accepted that it is found with a wider application outside that period and in non-official contexts (Cadbury s.v.), and so its use here does not prove that Theophilus was a Roman official. Certainly in scientific prefaces it is hard to see any evidence of strict attention to rank in the choice of epithets: Galen's Hieron (not a Roman name) is addressed successively as ὦ Ἱέρων φίλτατε, Ἱέρων κράτιστε and ὦ Ἱέρων (*De Meth.Med.* I, II, III = K X pp. 1, 78, 157), despite the fact that φίλτατε in letters is used regularly to address a person lower in rank than oneself (Koskenniemi, 1956, p. 99f.).[36]

The name of Luke's addressee is not a Roman one; it was very commonly, though not exclusively, used by hellenized Jews, cf. *Letter of Aristeas* 49; *CPJ* I p. xix; H. J. Leon, *The Jews of Ancient Rome* (Jewish Publication Society of America, Philadelphia 1960), no. 119 p. 104. It is listed as a slave name in Horsley, 1987, p. 178. Whether we can deduce anything more about Theophilus himself from the dedication and its parallels is a question we shall return to in chapter 9.

Interpretation

Once again the direct informational value of the main verb here (the grammatical pivot of the sentence) is minimal. Much more important is the hidden rhetoric of the participial and adverbial phrase, which Luke, like his contemporaries, uses to advance two claims about his book. The first relates to the status of his material, the second to its presentation. What precisely is Luke saying here?

The participial clause, as commentators have recognized, brings forward some sort of epistemological claim about the status of the material presented. The precise nature of this claim becomes clearer when we set it alongside the claims made at similar points by the writers of scientific prefaces. Serenus has a neutral, uninformative phrase which in some respects recalls Luke's ('such material as has come to my knowledge', cf. 'Structure', above); but there is an implied modesty in Serenus' phrase which Luke does not share. The structure of Luke's phrase is that of a boast rather than a disclaimer, as Cadbury rightly perceived. If Cadbury's reading of παρηκο-

---

[36] Cf. a similar variation between τιμιώτατε (used in strict letter-convention to address a person of higher rank than oneself, Koskenniemi, 1956, p. 101) and φίλτατε (strictly used for lower ranks) in Dioscorides, *Eup.* I p.151.3/II p.3.17.9. Further examples in Cadbury. Note also Libanius, *Hypotheses to Demosthenes*. pref., where the proconsular Montius (and therefore not equestrian but senatorial in rank) is addressed as κράτιστε.

λουθηκότι were right, Luke's claim would be more like the claim to personal experience found in Galen, Dioscorides and Artemidorus (see 'Structure', above): he would be claiming to substitute material discovered by himself for the traditional material passed on by the authorities mentioned in verse 2. But Cadbury's interpretation seems semantically unlikely (above, s.v.) and creates difficulties when we come to ask how a claim on Luke's part to have participated in the events he describes relates to the Gospel to which the preface most immediately belongs. Moreover to read such a claim in to this part of the sentence would be to go against all that we have discovered about its overall structure: Luke is ranging himself *alongside* his predecessors in verses 1–2, not setting himself against them.

Παρηκολουθηκότι then is best understood either as a general claim to thorough and accurate understanding (in accordance with the best-attested use of the compound in Greek) or possibly as a claim to be 'following in the footsteps' of the sources already identified in verse 2. Either way, what we have here is a claim to fidelity and comprehension in transmission rather than to any personal contribution by the author: Luke is proud to have 'received and understood' the message passed on to him by the 'eyewitnesses and ministers of the word'. Similar claims are found both in Vitruvius and in Luke's contemporary Hero, although Luke does not share their concern to evaluate the tradition and to differentiate his own contribution.[37] We may also compare the claims of Philo and Apollonius of Citium to be following tradition (see above, 'Structure' verse 2). Luke's claim here thus falls well within the attitudes to tradition which we have documented in the scientific authors.

Secondly, what kind of claim is Luke making about the presentation of his work? What significance should we attach to the words καθεξῆς σοι γράψαι? Some commentators have linked the adverb with Papias' observation that Mark wrote down Peter's preaching 'but not in order' (οὐ μέντοι τάξει), with the implication that Luke is here stating his intention to improve on Mark (who is, on this

---

[37] E.g. Vitruvius X 11.2; Hero, *Spir.* I p.2.8f. Hero, *Dioptr.* p.188.5ff. distinguishes three categories of material: what has been 'received by those before me', and is useful, will be written down; what is 'difficult in expression' will be put into an easier form; and what is wrong will be corrected. But note that Hero explicitly refuses the polemical role of open discussion of others' mistakes: 'those who wish to do so', he says, 'may read them and judge the difference' (12f.).

hypothesis, one of the 'many' of verse 1) by writing 'in order'.[38] The
adverb on this reading would be emphatic, much as in Plato,
Politicus 281d5 ἵν' ἐφεξῆς ἡμῖν ὁ λόγος ἴῃ, and would constitute the
major point of difference between Luke's work and that of his
predecessors. But Luke does not place the adverb here in an emphatic position; to interpret this single word as promising a programme
of chronological (or any other) reordering of Mark's work would be
to press it to an unjustified extent.[39] Moreover it is hard to see in
what Luke could have felt Mark's order to be deficient, since his
own (unlike Matthew's) is substantially the same.

It seems that we must look for a less polemical interpretation.
This central part of the sentence is its weakest in terms of interest
(especially since γράψαι has no object), and Luke has taken some
pains to get the aural balance right and to buffer the enclitic σοι
between two heavier words. The simple γράψαι provides an
effective contrast with the complex ἐπεχείρησαν ἀνατάξασθαι
διήγησιν, but it risks being too weak for its central position. We
have already noted the facility with which scientific writers vary
their terms for recounting and composing (above ch. 5, pp. 100–1),
and their fondness for verbs which imply the ordering, rather than
the mere retailing, of their material (above ch. 5 p. 95). We would
suggest, therefore, that Luke's καθεξῆς γράψαι should be taken
closely together as simply another variation on this theme: compare
Hero's εἰς τάξιν ἀγάγειν (Spir. I p.2.9).

Luke then shares with the scientific tradition an ideal of 'orderly'
presentation, but this need not imply any particular criticism of his
predecessors. There is nothing in the preface to lead us to believe
that the order Luke offers is conceived as better than or even
different from the order the material had in any other version, much
less that the order of Luke's narrative is closer to a presumed

[38] Papias ap. Euseb. HE III 39.15. See e.g. F. Blass, Evangelium Secundum Lucam
(Teubner, Leipzig, 1897), ad loc.; J. Drury, Tradition and Design in Luke's Gospel
(Darton, Longman & Todd, London, 1976), p. 121; M. D. Goulder, Luke: a New
Paradigm (JSOT suppl. 20: Sheffield (Sheffield Academic Press) 1989), vol. I
pp. 199–200. For a rather different attempt to make sense of the words on these lines,
Kümmel, 1966, pp. 96ff.
[39] Contrast the Politicus passage just quoted, where the adverb is certainly emphatic, but is placed in a predicative position. In Galen, K XIV pp. 106–7 the sense is
rather, 'one after another', 'one by one', and the reference is to a list of items rather
than to a connected narrative. J. Kürzinger, 'Luke 1, 3 ... ἀκριβῶς καθεξῆς σοι
γράψαι ...', Biblische Zeitschrift 18/2 (1974), pp. 249–55, p. 251, rightly casts doubt
on interpretations which, while they may reflect profound analysis of the Lucan
achievement, cannot be derived from the word itself.

historical order of events. If any contrast is implied, it is worth remembering that Luke never says that his predecessors had produced *written* accounts (above, 'Interpretation' verse 1); the contrast may simply be between the shape of any written Gospel and that of the underlying tradition. Καθεξῆς suggests the linear progression (*seriatim*, 'in succession') unavoidable in a written narrative: the physical constraints of the medium ensure that the writer has to recount events 'one after another' in a narrative sequence, and cannot reproduce the fluidity and flexibility of oral storytelling.

Verse four

... ἵνα ἐπιγνῷς περὶ ὧν κατηχήθης λόγων τὴν ἀσφάλειαν.

... so that you may have assured knowledge about the things in which you have been instructed.

Structure

The final clause of the preface centres on Theophilus: Luke is writing, he says, 'so that you may know ... ' Scientific writers regularly use this way of relating the subject of the book to the dedicatee; see above ch. 5 pp. 74–5. The content of the 'so that you' clause varies, but most commonly it refers to the enhanced understanding of the subject which the dedicatee will gain from the book. Formally speaking Luke is closest to Hero's *Pneumatica* I, where the purpose clause is bound in with the 'decision' sentence, albeit in a generalized form where there is no dedication: 'for thus it will come about that those who subsequently wish to be involved in mathematical studies will find assistance' (Hero, *Spir*. I p.2.10–12). Cf. *Bel*. W 73.11 'so that the tradition may be easy to follow (εὐπαρακολούθητος) for all'; Galen, *De typis* K VII 463, 'thinking that in this way the matter would be easy to recount and easy to learn for those just entering the profession'; Vettius Valens pp.157.30, 290.35.

In content this final clause is not very informative. This is not in itself unusual, as the examples just cited show. But Luke has not so far given his readers any very precise idea as to what his book is about, and we might have expected some information here (cf. Ps.-Scymnus 73ff., where the 'so that you' clause is used for a detailed statement of the subject of the book). Luke's determined reticence only serves to reinforce the impression that he is not writing for complete outsiders, but for a group in which his vague phrases ('the matters which have come to fruition in our midst', 'the things in which you have been instructed') would be immediately understood. Theophilus above all, we must presume, knows what to expect; he has already received some kind of information about all this. The phrase περὶ ὧν κατηχήθης λόγων recalls Hermogenes' περὶ ὧν ἤδη σοι φθάνω καὶ δι' ἐμαυτοῦ πολλάκις τεχνολογήσας (*Inv.* III p.126.3ff.); a similar situation is presupposed in several passages where Galen speaks of writing a book for friends who have heard his lectures or seen his demonstrations, as a 'reminder' of 'what you have seen'.[40]

Vocabulary and style

Luke's final clause is shorter and simpler than the preceding ones. There is still a tendency to prefer the heavier, compound word or phrase (ἐπιγνῷς ... τὴν ἀσφάλειαν), but the basic formula used here ('I decided to write to you so that you might know ... ') is not far from a phrase familiar in papyrus letters (Koskenniemi, 1956, pp. 78–9); the preface-convention may ultimately derive from this letter-formula. Luke's vocabulary here is also closer to the papyri than to classical literature.

ἵνα ἐπιγνῷς: **'so that you may know'.** The compound and its cognates are found in scientific prefaces with reference to the dedicatee:

> Philo, *Bel.* Th. 56.16–17 συμβήσεται δέ σοι ... ἐπιγνῶναι. ibid. Th. 59.1–2 περὶ ὧν τὴν ἐπίγνωσιν ἕξεις.
> Apollonius of Citium p.64.10–12 ἵνα ἔχῃς ... τὴν ... περὶ τῶν ἄρθρων ἐπίγνωσιν.
> Artemidorus p.300.20 εὐεπιγνώστων σοι ἐσομένων.
> Vettius Valens p.352.34ff. ὅπως ... ἐπιγνόντες; cf. also pp.176.16, 351.26f.

But Luke's precise meaning cannot be determined from the parallels alone.

In classical usage, the compound meant either 'to recognize' (with a person as object) or 'to realize/recognize/find out/ascertain' (with a fact as object). All these uses are found in the NT, as well as the weakened hellenistic use in which the verb is simply a variant for γινώσκειν (cf. e.g. Rom. 1.32). Luke is fond of the word (it occurs 7 times in the Gospel and 13 in Acts, as against 22 in the rest of the NT) and seems to use it fairly

[40] Cf. ch. 4 pp. 62–3 and nn. 40, 41.

precisely. We should therefore expect either 'recognize' or 'ascertain' as a meaning here, producing a translation on the lines of 'to recognize the reliability of the accounts you have heard' (cf. Xen. *Mem.* IV 6.15 where ἀσφάλεια λόγου means the 'convincing nature' of an argument (LSJ s.v.)). I Tim. 4.3 provides a parallel use of the verb with the abstract noun 'truth' as object. But Luke does not normally use the verb in this way, and ἀσφάλεια is not a true parallel to ἀλήθεια; moreover, περὶ ὧν should probably not be spelt out as τῶν λόγων περὶ ὧν (see below).

An examination of evidence from the papyri and Acts suggests that verb and noun should be taken more closely together. The combination ἐπιγν-ῶαι τὸ ἀσφαλές occurs in three passages from papyrus letters of the second century AD: P. Giss. 1.27, P. Amh. 131.3f., 132.5f. (Cadbury s.v.; Klostermann, 1929, *ad loc.*; van Unnik, 1955, pp. 330ff.). The noun here is functioning more or less as an adverb, 'to find out *for certain*'; it is followed in one case by a genitive (τοῦ πράγματος), in another by an indirect question. Luke uses a similar phrase (with the simplex rather than the compound) at Acts 21.34, 22.30,[41] and it seems best to read the phrase in Luke 1.4 in the same way. However περὶ ὧν is resolved (see below), the sense is much the same; cf. P. Amh. 131, where ἐπιγνῶ τὸ ασφαλές τοῦ πράγματος means 'find out for certain about the matter', not 'find out that the matter is certain'. This interpretation accords with Luke's normal practice except for the use of the compound: it is as if he had written 'to ascertain for certain'. But we have already noticed a preference for compounds in the preface, and may compare Bauer's remarks (BAG s.v. ἐπιγινώσκω 2d) on Acts 25.10 where 'the influence of the adverb causes the compound to sink to the level of the simplex'.

περὶ ὧν: 'about [the things] in which'. The attraction of the relative is classical, but it is also regular in the NT and papyri (Blass–Debrunner, 1961, §294). The phrase is common in papyrus letters (Koskenniemi, 1956, p. 68), and Luke may not have had a clear idea in his own mind about its resolution. This really depends on the construction to be expected with κατηχήθης. Acts 21.21, 24 have the verb in the passive with περὶ σοῦ, so that τῶν λόγων περὶ ὧν κατηχήθης is grammatically possible (cf. Plut. *De fluviis* 7.2, 8.1, 17.1). The verb is also found with an accusative in Acts 18.25 and Gal. 6.6 (cf. also Jos., *Vita* 366), and possibly with a genitive in Acts 21.24. The accusative will clearly refer to the internal object, the content of the *catechesis*, while the περί-construction would refer to the general subject which the *catechesis* is 'about'. It seems more reasonable to treat τῶν λόγων as internal object, 'the words in which you have been

---

[41] Cf. also Acts 25.26; 2.36. Compare the phrase ἀσφαλῶς ἰδέναι which occurs in the fourth line of an inscription from the temple of Mandulis Aion at Talmis (modern Kalabsha): text in Nock, 1972, I pp. 364–5, further Nock, 1933, pp. 109f., 289f. Nock dates the text as third-century AD at the latest (1972, I p. 368) and describes it as 'written in vulgar Greek' (1933, p. 110).

instructed': otherwise the 'words' and the 'instruction' seem to be two different things. The phrase is thus probably best resolved περὶ τῶν λόγων οὓς κατηχήθης; but the sense is little affected either way.

κατηχήθης: 'you have been instructed'. The verb does not occur (except in a purely technical sense in Vitruvius V 8.1) before the first century AD. Besides the NT and Philo, Agrippa's letter to Josephus in *Vita* 366 provides our earliest example: 'when you meet me, I will myself by word of mouth inform you of much that is not generally known'.[42] In the NT, the verb is used in two distinct contexts: in a forensic or official context, where it means 'to lay information' (Acts 21.21, 24); and in a religious context, where it means 'to instruct' (Gal. 6.6, Rom. 2.18, I. Cor. 14.19, and probably Acts 18.25); in Romans and in I Corinthians, where it is used absolutely, some kind of pregnant use is required, 'to give [Christian] instruction'. A similar range of contexts is found in secular literature. The verb is used of 'instructing' a rhetor in a forensic situation in P. Lips. I 32.1 (third century AD). But the noun κατήχησις, which is current from the first century BC onwards, normally refers to instruction in a school context, whether rhetorical (Dion. Halic. *Dem.* 50, *Din.* 7), medical (Hipp. *Praec.* 13) or philosophical (Athenaeus *ap.* Oribasius, *Collect.Med.* 21.6/*Raeder* IV p.139.17).[43] Cf. also Clement's use with reference to pagan philosophers (*Strom.* V ii, 15.3). Both meanings have been suggested here. Cadbury (1921, pp. 431–41 *passim*) argued that it meant 'hostile reports' by analogy with Acts 21.22, 24, but the false accusations there belong to the context, not to the word itself. Its combination here with τῶν λόγων suggests rather a parallel with Galatians 6.6 κατηχούμενος τὸν λόγον. Certainly it makes sense to regard Theophilus as having already received some instruction in the Gospel (not of course in the later technical sense); but the plural 'the words' is not quite the same as 'the Word', and the more neutral 'things of which you have been informed' is equally possible. See further below, 'Interpretation'.

λόγων: 'the things'. If Luke wishes to refer to Christian instruction here, he avoids the most obvious ways of doing so; perhaps the language is deliberately colourless. Nevertheless it is perfectly possible to use the plural of

---

[42] Tr. Thackeray (LCL). Note that Thackeray understands the verb to mean 'inform *by word of mouth*'; and that he described Agrippa's Greek as 'vulgar and obscure'.

[43] Cf. LSJ s.v. The Hippocratic *Praecepta* (Littré IX p.268.10) does not strictly speaking describe a school setting, but gives a comic picture of a pompous 'late-learned' doctor 'lecturing' his unfortunate audience. The text should probably be dated in the first century BC or AD: V. Fleischer, *Untersuchungen zu den hippokratischen Schriften παραγγελίαι, περὶ ἴητρου und περὶ εὐσχημοσύνης* (Neue Deutsche Forschungen 240, Berlin, 1939), p. 24. Cicero (*ad Att.* XV 12.2) and Chrysippus (*ap* Galen K V 463) appear to use the word more generally of 'education' or 'upbringing', but it still has a decidedly scholastic flavour. On Cicero's value as a source for

Christian teaching (e.g. I Tim. 4.6, II Tim. 2.13), and semantically there is
no reason why it should not be so used here. More generally, λόγοι is used
for 'stories/reports/rumours', with the stress more on the events reported
than on the report itself (Cadbury *ad loc.* BAG s.v.). Grimm aptly compares
I Macc. 3.27, 7.33, 10.88. In English 'things' is often the best translation (cf.
RV).

τὴν ἀσφάλειαν: **lit. 'the certainty';** 'so that you may have assured knowledge'. We have argued above that the abstract noun here should be
regarded as equivalent to τὸ ἀσφαλές, and is to be taken closely (effectively
as an adverb) with ἐπιγνῷς. The choice of the abstract noun is probably a
matter of sound and weight: as Cadbury observes, the noun provides a
better ending to the sentence. Stylistically τὸ ασφαλές is more classical, as
well as being a common cliché in contemporary use (Pelletier, 1962,
pp. 122–4). The noun appears frequently in legal documents (in the concrete sense, 'a security') and is found as a loan-word in Aramaic.[44] Luke's
phrase thus reflects contemporary *Koine* rather than literary style. There is
no evidence that the word was ever adopted by historians (Herkommer,
1968, p. 138 n. 4 can cite only this passage and Eunapius), and it does not
appear in the scientific prefaces studied, except in Dionysius Calliphontis
12.

Idiomatically, the phrase simply means 'to find out for certain'; our
translation, 'to have assured knowledge', is more formal. But it has been
suggested that ἀσφάλεια itself has the connotation of the greater 'security'
of written document over against oral report. Aberle, 1863 (cf. ch. 1 n. 3)
p. 104 quotes 'an ancient scholiast' (in Cramer, *Cat. Gr. Patr.* Appendix
p. 417) who interprets ἀσφάλεια as 'the higher security which is preserved
by the written document as opposed to the purely oral statement'. This
would certainly make sense in P. Giss. 1.27 (Cadbury, 1922a, p. 509), where
the writer is sending his letter explicitly in order to find out for certain (ἵνα
τὸ ἀσφαλὲς ἐπιγνῶ) about the 'good news' of a victory (εὐαγγελίζοντι τὰ
τῆς νείκης αὐτοῦ) of which he has only oral reports. We may also compare
'Aristeas' 28 where the word is linked with the painstaking accuracy of
Egyptian royal records: and van Unnik, 1963, p. 18 n. 75 notes a contrast
with hearsay evidence in Polyb. IV 2.3. If this is right, then Luke's stress on
ἀσφάλεια would reflect a contrast not with other written Gospels but with

contemporary spoken *Koine*, see H. J. Rose, 'The Greek of Cicero', *JHS* 41 (1921),
pp. 91–116.

[44] See 5/6 Hev. 1 (a letter from Shim'on bar Kosiba) where it apparently occurs
three times (Y. Yadin, 'The expedition to the Judean desert 1960: expedition D',
Israel Exploration Journal, 11 (1961), pp. 36–52, pp. 41–2; E. Y. Kutscher, 'The
language of the Hebrew and Aramaic letters of Bar Koseva and His Contemporaries', *Lešonenu* 25 (1960), pp. 117–33, p. 119). The word also occurs in Rabbinic
Hebrew (e.g. Deut. R. VII 1): further, S. Liebermann, *Greek in Jewish Palestine*
(Jewish Theological Seminary of America, New York, 1942), p. 8.

the oral instruction (κατήχησις) which Theophilus has received. This is certainly consistent with a common pattern of book production in the scientific tradition: see further below, ch. 9.

Interpretation

Choices are limited on the interpretation of this relatively straight-forward verse. The only real question regarding Luke's vocabulary is over the meaning of κατηχήθης: does it mean 'you have been informed' or 'you have been instructed'? If the former, then Luke could be promising to correct rumours or reports about Jesus and the apostles, mistaken or even hostile, which have come to the ears of Theophilus in some unspecified manner: Theophilus will be an 'outsider' to whom the detailed story which Luke is about to unfold will be more or less new. If the latter, then Theophilus is an 'insider' who has already received some Christian instruction in oral form: the material he is about to read will not be new to him in quite the same way, and the 'security' he is promised is not that of new, previously unknown facts or investigation but of having in his hand a full written text of the tradition as handed down by the 'ministers of the word'.

This is not a question that can be settled by vocabulary study alone. As we have seen, the word in context could bear either meaning; extra-textual factors will have to be invoked to resolve the dilemma. Both interpretations have their problems. Cadbury's picture of Theophilus as an official who has received hostile reports about Christianity (1921, pp. 431–41) seems to apply more closely to Acts than to the Gospel (although there may be an apologetic slant to Luke's picture of the political innocence of Jesus as well as that of Paul). Conversely, if we stress the traditional or confessional nature of the 'instruction' Theophilus has received, it is less clear how the words would apply to Acts: was the story of Paul also part of Christian 'instruction'? In favour of the second option, we may point out that this difficulty applies equally to other parts of the preface, with its stress on traditional material; either the stories of Acts *were* in some sense 'traditional' in Luke's circle (a suggestion not as far-fetched as it might seem,[45] or the preface does not refer to

---

[45] There is a growing recognition that some at least of the stories in Acts have been shaped by a process of community retelling not unlike that of the Gospel stories (Jervell, 1962). It is worth asking whether we should not also think of a community ('School') setting for the repetition of Paul stories, whether in his lifetime or later in

the contents of Acts quite as directly as it does to the contents of the Gospel.

Ultimately our solution to this question will depend on the social framework we adopt for the creation of Luke and Acts. The whole thrust of this commentary has been to suggest that the scientific tradition provides the best matrix for understanding what is going on in the preface. If that is accepted, it will be logical to look to parallels within that tradition for the creation of a book as a written 'reminder' of oral teaching with which the reader is already familiar. Such parallels are not hard to find (above, 'Structure'; further, above pp. 62f., below ch. 9), and it is this fact which predisposes us to accept the sense 'instructed' for κατηχήθης. It may seem odd that Luke, if he does mean 'Christian teaching' here, has partially disguised the fact by adopting the most neutral words possible: but this is merely a further example of his apparent policy throughout the preface of avoiding explicitly sectarian language.

The other question which arises out of the discussion of this verse is, how seriously should we take it as an indication of Luke's controlling purpose? Both van Unnik (1955) and Cadbury (1921) lay some stress on the verse as a clue to Luke's intentions. This is of course what the verse is ostensibly about; but we have already seen that the rhetorical function of statements in this highly conventional preface is not always the same as their ostensible content. The purpose-clause, expressed in very similar terms to Luke's, was a standard feature of scientific prefaces. It could have a positive informational function (for example if it was used to list the contents of the book), but in most cases it was little more than a flourish, a conventional afterthought designed to complete the balance of the sentence rather than to add anything of substance to the sense.

Acts 1.1

Τὸν μὲν πρῶτον λόγον ἐποιησάμην περὶ πάντων, ὦ Θεόφιλε, ὧν ἤρξατο ὁ Ἰησοῦς ποιεῖν τε καὶ διδάσκειν ...

The previous treatise which I wrote, Theophilus, about all that Jesus began to do and to teach ...

---

the group(s) responsible for the Pastorals. But there is still a great gulf between the nature of Acts and that of the Gospel which makes it easier to apply the words of the preface to the Gospel than to Acts.

Structure

Acts begins with a secondary preface, repeating the address to Theophilus and alluding to the contents of the previous work. The opening words recall the recapitulations found in many scientific and other texts. Luke is only unusual in that he fails to complete the summary with a description of the contents of the current work: his τὸν μὲν πρῶτον λόγον is left without its expected νῦν δέ and we plunge directly into the narrative. We have not found this form of anacolouthon in the scientific prefaces studied, though there is a partial parallel in Vettius Valens p.294.4 where a μέν is left hanging at the end of Book VII. There are however several prefaces where some sort of anacolouthon must be allowed;[46] as we have already seen, syntactical difficulties were often experienced by scientific writers unaccustomed to coping with complex periods. None of the attempts made to emend Luke's text is satisfactory, and it seems best to allow the anacolouthon to stand (Kümmel, 1966, pp.109–11). We have incorporated an analogous anacolouthon into our translation.

The practice of beginning each new book with a recapitulation is foreign to the classical Greek and Roman historians (see above ch. 3). Some hellenistic historians do use recapitulations, but only at specific points and for specific purposes.[47] In scientific treatises, on the other hand, the recapitulation is regular and common; it is in fact at home in these texts in a way that it never was among the historians. It serves the essentially practical purposes of clarity of exposition and ease of reference, and may be related both to the widespread concern for systematization and to the Aristotelian concern for relating each branch of knowledge to its parent philosophy (above ch. 4). Formally, it is a simple development from the regular practice of announcing the subject in the opening words. It was never easy to render such recapitulations into elegant and varied prose, but this was not a major consideration for scientific writers in the way it was for historians. Recapitulations are found already in Theophrastus (e.g. *De ventis* 1), and they recur frequently in the authors studied: cf. Hipparchus Books II, III; Philo, *Bel.*; Apollonius of Citium Books II, III; Hero, *Mech.* III p.200.4; Dio-

[46] E.g. Apollonius of Citium, Book I pref. (see note in Appendix B). Cf. Hero, *Metr.* I p.4.16; *Catoptr.* p.318.28–33, p.320.5–8.

[47] Recapitulations: for Book II of a multi-volumed work where the first formed an extensive introduction; for a later book where an addition was made to the original plan; or, in the case of Diodorus, only for the introductory books which lacked the strong narrative thread of the main text.

scorides, *Mat.Med.* Books II, III, IV, V; Hermogenes, *Inv.* IV; Artemidorus Books II, III; Vettius Valens Book II; Galen K VIII 695, 823, 878, 917; IX 55, 105, etc. These summaries do not always take the tabular form used, for instance, by Dioscorides, and they are not limited to the later volumes of a single work. There was a tendency to regard an author's whole output as an ongoing corpus and to relate each new work to the previous one: cf. Theophrastus, *De ventis, De signis temp.*; Archimedes, *Sph. Cyl.* I; Galen K VIII 766. Conversely, not all separate volumes bear a summary, and we do sometimes find a preface attached to a part of a larger work which makes no reference to the previous volume or to the work as a whole (Philo, *Pneum.*).

Vocabulary and style

Τὸν μέν: 'The [on the one hand] ... ' The classical particle μέν (which is untranslatable) is common enough in the NT, normally with its expected δέ, sometimes with καί, ἀλλά or πλήν. But it is not unusual in the NT to find it alone, as here: cf. e.g. Acts 21.39, 27.21; Rom. 1.8. Acts is especially fond of the pair μὲν οὖν with no corresponding δέ (e.g. Acts 1.6).

πρῶτον: 'previous'. The earlier writers tend to use the adverb πρότερον (Theophrastus, *De ventis* 1; Apollonius of Perge, *Con.* IV p.2.3; Archimedes, *Sph. Cyl.* II p.168.3). Later, a common form of expression is the phrase ἐν τῷ πρὸ τούτου βιβλίῳ or equivalent: cf. Apollonius of Citium p.38.3; Artemidorus p.100.1; Dioscorides, *Mat.Med.* II p.121.2 (with πρώτου as variant reading). Here Luke's πρῶτον is used, as so often in the *Koine*, for πρότερον, and does not necessarily indicate that he had more than one volume in mind (F. F. Bruce, *The Acts of the Apostles: the Greek Text with Introduction and Commentary*, 2nd edn (Tyndale Press, London, 1952), *ad loc.*; 1988, *ad loc.*; BAG s.v.; and add P. Brem. 61.55f.). Adjectival πρότερος is not found in our texts.

λόγον: 'treatise'. The word has a wide variety of applications. Herodotus uses it in the sense 'tale, narrative', both written and oral (LSJ s.v. V 3); thus in Herod. V 36 ὁ πρῶτος λόγος means 'the earlier part of my tale' or 'in the first book'. This use is not cited, however, for any historian after Herodotus. A similar use appears in Aristotle (LSJ s.v. VI 3), where λόγος meaning 'discussion, debate' is already used concretely; hence it comes to be used of a section or division of a dialogue or treatise. This is presumably the origin of the common use of the word in scientific treatises: cf. e.g. Philo, *Bel. Th.* 68.2–3 ποιήσομαι τὸν λόγον σοι; Dioscorides, *Mat.Med.* II p.121.3ff. παρεδώκαμεν τὸν περί ... λόγον; *Mat.Med.* V pref. Ἀποδόντες ... τὸν περί... λόγον; Galen K VI p.554.7 κἀγὼ περί... ἐν τῷ πρώτῳ λόγῳ διελθών; K IX p.55 περὶ μέν ... διὰ τοῦ πρώτου δεδήλωται λόγου; K XIII p.652 ὁ μὲν πρῶτός μοι λόγος ἐτελεύτησεν; Artemidorus p.100.5 περὶ πάντων ... ἐποιησάμην τὸν λόγον; Vettius Valens p.244.23 ἐποιησάμην τοὺς λόγους. In many of these examples the λόγος is abstract: the 'discussion' takes place *in* the book. But in Galen it is clearly used concretely on occasion as an equivalent to βιβλίον, a usage also found in Philo Judaeus, *Quod omnis probus* pref. Here in Acts 1.1 the word could be taken either way.

ἐποιησάμην: 'I wrote'. For parallels, cf. Galen K IX p.157.7, K XIII p.14.5, and the examples from Philo, Artemidorus and Vettius Valens cited in the previous paragraph.

ὦ Θεόφιλε: 'Theophilus'. See note above on Luke 1.3 for the variation in style of address between different books. The form used here is classical both in its lack of epithet and in the use of ὦ without exclamatory overtones (Blass-Debrunner, 1961, §146). Parallels can be found in scientific prefaces of all periods: cf. Hipparchus p.120.24; Hypsicles p.2.1; Demetrius p.1.2; Dionysius Calliphontis 1; Artemidorus p.300.18; Galen K I p.224.1; K V p.806.1 = SM III p.33.1; K V p.899.1f. = SM I p.93.2. The placing of the address late in the sentence conforms with the practice of later prefaces (above 'Structure' verse 3); but the positioning between πάντων and ὦν, rather than at a more definite break in the sense, is stylish.

Interpretation

We are concerned with Luke's use of preface-convention here, not with the wider issues of interpretation which these opening verses raise. One potential problem has already been dealt with. Commentators in the past have argued from Luke's πρῶτον (literally 'first') that Luke meant to write a third volume in his history of the early church; but most now accept that this is simply the loose *Koine* equivalent to πρότερον, and cannot prove anything one way or the other.

The only remaining question concerns the unity of Luke–Acts itself. It is axiomatic to most contemporary scholarship that the Gospel of Luke and the book of Acts are two volumes of a single work, conceived as one major enterprise and forming together the largest literary unit in the New Testament. There is of course no question about the single authorship of the two texts; but our study of recapitulations in scientific treatises makes it less clear that the two are necessarily so closely linked. Things seem to have been looser in practice than logic might demand. Not all multi-volumed works have recapitulations; and conversely, not all recapitulations signal a close literary unity of the type presupposed in current study of Luke–Acts. The critic who finds a unitary conception in the texts themselves may indeed find confirmation for this unity in the two prefaces. But it needs also to be stated clearly that the critic who finds that the two works, while complementing each other, are none the less very different in conception, need not find the prefaces a stumbling-block. The connection between two successive works of a corpus linked by recapitulations is not always as tight as we might expect. This is particularly relevant to the interpretation of the preface to the Gospel which in many respects, as we have seen, applies much more directly to the Gospel than to Acts. We have to acknowledge it as a possibility (at least as far as preface-convention is concerned) that Luke did not have the narrative of Acts immediately in mind when he wrote Luke 1.1–4.

7

PREFACES IN HELLENISTIC JEWISH LITERATURE

A stylistic hybrid?

We are now in a position to see in what respects Luke's preface approaches those of the scientific writers. In structure, it is remarkably close; its linguistic usages are of a broadly similar type, and many of its concepts and key words can be elucidated from the conventions of scientific prefaces. Moreover, there are points where it is clear that Luke fits specifically into the practice of the later scientific writers rather than the earlier, that is into the conventional pattern of the Greco-Roman period rather than that of the hellenistic. These points include the brevity and compression of Luke's preface; the placing of the vocative; the lack of specific information about the subject of the book; the use of the opening clause to refer to predecessors rather than to the disposition of the dedicatee; and the use of *autoptai*. Within that later group, Luke's preface may be distinguished from the more extravagant examples of the genre (Erotian, Thessalus, Artemidorus): his language is simple and modest, and there are no excessive claims. Probably the closest parallel overall is with the prefaces of Hero of Alexandria, which date from around AD 70 – which is, of course, well within the range of dates probable for Luke's literary activity.

There are, however, as we have seen, points in the Lucan preface which do not fit into the pattern of scientific preface-convention. The choice of πεπληροφορημένων cannot be explained by reference to scientific convention; the underlying idea here seems to be a Christian one, as again with ὑπηρέται τοῦ λόγου. But these features are no more explicable by reference to any other point on the Greek cultural axis: they are equally far away from the conventions of Greek historical literature, and do not recall any of the characteristic terms used in pagan religious propaganda.

Luke's preface may thus be described as a stylistic hybrid: wholly

Greek in structure and largely Greek in content, it yet contains elements which are irreducibly (if not explicitly) Christian. Moreover, it is attached to a narrative whose tone is emphatically biblical and whose message is clearly religious. This combination of secular Greek preface-convention and biblical narrative immediately calls to mind the literature of hellenistic Judaism, where we find a comparable mixture: biblical narrative or discourse is embellished with stylistic features reminiscent of Greek literature. Among these hellenistic Jewish texts are a number of formal prefaces clearly influenced by Greek preface-convention. Could Luke have derived his knowledge of Greek preface-conventions, as he did so much else, from the Greek Bible and kindred texts?

The suggestion is an attractive one. We have already noted certain verbal similarities: the use of ἡμῖν in Luke 1.1 is paralleled in Josephus (above ch. 6 s.v.); the word διήγησις is used in the opening sentence of the *Letter of Aristeas*; and κατηχέω appears in a letter from Agrippa quoted by Josephus (above ch. 6 s.v.). Parallels from Josephus, II Maccabees and the preface to the Greek ben Sira are noted by several commentators (ch. 1 n. 18). Moreover, there is something very persuasive about an hypothesis which so effectively limits the number of extraneous literary influences on the evangelist. It is fairly clear that Luke read the Greek Bible and used it as a stylistic model for the narrative which begins at Luke 1.5. It would be a neat and economical conclusion if we could demonstrate that the Greek Bible – or some related text from the world of hellenistic Judaism – also provided the model for the prefaces to the Gospel and Acts. In this chapter we shall examine each of these prefaces in turn.

II Maccabees 2.19–32

The earliest Greek-style preface in the Greek Bible is the one composed by the anonymous epitomator who created II Maccabees out of the five-volume narrative of Jason of Cyrene (2.23). This preface appears in the present text at II Maccabees 2.19–32; the text as it stands begins with two letters addressed to the Jews in Egypt from Jerusalem (1.1–9, 1.10–2.18). Neither mentions the book itself: they are concerned to commend the observation of the Feast of Tabernacles (1.9, 1.18) and the celebration of the purification of the Temple (1.18, 2.16–18). No manuscripts transmit the text without these letters, which must have been attached at an early stage. The status of 2.19–32 as a 'preface' is thus ambiguous: though clearly prefatorial in content, it does not actually stand at the beginning of the work, in the proper prefatorial position.

Demarcation

The preface is a self-contained unit, clearly marked off from the beginning of the text by a transition-formula (2.32) which makes a piquant link between the rhetorical ideal of brevity and the aims of the epitomator: 'it is truly stupid to expatiate in introducing a history and then cut short (ἐπιτεμεῖν) the history itself' (tr. Moffatt). The preface is in fact 14 verses long, more than four times the length of Luke's in the *Jerusalem Bible* layout. The book ends with a brief epilogue (15.37–9).

Personalization

Although the narrative of II Maccabees normally uses the third person, in the preface the epitomator speaks of himself in the first-person plural (verses 23, 25, 27, 32), slipping into the first-person singular at verse 29. The first person recurs at points of transition in the narrative (10.10) and in the brief epilogue (15.37–9). There is no second-person address.

Structure and content

(a)   The long opening sentence (verses 19–23) gives a detailed list of the contents of the book, syntactically presented as the object of the literary activity of Jason and his epitomator. This inevitably results in a clumsy sentence, recalling the overlong list of contents in Ps.-Scymnus 69–97 (an epitome of comparable date).

(b)   The author's purpose is outlined in verses 24–5 in terms of the difficulty of Jason's original and the advantages which will accrue to prospective readers from the epitome, a seductive cocktail of 'entertainment' (ψυχαγωγία), 'ease' (εὐκοπία) and 'usefulness' (ὠφέλεια). This is a neat expression of the 'profit with delight' *topos*, which is a commonplace of ancient literary theory, discussed among poets (cf. Horace, *Ars poetica* 343–4) and historians.[1] Ps.-Scymnus

---

[1]   On the Horace passage, see C. O. Brink, *Horace on Poetry: The 'Ars Poetica'* (Cambridge University Press, 1971) pp. 352–8. Brink traces the *topos* back to 'poetic

92–3 echoes the same theme: as a geographical epitome written in verse, he considers his work to be an ideal combination of 'pleasure' and 'usefulness'. But the scientific writers in general are keener to stress the 'usefulness' of their work as a purely utilitarian ideal (cf. above ch. 5 p. 97); as Vitruvius puts it (V pref. 1–2), a work on architecture cannot hope to 'captivate' or 'delight' the reader in the way that history and poetry naturally do.[2]

(c)   Another favourite preface-*topos* appears in verses 26–8, where the author describes his work as 'a matter of sweat and sleepness nights': compare Janson on this theme in later Latin prefaces (1964, pp. 97, 147–8.). Janson in fact attributes the creation of the word used by our epitomator, ἀγρυπνία, to the Alexandrian poet Callimachus (p. 97).[3] The theme is reinforced by a simile which makes a comparison with the selfless labour of the host who prepares the dinner-party (συμπόσιον) for the good of his guests (verse 27).

(d)   A reminder of the nature of the work (verse 28) ushers in another poetic simile (verse 29) in which the epitomator is likened to a house-decorator, whose job is only to embellish, in contrast with the builder who is responsible for the underlying structure of the new house. The point of the comparison becomes clear in verses 30–1: it is a rather convoluted form of self-deprecation which allows the author simultaneously to profess a becoming modesty about his own abilities and to forestall any criticism of the substance of his work. Perhaps for this reason, there is no attempt to claim any special aptitude as an historian: our author's only object is to

theory in the Hellenistic age', cf. Neoptolemos of Parium *ap.* Philodem., *Poem.* V 13.8ff. (cf. *Prol.* 55 (Neopt. no. 10), 128f., 135); καὶ πρὸς ἀρετὴν δεῖν τῷ τελείῳ ποιητῇ μετὰ τῆς ψυχαγωγίας τοῦ τοὺς ἀκούοντας ὠφελεῖν καὶ χρησιμολογεῖν. Eratosthenes, according to Strabo, held that poets were only interested in ψυχαγωγία (Strabo I 2.3 (15–16)). For the debate in the historians, see Avenarius, 1956, pp. 13–29; Herkommer, 1968, pp. 128–36, esp. p. 128 n. 1 and p. 135 n. 5. Polybius was particularly fond of 'the rhetorical contrast between χρήσιμον and τερπνόν, cf. I 4.11; VII 7.8; IX 2.6; XI 19a.1–3; XV 36.3; XXXI 30.1' (Walbank, 1972, p. 6 n. 24; further, pp. 34–40).

[2] Vitruvius V pref. 1–2 (tr. Morgan): 'Writing on architecture is not like history or poetry. History is captivating to the reader from its very nature; for it holds out the hope of various novelties. Poetry, with its measures and metrical feet, its refinement in the arrangement of words, and the delivery in verse of the sentiments expressed by the several characters to one another, delights the feelings of the reader, and leads him smoothly on to the very end of the work. But this cannot be the case with architectural treatises . . . '

[3] Paul uses the noun twice in the rhetorical 'boasting' passages of II Cor. 6.5 and 11.27. But clearly by the first century AD the related verb had a wider range of uses: cf. Mk. 13.33, Lk. 21.36, Eph. 6.18, Heb. 13.17.

abbreviate. This feature too can be paralleled in later Latin prefaces, particularly in epitomes: compare Janson, 1964, 151–2.

Language and style

This preface contains scarcely a trace of the themes familiar to us from scientific prefaces, beyond the listing of contents and the 'decision to write' (πειρασόμεθα verse 23) which are of course found in many different types of literature. The preface contains a number of literary *topoi* which are not found in scientific prefaces, as well as the two similes (with a third in the epilogue) and a range of vocabulary which mark it out as distinctly more poetic in tone than most of the prefaces we have studied. Despite his literary pretensions, however, the author's scope and subject-matter are explained clearly and unambiguously: unlike Luke, he makes no attempt to conceal the fundamentally religious character of his work (cf. verse 22).

Ecclesiasticus: the Wisdom of Jesus ben Sira

It was the Greek translator of ben Sira's wisdom, the author's grandson according to his own story (Prol. 7), who added a Greek preface to the text to explain his reasons for publishing the work and the difficulties encountered in translation. Not all the manuscripts and versions contain the prologue as we find it in our texts: it is missing in Armenian and Ethiopic, and in a number of minuscules.[4] In 248 it is replaced by an entirely unrelated 'prologue',[5] a third-person narrative which gives a number of biographical details about the translator and his grandfather. In this alternative prologue, the date of the translator is determined very roughly in terms of biblical chronology ('after the captivity and return, and after almost all the prophets'), and there is a noticeable concern to establish a reliable chain of tradition. Thus we are told that the book was entrusted to the younger Jesus by his father Sira, who had in turn received it from his father Jesus; Jesus himself compiled it out of the *apophthegmata* of earlier sages as well as out of his own wisdom; and he was a 'follower' of Solomon, with whom his wisdom is compared.

---

[4] J. Ziegler (ed.), *Sapientia Iesu Filii Sirach* (Göttingen Septuagint vol. XII, 2, Göttingen, Vandenhoeck und Ruprecht, 1965) *ad loc.*. The preface was also missing in the tenth-century 443, but was added by a later hand.

[5] Ibid. p. 127.

Despite the author's command of Greek (note the poetic ὀπαδός), this bears no resemblance to the first-person prefaces we have been studying: it recalls rather the biographical annotations found in the manuscripts of many classical authors, and is probably Byzantine.

Demarcation

The translator's preface is clearly demarcated from the text itself both in style and in content: the change to a biblical 'proverb' style at 1.1ff. is very striking after the three long and convoluted Greek periods of the preface.

Personalization

The preface is written in the first person, though only the last sentence (27–36) concerns the translator himself; the first sentence (1–14) oddly describes not the author's own 'decision to write' but that of his grandfather. There is no dedication, but there is a direct exhortation to the readers (plural) in line 15.

Structure and content

(a)   The first sentence (1–14) begins with a ponderous genitive absolute (Πολλῶν καὶ μεγάλων ...) extolling in the most general terms the magnitude of the biblical wisdom tradition (1–3) and its usefulness both for its readers and for 'those outside' (4–6). This provides both the justification for the author's project and his subject-matter: at this point the author introduces his grandfather as the subject of a classic 'decision' sentence (above ch. 5, pp. 70–1). The decision forms the main verb of the sentence (12: προήχθη καὶ αὐτὸς συγγράψαι); the author's qualifications precede this verb in the form of a participial clause (7: δούς); and the sentence closes with a purpose-clause detailing the advantages which the project is designed to ensure for the *philomatheis* (13–14).

(b)   The second sentence (15–26) makes a direct appeal for the goodwill and attention of the readers, who are asked to pardon any shortcomings in the translation. The author's remarks on the difficulty of achieving 'dynamic equivalence' (21: ἰσοδυναμεῖ) in translating from Hebrew to Greek are individual and fascinating, but the motif of asking the reader to pardon any failure in the books is a commonplace in later Latin prefaces.[6] The general tone here, however, recalls not so much the characteristic modesty of the preface-writer as the exhortations of the preacher and religious teacher: note παρακέκλησθε (15).

(c) In a final sentence (27–35) which mirrors the structure of the first, the author explains his arrival in Egypt (27–9), his 'decision' (30: ἀναγκαιότατον ἐθέμην καὶ αὐτός) to undertake the work of translation (30–1), the skill and hard work involved (32), and the purpose of the enterprise (33–5). The theme of 'sleepless nights' (32: ἀγρυπνία) is a preface-*topos* which also appears in II Maccabees 2.26 (p. 150 above). The purpose-clause echoes that of the opening sentence: compare τοῖς ... βουλομένοις φιλομαθεῖν (34) with ὅπως οἱ φιλομαθεῖς (13) and ἐννόμως βιοτεύειν (35) with διὰ τῆς ἐννόμου βιώσεως (14).

Style and language

Ben Sira's grandson is less influenced by Greek literary convention than is the epitomator of II Maccabees, a fact which probably relates to the respective genres of the two works: the historical epitome is a recognizable genre in terms of Greek literature, while a biblical wisdom-text like ben Sira's is not. Nevertheless, this preface has a distinctively 'Alexandrian' style which is certainly not biblical, and which probably reflects a characteristic style of Greek which has become naturalized in the Jewish community of Alexandria. It is 'Alexandrian' in its rich and varied vocabulary, including the Calli-machean ἀγρυπνία; unlike Luke, it is openly religious, but has developed its own *Greek* vocabulary for distinctively Jewish relig-ious ideals (14, 35), while cheerfully taking over *topoi* and phrase-ologies more widespread in Greek scholastic literature. These linguistic phenomena raise the question of the existence of Alexan-drian Jewish 'schools' of wisdom offering a Jewish *paideia* parallel to that of the Greek schools: note that ben Sira claims to have found his grandfather's book in Alexandria, not in Palestine.

Ben Sira's prologue, despite its lack of a dedication, is compar-able in some respects with the 'scientific' prefaces studied. The struc-

6 Janson, 1964, pp. 124–41. Note the difference here, though: later Christian writers excuse the deficiencies of their Greek on the grounds of over-immersion in Hebrew or in the stylistically deficient Christian Scriptures, whereas ben Sira is more concerned that his Greek translation will not do justice to the force of the Hebrew original.

ture of the two 'decision' sentences can easily be paralleled (cf. above ch. 6 on Luke 1.3): as we noted in the case of Luke, even the language of 'necessity' which the writer uses here (verse 30), and which is so familiar in Greek prefaces, takes us outside the normal linguistic register of the Greek Bible. The final purpose-clause in each sentence may also be paralleled without difficulty (cf. above ch. 6 on Luke 1.4); as in Hero, this clause, which often referred to the beneficial results to be gained from the book by the dedicatee, is redirected to the readers in general. The description of these readers as *philomatheis* is also interesting: compare ch. 5 p. 100 on this term in scientific prefaces. As with II Maccabees, there is no attempt to hide the distinctively religious and Jewish nature of the subject-matter: on the contrary, the preface is openly laudatory of Israel's wisdom-traditions (verse 1).

The 'Letter of Aristeas'

As is widely recognized, the common name is a misnomer: the 'Letter' is in fact a dedicated treatise, addressed throughout to the fictive author's brother Philocrates. Most accept, following Bickermann,[7] that the real date of the treatise is between 145 and 100 BC. Little attention has been given to the question of genre. The work is generally categorized as 'apologetic' and 'propaganda' for the LXX, or for some other cause.[8] However, Bickermann (*op. cit.* n. 7) points out that the story of the translation of the Septuagint is assumed rather than described; the tale is told briefly in the last seven chapters of the book, and 'Aristeas' devotes substantially more time to the geography of Jerusalem and Palestine, the description of the treasures and the sympotic questioning of the Jewish sages. As Bickermann observes, all this has the flavour of the 'traveller's tales' or 'exotica' popular in the hellenistic period. The fictive setting evokes the more novelistic 'court tales' of Jewish literature (Nehemiah, Daniel, Esther, Joseph and Aseneth), where a prominent Diaspora figure is accepted at the court of a pagan king and exploits his position in the Jewish cause: in this case, however, the narrator (and successful courtier) is presented not as a Jew but as a

[7] E. Bickermann, 'Zur Datierung des Pseudo-Aristeas', ZNTW 29 (1930) pp. 280–98, pp. 289–93.

[8] For a survey of recent suggestions as to the *Tendenz* of 'Aristeas', see W. Schmidt, *Untersuchungen zur Fälschung historischer Dokumente bei Pseudo-Aristaios* (Bonn, Habelt Verlag, 1986), pp. 11–13.

Gentile sympathizer, and the Jewish wisdom which sweeps all before it is ascribed not to him but to the seventy sages whom he is instrumental in bringing to Egypt.

The audience of the book is equally uncertain: Greeks, Jews, or a combination of both at the Ptolemaic court have all been suggested (see n. 8). It is widely agreed, however, that Alexandria provides the real-life backdrop for the book as well as its fictive setting.

Demarcation

The preface (chs. 1–8) is marked off from the main narrative by a formulaic transitional phrase similar to that of II Macc. 2.32: 'But lest we create mere idle chatter by prolonging the introduction, we shall press on to the continuous part of the narrative' (§8).

Personalization

The narrator speaks in the first person in the preface, and the first-person narrative continues throughout the treatise. The second-person address to Philocrates is classically placed after the first two words of the opening sentence, and is recalled at §§120 and 295 and in the Epilogue at §322.

Structure and content

(a) The content of the first sentence (§§1–2) is classic for a dedicated preface of the hellenistic period: the main verb expressing the author's decision in a conventionally modest form ('I have tried to set [it] out clearly for you') is surrounded by a nest of subordinate clauses. The decision rests first on the noteworthiness of the subject-matter ('Αξιολόγου ... συνεσταμένης), secondly on the disposition of the dedicatee, which is mentioned twice (διὰ τὸ σέ ... διὰ τί and κατειληφὼς ἣν ἔχεις φιλομαθῆ διάθεσιν ...). (Note φιλομαθῆ.) The latter point is amplified by a poetic citation, expanded with a brief allusion to the familiar distinction between first-hand experience and *historia*. The awkwardness of the opening clause[9] may indeed be partially explained by the conventional nature of these phrases: our author is aware that both points can be made at the

---

[9] G. Zuntz, 'Zum Aristeas-Text', *Philologus* 102 (1958), pp. 240–6, repr. in *Opuscula Selecta* (Manchester University Press, 1972), pp. 102–9, p. 107.

beginning of a preface, but is not quite sure how to combine them neatly.

(b)   The opening clause leaves the reader in little doubt about the religious subject-matter of the narrative ('our visit to Eleazar the high priest of the Jews'), and the second sentence underlines this: the *philomatheia* which our author values has a lot to do with εὐσέβεια, 'piety' (§2).[10]

(c)   'Aristeas' then proceeds to a personal narration (§§3–4) which sets the scene for the story which follows. Perhaps the closest parallel to this in the texts we have studied is in the anecdotal 'discovery-narratives' which occur in the letters of Archimedes and Apollonius of Perge: these did not become a regular feature of scientific preface-convention, but interestingly they are of approximately the same date as the fictional date of 'Aristeas', and (at least in the case of Archimedes) they also have an Alexandrian connection. Here the narration also has the advantage of highlighting indirectly both the pious disposition of the narrator and his first-hand knowledge of the material he is about to relate.

(d)   The disposition of the dedicatee is highlighted again (§§5–6), both in terms of his interest in Jewish Law and in terms of a favourable inclination towards the Jews themselves, which may be linked to the efforts of 'Aristeas' on behalf of the Jewish captives (§§12–27). In §7 a second, simpler 'decision-sentence' (δέον ἐστὶ μεταδιδόναι) relates the whole enterprise directly to the *philomatheia* of the dedicatee, in which he is treated as representative of 'all like-minded persons'.

(e)   The preface finishes with a rather trite observation on the relative usefulness (ὠφέλεια) of education (παιδεία) and gold (§8).

Language and style

The demarcation between preface and text is not so clear at the stylistic level as it is with ben Sira: the Greek of 'Aristeas' is of a piece throughout the treatise. The author writes a good literary *Koine* reminiscent of the language of Polybius, Diodorus Siculus and Plutarch, showing a typically hellenistic love of double compounds, and with some vernacular and documentary elements to

[10]   A. Pelletier, *Lettre d'Aristée à Philocrate* (Sources chrétiennes 89, Paris, Ed. du Cerf, 1962), pp. 101–2 n. 4.

which papyri and inscriptions provide the best parallels.[11] Nevertheless there are linguistic 'clusters' which mark out the preface and other transitional passages: 'in the Preface and Epilogue certain words and phrases are repeated, suggesting either that the Epilogue echoes the language of the Prologue, or, what is more probable, that some of the terms common to both are used in a semi-technical sense, having become more or less fixed by conventional usage'.[12] As Zuntz observes, it is in these passages that the limits of our author's stylistic competence become clear: 'in the attempt to reproduce with full rhetorical *éclat* the traditional commonplaces of a literary Prooemium ... the narrow limits of his stylistic abilities make themselves painfully clear'.[13]

A marked feature of the preface is its heavy insistence on piety: *philomatheia* here gains a distinctively Jewish colouring as it is interpreted in terms of devotion to the Law and hence to 'divine things' (§3). We have observed a similar phenomenon in *Ecclesiaticus*. Unlike ben Sira's grandson, however, this author has a clear sense of writing for a non-Jewish audience, at least in the fictive person of Aristeas, which gives his religious vocabulary a peculiar twist (see esp. §§15–18).[14] In the preface, this results in the use of language characteristic of Greek rather than Jewish piety: εὐσέβειαν (§2), σεμνότητα (§5).

Philo of Alexandria

Wilhelm Bousset observed long ago that the Philonic corpus bears many resemblances to the school literature of the hellenistic world.[15] It is therefore no surprise to find that the corpus exhibits a number of similarities to Greek school literature in the matter of prefaces.

First, a significant number of treatises have no prefaces at all. Most of the texts in the *Allegory of the Laws* have no prefatory material, but begin *in medias res* with the biblical *lemma* which

[11] H. G. Meecham, *The Letter of Aristeas* (Manchester University Press, 1935), pp. 49–50, 161–3.

[12] Ibid. p. 163.

[13] Zuntz (as cited in n. 9 above) p. 107, my trans.

[14] Shutt's translation in J. Charlesworth (ed.), *The OT Pseudepigrapha* (Doubleday, New York, 1985), p. 13 is seriously misleading at this point.

[15] Wilhelm Bousset, *Jüdisch-christlicher Schulbetrieb in Alexandria und Rom* (Göttingen, Vandenhoeck and Ruprecht, 1915), pp. 1–7.

forms the first exegetical subject of the text.[16] The *De opificio mundi*, which may well have functioned as an introduction to the more accessible *Exposition of the Laws*,[17] begins with a more general philosophical introduction (§§1–12), but there is no separate personal preface.

Secondly, Philo makes extensive use of summary and recapitulation sentences. As we have shown above, (ch. 4 p. 45), the use of these *proektheses* to link succeeding works in a school corpus is common from the fourth century BC onwards, and predates the appearance of the personal prefaces which formed the subject of our study in chapters 4 and 5. About two-thirds of Philo's treatises begin with a sentence of this type.[18]

Personal prefaces, on the other hand, are rare in the corpus. Only one of the surviving treatises bears a dedication, and that is the youthful *That Every Good Man is Free* (*Quod omnis probus*); it is fair to assume that its lost predecessor, *That Every Bad Man is a Slave* was also dedicated to Theodotus. It is worth noting that Philo's only dedicated writing is untypical of his work in many aspects: it is a philosophical treatment of a well-known Stoic paradox, and contains only five biblical allusions (LCL vol. IX p. 5). The most developed of Philo's prefaces is that of the encomiastic *De vita Mosis* I, which may well have been intended for a more general audience.[19]

Demarcation

There is no stylistic change between introductory sentences and discourse, and in most cases the introductory sentence leads directly into the exposition. In the *De vita Mosis*, however, a transitional formula marks the beginning of the discourse proper (§5).

[16] No preface: *Opif., Leg. All., Cher., Sacr., Quod det., Post., Gig., Quod Deus., Agr., Migr., Congr., Fuga, Mut.*

[17] Cf. *De Abrahamo* 1, with Colson's note (LCL vol. VI p. ix note a); E. R. Goodenough, *An Introduction to Philo Judaeus*, 2nd edn (Oxford, Basil Blackwell, 1962), pp. 35–8.

[18] Cf. e.g. *De sobrietate* 1, *De plantatione, De ebrietate, De confusione linguarum, Quis rerum div.heres, De somniis* I and II, *De Abrahamo, De Josepho, De vita Mosis* II, *De decalogo, De spec. leg.* I, II, III (ch. 2), IV, *De virtutibus, De praemiis, De vita contemplativa.*

[19] E. R. Goodenough, 'Philo's Exposition of the Law and his De Vita Mosis', *HTR* 26 (1933), pp. 109–25; *idem, An Introduction to Philo Judaeus*, 2nd edn (Oxford, Basil Blackwell, 1962), pp. 33–5; S. Sandmel, *Philo of Alexandria: an Introduction* (Oxford/New York, Oxford University Press, 1979), p. 47.

Personalization

Philo favours an impersonal style of exposition, with free use of impersonal verbs and passives, and his *proektheses* tend to follow this style (e.g. *De confling.*), interspersed with the occasional routine first-person plural (e.g. *Quis heres?*). First-person singular is rare but does occur, e.g. at *De Josepho* 1, *De vita Mosis* II 3. Both the *Quod omnis probus* and the *De vita Mosis* I have a noticeably higher proportion of first-person singular forms than is usual for Philo. The second-person address in the *Quod omnis probus* is inserted classically after the first six words, but the dedication has no further effect on the treatise.

Structure and content

(a) *Quod omnis probus.* In content, Philo's only dedicated preface is no more than a rather flowery *proekthesis* marking the transition to the second of two books: 'The present treatise is closely akin to [the former], its full brother, indeed we may say its twin' (tr. Colson). Like Luke and many other writers, Philo describes the previous work as a λόγος (cf. above ch. 6 on Acts 1.1); unlike Luke, he uses the classically correct πρότερος rather than the debased πρῶτος.

(b) *De vita Mosis.* This preface makes no reference to other works in the corpus, but introduces the subject directly and aggressively, praising Moses (§§1–2) and attacking the Greek writers who have misrepresented him (§§2–3). Philo's own account will be be based on his own learning, 'both from the sacred books ... and from some of the elders of the nation; for I always interwove what I was told with what I read, and thus believed myself to have a closer knowledge than others of my nation's history' (§4). Despite some similarities in content (decision to write; predecessors; author's qualifications), this preface bears only the slightest resemblance in form to the prefaces we have found in scientific texts.

Language

Philo is master of a much more complex Greek style than most of the scientific writers studied, and his prefaces can at times verge on the flowery, with rhetorical *variatio* (aided by a copious and recondite vocabulary) at a premium. Generally speaking, however, his recapitulations use the familiar lexical stock for such sentences, with a wide variety of multiple compound verbs for 'writing up' or 'recounting' and a varied repertoire of standard phrases for presentation. Noteworthy are:

> deprecatory phrases: ὅσα καιρὸς ἦν (*Plant.* 1); ὡς οἷόν τε ἦν (*Ebr.* 1, *Abr.* 1, cf. *Plant.* 1, *Somn.* I 1); ὡς ἐνῆν (*Quis rerum* 1); ὅσα καίρια (*Virt.* 1), cf. *Spec. leg.* II 262; ὡς γε ἐμαυτὸν πειθω (*Spec.leg.* IV 1).
>
> concern for order: κατὰ τὸ ἑξῆς (*Jos.* 1); κατὰ τὰ ἀκόλουθα ἑξῆς (*Dec.* 1); ἀκολουθίᾳ τῆς πραγματείας ἑπόμενος (*Vit. cont.* 1); cf. the use of προσαρμόττειν (*Sobr.* 1) and ἐφαρμόττοντες (*Spec.leg.* II 1), and the frequent use of σύνταξις and its verb (e.g. *Vit. Mos.* II 1).
>
> concern for accuracy: the *akribēs* word-group is common, e.g. *Quis rerum* 1, *Abr.* 1, *Dec.* 1, *Spec. leg* I 1.

There may be an echo of the familiar courtesies of hellenistic patronage in the puzzling φιλομαθοῦς ἐπιστήμης of *Dec.* 1.[20]

Josephus

Josephus writes as a historian in the classic Greek manner of Polybius and Thucydides, and in that respect many aspects of his prefaces fall under the historiographical conventions discussed in chapter 3. However, he has been cited by a number of authorities as a possible model for the Lucan preface (ch. 1 n. 18), and for that reason it is worth returning to these prefaces briefly to ask what formal points of comparison there are.

Demarcation

Josephus' prefaces are clearly demarcated from their texts, often with a simple transitional sentence to mark the beginning of the text (*Antiquities* I 26; *BJ* I 30). The *Bellum Judaicum* has a general introduction (I 1–16), followed by summary of contents (I 17–30). There is an epilogue of two sentences at the end of Book VII

---

[20] On *philomatheia*, see above ch. 5 p. 100. The whole phrase looks like a rather convoluted Philonic form of the common courtesies of a dedicated preface, adapted for general use. On the difficulties of the phrase, see Colson's notes, LCL vol. VII p. 7 note c and on p. 609.

(454–5), reasserting the accuracy and truthfulness of the narrative and deprecating any deficiencies of style. Intervening books have no prefaces. The *Antiquities* has an introduction of a similar length (I 1–26). Subsequent books have no prefaces, but the whole ends with a brief one-sentence epilogue (with address) which is a simple closing-formula (see (b) below). The two books of the *Contra Apionem* have shorter prefaces (I 1–5; II 1–7), and each ends with a single-sentence epilogue.

Personalization

(a) First person. When speaking as the author in his preface, Josephus follows the classical historiographical convention by giving his own name (*BJ* I 3, cf. above ch. 3 pp. 27–7); unlike Thucydides and Herodotus, however, he uses the first person for this *sphragis* as he does throughout the preface. Later in the narrative the third person is used when the author appears as a character (e.g. *BJ* II 568–646): there are no 'we-passages' in Josephus. For the *Antiquities* this ancient convention is unnecessary: although the narrative is largely impersonal, authorial interjections using the first person occur occasionally (e.g. *Antiquities* I 29). The *Life* and the *Contra Apionem* use the first person throughout.

(b) Second person. Histories were not dedicated, and Josephus does not break the formal convention on this point (see above ch. 3 pp. 27–9). Thus the *Bellum Judaicum*, the most self-consciously Thucydidean of his works, contains no hint of a dedication. In the *Antiquities*, which fall rather into the category of 'archaeology',[21] Josephus' patron Epaphroditus does make an appearance in the preface (I 8–9). But even here Josephus is reluctant to break with convention and address Epaphroditus directly in the second person; the third person is used throughout, and it is only at the end of the *Life*, which formed an appendix to the *Antiquities*, that we learn that the whole work was actually dedicated to him: 'Having here, most excellent Epaphroditus, rendered you a complete account of our antiquities, I shall here for the present conclude my narrative' (*Life* 430, tr. Thackeray).

The only dedicated prefaces in Josephus are therefore those of the *Contra Apionem*, which are also addressed to Epaphroditus. In both cases the opening sentence takes the form of a resumptive summary

[21] For the distinction, cf. Momigliano, 1969, pp. 3–5.

of previous works, with the vocative inserted after ten words (Book
I) or six words (Book II). Note the variation in epithet between
κράτιστε and τιμιώτατε. The effect of the dedication on the content
of these addressed prefaces is minimal. It is interesting, however, to
find some of the conventional courtesies of dedication appearing at
Ant. I 8–9: the disposition and learning of the dedicatee are familiar
to us from scientific writers, but the twin themes of the reluctance of
the author and his yielding to persuasion are more characteristic of
Latin prefaces (Janson (1964) pp. 27–8, 53, 117–20), and perhaps
show the force of Roman influence on Josephus.

Structure and content

A full-scale analysis of Josephus' prefaces is impossible here. We
can note, however, the appearance of a number of well-known
preface-topics.

(a)   The magnitude of the subject. This central *topos* of historical
prefaces is used to create a striking opening to the preface of the
Bellum Judaicum (I 1,45). Cf. above, ch. 3 p. 31.

(b)   In the *Bellum Judaicum*, Josephus stresses his own experience as
a major qualification for writing (I 2–3, 18), and this is repeated in
more polemical terms in *Antiquities* I 4, in *Contra Apionem* I 53–6,
and in *Life* 357–67. It is only in the latter two places that we learn of
Josephus's reliance on the *hypomnēmata* (*commentarii*) of the Roman
commanders (*Life* 358, *Contra Apionem* I 56): in the *Bellum Judaicum*
itself, in true Thucydidean fashion, Josephus highlights personal
involvement in events rather than documentary research.[22] Even in
the preface to the more 'archaeological' *Antiquities*, documentary
authentication is little in evidence: unlike Philo (*De vita Mosis* I 4),
Josephus does not here stress his qualifications for the task in terms of
priestly tradition or access to archives. See further above, ch. 5
pp. 78–87 on the different ways in which this theme is treated in historical and antiquarian works and in the scientific tradition.

(c)   Predecessors. Polemic against other writers forms a substantial
topic of all the prefaces. In the *Bellum Judaicum* Josephus' predecessors are introduced after the opening theme of the magnitude
of the subject, as the grammatical subject of the opening Ἐπειδή

[22] Cf. Thackeray (LCL vol. II p. xix): 'The *War* contains no allusions to authorities such as are interspersed throughout the *Antiquities*.'

clause (I 1–2); he reverts to the theme at I 6–8. The *Antiquities* begins with a grandiose general statement about 'Those who essay to write histories' whose relevance to Josephus himself only becomes clear at I 4. The *Contra Apionem*, on the other hand, is polemical in tone throughout: the attack on other writers occupies the foreground through much of the preface, and is continued through both books.

(d)   Author's decision. The 'decision' sentence which we have found to be so common among scientific writers is also found in Josephus' prefaces, though it does not dominate them. The long opening sentence of the *Bellum Judaicum* is of the structure 'Since others have written about the war of the Jews against the Romans, I decided (προυθέμην ἐγώ) to tell the tale (ἀφηγήσασθαι) . . .' (I 1–3). Inserted participial clauses convey additional information about the magnitude of the war, the inadequacies of the competition, the translation of the original Aramaic edition, and the author's personal experience of the events of the war. The historiographical *sphragis* or author's name is rather clumsily attached to this first-person 'decision'. Clearly this complicated sentence bears some relationship to the prefaces we have studied; in fact its extreme awkwardness seems to result from the half-hearted blending of two distinct types of literary convention, deriving respectively from 'history' proper and from the broader, Aristotelian *historia*-tradition. There is another recognizable 'decision-sentence' at *Contra Apionem* I 2–3: 'Since I observe that a considerable number of persons (ἐπεὶ δὲ συχνοὺς ὁρῶ) . . ., I consider it my duty to devote a brief treatise to all these points . . .'

Language and style

Thackeray's judgement on the style of the *Bellum Judaicum* is worth quoting in full:

> The style is an excellent specimen of the Atticistic Greek fashionable in the first century . . . A choice vocabulary, well-knit sentences and paragraphs, niceties in the use of particles and in the order of words, a uniformly classical style but without slavish imitation of classical models, these and other excellences tax and often defy the powers of a translator. Writing for educated [Greek and Roman] readers, Josephus boasts of having immersed himself in

> Greek literature and taken extraordinary pains to cultivate
> style.   (*Josephus* vol. II (LCL) pp. xiii–xiv, referring
>   to *Antiquities* XX 263 and XIV 2)

The avoidance of hiatus is a particularly marked feature of the
Bellum (ibid.). These features suggested to Thackeray that we
should take seriously Josephus' own admission that he had used
'assistants for the sake of the Greek' (*Contra Apionem* I 50).
Whether we accept this at face value or not, it is a testimony to the
difficulty of large-scale composition in literary Greek for a first-
century Jew, and to the high level which is achieved in these texts.
Even in the *Antiquities* there is a clear predilection for literary
language and classical allusion, and the *Contra Apionem* exhibits
'choice diction, recondite classical lore, and excellent arrangement
of subject-matter' (Thackeray, *Josephus* vol. II (LCL) p. xv). On the
'Atticism' of Josephus, see further Pelletier, 1962.

It follows that there is no clear stylistic demarcation between the
prefaces and the texts to which they are attached. The prefaces share
in a level of linguistic sophistication which clearly outshines that of
the majority of the authors studied (Galen and Hermogenes perhaps
being the closest parallels). Thus even when we have an apparent
parallel to Luke in content or structure (as in the two sentences
analysed above p. 63), the choice of vocabulary and variety of
expression make it impossible to believe that Luke's preface could
be derived directly from Josephus': it is only because of our knowledge of Greek literary conventions on the wider plane that we are
able to recognize any affinity between them.

Conclusions

It must be clear at once, even to the casual reader, that there are
both similarities and differences between Luke's prefaces and those
of the hellenistic Jewish texts studied in this section. What is the best
way of accounting for these similarities and differences?

Do the phenomena support the thesis of direct dependence? Are
the similarities such as to suggest that Luke's preface could be
derived from one or more of these models without recourse to the
wider world of Greek literature? If so, the existence of these prefaces
in the LXX and in other hellenistic Jewish texts could provide a
sufficient explanation for Luke's preface, and we could describe

Luke's adoption of this style simply as copying or direct influence from this text or group of texts.

As we observed above, there is a certain attractive economy about this suggestion: nevertheless, closer examination of the texts shows that it cannot be upheld. When we come down to detail, none of these prefaces is actually very like Luke's. Dedicated prefaces are few and far between in this literature: only 'Aristeas', Philo's *Quod omnis probus*, and Josephus' *Contra Apionem* qualify, and none of them is close enough in language to be a convincing model, quite apart from considerations of date. If we broaden the view to include first-person prefaces without dedication, there are still too many points of dissimilarity to make the hypothesis of direct dependence a plausible one. The similarities which we have noted are chiefly at the level of deep structure, perceptible with hindsight and with our own broader knowledge of Greek prefaces: but it is hard to believe that a reader without that broader knowledge could ignore the many significant differences in vocabulary, in syntax, in content and in style.[23] At most, these prefaces might have served to create a precedent for the idea of using a Greek-style preface for a biblical-style book; but Luke's detailed knowledge of Greek preface-convention must be derived from elsewhere – and once we admit that, we lose the economy of explanation which was a major attraction of the thesis.

But what about a more diffused dependence? Hellenistic Jewish literature was of course much more extensive than the surviving texts, and it is likely that there were other prefaces in texts now lost to us. Could Luke have encountered the conventions we have observed through his reading of this wider body of literature, and perhaps have found a model for his preface in a work now lost? Or should we simply say that since Greek preface-conventions are well entrenched in the judaeo-hellenistic literary tradition in which Luke writes, we need look no further to explain Luke's acquaintance with these conventions? On this analysis, the link which we have postulated with the prefaces of the scientific tradition will be operating at one remove, and Luke's knowledge of this type of preface will have been mediated to him through hellenistic Jewish literature.

This modified form of the thesis is clearly more plausible, and

[23] The uncertain status of the prefaces to ben Sira and II Maccabees should also be borne in mind when assessing the likelihood of Luke's using either or both as a model: see above.

indeed the untestable hypothesis of a lost model makes it technically irrefutable. Even so, detailed consideration of the prefaces we do know suggests that it is not the best way to account for the data. First, it ignores the fact that we have discovered detailed points of similarity between Luke's preface and those of the 'scientific tradition' which are not found in any of the extant hellenistic Jewish prefaces. Greek prefaces are not all the same: there are distinct styles within the broader genre, and Luke's is closest to the particular style which we have called 'scientific'.[24] If Luke's knowledge of Greek convention were mediated through the hellenistic Jewish tradition in general, we should not expect to find that his preface is so unlike the one group and so much closer to the other. It is of course true that the influence of the 'scientific' preface-style can also be seen in some hellenistic Jewish prefaces; but it is significant for our purposes that Luke shows this influence more closely than they do and at different points.

Secondly, it is dangerous to assume that hellenistic Jewish literature itself forms a homogeneous literary tradition. The term is useful as a label; but on the evidence of these prefaces at least, what it seems to cover is a diverse group of Jewish writers whose prefaces plug in to Greek literary convention in different ways. Each writer draws on different aspects of the Greek style according to his time and place, his individual style, and the genre and occasion of his writing. The one point where there is some community of expression which we might label 'hellenistic Jewish' is also one of the major points which Luke does not share with these texts: they show a readiness to use religious language (Jewish or Greek or both) and to be explicit about the Jewish content of their work which contrasts markedly with Luke's muffled allusions to Christian beliefs and institutions.

We would suggest, then, that the most economical explanation for the data is that individual hellenistic Jewish writers drew their knowledge of Greek preface-convention from their own individual contacts with contemporary Greek literature, and that Luke did the same. Inevitably, that makes for a family resemblance: but what we

[24] Generalizations such as that found in P. W. Skehan and A. A. DiLella, *The Wisdom of Ben Sira* (Anchor Bible Commentary, Doubleday, New York, 1987), p. 132 do nothing to advance our understanding of the intricate network of relationships linking the biblical writers with Greek literary culture. As we have endeavoured to demonstrate throughout this study, Herodotus, Thucydides, Polybius, Dioscorides, Hippocrates, Aristeas, Josephus, ben Sira and Luke did not all write the same kind of preface.

are dealing with here is not paternity or maternity but a lateral relationship of siblings or cousins within the wider extended family. And with the benefit of our knowledge of the wider 'family' (in this case, the broad range of Greek prefaces which we have tried to look at in this study),[25] it is possible to see certain smaller family group-ings within the larger kinship-group. In the last analysis, only a thorough reading of a wide range of texts can make a judgement possible, and there will always remain a degree of subjectivity. But viewed against that wider range, Luke's preface-style seems to be more closely related to that of the 'scientific tradition' than it is to that of hellenistic Jewish literature or to any other Greek literary tradition.

One final point. There is a family resemblance between Luke and the hellenistic Jewish writers, and this should warn us to be wary of certain well-worn assumptions of Lucan scholarship, such as the assumption that a writer who adopts a Greek preface-style must be making a direct appeal to the wider cultural world of the Greeks, whether apologetic or polemical. Some hellenistic Jewish writers were of course doing exactly that: Josephus is the prime example among those we have looked at in this chapter. 'Aristeas', likewise, involves a fictional appeal to a non-Jewish audience through the medium of a non-Jewish fictional narrator; and Philo's *De vita Mosis* may have a wider audience in mind that his *Allegory of the Laws* (above n. 19). But the same cannot be said of all the texts reviewed. Neither *Ecclesiasticus* nor II Maccabees shows any sign of being directed at an audience outside the community, despite their Greek prefaces, and the real audience of 'Aristeas' and Philo is as likely to be Jewish as Gentile.[26] It would be well to bear this in mind when we return to the question of Luke's audience in our final chapter.

[25] As we stressed in ch. 2, we have made no attempt to survey all Greek prose prefaces in this study, but have concentrated on those most plausibly cited as parallel to Luke's.
[26] 'Aristeas': see n. 8 above. Philo: Sandmel (see n. 19) p. 47; D. L. Tiede, *The Charismatic Figure as Miracle Worker* (SBLDS 1, 1972), pp. 105–8.

8

THE SOCIAL MATRIX OF LUKE'S PREFACE

Isolated phenomenon or historical pattern?

In an address to the British Academy in 1954, the great papyrologist C. H. Roberts made the observation that the early Christian groups were among the first to use the codex regularly in preference to the roll for substantial texts. Roberts' observation was confirmed by E. G. Turner in 1968 (E. G. Turner, 1968, pp. 10ff.), and is documented more fully in Roberts and Skeat, *The Birth of the Codex* (1987). For the historian of the early church, this observation poses a problem. Is it simply an isolated phenomenon or does it form part of a pattern? And how many such observations do we need before we can reasonably claim to have discovered a historical pattern?

We might compare the position of the historian here with that of an archaeologist faced with a collection of broken potsherds. Reconstruction of a whole pot would be nice, but the archaeologist does not even know at the outset if the fragments in the pile are all part of one pot: they might be the remnants of two or three pots, or be a completely random collection with no links whatever. Thus the archaeologist is not in the position of the jigsaw-doer, who is able to start with the presupposition that all the pieces in the box will make up a single picture. The patterns constructed by the historian, moreover, based as they are on scattered empirical observations, will always fall short of rigorous or final proof; the reconstructed pot may have to be broken and reassembled more than once if new pieces of evidence appear. Nevertheless, as historians we cannot absolve ourselves of the obligation to try to make reconstructions, as sensitively and as economically as we can.

That is the broad obligation which we shall try to discharge in these last two chapters. Our observations about the literary affinities of the Lucan preface present us with a problem analogous to that of the papyrologist – or the archaeologist. We have concluded that Luke's preface is not to be aligned with the prefaces of the Greek historians, but with those of that miscellaneous tradition of technical prose which we have called 'scientific'. By itself, this conclusion is no more than a random item of historical information: we have yet to see whether it can be combined with other pieces of information to create an historical pattern. We begin by surveying a range of data outside the preface, divided roughly into three areas: language; literature; social class and culture. At all levels, we shall argue, it can be seen that our analysis of Luke's opening verses fits into a wider pattern of observations made by others about the early church – including Roberts' observations about the codex, to which we shall return.

Language

Our most accessible data are the New Testament texts themselves and, first of all, the language they are written in. Outside the preface, what kind of Greek does Luke write? It is clear that a high proportion of his vocabulary, as of the whole New Testament, deals with matters of Christian concern and thus constitutes in some sense a 'technical vocabulary' heavily dependent on biblical roots. This is in itself a subject for detailed investigation (cf. Malherbe, 1983, pp. 36–8), but it is not our concern here. Our question is, how is Luke's language to be classified in terms of non-biblical – that is classical and hellenistic – Greek culture?

The Gospels and Acts are manifestly not written in the language of the Greek classics or of the 'belles-lettres' of their day. Since the pioneering studies of A. Deissmann in *Light From the Ancient East*, 1927 (ET Lionel Strachan, 4th edn (rep. Baker Book House, Grand Rapids, Michigan, 1965)) it has been customary to classify the Greek of the New Testament as 'Volkssprache', indeed to regard the New Testament, along with the papyri, as one of our most valuable records of the Greek spoken by ordinary people in the first century. Only relatively recently have scholars begun to refine on that rather over-simplified judgement. First, there is a methodological problem: how can written documents represent the spoken language of the illiterate? In the perceptive words of a recent scholar, 'The "people" itself cannot reproduce "popular speech" in writing: it takes a sharp-eared *littérateur* to convey a true conception of popular syntax and style.'[1] Even the letters and documents preserved in papyrus form, invaluable as they are, cannot be assumed to reveal how ordinary people actually spoke: the really illiterate (as well as the many functional illiterates in ancient society) would have had their letters written for them by a professional letter-writer (E. G. Turner, 1968, pp. 82ff., 130 and notes; further now Harris, 1989).

Secondly, a series of careful linguistic studies on hellenistic Greek have enabled us to refine on Deissmann's division between literary language and 'Volkssprache': see especially Malherbe, 1983, pp. 38–41. Particularly interesting for our study is Lars Rydbeck's work on *Fachprosa, vermeintliche Volkssprache und neues Testament* (Uppsala, 1967) (which I was not aware of until after the completion of my work on scientific prefaces). Rydbeck argues that the language of the New Testament is on the whole representative of the contemporary written *Koine*, a literate but not literary language which even displays some phenomena classified in New Testament studies as 'Semitisms'. Besides the New Testament and the official papyri, the main surviving witness for this language is what Rydbeck calls 'Fachprosa', the language used by scientific and technical writers: that is, the same group whose prefaces we have been analysing.

Rydbeck investigated selected grammatical and semantic phenomena found in all these groups. *Pace* N. Turner (1976, p. 159), his study in no way conflicts with the observation that there are differences in style between one New Testament writer and another: thus, for example, in one case Rydbeck finds (1967, pp. 174ff.) that Luke is closer to the language favoured by officialdom, where Mark is closer to the usage which was standard in classical Greek and remained part of the ordinary spoken language. Rydbeck does not undertake a systematic comparison between Luke and the other evangelists, but he does tend to find Luke's writings particularly full of parallels to the usage of official documents and technical prose (e.g. pp. 39ff., 100ff.); Malherbe (1977, p. 41 n. 28) notes that 'almost half of R.'s references are to Luke and the Acts of the Apostles'. In general, therefore, Rydbeck's study tends to confirm the earlier demonstration of Albert Wifstrand that the linguistic differences between Luke and the other Synoptists do not reveal aspirations towards 'Atticism' or

---

[1] 'Das Volk selbst kann "Volkssprache" schriftlich nicht wiedergeben; nur ein hellhöriger Schönliterat kann eine wahre Auffassung von volkstümlicher Syntax und Stil vermitteln' (Rydbeck, 1967, p. 187 n. 2: my trans.).

'Classicism' on Luke's part: on the contrary, 'the difference ... is that which distinguishes a well-used, careful written language from an everyday and vulgar language'.[2] It is vital not to blur either side of this distinction: the fact that Luke's language manifestly differs from that of his fellow-evangelists does not automatically mean that he is to be placed among the *littérateurs* of his day. It is the distinctive and valuable contribution of these (and other) Swedish scholars to have directed our attention towards a linguistic 'middle zone', a 'Zwischenprosa' which is by no means vulgar, which bears the marks of a well-used written language (it has been called a 'Schreibtischprodukt'),[3] but which is distinct from the literary Greek of the period.

Rydbeck's study does not mention Luke's preface; as he insists, it is concerned with 'linguistic-grammatical facts', not with a 'technical prose *style* as such' (my translation). We may therefore legitimately take his work as independent confirmation for our suggested alignment of Luke with the Greek scientific tradition. If Luke's language in general shows strong affinities with 'technical prose', it is not so strange that his preface too should be best understood in terms of its conventions. At the linguistic level, at least, it looks as if we are not dealing with an isolated phenomenon but with a broader pattern. Moreover, the convergence of these two lines of investigation suggests that the significance of the preface as a piece of 'literary' Greek has been wildly overstated, both in absolute terms and in comparison with the Greek of the New Testament in general. Certainly there is a contrast in style between the preface and the text which follows it, as there is between Luke's language and that of other New Testament writers. But we are beginning to appreciate the importance of locating the various styles of New Testament Greek within a broad linguistic 'middle zone', rather than accepting the fatally attractive polarities of 'Volkssprache' and 'Hochliteratur'.

It is worth considering at this point the related data concerning

[2] A. Wifstrand, *L'Eglise ancienne et la culture grècque* (French trans. by L.-M. Dewailly of *Fornkyrkan och den grekiska Bildningen*, Stockholm, Svenska Kyrkans Diakonistyrelses Bokforlag, 1957; Paris, Ed. du Cerf, 1962, p. 46 (my trans.); the argument against Norden's view of Luke as an 'Atticist' is summarized on pp. 43–7. The full argument is set out in the major Swedish study of 1940, *Lukas och Klassicismen, Svensk Exegetische Årsbok* 5 (1940), pp. 139–51.

[3] 'Schreibtischprodukt': Palm, 1955, p. 196 (on the language of Diodorus Siculus); more generally, pp. 175f., 207f. For a general description of this 'Zwischenprosa', cf. Rydbeck, 1967, pp. 177, 189–90.

the physical properties of early Christian manuscripts, which in some respects mirror Rydbeck's observations on the lingustic level of the New Testament writers.

> The Christian manuscripts of the second century, although not reaching a high standard of calligraphy, generally exhibit a competent style of writing which has been called 'reformed documentary' and which is likely to be the work of experienced scribes, whether Christian or not; certainly there is nothing in the nature of privately made copies such as the celebrated manuscript of Aristotle's Constitution of Athens.[4]

Even the adoption of the codex has suggested to some scholars a degree of alienation from standard expectations about literary texts: outside the Christian church, the codex was slow to gain acceptance as a receptacle for substantial writings, and the earliest lists of codices contain 'a high proportion of technical or professional texts'.[5]

Literature

With the preface, however, we move from a linguistic affinity to a literary one. Isolated grammatical/semantic points of contact, of the type observed by Rydbeck, show only that two works belong to the same broad linguistic stratum; but the adoption of a literary convention, involving choices as to form, style and content, demands a closer relationship. Literary conventions are not inhaled from the atmosphere: at the very least, on our hypothesis, the author of Luke

---

[4] Roberts and Skeat, 1987, p. 46; Roberts, 1977, pp. 15–19. M. Hengel, *Studies in the Gospel of Mark* (SCM, London, 1985), pp. 78–81 rightly notes the importance of these phenomena for our understanding of early Christianity.

[5] The case for a link between the codex and technical or school texts seems better supported than the broader thesis of a link with 'popular literature', as argued by G. Cavallo in *Libri, Editori e Pubblico nel Mondo Antico: Guida Storica e Critica* (Rome, 1975). The latter has to contend with the fact that the overwhelming majority of 'popular' texts (however they may be defined) are still written in rolls up to the fourth century and beyond (Roberts and Skeat, 1987, pp. 69–71): social class alone is not sufficient to account for the early Christian preference for the codex (Harris, 1989, p. 296). In fact, besides two novels, the list of codices from the second century AD (Roberts and Skeat, 1987, p. 71) includes two grammatical manuals and two medical treatises, plus a commentary on Demosthenes, a lexicon to Homer and a *Homeromanteion*. The remainder are copies of classical authors, ranging from Homer to Demosthenes: none of them is later than the fourth century BC, so even the literary texts in the list are of authors widely studied in school, not of contemporary writers.

1.1–4 must have had some direct contact with Greek scientific literature. Our next question, then, is: how does Luke's adoption of this literary convention assist us in the attempt to chart his position on the map of Greco-Roman culture?

The first necessity is to establish what precisely is involved in the use of such a convention.[6] The simplest explanation of the phenomenon, but socially the least revealing, would be to say that Luke had seen a preface like this in some other text and was imitating that single model. This suggestion was in fact made by Lagarde in *Psalterium Hieronymi* in 1874 (p. 165), where he argued that Luke 1.1–4 is a bad imitation of Dioscorides' preface. Such an explanation, depending essentially on a chance collocation of individual texts, would not provide us with a social matrix for our author. It is however unlikely to be the true one, for as our analysis has shown, the points of comparison which Lagarde saw in Dioscorides could be paralleled and bettered in a number of technical prefaces.[7] What we have is not a copy of any single preface but a close affinity with a wide variety of prefaces and authors; and, despite its obscurities, Luke's own composition does make sense in its own terms. We should see him, then, not as the inept imitator that Lagarde saw, but as an independent author composing freely: he is constrained not by the effort to copy a single model but by an awareness of an appropriate style and structure for prefaces which is widely distributed in a particular literary tradition.

We have, then, an author who is thoroughly at home in Greek technical literature, so much so that he naturally falls into its style and adopts its preface-conventions when he finds himself at the beginning of a major literary undertaking. The sociolinguistic concept of 'register', can be usefully brought into play here: as a linguistic style is chosen (whether consciously or not) 'according to what a person is doing at the time',[8] so, we might say, a literary convention is chosen because it is perceived to be appropriate to a

---

[6] For a fuller discussion of this point, see Alexander, 1986, pp. 63ff.

[7] The same argument holds against the suggestion that Luke's preface is based directly on one of Josephus': cf. Schlatter, 1931; H. J. Schonfield, *The Pentecost Revolution* (Macdonald & Jane's, London, 1974); F. G. Downing, 'Redaction criticism: Josephus' *Antiquities* and the Synoptic Gospels', (II) *JSNT* 9 (1980) pp. 29–48, pp. 30–1.

[8] Cf. the definition given by M. A. K. Halliday, *Language as Social Semiotic* (London, Edward Arnold, 1978), p. 110: 'The dialect is what a person speaks, determined by who he is; the register is what a person speaks, determined by what he is doing at the time.' P. Trudgill, *Sociolinguistics: An Introduction* (Harmondsworth, Penguin, 1974), p. 104 gives a rather more restricted definition of 'register'.

particular occasion. That occasion could be defined in purely literary terms (i.e. appropriate to the genre of the text), but it also has a social dimension: every text takes shape in a particular social context and has a social function or functions within that context. The adoption of a formal literary convention can be seen as the author's response to the nature of the communication taking place in his or her original context. Thus if Luke chooses something that looks like a 'scientific' preface for the beginning of his Gospel, it is because, for him, this preface fits the context as he sees it. In other words, his situation in presenting his Gospel in written form must have been in some important sense like the situation of other writers who used the same sort of preface.

This conclusion obviously has important implications for our estimate of the 'occasion' of Luke–Acts, that is for the literary genre of the work and the immediate social context in which it was composed. We shall explore these further in chapter 9. Here we are still concerned to see if it is possible to establish a broader social matrix for Luke's literary activity. Does Luke's adoption of this particular preface-style enable us to make any suggestions about the general socio-cultural level of its author and his readers?

The preface alone, of course, is not sufficient to indicate the general level of its author's literary abilities. A writer familiar with a far wider range of Greek literature might choose this style for particular purposes, as, among our writers, Hermogenes uses elements of the 'scientific' preface-style for a handbook of rhetoric. In this case, the adoption of this style simply indicates that the text is informative rather than literary, not that the writer is incapable of writing more rhetorical Greek.[9] In sociolinguistic terms, the preface is indicative of a particular literary 'register' (technical prose) but is not necessarily representative of the 'dialect' of the author, if by that we mean the habitual style of a particular social group (n. 8 above). Theoretically speaking, we could see Luke as a highly educated writer, hiding his literary light under a bushel because for some reason it suits him to write a preface in the 'scientific' style. But this is to reverse the actual state of our evidence. Luke's preface is not normally seen as being 'below' the literary level of the rest of the

---

[9] The non-literary *Koine* of the scientific handbooks was regarded as appropriate for a technical manual, even in the rhetorical schools: cf. R. Browning on Apollonius Dyscolus (*OCD*[2] p. 86): 'He himself writes Hellenistic *koine*, as befitted a technical writer. Atticism was confined to belles-lettres ... A. takes no thought for style ... '

New Testament, but 'above' it: it is the exceptional nature of the preface which has convinced scholars that Luke and his readers must be placed on a higher educational (and therefore social) plane than those of other New Testament writings (above, ch. 1 pp. 8–9). If the style of the preface turns out to belong (as we have argued) not to high literary historiography but to the broader tradition of technical and scientific prose, then this argument falls to the ground. Taken on its own, the preface provides no grounds for saying that with Luke the Gospel is 'leaving the milieu of "ordinary people" and entering the world of literature, the cultural world of antiquity' (Haenchen, 1971, p. 136).

It is worth stressing that our negative conclusions about the literary level of the preface are consistent with a wider range of observations on Luke's literary interests. In the preface itself, as our study has shown, the literary competence of its author is easily overvalued. Although he is composing freely, his freedom to use and adapt conventions is only relative (and here Luke may profitably be contrasted with Hermogenes, who quite clearly uses the form from choice and adapts it for his own purposes). Once the preface is over, Luke reverts with startling suddenness to a 'biblical' style with which he clearly feels much more at home. The contrast in style and language between preface and text has often been observed; what is less often remarked is that, like the scientific writers but unlike Arrian, Philostratus or Josephus, Luke shows no sign of wishing to apologize for any falling away from the 'purer' Greek of the preface, or even of being aware of it.[10] His narrative style in the Gospels derives from models right outside the world of Greek rhetorical literature, the Greek Bible and the synoptic tradition.[11] Even in Acts, his style is far less rhetorical than that of much hellenistic Jewish literature, and shows little sign of acquaintance with any rhetorical structures other than those widely disseminated through the language of officialdom.[12] More 'literary' passages, like the

[10] Apologies for defective style in Arrian, *Discourses of Epictetus*, pref.; Josephus, *Ant.* I 7, *C. Ap.* I 50; Philostratus, *Life of Apollonius of Tyana* I 3. Even if the *hypomnēmata* of Damis are a literary fiction, Philostratus' view of the necessity of rewriting is significant, as is his insistence that his hero was a natural Atticist, uncorrupted by the local dialect (*Vita* I 7).

[11] Luke's 'Septuagintal' style is well known: cf. H. F. D. Sparks, 'The Semitisms of St. Luke's Gospel', *JTS* 44 (1943), pp. 129ff.; 'The Semitisms of Acts', *JTS* NS 1 (1950) pp. 16ff. and Plümacher, 1972, on the LXX as Luke's literary model (cf. ch. 9 n. 23). On the 'synoptic' influence on Luke's style, cf. ch. 9 n. 21.

[12] Cf. above, ch. 6 (Verse one) on ἐπειδήπερ.

shipwreck scene of Acts 27, evoke the world of the popular novel as much as that of high classical literature.[13]

Furthermore it is clear that the author of Luke–Acts is either little acquainted with Greek classical literature or little interested in it. There is only one explicit poetic citation (Acts 17.28), and that is from the pseudo-scientific (and hugely popular) Aratus; and even this line may be quoted second hand, since we know that it formed part of a collection of *testimonia* already assembled in Alexandrian Jewish missionary literature.[14] Luke shows no evidence of direct acquaintance with the school classics, not even with that staple of Greek education from the primary level upwards, Homer.[15]

Negatively, then, there is little evidence that Luke knew any Greek secular literature apart from the novelistic tales and the handbooks of the school and craft traditions which had prefaces similar to his. In terms of Greek culture, this means that he himself presents us with no reason to place him any higher up the social scale than the groups which produced and/or used this type of literature. Furthermore, on the positive side there are significant pointers which link the early church with the social world of the crafts and professions of the Greek East, rather than with the status-conscious and culturally exclusive circles which were producing and reading the literary Greek of Luke's day.

Culture and social class

It will be clear immediately that our reading of the preface accords well with the traditional belief that the author of Luke–Acts was the

[13] For affinities with the Greek novels, long ago noticed by Dibelius (1956, pp. 1–25), see now Pervo, 1987; on the 'shipwreck style' of Acts 27, cf. V. Robbins, 'By land and by sea: the we-passages and ancient sea voyages', in C. H. Talbert (ed.) *Perspectives on Luke–Acts* (Macon, Ga., Mercer University Press, 1978), pp. 215–42. On the 'middle-class' audience of the novels cf. B. E. Perry, *The Ancient Romances* (Berkeley, University of California Press, 1967), e.g. pp. 33, 40, 56; Tomas Hägg, *The Novel in Antiquity* (Oxford, Basil Blackwell, 1983), ch. 3 is more circumspect, but still stresses that the genre aimed originally at 'a broader audience which made no strenuous demands on literature' (p. 107).

[14] Cf. N. Zeegers-Vandervorst, *Les citations des poètes grecs chez les Apologistes Chrétiens du II siècle* (Recueil de Travaux d'Histoire et de Philologie, IV, Fasc. 47, Université de Louvain, 1972), p. 187 n. 7 (on the use of Aratus in Aristobulus); the apologists are contrasted with the NT evangelists on pp. 134–5. For the literary interests of Josephus, cf. *C. Ap.* I 12; II 14, 155, 256.

[15] See especially G. Glockmann, 1968, pp. v., 17ff. (on Homer's place in Greek culture) and 59ff. (on Luke). Even the Rabbis had apparently heard of Homer (m. Yad. IV 6; y. Sanh. X 1/27c. 17–20) – though the significance of these passages is

'beloved physician' of Col. 4.14. It does not of course constitute a proof of that tradition. All it provides is the collateral observation that Luke's preface is the kind of preface a doctor might write, especially if he was a doctor whose acquaintance with Greek literature went little further than the handbooks of his trade. But for our purposes the general social observation implicit in the tradition is more important than the identification of the author with a particular individual in the Pauline retinue. Medicine in the ancient world was a craft before, and as much as, it was an intellectual discipline (Temkin, 1953): the doctor, even though his profession might bring him into the service of the great, was a *technitēs*, a craftsman who earned his keep by the exercise of his profession. Galen's public career as a *iatrosophistēs*, which briefly raised the medical lecture to the status of a rhetorical display, was exceptional (Bowersock, 1969, ch. 5).

The 'Doctor Luke' tradition is not the only link between the early church and the *technitae* of the ancient world. Celsus' complaint about the Christians in the second century includes the fact that they meet in 'cobblers' shops and fullers' shops', and Tertullian lists a wide variety of crafts practised by Christians (and causing problems of conscience) including those of plasterers, painters, marble masons and bronze-workers.[16] Luke's own narrative features a number of craftsmen and women in leading roles: Aquila and Priscilla, Lydia and Paul himself are presented as artisans or traders (Acts 16.14, 18.1–3). Paul's own reasons for adopting the profession of tentmaker may have been as much ideological as social (Hock, 1980): but there is no polemic or ideological justification of Paul's position in Luke's narrative. For Luke, as much as for the other evangelists, Jesus the carpenter's son and Paul the leather-worker figure without a trace of irony as actors in and mediators of events of world-shattering religious significance. Such heroes could never be taken seriously by the aristocratic readers who shared Celsus' attitude to 'banausic' occupations and his disdain for the taste of their practitioners – an attitude which was endemic among the

---

disputed, cf. Liebermann, 1962, pp. 105–14. For other Greek authors in the NT, see Malherbe, 1983, pp. 41–5. Note the warning of Lane Fox (1986, p. 100): 'although Acts' author has been given some odd disguises, none is odder than that of a man who knew fragments of Ovid and their Greek sources and distorted them to suit his picture of St. Paul'.

[16] Celsus: Origen, *Contra Celsum* III 55; Tertullian, *De idol.* VIII 2–4. Further, Hengel, 1974, ch. 9.

educated classes.[17] It seems only reasonable to conclude that Luke and his readers do not belong to this group any more than their heroes do.

It may be objected at this point that we are pitching Luke's social level too low. Does not the recently emerged consensus on the social composition of the early churches assign a rather higher social standing to their members? It is true that recent studies in this area have been concerned to correct Deissmann's romantic view of early Christianity as 'a movement among the weary and heavy-laden, men without power and position, "babes", as Jesus himself called them, the poor, the base, the foolish . . .'. Thus Malherbe can speak of 'a new consensus . . . that the social status of early Christians may be higher than Deissmann had supposed' (Malherbe, 1983, pp. 31–2, from which the above quotation is also taken). But there is a danger here of overcorrection. Current scholarship has produced estimates of the social constituency of the early Christian groups in the cities of the Empire which correspond remarkably well with the evidence of Celsus and Tertullian: thus, for example, Kreissig (1967, p. 99, my trans.) speaks of 'the urban circles of well-situated handworkers, traders, and members of the liberal professions'; Hengel (1974, ch. 9) says that 'the early Christians were petty bourgeois: manual workers and craftsmen, small businessmen and workers on the land, all of whom had a great respect for honest toil'; while Meeks (1983, p. 270) describes the typical member of the Pauline churches as 'a free artisan or small trader'.[18]

In social terms, these groups function at a level precisely analogous to the 'intermediate' zone to which the linguistic and literary data point. They are by no means destitute (though they may not have had much to cushion them against economic disaster); they probably owned slaves and may have employed other free labourers. But this does not make them members of the upper classes of the Greek cities, the wealth-owning and office-holding classes estimated in a recent study at about five percent of the adult male population (Lane Fox, 1986, p. 57). Wealth is a relative thing. A prosperous artisan is a long way off acceptance in a fundamentally aristocratic

[17] 'Banausic' occupations: cf. Cicero, *De officiis* 150; Burford, 1972, pp. 12, 25–6, 29ff., 128ff. and n. 334; Hock, 1980, pp. 35–6; Oleson, 1984, pp. 399–400.
[18] See further, Gager, 1972; A. H. M. Jones, 'The social background to the struggle between paganism and Christianity' in A. Momigliano (ed.), *The Conflict Between Paganism and Christianity in the Fourth Century* (Clarendon Press, Oxford, 1963), pp. 17–37; Dodds, 1965; Malherbe, 1983, ch. 2; Judge, 1960; Stambaugh and Balch, 1986, p. 112.

society, especially if he (or she) does not even have citizenship in the place of his/her trade; the geographical mobility of many artisans and traders (people like Lydia and Priscilla and Aquila) must have meant that large numbers were effectively disfranchised in their place of residence.[19] Looking down from above, in the words of Lane Fox, there was 'little to span the gap between the rich few and the dependent, or servicing, many'. Upward mobility was rare, and the competition of slave labour kept profit margins low.[20] Even if there were one or two highly placed individuals in the church in the first and early second centuries, this would make little difference to the overall picture that Christianity at this date barely affected the educated classes of the Empire.[21]

But have we not moved too fast in equating cultural level with social class? Is it not too facile to make a simple correlation between the production of a certain type of literature and a particular stratum of society? In many ways, of course, it is. We are ignoring the complexities in the social status, say, of a teacher of rhetoric, whose subject was of the highest social standing but who might be himself a slave or freedman, a Greek in Roman society, a professional obliged to support himself in a society which valued the leisured more highly than the worker. We have not yet considered (and cannot consider here) the variations in social status between one technical subject and another, or the question of how far the

[19] The mobility of these groups is stressed particularly now by P. McKechnie, who includes both 'Mobile skilled workers' and 'Traders' among the 'outsiders' of his study, *Outsiders in the Greek Cities in the Fourth Century BC* (Routledge, London and New York, 1989); and their continued marginality is emphasized by H. W. Pleket, 'Urban elites and business in the Greek part of the Roman Empire', in P. D. A. Garnsey, K. Hopkins and C. R. Whittaker (eds.), *Trade in the Ancient Economy* (London, Chatto & Windus, 1983), pp. 131–44.
[20] Lane Fox, 1986, pp. 57–9. Note that in speaking of these groups as 'intermediate' we must be careful to avoid the assumption that they constituted an *economic* 'middle class' in the sense employed in analysis of modern European society. The fundamentally dependent position of these craftsmen and traders is well brought out by Oleson, 1984, ch. 6, esp. pp. 398ff.; Burford, 1972, ch. 4.
[21] A. Harnack, *The Mission and Expansion of Christianity in the First Three Centuries I-II*, tr. and ed. J. Moffatt, 2nd edn (William & Norgate, London, 1908), II pp. 34–42 (also pp. 64–8) tends to maximize the small amount of evidence for conversion among the upper classes in the first century. As Gager (1972, pp. 112ff.) correctly insists, wealth does not necessarily indicate a high social position. It is also worth making a reverse deduction, so to speak, from later notices of the conversion of the eminent. The conversion of Victorinus is still hailed as a major triumph even at the time of Augustine (*Conf.* VIII i-ii [3–9, esp. 5]). It is hard to believe the fourth-century church would have reacted like this had such men been common; it is also hard to believe that, had there been more evidence of converts like this in the early period, the Fathers would have kept quiet about it.

writer of a *Technē* could be said to belong to the same social class as the practitioner of the craft it describes.[22] Nevertheless on a broad front it is only realistic to recognize the social dimension of education. Ancient education was not free. If the literary basis of the primary levels meant that even those with the minimum of education would share a common literary grounding (Marrou, 1964, *passim*), it is still true that relatively few would be able to afford to stay in the system to complete the tertiary level of full rhetorical training.[23] Technical education, in so far as anything is known about it, seems to have bypassed the gymnasium system altogether; it was certainly not catered for by the gymnasium curriculum.[24]

To ancient writers, therefore, the correlation between education (as revealed by literary prowess) and social class was both inevitable and obvious. This may be seen particularly clearly in a number of texts in which the Fathers of the church discuss the literary merits of the Gospels and Epistles. These later Christian commentators, at home in Greek *paideia* themselves, make no bones about the fact that the earliest Christian writers must have lacked that *paideia*. The literary deficiencies of the earliest records of the faith were a common taunt for its opponents, from Celsus onwards. Just as the church was composed of 'vulgar and illiterate persons', so, Celsus complains, its writings are the work of 'sailors' (*nautae*). That this was a literary judgement, not simply a reflection of social prejudice, may be seen from Origen's reply.[25] It is echoed by others, for whom

---

[22] The whole subject of the social context of technical literature is one which would repay study in much more depth than is possible here; Harris (1989) is one of the few scholars to have considered it, and his concept of 'craftsman's literacy' (pp. 7–8 and *index*) is a useful counter to the too easy assumption that all such written texts must have been directed at the educated amateur rather than at the *technitai* themselves. Further on this, below, ch. 9 pp. 191–7. On the social world of the crafts in general, see Burford, 1972, and Oleson, 1984, ch. 6 'The social context' with the literature there mentioned. McKechnie (see n. 19 above) also contains much valuable material.

[23] A fact which is sometimes forgotten when broad assumptions are made about the rhetorical education of New Testament writers. The whole subject is discussed with great sensitivity by Malherbe, 1983, ch. 2. The situation as regards *rhetoric* in particular is complicated by the fact that rhetoric (like opera in nineteenth/twentieth-century Italy) was a public art and certainly attracted popular acclaim and censure (Aune, 1987, pp. 12–13; F. G. Downing, '*A bas les aristos:* the relevance of higher literature for the understanding of the earliest Christian writings', NovT XXX (1988), pp. 210–30). But the ability to appreciate a good speech is not the same as the ability to write one.

[24] Marrou, 1964, II/ix pp. 262ff. For apprenticeships in the crafts, cf. Burford, 1972, pp. 82–91.

[25] Origen, *Contra Celsum* I 62. Cf. Norden, 1909, II p. 516 and n. 1; Janson, 1964, p. 129 and n. 11.

the apostles are *rudes et indoctos*, ἀμαθεῖς or ἀπαίδευτοι, their writings 'barbarous' and full of unacceptable neologisms, solecisms and grammatical faults.[26] What is striking is that the Fathers make no attempt to rebut these charges. Their defence is rather on the lines laid down by Paul in I Cor. 2.1ff., making a theological virtue of a social necessity; it remains a simple fact, as clear to them as to their opponents, that the earliest writings of the church could not measure up to the standards of Greek literary culture. From this position it is a fair (if not an inevitable) deduction that their authors, judged purely by the writings they produced, did not participate in that culture.

It is precisely here, however, that we can begin to see the importance of nuancing our understanding of the 'middle zones' of Greco-Roman society; for it would be a mistake to accept these judgements without further qualification. They are of great importance in so far as they reveal clearly and unequivocally the reaction of *homines litterati* to the New Testament writings. In so doing, they bear witness to the reality of the social and cultural divide described above. But they can also have a distorting effect, for they necessarily reflect a limited viewpoint. One distortion is easily corrected by the modern critic, namely the lack of appreciation for the biblically based cultural milieu of the New Testament writers. Despite the explanations of Jewish and Christian apologists, the 'great tradition' of the Hebrew Bible remained simply 'barbarous' to most educated pagans (cf. Jos., *Ant.* I 129). On this side, twentieth-century criticism has redressed the balance. It has, however, generally failed to face up to the equal distortion or 'foreshortening' implicit in the judgement of the *litterati* along the Greco-Roman socio-cultural axis. Celsus' 'vulgar', for example, were not necessarily either poor or uneducated, at least if by 'uneducated' we mean incapable of reading and writing; cf. Martial, *Epigr.* IX 73.7, which apparently refers to a cobbler whose parents, too poor to send him to school, taught him the elements themselves. The story shows that literacy at least was possible outside the school system; it also shows the ambiguity of the term 'educated', for to Martial these intelligent and resourceful parents are still 'ignorant' (*stulti*).

Literary judgement could show a similar foreshortening. The phenomenon is clearly visible in a small group of texts collected by Rydbeck, commenting on the language of medical writers. Here we

---

[26] The passages are listed by Norden, 1909, II pp. 517–25, also p. 535. Cf. also Eusebius, *HE* III 24.3; Harris, 1989, pp. 302–3.

find much the same sort of blanket condemnation as that incurred by Christian texts of the same period. Phrynichus complains of solecism and describes these medical writers as ἀμαθεῖς, while Galen even suggests that Dioscorides was imperfectly acquainted with the Greek language. This last suggestion, as Rydbeck rightly observes, need hardly be taken seriously: there is no indication of Semitic or any other non-Greek influence on Dioscorides. What it does is to illuminate the highly select standards operated by Galen. For him, as for the whole group of 'men of taste' with whom he aligns himself here (though not everywhere: cf. n. 27 below), the determination of the essence of pure Greek was an exact and painstaking discipline. 'Greek' in this sense is not the common tongue of millions throughout the empire but a purified 'Attic', resurrected primarily (though by Galen's time not exclusively) for the composition of literature. This standpoint, with its combination of social and lingustic snobbery, is perfectly described by Galen himself:

> I had a father who was rigorously correct in the language of the Greeks, and my teacher and *paedagogus* were Greeks too. I was reared on these words. I do not recognize yours. Don't quote me the usage of merchants or tradesmen or tax-collectors – I haven't mixed with such people. I was brought up on the books of the men of antiquity.
>
> (K VIII p. 587, my trans.)

The problem of 'Atticism' and the correct use of words is not the only point at issue in the ancient judgements on the literary defects of the earliest Christian writers, though it is one of their major concerns. Nevertheless these passages may be taken as a good illustration of the viewpoint of this limited and select group, for whom even minor solecisms served to classify the perpetrator as socially and culturally beneath them. As Rydbeck correctly observes, chronology plays a large part in these unfavourable judgements. Galen and Phrynichus, writing after the triumph of Atticism, simply failed to appreciate that when Dioscorides was writing in the mid-first century, the canons of strict Atticism were not applied to writings like his. But Atticizing influences were already at work in the first century and earlier, as may be seen from Josephus (Pelletier, 1962). What Galen is doing in these passages, and what critics of the New Testament have persisted in doing from Celsus onwards, is to apply universally the standards of Greek *paideia*, that is of that classical culture which was so predominantly literary that it viewed even philosophy, rhetoric's traditional opponent, in this light, and so influential as to affect even the avowedly anti-rhetorical Galen.[27] From one standpoint the criticisms are perfectly correct: the writings in question do not measure up to the required literary standards, and in this sense their authors can justly be described as 'uneducated', ἀπαίδευτοι: i.e. lacking παιδεία. What is not correct is to accept these standards as universal.

It is now becoming clear that our analysis of the literary affinities of Luke's preface is actually rather useful in defining a little more precisely where he and his work fit on the Greco-Roman socio-cultural axis. Within the church, Luke was regarded as the evangelist who wrote 'for the Greeks' (although it is not entirely clear what the phrase means), and Jerome comments that he knew more Greek than the other evangelists.[28] Despite this, most of the Fathers seem to accept that Luke–Acts, broadly speaking, shares the stylistic inadequacies of the rest of the New Testament. Certainly there is no polemical attempt to quote Luke's work as an exception to the low cultural level derided by Celsus. This is exactly what we should expect. The preface does provide a link with Greek culture, but not with the high literary culture of the upper classes. Rather it reveals a connection with an 'alternative' culture, despised by its contemporaries and largely ignored by subsequent scholarship,[29] a culture which consciously holds itself aloof from the prevailing passion for rhetoric, while admitting the usefulness of a limited number of rhetorical devices at certain formal points of composition.

The full investigation of that culture will have to be deferred to

[27] On the widespread influence of rhetoric on education, cf. Marrou, 1964, part II chs. 10 and 11, esp. pp. 289f. But note that Galen's own attitude to 'Atticism' is less clear-cut than the above quotation would suggest: elsewhere he allows that 'it is not necessary (as some believe) that everyone should atticize, even if they are doctors, musicians, lawyers, philosophers, geometers or simply rich people or *euporoi*': *De ordine librorum suorum* 5, K XIX 60–1 = SM II 89. On Galen and rhetoric, cf. further J. Kollesch, 'Galen und die zweite Sophistik', in Nutton, 1981, pp. 1–11.

[28] Jerome, *Ep. XIX ad Damasum* 38, '(Lucas), qui inter omnes evangelistas graeci sermonis eruditissimus fuit ...' Cf. further Aland, 1968, pp. 533, 539, 540. The 'quasi litteris studiosum' which is sometimes cited from the Muratorian canon as evidence of Luke's superior education is a conjecture for 'quasi iuris studiosum', which should almost certainly be retained: see A. Ehrhardt, *The Framework of the NT Stories* (Manchester University Press, 1964), pp. 16–18. (I am indebted for this reference to Professor F. F. Bruce.)

[29] On the tendency to ignore this 'alternative culture', cf. Neugebauer, 1969, *passim* and esp. p. 152; M. Fuhrmann, Review of Janson, *Latin Prose Prefaces*, in *Gnomon* 38 (1966), pp. 466–9 (p. 467).

another occasion; as we observed above, our study of the prefaces to scientific texts has perforce left many questions unanswered, and it must be regarded as a task of some urgency to follow up the literary analysis with a serious exploration of the social contexts of the technical writings studied. But it is now clear, I believe, that such an investigation would be immensely fruitful for our understanding of the social matrix of the earliest Christian writings. We shall conclude here simply by noting three early Christian phenomena which may be illuminated by placing them within the same broad social matrix as 'the scientific tradition': attitudes to rhetoric, attitudes to manual labour and attitudes to the written word.

Attitudes to rhetoric

The question of Luke's attitude to Greek literature is pointedly raised by Glockmann's study on Homer in early Christian literature (1968, pp. 59ff.). We have suggested above that the lack of literary allusion in Luke's work may be taken as an indicator of his educational and cultural level. Yet it remains a puzzle (for Paul and other New Testament writers as well as Luke) how they could achieve the level of Greek education which they evidently have, while being so little affected by the literary concerns which dominated Greek education from the primary level onwards. Glockmann finds it inconceivable that Luke should be completely ignorant of Homer (p. 65), and suggests that the absence of poetic citations in the Gospel may be deliberate (pp. 59ff.). His suggestion receives some support from a parallel with Apollonius of Citium, who omitted or curtly summarized Homeric and mythological allusions which he found in the text of Hippocrates (*Art.* 8, 53). Apollonius is clearly operating within a value system which did not rate literary allusion very high (even though his work is an elaborate and costly presentation to a monarch). The attack on *logos* which emerges at other places in the scientific tradition (above ch. 5 pp. 66, 88–91) confirms that there is an element here of deliberate choice (cf. also Galen, *On the Errors of the Soul* vii, K V 102–3 = SM I 80f.). Interestingly, similarly negative attitudes to rhetoric, using very similar language, appear later in Christian writers.[30] These attitudes

---

[30] E.g. Theodoret, *Rel. Hist.* pref. (*PG* LXXXII 1292C–1293A); Mark the Deacon, *Vita Porph.* pref.; Theophilus of Antioch, *Ad Autol.* III 2 (discussed in Alexander, 1978, pp. 249–52). Further Janson, 1964, pp. 127–41.

were in part forced on the church by the lack of recognizable formal rhetoric in the Bible, but it is worth noting that the Christians were not the only ones, and not the first, to express such views.

Attitudes to manual labour

The flip side, so to speak, of this negative attitude to rhetorical culture is the attitude of respect for manual labour shown by many Christian writers. Not only are many of the heroes of the New Testament story manual workers, but there is a strong current of respect in Christian ethics for 'earning one's bread' by honest toil: cf. I Thess. 4:11, II Thess. 3:6–13, Didache xii (Hengel, 1974, ch. 9). This attitude can of course be paralleled in rabbinic Judaism and, in an idiosyncratic form, in Cynic philosophy (R. F. Hock, 'Simon the Shoemaker as an ideal cynic', *GRBS*, 17 (1976), pp. 41–53; 1980, pp. 39–41). But there is no doubt that in the Greco-Roman cultural sphere its natural place is among the craftsmen themselves. Their own positive evaluation of their work can be documented from a study of sculptured reliefs;[31] for an expression of similar respect in literary texts (and without any trace of the tone of philosophic condescension found in the Cynic passages) we have to turn to the writers of the scientific tradition: cf. e.g. Philo, *Bel. Th.* 51.9ff.; Vitruvius X 2.11–14; X 13.2; X 16.3–8; Galen, *De comp. med. sec. loc* VI 1 (K XII 894); and note the part played by the *architekton* at the end of *On the Errors of the Soul* (K V 98–103 = SM I 77–81). It is instructive to compare Galen here with his contemporary Plutarch, who despises even the great classical artists for their involvement in 'mean occupations' (Plutarch, *Pericles* 2; compare *Marcellus* 14, on Archimedes' practical inventions, and Valerius Maximus VIII 14.6, on Q. Fabius Pictor) (cf. n. 17 above). It is Plutarch, not Galen, whose views are more representative of Greco-Roman literary culture: indeed, one student of the period has 'investigated changes in the cultural opinion of manual labour throughout classical antiquity and found the growth of a positive evaluation only in the context of Christian doctrine'.[32]

---

[31] M. Reddé, 'Les scènes de métier dans la sculpture funéraire gallo-romaine', *Gallia* 36 (1978), pp. 43–63.

[32] Oleson, 1984, citing A. T. Geoghegan, *The Attitude towards Labor in Early Christianity and Ancient Culture* (Catholic University of America, 1945: Studies in Christian Antiquity 6). I have not been able to see a copy of this book.

Attitudes to the written word

An early Christian attitude of scepticism about written tradition is expressed clearly in Papias' famous phrase about preferring the 'living voice' to anything he could learn from books (Eusebius, *HE* III 39.4). At first sight this seems decidedly odd in a cultural climate as bookish as that of the second-century empire, so much so that Gerhardsson (1961) suggested it should be linked particularly with the practices of the rabbinical schools. But the scientific tradition provides ample evidence of a prejudice against 'book-learning' which closely parallels Papias'; the closest parallel of all, verbally, occurs in a saying quoted by Galen as 'a proverb current among the majority of craftsmen'.[33] What we seem to have here is a widespread cultural phenomenon which links Papias with the craftsmen of the Empire – and also, as I have argued elsewhere (Alexander, 1990), with the schools of the Greco-Roman world as well as those of rabbinic Judaism. We shall return to this point in our final chapter.

[33] Galen, *De comp.med.sec.loc.* VI pref. (K XII 894). The passage is fully discussed in Alexander, 1990, pp. 224–5.

9

THE APPROPRIATE FORM OF WORDS FOR THE OCCASION

We turn now from the general to the particular. In chapter 8 we argue that Luke's 'scientific' preface can be seen as part of a wider pattern reflecting general socio-cultural aspects of the life of the first-century churches. We are now in a position to return to the questions adumbrated in chapter 1 concerning the immediate context of the preface. We have suggested that a 'minimal' conclusion to be drawn from Luke's use of scientific preface-convention might be formulated thus: 'If Luke chooses a "scientific" preface for the beginning of his Gospel, it is because, for him, this is the appropriate form of words for the occasion.' In this final chapter we shall consider in more detail what the occasion was: first in relation to the dedication and its social context, and then in relation to the text itself and the literary expectations aroused by the preface.

The social occasion: Luke and Theophilus

It is easy to forget that the primary announcement of purpose in Luke–Acts comes in the preface, with the statement that Luke is writing 'so that you (that is, Theophilus) may have assured knowledge about the things in which you have been instructed'. At the surface level, the text is a personal communication to a named individual. As we have demonstrated above, that does not mean that it is a private communication for one reader only; dedication is a widely recognized literary courtesy by means of which a text is 'personalized' as a gift or communication to one individual, without thereby negating its inherent literary character (whatever that might be). Nevertheless, for most readers, certain specific questions still need to be answered before we can leave the preface. Why did Luke choose this particular form of courtesy, and what does it tell us about the immediate social context of his work?

187

Was Theophilus a real person?

Yes: this is one of the few facts about Theophilus on which we can be reasonably certain. The name is a real one: although it looks superficially as if it might be chosen to represent a 'typical' Christian ('lover of God' or 'dear to God'), the right adjective for that would be θεοφιλής. And, more fundamentally, to say that dedication is a convention is not to say that it is a fiction. There is nothing in the ancient evidence to suggest that the dedicatees named in these texts did not exist, or that they did not receive copies of the texts addressed to them (whether they read them is another question to which there is strictly speaking no answer). The fact that there are some apparently fictional dedications, like that of Thessalus to the emperor, does not mean that all dedications are fictitious. On the contrary: the fiction apes a real situation and could not function without it.[1]

Was Theophilus Luke's social superior?

This one is more difficult, though certain negative points are clear. First, there is no justification for the common assumption that Theophilus was a Roman. The name is not Roman but Greek, and typical of the theophoric names popular among Jews of the Diaspora (ch. 6 s.v.). Similarly, the epithet κράτιστος does not by itself indicate a position in the Roman hierarchy. When used in dedications, it is not a strict indicator of rank (above ch. 6 s.v.); and the mere fact that it sometimes occurs in official documents does not mean that every occurrence indicates an 'official'. As to status, the fact that the name occurs among slaves (ch. 6 s.v.) should warn us against easy assumptions regarding Theophilus' social position, although of course there is no proof that the name was exclusive to slaves, and in any case a slave origin would not preclude a subsequent rise up the social ladder. More significant perhaps is the simple fact that early Christian tradition knows so little of Theophilus' identity: given the delight taken in the early centuries over the conversion of prominent members of society (above ch. 8 n. 19), it is

[1] As may be seen from the fictional dedications of the *Rhetorica ad Alexandrum* or of the *Letter of Aristeas*. In the former, the dedication to Alexander was added subsequently to the book's production, cf. above ch. 4 n. 4. In the latter, Aristeas' address to Philocrates is a fiction essential to the author's purpose. But in both cases, the fiction only works by relating the text to real 'historical' characters in a realistic social situation.

difficult to believe that any favourable information about Theophilus' status would have been lost.

Lacking any information about Theophilus himself, then, we are left with indirect evidence. We have already demonstrated (above ch. 8) that the type of literature indicated by the preface is not in itself socially pretentious. We can thus dismiss the line of argument represented by Wengst (1987, p. 101; above, ch. 1 p. 8–9), which reasoned that the mere fact of the preface showed that Luke had aspirations to produce 'Literature' for an educated public. Luke's dedication, it is now clear, will only show social pretension to the extent that dedication within the scientific tradition shows such pretension. But here it is less easy to reach an unequivocal conclusion. Our focus in this study has been largely on linguistic and literary phenomena in the small body of scientific prefaces discussed; a full analysis of the social realities lying behind these dedications is impossible within the confines of the present work, and would have to take into account a far wider range of evidence than we have been able to do here.[2] However, we have devoted sufficient attention to this issue (above, ch. 4 pp. 50–63) to demonstrate the complexity and variety of the social situations of scientific writers and the difficulty of moving direct from the literary phenomenon to the real world of writer and addressee.

It is clear that some dedications among the scientific prefaces analysed indicate some degree of social pretension: dedications to monarchs or their sons are the most obvious (Diocles, Bito, Archimedes' *Psammites*, Apollonius of Citium, Ps.-Scymnus, Vitruvius, Thessalus), but we might add Erotian's dedication to Andromachus (a colleague with a court position), or Artemidorus' decision to address the first three books of his *Interpretation of Dreams* to the rhetor Cassius Maximus. But, as we showed in our analysis in chapter 4 above, the scientific tradition also contains from its earliest stages a number of works addressed to peers, as in the letters of Archimedes and Apollonius of Perge: and there is no evidence to justify the assumption that this type of dedication died out after the

---

[2] Including epigraphic and fragmentary evidence, which we explicitly excluded from our study (above ch. 2 p. 11). Roman evidence was also largely excluded for a different reason, namely that linguistic parallels to Luke should primarily be sought in Greek texts. See now Rawson, 1985; Gold, 1987; and, on Roman patronage in general, R. P. Saller, *Personal Patronage under the Early Empire* (Cambridge University Press, 1982). In addition, however, much material on the social context of the scientific writers studied has been perforce omitted for reasons of space; I hope to return to this material at a later date.

early period. Thus, for example, at the end of the second century AD we find Vettius Valens addressing his collection of horoscopes to his pupils, while Artemidorus addresses the last two volumes of his dream-book to his own son, not to an influential outsider. Many of the dedicatees in the texts studied are and remain, like Theophilus, just names (cf. Philo, Hero, Demetrius, Serenus and many of Galen's dedicatees); the fact that we can identify a few well-known and influential figures should not lead us to conclude that all dedicatees were well known. Significantly, as we have noted above, Greek names (and slave names) tend to predominate even in the Roman period (above ch. 4 pp. 60–1), a fact which confirms the observation that teachers and writers from the eastern end of the empire, even in Rome, tended to associate most with their own compatriots. It is thus not possible to state decisively that Theophilus was in a position of social superiority; there is a degree of probability that this was the case, but without further research we cannot be certain.

Was Theophilus a patron?

As we have demonstrated above (ch. 4 pp. 52f., 57), the relationship between dedication and patronage is complex: not all dedicatees are patrons, and not all patrons receive a dedication.[3] However, some dedications are certainly linked, if indirectly, with patronage; and if Theophilus was a person of some social standing, we could quite easily construct a Christian scenario in which the concept of patronage would make sense. The role of the patron (*prostatēs/prostatis*) in the life of the first churches is well known from Acts and the Epistles, and is receiving confirmation from inscriptional evidence.[4] This kind of patronage should not necessarily be assimilated to the more formal *clientela*-system of the capital. In the cosmopolitan Greek cities of the Roman Empire, the patron could provide more nebulous benefits in the form of social identity and security for a

---

[3] A similar complexity is noted in Gold's study of the relationships between poets and patrons: Gold, 1987, ch. 1.

[4] Patrons: Meeks, 1983 (*Index* s.vv. 'Benefactors', 'Patrons of churches'); Horsley, 1987, pp. 241–4; Stambaugh and Balch, 1986, pp. 55, 140. Women particularly tend to figure in this role: Ben Witherington III, *Women in the Earliest Churches* (SNTSMS 59, Cambridge University Press, 1988), pp. 145–6; H. Lawrence, 'Women as Leaders in the Church(es) of Asia Minor', Diss. submitted to the University of Sheffield as part of the Degree of Master of Arts, Dept. of Biblical Studies, 1987 (unpublished) ch. 4.

small non-citizen group, as well as hospitality for visitors and a kind of informal 'embassy' in a foreign city, without being a member of the ruling hierarchy himself/herself: Junia Theodora in Corinth provides a good example, aptly cited as a parallel to Christian patrons like Phoebe or Lydia.[5] Theophilus could well be such a patron, a provincial rather than a member of the Roman governing classes, but sufficiently well established in his local community to provide house-room for Christian meetings and such other *beneficia* as his position demanded (cf. A. J. Marshall (cited n. 5 below), pp. 123, 125–6). Once again it is worth noting the preponderance of Greek names among scientific dedications in the Roman period (above ch. 4 pp. 60–1): if these dedications do presuppose some kind of patronage relationship, the patrons chosen are compatriots, not Romans, and their connections with the Roman web of power operate at some remove. Nevertheless it must still be stressed that patronage is an assumption in these cases, not a certainty, and that the assumption can only be verified (or disproved) by further investigation.

<h2 style="text-align:center">Was Theophilus an outsider?</h2>

This is really the crux of the question for many interpreters, who have shared Corssen's assumption that Luke's preface and dedication mark a decisive step in the communication of the Christian gospel, a breaking out from 'the darkness of the conventicle' into the wider world of 'the educated public' (Wengst, 1987, p. 101: cf. above, ch. 1 pp. 8–9). This is not quite the same as the question of social status or patronage, although they are often perceived as the same. Theophilus could well be both a social superior and a patron without being an 'outsider' in this sense: if he were patron to a Christian group in the manner just described, he would

[5] On Junia Theodora, see D. I. Pallas, S. Charitonidis and J. Venencie, 'Inscriptions Lyciennes trouvées à Solômos près de Corinthe', *Bulletin de Correspondance Hellénique*, 83 (1959), pp. 496–508; A. J. Marshall, 'Roman women and the provinces' (*Ancient Society*, 6 (1975), pp. 109–27), pp. 123–6. I am indebted to Lawrence (cited in n. 4, pp. 87–9) for bringing this instance to my attention. The inscription published by Pallas *et al.* dates from the first century AD, before AD 43 (pp. 505–6). Junia Theodora lived in Corinth and was honoured by the Lycian confederacy and several Lycian cities for services to Lycians visiting Corinth, whether singly or in groups. One of these services is described as 'making the Roman authorities (*hēgoumenoi*, 1.5, cf. p. 507n.) friendly towards our nation', which (quite apart from her gender) makes it clear that she acts as an intermediary rather than being an authority figure herself.

presumably have heard some account of the Christian message already.

In fact the preface itself makes it clear that Luke's dedicatee is not being introduced to Christianity for the first time. Its allusive and elliptical character make it ill-adapted for such a purpose (above ch. 6, *passim*), and if our interpretation of verse 4 is correct, the *catechesis* which Theophilus has already received should be understood as some kind of Christian 'instruction' rather than neutral or hostile 'information' (ch. 6 s.v.). The situation is paralleled in both Galen and Hermogenes, where the text is presented to the dedicatee as a written version of something already familiar to him, whether as oral teaching or practical demonstration: in this situation the text itself is a 'reminder' of teaching already received, rather than a first introduction to a new subject (above ch. 4 pp. 62–3). What Theophilus is being offered, on this hypothesis, is the greater 'security' (ἀσφάλεια) of a written text over against oral teaching (above ch. 6 s.v.).

Whether patron or not, then, Theophilus is not in the most obvious sense an 'outsider' to the Christian message. It may be objected that there is an inconsistency here: does not the very existence of a preface, even within the terms of scientific convention, indicate a move outwards from a self-explanatory 'school' situation to the wider world? Certainly, as we argued above (ch. 2 pp. 18–22), it is plausible to link the origins of explanatory prefaces with such a move. But we must bear in mind the distinction between the reasons for the origin of a literary convention and the reasons for its continued existence. It seems clear that within the scientific tradition preface-writing, once established, became something of a habit, so that its appearance in later texts points simply to conformity with the established usage of a tradition, and not necessarily to the real circumstances of the writer. Thus in the later scientific texts it is impossible to identify a clear demarcation between texts for 'outsiders' and texts for 'insiders' of the sort visible in Archimedes (above ch. 4 pp. 50–1). Only where the actual circumstances of the dedication are known can we be sure whether the dedicatee is in any respect representative of an 'outside' audience.

Given the general paucity of information on the social context of scientific texts, the evidence of Galen deserves particular attention here (above ch. 4 pp. 62–3). Galen's relationships with Boethus, Eugenianus and other addressees would repay a more substantial investigation than we are able to give them here, and might well provide some illuminating parallels to the relationship between Luke and Theophilus. In particular, it is important to ask just what is meant by 'insiders' and 'outsiders' in the case of a work like the *De anatomicis administrationibus*. Boethus is presented as a reader who has already heard the essential context of the text. But is he representative of the primary audience of the text? Galen makes it clear that he has at least two distinct audience groups in mind, both as speaker and as writer, and the same double audience is clearly presupposed by a number of the writers in our study (above ch. 4 pp. 57–60). Boethus, as a *philiatros*, is representative of Galen's fan club among the cultured classes: he has heard Galen's public lectures, but is not a pupil or a would-be professional. He is therefore an 'insider', but only in a limited sense. But it should not be assumed that the written text somehow depends for its existence on this more educated but 'amateur' audience. It is clear that the production of medical text-books, although secondary to his oral teaching activity, was an integral part of Galen's educational world at every level.[6] Texts were produced, by one means or another, both for amateurs and for professionals, both for pupils and for the educated public: both can be described as *hypomnēmata*, and both sometimes bear prefaces and dedications. Making a firm correlation between prefaced works and 'outsiders' is far too simple.[7]

Was Theophilus Luke's publisher?

Is Theophilus being requested, in a covert way, to publicize or even 'publish' Luke's work? This last suggestion was made by Goodspeed in 1954; it has received little direct support, though the idea of a more nebulous duty of the patron to publicize the work remains popular (above ch. 1 pp. 6–8). In one sense the question is unanswerable: the concept of 'publication', like Corssen's concept of the 'book-market', is so misleading in the context of ancient book production that we have thought it better not to introduce either

[6] As is clear from his two small treatises *De libris propriis* (K XIX 8ff. = SM II 91ff.) and *De ordine librorum suorum* (K XIX 49ff. = SM II 80ff.). Galen's prolixity was famous in his lifetime: Athenaeus, *Deipnosophistae* I 1.e–f. Further on Galen's attitude to books: Alexander, 1990.

[7] *Pace* e.g. Gerhardsson, 1961, p. 196 and n. 4. The whole question of the literary status of *hypomnēmata* needs urgent reconsideration in the light of the literary praxis of the scientific tradition, and of new evidence emerging from the papyri.

into our discussion so far.[8] Nevertheless, as we stressed in chapter 1, the question of publication does raise the vital issue of the social framework in which texts come into existence and are disseminated and preserved. 'Publication' in the modern sense, a complex process dependent on the technology of printing and involving a large financial outlay, is clearly the wrong model to use when looking at the ancient world; but it is right to look for some equally concrete model to put in its place.

Recent studies of the Roman world have stressed the complexity of the relationships between literature and patronage (Gold, 1987; Rawson, 1985), and provide an increasingly detailed understanding of the institution of patronage itself and its mutual duties and obligations (R. P. Saller, *Personal Patronage under the Early Empire*, Cambridge University Press, 1982). But neither these studies nor our own readings in the scientific tradition afford any justification for the common assumption that a dedicatee-patron had an obligation to 'publish' the book presented to him or her.[9] What is clear, however, is that the patron's provision of support for the author frequently had the additional effect of providing a social context for the work itself, so that the patron's function vis-à-vis the work can be subsumed under his or her functions towards the author or the group in which it was produced.

Patronage for scientific writers might involve tangible support for the writer, in the form of finance or (more commonly) subsistence: or it might take the more nebulous form of support for the 'subject'. Probably the best-known example of this form of patronage in the hellenistic world was in Alexandria, where the munificence of a succession of Ptolemies supported huge numbers of poets, scholars,

[8] On publication in the early church in general, see Marrou, 1949; van der Valk, 1957. It is important to keep in mind the practical conditions of ancient book production: it was a haphazard affair, frequently chaotic, especially in the sub-literary area. Galen gives a vivid picture in *De libris propriis* of the way in which his own writings circulated among his friends and pupils. Notes from his lectures were copied (with or without his knowledge or permission), passed on, lost, mutilated and found again. The book trade as such seems more or less irrelevant to the process: the one work bearing his name which Galen records having found on a bookstall turned out not to be by him (above, ch. 6 n. 5). Cf. van Groningen, 1963.

[9] Cf. Rawson, 1985, pp. 98–9; Gold, 1987, p. 174: 'It is hard to estimate the nature, value and consequence of gifts because [Roman] writers were reluctant to bring up this potentially embarassing subject; when they did, it was often in a vague and teasing way. Material gifts obviously mattered more to certain writers such as bards in Homer's Greece or Plautus; other writers were more concerned with amenities or introductions to important friends; some writers needed nothing apart from the inspiration that a patron provided. Such things are never made clear.'

scientists and technicians. But this was only an unusually lavish extension of the simplest and most archaic form of paronage, the hospitality (or 'hearth': Pindar, *O*. I 11) of a court or wealthy house. An invitation to such a court, for a bard or lyric poet, meant not only support in the form of subsistence for the time that he was there, but also, and just as important, the provision of a social occasion for the performance of his work. The pattern is as old as Homer and Pindar (Gold, 1987, pp. 15–30); it persists in different forms throughout antiquity, whether we see it exemplified in the Greek householders who gave short-term hospitality to the itinerant sophists and philosophers of the Greek world, or in the wealthy Romans who gave so many Greek intellectuals a (dependent) position in their households.[10] In both cases the provision of hospitality also meant the provision of opportunity to practise one's profession, whether in teaching, in philosophical debate or in rhetorical performance.

It hardly needs to be stressed that this form of patronage was also vital to the spread of the Christian gospel: the patrons of the earliest mission not only provided board and lodging for the missioners, but also created and sustained the social context essential to their work through their willingness to host the meetings of the Christian group. We might loosely compare the picture drawn so vividly by Ps.-Scymnus, where the 'hearth' of the Bithynian king Nicomedes (Ps.-Scymnus 63) – in other words, the hospitality of the court – is seen as providing the essential social setting for exchange of ideas among 'lovers of learning' (62–3). Thus when Ps.-Scymnus claims that through his dedication to Nicomedes 'I will provide *through you* a useful facility common to all who wish to study' (7–10), he almost certainly does not mean that the king was expected to 'publish' the poet's work, if by that we mean arranging for the dissemination of

---

[10] For the Sophists, cf. G. B. Kerferd, *The Sophistic Movement* (Cambridge University Press, 1981), pp. 18–19. Protagoras, in Plato's dialogue of that name, is shown as using the house of his patron to make his initial contacts and to hold semi-public debates and instructional sessions (*Prot.* 314b6–316b6; see further, Kerferd, *op.cit.* pp. 17–23). Hospitality also played a part in the teaching activity of the Cynics, since an invitation to join a rich man at dinner could mean an opportunity for further discussion and further spiritual therapy for the host (Diogenes, *Ep.* 38.3–5: Malherbe, 1977, p. 163). We also hear of more long-standing associations with Cynic teachers, such as that between the first-century Roman senator Thrasea Paetus and Demetrius the Cynic (Tacitus, *Ann.* XVI 34). For other Greeks in Roman households, see Rawson, 1985, and Gold, 1987, *passim*, and add Rawson, 'Roman rulers and the philosophic adviser', in M. Griffin and J. Barnes (eds.), *Philosophia Togata* (Oxford, Clarendon Press, 1989), pp. 233–57.

multiple copies of a text: here the duty of the patron to 'publicize' the work is included (and already discharged) in his wider role as patron of the social group.

Up to this point we have deliberately refrained from talking of a paton's duties towards a *book*: the primary and most public form of the 'work', in all the cases mentioned so far, will be oral, not written. But in the case of Ps.-Scymnus we are clearly dealing with a written text, not with an oral performance. Does Ps.-Scymnus have in mind any more specific duties towards his text, that is toward the book he has so painstakingly composed? The answer, I would suggest, probably lies in the royal library. We know that the libraries of the hellenistic monarchs played a crucial role in the preservation and facilitation of scholarship in the hellenistic world, and any text deposited in such a library would be not only preserved (at least until the demise of the court) but also (presumably) available for study to other scholars enjoying the hospitality of the court.[11] Among our texts, the Hippocratic commentary of Apollonius of Citium might also be a candidate to be regarded as a text designed for a royal library: the illustrations which form an integral part of its conception must have made this an expensive book.[12]

Patronage could thus provide a public platform for an author's work in two ways: certainly through the facilitating of an occasion for the public recitation of his work, and probably (for this is no more than a conjecture) through the possession of a library in which a book could be preserved and made available for study. But it would be a mistake to assume that these were the only means of dissemination available to the writers who have formed the object of our study, as if their work could receive no publicly visible form without the provision of such favours. The court scenario described by Ps.-Scymnus is by no means the only kind of social situation envisaged in our texts. In many cases it is clear that the book has its own lines of communication with an audience quite separate from the dedicatee, as in the passages from Vitruvius and Pliny quoted

[11] On publication as 'deposition' in a library, cf. Liebermann, 1962, pp. 83–99, esp. p. 85. On libraries in private houses, see Kenyon, 1951, pp. 82–4; Rawson, 1985, pp. 39–44.

[12] And the establishment of a library may have seemed a natural course of action for Apollonius' dedicatee who was (it is presumed) holding court in Cyprus while temporarily estranged from Alexandria. But it should not necessarily be assumed that all illustrated books in antiquity were luxury items: John M. Riddle, *Dioscorides on Pharmacy and Medicine* (University of Texas Press, Austin, 1985), pp. 176ff. Pliny speaks of illustrated books in a fairly matter-of-fact way: *NH* XXV 4.8, XXXV 11.

above, ch. 4 p. 58. Here the dedication is quite clearly peripheral to the book's real business, and the author is in no sense writing solely for his patron. Galen's double audience of amateur *philiatroi* and professionals is paralleled in many of our texts, and for most of them (including the great bulk of material without any prefaces or dedications) the primary means of dissemination must have been via the channels provided by the profession itself.

Space here precludes a full investigation of what these channels actually were: that important task will have to wait for another day. But enough has been said of the nature of the scientific tradition (above ch. 4 pp. 42–6) to make it clear that many of the texts we have studied emanate from a 'school' context. 'School' can be used in the broadest sense to include any teaching situation; we can speak of 'tradition' whenever we have a succession or passing on of teaching from one teacher to another, as pupils become teachers and pass on and improve what they have learnt.[13] As with the courts, the primary form of presentation for which the schools provided a social context was oral 'performance' in the shape of teaching or practical demonstration: the role played by written texts in this process was secondary (cf. Alexander, 1990). But it is sufficiently clear that we must also reckon with the 'school' as an alternative social context for the preservation and dissemination of texts. The hellenistic courts were not the only institutions to have libraries: the schools also acted as vital repositories, and channels of transmission, for the accumulated wisdom of their traditions.[14]

Locating Luke's dedication within the framework of the scienific tradition, then, enables us to construct a number of realistic social models for the composition of Luke and Acts. These models should not be thought of as mutually exclusive but as mutually overlapping, each illuminating a different aspect of the complex relationships between the first Christians and their social world. First, the 'hellenistic court' model recognizes the importance of hospitality in

[13] I have attempted to clarify and define the terminology used in this area in my ABD article, 'Schools, hellenistic'.
[14] School libraries: probably the best-known example is that of Aristotle (Strabo XIII, 54; Plutarch, *Sulla* 26.1): described as 'the prototype of all the great libraries of antiquity': W. D. Ross, 'Aristotle', *OCD*, p. 94b. Cf. F. Grayeff, *Aristotle and his School* (London, Duckworth, 1974), ch. 4. David Sedley ('Philosophical allegiance in the Greco-Roman world', pp. 97–119 in M. Griffin and J. Barnes (eds.), *Philosophia Togata* (Oxford, Clarendon Press, 1989), p. 100 argues that the loss of the school's 'scriptures' was a major factor in the decline in Peripatetic fortunes after Theophrastus.

creating a social context for many kinds of literary and intellectual activity, whether in the courts or on the more modest scale of a prosperous household. Within the context of early Christianity, this model suggests a Theophilus who, as patron to a local house-church, is already discharging his duties as patron by facilitating the promulgation of Christian teaching in his house. He is familiar with the Christian teaching which Luke now presents to him in written form and which, Luke assures him, is a reliable collection of tradi-tional material. On this hypothesis the two books which Luke dedicated to Theophilus could have become part of his library, available to the church which met in his house, and ultimately becoming the nucleus of that church's library.[15]

The advantage of this model is that it locks easily into the 'household' model already recognized as fundamental to the social structures of the early Christian groups (Meeks, 1983, pp. 75–7). We need also to bear in mind, however, the more open-ended social model suggested by Galen, which we might call the 'public lecture' model. On this model the dedicatee is a more ambivalent figure, an odd mix of 'outsider' (to the profession) and 'insider' (to the lectures), and the writer (in Galen's case also the speaker) has an independent professional position of his own. This model also provides obvious analogies with phenomena known from early Christianity. Theophilus may have acted as host, and thus as patron, to a travelling Christian teacher, as so many of the char-acters in Acts do for Paul.[16] (It is surely significant that the ambiva-lence of the relationship between Galen and Boethus looks very similar to that which characterizes Paul's relationships with local patrons.)[17] Or he may have been simply an auditor at a Christian

---

[15] Church 'libraries' are mentioned in second-century martyr-acts: cf. *Acts of the Scillitan Martyrs* §12 (H. Musurillo, *The Acts of the Christian Martyrs* (Clarendon Press, Oxford, 1972), p. 88.14–15). For more general observations on the part which must have been played in the development and distribution of early Christian literature by the house-churches, cf. D. W. Riddle, 'Early Christian hospitality: a factor in the gospel transmission', *JBL* 57 (1938), pp. 141–54; Hengel, 1985, 77–8.

[16] The idea of Paul as a travelling 'sophist' was put forward by Judge (1961) and has been developed by B. Winter, 'Paul among the Sophists: a Hellenistic Jewish and a Christian response' (unpublished Ph.D. thesis, The School of History, Philosophy and Politics, Macquarrie University 1988). Cf. also more generally Stambaugh and Balch, 1986, pp. 143–5.

[17] It was not only the Cynics who felt unhappy about the relationship between the philosopher and the wealthy patron (Malherbe, 1977, pp. 103f., 161f.; Hock, 1980). The phenomenon should be considered also in the context of a wider unease about the relationship between patrons and writers, artists and teachers: who was bestow-ing *beneficia* on whom? See further Gold, 1987.

'lecture', like the *equites* whom Clement describes listening to Peter in Rome and asking Mark afterwards for an *aide-mémoire*.[18] Whatever the historical value of notices like this, we should take seriously ancient perceptions that this was the kind of process which could plausibly lie behind the production of a written Gospel. Galen also provides evidence (which can be supplemented from other school writers) of other material factors which we tend to forget if we ignore the conditions of ancient book production: the widely recognized role of disciples (auditors) in the production of written texts,[19] and the importance of the mobility of the lecturer as a motive for committing the content of an oral presentation to writing.[20]

But it is vital to remember that neither the patron nor the 'amateur' auditor should be allotted an exclusive role in the production of texts of the 'scientific' type. The social context provided by the dedication (whatever that was) is not sufficient to account for the existence of the text. If it were, we should have no scientific texts which were not dedicated: but in fact, as we stressed at the beginning of our investigation (ch. 4 p. 46), there are many such texts, and in the later hellenistic and Roman periods many of them are indistinguishable in form and content from dedicated texts. The position with regard to the Gospels is very similar: we have three synoptic Gospels of which only one is dedicated, but the dedicated Gospel is closer in form, content and vocabulary to the other two Gospels than it is to the author's other work.[21] In other words, the 'personalizing' of a dedicated text tends to be limited to superficialities, and often, as with Luke's, to the preface; it cannot therefore automatically be assumed to give us a key to the nature of

---

[18] Clem. Alex., *Adumbrationes ad I Petr.5.13* (Aland, 1968, p. 539): 'Marcus, Petri sectator, praedicante Petro evangelium palam Romae coram quibusdam Caesareanis equitibus et multa Christi testimonia proferente, petitus ab eis, ut possent quae dicebantur memoriae commendare, scripsit ex his, quae a Petro dicta sunt, evangelium quod secundem Marcum vocitatur ...' Cf. the Greek passage quoted by Aland, ibid.: ὡς ἂν καὶ διὰ γραφῆς ὑπόμνημα τῆς διὰ λόγου παραδοθείσης ... διδασκαλίας ... The only element in the story for which there is an obviously tendentious motive is the name 'Peter'. Papias suggests a similar picture. (There is no need to read Papias as meaning that Mark wrote his 'recollections' after Peter's death: ὡς ἀπεμνημόνευσεν means 'as [Peter] recounted', not 'as [Mark] remembered'.)

[19] Galen, *De libris propriis* pref. and ch. I (K XIX 10–12 = SM II 92–3. Compare Quintilian, *Inst.or.* I pref. 7–8; Arrian, *Epict.* I pref.

[20] Apollonius of Perge, *Con.* I pref., II pref.; Galen, *De libris propriis* II (K XIX 17 = SM II 97f.).

[21] A. J. P. Kenny, *A Stylometric Study of the New Testament* (Clarendon Press, Oxford, 1986), p. 72: 'The Acts of the Apostles is closer to Luke than it is to any of the other works of the NT, including the synoptic Gospels; but Luke, while being very close to Acts, is slightly closer to Matthew and Mark than it is to Acts.'

the text itself. Failing any other clear references to Theophilus or his interests in the text, it would be dangerous to assume that Luke's point of view throughout his narrative was determined by a wish to please this particular reader. As with the scientific texts we have studied, the nature of the text as a whole is not determined solely by the dedication, but must be considered also in relation to the broader socio-literary context of the tradition in which it stands.

The literary occasion: preface and text

We turn now to the relation of the preface to its literary occasion. Why does this particular preface appear at the head of this particular text? In an earlier article, we posed the question from the author's point of view: why did Luke choose to begin with this preface? (Alexander, 1986, pp. 63ff.). Here we shall rephrase it in terms of the readers. It is the job of a preface to arouse readers' expectations and to give them certain clues, implicit or explicit, as to what is to come. Would the informed ancient reader (i.e. the one attuned to the implicit signals given by literary convention) have been disappointed by the text which follows the preface? Does the preface arouse expectations which the text fails to fulfill?

Readers and expectations

The underlying assumption of most twentieth-century criticism of the preface has been that alongside its comparatively simple surface message the informed reader would also pick up covert messages about the genre of the work in hand. At this level, as we saw in chapter 1, the preface has long been a determining factor in the critical decision to read Luke–Acts as 'Greek history'. But if our argument is correct, then most of the varied approaches to reading Luke–Acts as 'history' in the Greco-Roman tradition are based on a misreading of the preface. The signals it is sending out have been misinterpreted by twentieth-century critics in a way that would not have been possible for the informed contemporary reader.

It is perhaps worth pausing at this point to make clear what we are saying here. The point so far is a purely negative one: the preface does not point towards a reading of the following text in terms of Greco-Roman historiography. That statement says nothing in and of itself about historical accuracy, which is not (and never was) coterminous with Greco-Roman historiography. Neither does it exclude the possibility that the text might contain other clear signals which would point in that direction. But in point of fact, I believe, the preface has always held a key position in the argument.[22] Once the preface is removed, other 'historiographical' elements carry less conviction, and readings in terms of other literary traditions may begin to seem more compelling: the multiple dating at Luke 2.1ff. for example, may be modelled not on Thucydides but on the datings of prophetic oracles in the Greek Bible, and the speeches, dramatic episodes and characterization of Acts may prove to be best paralleled in the Septuagint and in the novelistic tales familiar to both Jewish and pagan readers.[23] And this brings us from the negative to the positive: if the signals given by the preface point (in terms of Greco-Roman literature) not to the historiographical but to the scientific tradition, what would the informed reader expect in the text which follows?

It is worth reminding ourselves at this stage that at surface level the preface actually does little to arouse anybody's expectations, at least as regards the content of what is to follow. Unlike the openings of Matthew, Mark and John, it contains no promise of revelation, no mention of Jesus, no overtly religious language at all: such possibly 'Christian' terms as there are (πεπληροφορημένων, ὑπηρέται τοῦ λόγου) would be opaque to the outsider unfamiliar with the argot of the Christian tradition, deliberately muffled by the predominantly neutral, secular terminology (διήγησιν, πραγμάτων, αὐτόπται, ἀσφάλεια). All the reader is told to expect is an account of tradition, carefully (or accurately) 'followed' and then written down 'in an orderly fashion', a written confirmation of something the dedicatee (and by implication the reader) has already heard.

If these expectations are modest, they are also perfectly fitted to the traditional account which follows and to the Christian narrative

---

[22] Cf. e.g. Dibelius, 1956, 146–7; Conzelmann, 1966, esp. p. 218; Nineham, 1960, pp. 253ff.; Plümacher, 1972, p. 137; Cadbury, 1927, *passim*.

[23] Dating: the date at Luke 3.1–2 is attached to the coming of 'the word of the Lord' to the prophet John, i.e. it corresponds to the dating found at the beginning of many of the biblical prophetic books. An interest in chronology is characteristic of the OT as of other near eastern histories, and appears even in such apparently timeless stories as that of Tobit (1.2; cf. Judith 1.1–2). Gärtner (1955, ch. 1) noted that Luke's speeches fit the biblical pattern of 'sermonizing' better than the Thucydidean habit of speech-writing; cf. also Cadbury, 1927, pp. 191–3 on septuagintal parallels to Luke's insertion of songs and prayers into his narrative. The 'novelistic' element in Acts was noted by Dibelius, 1956, pp. 1–25, and has recently been examined in depth by Pervo 1987. Further, Alexander, 1978, ch. 4.2 n. 4.

world which it creates. For the reader who is an 'insider', the reassurance lies precisely here: this is an accurate account *of the tradition*. The text is not set against the tradition but in alignment with it. Luke promises not independent 'investigation' but faithful recording of received tradition (verse 2); he does not challenge his predecessors but ranges his own work alongside theirs ('it seemed good to me also'); the 'order' that he promises is probably no more than the inevitable concomitant of the move from oral storytelling to written narrative.

But, it may still be asked, is not our hypothetical informed reader still going to be disappointed, or at the very least puzzled, when the narrative which unfolds proves to be so very unlike the mathematical or medical treatises which begin with prefaces like this? The objection is a serious one, and caution might encourage us to rest content with the negative conclusions just outlined. The appearance of these prefaces in the scientific tradition, we could argue, shows only that their use reveals nothing about the genre or provenance of the texts to which they are attached. If direct dependence of Luke's preface on the prefaces found in hellenistic Jewish literature is unlikely (above ch. 7), nevertheless those parallels do suggest that use of explanatory prefaces similar to the 'scientific' preface-type has become fairly widespread by the first century AD. This would be a reasonable, and, on the face of it, a satisfactory conclusion to our study. To stop there would at least have the merit of taking us no further than the strictest interpretation of the evidence permits. I believe, however, that Luke's preface is significantly closer to those of the scientific writers (especially to those of his contemporary Hero of Alexandria) than to any other group, and that his links with the scientific tradition go deeper than the mere adoption of a conventional form of words (ch. 8 pp. 172–4). Our final task must be to construct a positive model for understanding how these links might work.

Biography in the scientific tradition

The most obvious way to tie in Luke's work with the scientific tradition is to focus on its biographical character. Our question will then be: what place does biography play in the school tradition? Charles Talbert has done valuable work here in directing our attention to the lives of the philosophers as a literary parallel to the Gospel genre, with Acts as a parallel to the 'succession' narratives

found in Diogenes Laertius.[24] Talbert's argument is ingenious and
has much to recommend it, and he has rightly highlighted the
widespread biographical interest in the lives of great teachers, an
interest which was not confined to the philosophical schools. Thus,
for example, there was clearly interest in Cos in the biography of the
founder of antiquity's most famous medical school, Hippocrates,[25]
and there is some evidence of biographical interest in mathematicians like Archimedes and Hippocrates of Chios.[26] The role of such
biographical material within the school traditions should certainly
be explored in any future investigation of the literary genre of
Luke–Acts. There are however certain obvious difficulties in the
analogy, not only with regard to literary form,[27] but also, and more
seriously, with regard to function. Talbert points out, rightly, that
the lifestyle of a philosophical teacher was an important part of his
teaching. But as far as we can see the normal vehicle for this
exemplary material was the individual anecdote, not the full biography: in New Testament terms, the pericope not the Gospel. Where
there is evidence of a connected biography its function is clearly
ancillary to the bibliographical task of cataloguing the writings of a
philosopher.[28] It was the teaching tradition which was central in the
philosophical (and presumably other) schools, and biographical
material about the teacher was normally secondary to that.

Talbert's model thus works better for Acts than for the Gospel.
Luke's account of Paul's missionary activities could well be seen as a

---

[24] C. H. Talbert, *Literary Patterns, Theological Themes and the Genre of Luke–
Acts* (SBLMS 20, Scholars Press, Missoula, 1974), ch. 8; *idem*', 'Biographies of
philosophers and rulers as instruments of religious propaganda in Mediterranean
antiquity', *ANRW* II 16.2 (1978), pp. 1619–51; *idem, What is a Gospel?* (Fortress
Press, Philadelphia, 1977).

[25] Lives of Hippocrates: cf. *RE* VIII 2 s.v. *Hippokrates* no. 16 (1802–3) and *RE*
Suppl. VIA, 1292–1305, where Edelstein argues that the roots of the later *Lives* lie in
a Hippocratic legend of Coan origin arising in the second century BC. See now J.R.
Pinault, *Hippocratic Lives and Legends* (Leiden, Brill, 1992).

[26] Archimedes: cf. Plutarch, *Marcellus* 14f. Hippocrates of Chios: *RE* VIII 2 s.v.
Hippokrates no. 14 (1780–1801).

[27] The literary forms employed in this biographical activity appear to be (i) the
anecdote or single biographical episode and (ii) the collection of comparative lives,
lives of a school etc. The latter (which appear as early as the hellenistic period) seem
to be belletristic productions which must by their very nature have been composed
from a standpoint external to that of the school.

[28] A task which is also important to Diogenes Laertius. Andronicus' biography of
Aristotle seems to have been little more than an annotated bibliography: I. Düring,
Aristotle in the Ancient Biographical Tradition (Acta Universitatis Gothoburgensis/
Göteborgs Universitets Årsskrift LXIII (1957)/2), pp. 467, 413–25.

biographical/hagiographical appendage to the corpus of genuine and deutero-Pauline epistles, put together as an accompaniment to this pre-existent body of Pauline teaching. Acts would in fact make a lot of sense as the product of a 'Pauline school' which was also indulging in the typical 'school' activities of collecting a corpus of letters and expanding it along lines deemed to express the master's thought in changing circumstances.[29] But for the Gospel we lack the essential component of the analogy, namely a body of Jesus' teaching separate from and pre-existent to the narrative of his life. It is of course true that such a body has from time to time been postulated in Gospel studies ('Q'; the 'Logia'), and that the discovery of the Gospel of Thomas demonstrated that at least one (Gnostic) Christian group possessed a Gospel which consisted only of sayings. But the more we press the analogy, the further it seems to recede. Why was the central component, Jesus' teaching, lost so soon? Was it simply combined into the (Marcan) narrative by Matthew? If so, this was quite different from the procedure of the philosophical schools, and Luke, who is *ex hypothesi* closer to the world of the schools than Matthew, is even less systematic in his combination of teaching and biography.

The literary praxis of the scientific tradition

To explore these possibilities fully would of course take us outside the boundaries of the present study. But the difficulties involved in treating the Gospel as a 'philosophical biography' suggest that we should perhaps be looking in a different direction. If the Gospel is not a biographical appendage to a (separate) central core of Christian teaching, does it represent that central core itself? On this model, the biographical form of the Gospels simply echoes the form of the tradition which lies behind them: in the group or groups responsible for this material, the 'Good News' consisted of stories *about* Jesus, and it is this 'tradition' which Luke claims to be putting

[29] The idea of a Pauline 'school' was suggested by Conzelmann in 'Paulus und die Weisheit', *NTS* 12 (1965) p. 233: further, Meeks, 1983, p. 82 and p. 223 nn. 44, 45. Literary links between Acts and the Pastoral Epistles have been noted by e.g. J. D. Quinn ('The last volume of Luke: the relation of Luke–Acts to the Pastoral Epistles', in C. H. Talbert (ed.), *Perspectives on Luke–Acts* (T. & T. Clark, Edinburgh, Assoc. of Baptist Professors of Religion, Danville, USA, 1978), pp. 62–75); but as H. Gamble demonstrates ('The redaction of the Pauline letters and the formation of the Pauline corpus', *JBL* 94 (1975), pp. 403–18), few of the many scholars who talk of the redaction of the Pauline corpus have constructed a convincing social context for such an activity.

into written form for Theophilus.[30] The parallel with scientific literature, then, could be sought not in content or form but in literary praxis.

The advantage of this approach is that it enables us to make a comparison not with biographical material, which must always be to some degree peripheral, but with certain central features of the scholastic literary tradition. We have already observed (above ch. 4 p. 42) that there is little equivalence of form between the various areas which make up this tradition, just as there is little room for comparison as regards content between, say, the machines described by Philo of Byzantium and the surgical operations of Apollonius of Citium, or between Hermogenes' rhetorical precepts and Hero's technical mathematics. But what many of these writers do have in common is precisely what they also share with Luke. Luke's respect for tradition, his lack of polemic against his predecessors, his lack of concern for originality: all of these, as we have demonstrated above, can be paralleled in the scientific tradition (ch. 6). Behind the words of the preface lies a whole cultural world with a distinctive approach to literature, a world in which an oral teaching tradition is more important than written sources (ch. 5, pp. 82–5), a world in which even the *logos* so revered by most cultured Greeks is treated with suspicion (ch. 5, pp. 88–91). It is a world in which the *content* of the tradition, continually presented afresh and updated by the 'living voice' of a succession of teachers, is more important than verbal fidelity to any particular written crystallization of it (above ch. 4 pp. 42–4), and in which, therefore, the written text itself can be treated as transitional, subject to continual revision in the light of new insights or changing circumstances.[31]

Thus, to return to our starting-point, our hypothetical informed

---

[30] Whether that tradition was known to him as a fluid collection of independent anecdotes, or whether it was already structured as a full-length life-story of Jesus, is a separate question which does not concern us at this point. The point is that whether or not Luke knew and used a written source such as Mark's Gospel, what he talks about in the preface is 'tradition'.

[31] See further Alexander, 1990. The texts of both Erotian and Dioscorides were early recast into alphabetical form: see the introductions to the editions of Wellmann and Nachmanson, and, on Dioscorides, John M. Riddle, *Dioscorides on Pharmacy and Medicine* (Austin, University of Texas Press, 1985), esp. pp. 177–8. There is evidence for a similar ongoing revision process in the texts of Vettius Valens (see Kroll's introduction, p. xi; Simpson, 1930, p. 399) and Thessalus (Friedrich (1968) pp. 16, 26 n. 1). The phenomenon was widespread: cf. Heath, 1896, p. lxxvi; Keyes, 1935, p. 30. Further, Alexander, 1978, p. 146.

reader would find much that was familiar in the literary praxis of Luke–Acts. S/he would not expect to learn much from the preface regarding the particular shape of Luke's 'tradition'. A Christian reader, on our hypothesis, would already be familiar with its basic outline; an outsider would simply wait for the nature of the tradition to be made clear once the preface was over. Neither would be surprised by the abrupt change in style as the narrative begins at Luke 1.5: this is a normal feature in scientific texts (ch. 6, pp. 103–4). Likewise such a reader would not expect 'the familiar parade of proofs from the official archives' which, as Cadbury rightly noted, is so conspicuously absent in Luke–Acts.[32] As we have seen, that particular form of documentation belongs to the antiquarian side of Greco-Roman historiography and is alien both to rhetorical history and (for different reasons) to scientific literature (ch. 3, pp. 32–4; ch. 5 pp. 79–80). Within this literary framework, Luke's brief introductory description of his traditional sources would be deemed to provide both proper and sufficient warranty for the trustworthiness of his work.

It may reasonably be objected at this point that most of what has been said applies much more readily to the Gospel than to Acts – or to 'Luke–Acts', the single two-volume work which is normally reckoned as Luke's achievement. But this problem, as we have demonstrated in chapter 6, is integral to the exegesis of the preface itself, which in fact contains no positive pointer to the existence of a second 'volume'. Briefly, there are two ways of resolving it: either to show that Acts too is an account of traditional material, or to divorce Acts from the preface to the Gospel. Despite the predominance of the view that 'Luke–Acts' should be conceived as a single work, there are critics who are happy to accept the latter conclusion: Haenchen, for example, argued some time ago that 'the prologue to Luke applies only to the third gospel' (Haenchen, 1971, p. 136 n. 3; in more detail, p. 118–19; Conzelmann, 1987, p. 4). On the other hand, and for reasons that have nothing to do with the preface, there are also critics prepared to argue for a much greater amount of traditional material in Acts than is usually accepted

---

[32] Cadbury, 1927, p. 191: 'The absence in Luke of the familiar parade of proofs from the official archives is brought home to us by the contrast of Justin Martyr, who refers to the census records of Quirinius and the *acta* of Pilate as mentioning respectively the birth and the death of Jesus.' Cadbury is surely also right (1927, pp. 190–1) in classifying the letters in Acts with the speeches, rather than as documents. Similarly with the 'we-passages': these may or may not be based on authentic first-person documents, but Luke does not present them as such.

(notably, Jervell, 1962). The real problem is not the amount of such material but its form-critical status: New Testament scholarship has been reluctant to imagine a *Sitz im Leben* in which anecdotes about Paul and the Jerusalem apostles were treasured and repeated with anything like the care and attention accorded to anecdotes about Jesus. But it is not really difficult to construct a social context at least for Pauline material among a group of Pauline disciples/successors, perhaps the same as the one which was also to collect and extend the Pauline letter-corpus, perhaps a rival group: thus for example the story of Paul's dramatic change from persecutor to convert, which figures three times with varied detail in Acts, is also used by Paul himself in the letters for a variety of purposes, both parenetic and polemical (Gal. 1.13–23; Phil. 3.5–7; I Cor. 15.3–11). However we add it all up, the most extraordinary thing about Luke's literary achievement is simply that his double work combines tradition belonging to two specialist groups in early Christianity which otherwise appear to have few links, the Pauline group and the group (or one of the groups) associated with synoptic traditions; it is arguably just this combination which is Luke's most radical contribution in the development of early Christian self-definition.

The question of sources

The question of Luke's relationship to his sources needs a little more attention, however, before we leave the preface. Many would argue that it is precisely here that Luke's readers are most likely to find the preface misleading. Twentieth-century readers aware of the 'Synoptic problem' may well complain, like Lightfoot (1962, pp. 103–05), of Luke's cavalier handling of his major source: in Caird's words, 'The Markan Hypothesis involves the corollary that Luke used wide editorial freedom in rewriting his sources.'[33] Such readers find it frankly incredible that Luke's work should be regarded as a faithful following of tradition: and surely on any synoptic hypothesis the problem of Luke's relationship with the other Gospels is one that must colour our reading of the preface.

The first point to make, of course, is that we are not primarily concerned here with Luke's actual authorial achievement, or even with his intentions, but with the rhetoric of the preface itself. To examine the match between rhetoric and reality in Luke–Acts would

[33] G. B. Caird, *St. Luke* (Pelican Gospel Commentaries; Penguin Books, Harmondsworth, 1963), p. 23.

take us far beyond the scope of this chapter. But it is within the range of the question we have posed to ask how far first- or second-century readers would have been conscious of a mismatch regarding Luke's attitude to source material; and in fact I believe that such readers, whether or not they knew of the existence of other written Gospels, would have found the reality of Luke's work well within the range of the expectations aroused by the preface.

Scientific literature contains many examples of overlapping and parallel traditions of the type we have in the synoptic Gospels: Philo, Vitruvius and Hero provide good examples (above ch. 5 p. 80 n. 23 and p. 85 nn. 34, 35). In each case the preface stresses simply a general indebtedness to 'tradition': Philo speaks of what he has learnt from the master-craftsmen of Alexandria and Rhodes, Hero of 'the tradition of the ancients', and Vitruvius simply of 'what I have learnt from my teachers'. Critics have assumed that extensive literary borrowing actually underlies these texts, but it is significant that prefatorial rhetoric prefers to emphasize personal contact with teachers (further, ch. 5, pp. 78–87). The scientific tradition thus provides a literary matrix contemporary with the Gospels within which the nature of Luke's relationships with the other Gospels (and indeed the nature of synoptic relationships in general) could profitably be investigated.

In particular, the nature and function of the rewriting of predecessors within this tradition would repay detailed study. Cadbury's important treatment of this subject (1927, ch. 12) focusses on literary motives for rewriting: the importance of rhetorical *variatio*, and the need for stylistic improvement to an unpolished *hypomnēma* (1927, pp. 137–9; cf. 1922a, p. 15). But stylistic improvement is not wholly satisfactory as an explanation for the Lucan treatment of Mark, and in any case the finished result is still, from the ancient point of view, a *hypomnēma*.[34] Acquaintance with the scientific tradition suggests an alternative solution. Scientific texts share with the synoptic Gospels a puzzling combination of fixity and fluidity which has suggested at least to some Gospel critics an analogy with 'oral traditional literature' in which any given version of a story is not so much a reworking of a text as a new performance of material perceived as existing prior to and independently of the written text. This analogy was explored at some length by the Homeric scholar

---

[34] Tertullian describes Acts as a *commentarius*: 'in eodem commentario Lucae', *De ieiunio* x.3. On *commentarius* as the Latin equivalent to *hypomnēma*, see F. Bömer, 'Der *Commentarius*', *Hermes* 81 (1953), pp. 210–50).

Albert Lord at a colloquium held in 1977, on *The Relationships Among the Gospels*. In the debate which followed Lord's paper, attention focussed, *inter alia*, on the difficulty of locating such 'oral' processes within the highly literate society of the first-century Greco-Roman world.[35] More recent studies have made it clear, however, that the triumph of literacy over orality in the ancient world has been overestimated, and that many of the attitudes we would associate with a primary oral culture lingered on long after the fifth century BC.[36] One particular pocket where these attitudes survived, as I have argued elsewhere, was the hellenistic schools (Alexander, 1990).

We would suggest, then, that the similar treatment of 'sources' among the Gospel-writers and in the scientific tradition arises from similar origins in a social context where a living teaching tradition, conservatively preserved and yet constantly adapted to changing circumstances, has priority over written school texts.[37] The evidence suggests that, as with the 'oral folk literature' described by Parry and Lord (cf. n. 35 above). the process of writing down such a tradition would not be a simple stenographic operation: the written text, like each oral presentation before it, will be a new 'performance' in which the 'given' of tradition receives the individual stamp of the author.[38] Even after material of this sort is written down, its period of fluidity is not at an end: many of the texts in our study are described by their editors as 'school texts', with a confused and

[35] Albert Lord, 'The Gospels as oral traditional literature', in W. O. Walker (ed.), *The Relationships Among the Gospels*, (Trinity University Press, San Antonio, 1978, pp. 33–91); reply by Charles Talbert ibid., pp. 93–102, esp. pp. 101–2; seminar notes by L. E. Keck, ibid. pp. 103–22, esp. pp. 114–16.

[36] Thomas, 1989, Introduction and ch. 1; Harris, 1989, *passim*; and cf. O. Andersen, 'The significance of writing in early Greece', in K. Schousboe and M. Trolle Larsen (eds.), *Literacy and Society* (Copenhagen University Centre for Research in the Humanities, Akademisk Forlag, 1989), pp. 73–90. We should probably learn to think of points along a continuum ranging from 'oral' to 'literate' rather than a black and white distinction: as Talbert notes in the discussion cited in n. 35, Josephus and many other fully literate hellenistic writers betray an attitude to the rewriting of source material which is comparable to patterns found in oral traditional literature, though not (I believe) as close as the technical handbooks. But the whole subject would repay a much more thorough analysis than is possible here.

[37] The importance of the living teaching tradition for understanding Galen's attitude to the interpretation of Hippocrates is well expressed by Wesley D. Smith, *The Hippocratic Tradition* (Cornell Publications in the History of Science, Cornell University Press, Ithaca, New York and London, 1979), pp. 72–3.

[38] The readiness of scientific writers to correct and improve the 'tradition' which they claim to be preserving is significant in this respect: cf. n. 31 above and Alexander, 1990, pp. 235–7.

complex textual history which must at least in part be due to the fact that the written text was treated as open to improvement long after its first committal to writing (cf. n. 31 above). Noting a similar phenomenon in the 'Western' text of Acts, Dibelius argued that it was due to the fact (which he deduced from the preface) that Acts had circulated independently of the gospel 'in the book-trade' (Dibelius, 1956, pp. 84–92). As we have seen, there is no evidence for commercial publication for either Luke or Acts; but we would suggest that there is an explanation for the phenomenon far readier to hand in the parallel with the treatment of this 'Gebrauchs-literatur' within the schools.

Conclusions

As with all good quests, the end of our search for the social context of the Lucan preface is looking more and more like the beginning of a new one. Literary and social factors both seem to be converging towards one point: the need to look seriously at the world of the hellenistic schools and their literature as an essential element in the socio-cultural background of the New Testament. As Malherbe points out (1983, p. 16), literature, like language itself, needs to be understood in relation to a social context. Literary convention creates its own language, expressed or unexpressed: and this, like any other language, presupposes an audience. Thus the use of literary convention necessitates the existence of a shared world of discourse in which writer and readers can assume a certain basic level of understanding as a foundation for communication: the writer may take the reader along unexpected paths, but the journey cannot even begin unless the two have a basic level of mutual understanding.

In the broadest sense, that understanding is defined by language: Luke writes in Greek, and this means that his constituency, at its maximum estimation, encompasses a wide range of audiences in the first-century Mediterranean world. In chapter 8 we tried to narrow down the broad range by examining linguistic and cultural affinities within that world. The result was what we might call a general enabling thesis that on the external socio-cultural plane, Luke's use of literary convention is compatible with such evidence as we have about the social and educational level of most early Christians, and with the linguistic consensus on the 'literate but not literary' language of the New Testament (and of Luke–Acts in particular). The hellenistic school tradition can also plausibly be located within this broad social matrix. But the detailed comparisons suggested in this chapter presuppose a much more specific and concrete link with that tradition at the internal level of literary praxis. In other words, we are moving on from the observation that Luke–Acts and the scientific treatises studied belong to the same socio-cultural stratum of Greco-Roman society to the proposal that Luke is writing from within a Christian social context which is in significant respects like that of the hellenistic schools themselves.

This is not the place to argue in full the propriety of exploring the analogy between early Christian groups and the schools of the Greco-Roman world.[39] The comparison is not a new one; it builds on ancient perceptions[40] and can be structured in a variety of ways.[41] If we are to take it seriously again, as I believe we must, we must also take seriously the links and parallels between the hellenistic schools and the rabbinic, as well as the enormous variety of the hellenistic schools themselves. We must take into account not only the rarefied academic atmosphere of the Academy or the Museum, but also the humbler philosophical teacher whose class has been described as resembling a catechism class (M. L. Clarke, *Higher Education in the Ancient World* (Routledge & Kegan Paul, London, 1971), p. 96). We must look at medical schools as well as philosophical, and must bear in mind the largely undocumented training and apprenticeship schemes of the professions and crafts (Burford, 1972, p. 87–91). But wherever these explorations may take us, I believe that the comparison is important not only for the so-called 'sociological' understanding of the early Christians but also for our understanding of their literature. Some of the most basic questions about the New Testament demand a specific socio-literary frame-

[39] I have argued this point at more length in a paper presented at the British New Testament Conference in Bristol in September 1989 under the title, 'The New Testament and the hellenistic schools', and in my forthcoming paper, 'Paul and the hellenistic schools: the evidence of Galen' (*Paul and His Hellenistic Context*, conference held in Copenhagen June 1991: to be published by Fortress Press, ed. Troels Engberg-Pedersen).

[40] Cf. Philo, *Spec.Leg.* II, 62; Josephus, *BJ* II, 119–66; *Ant.* XIII, 171–3; *Ant.* XVIII, 11ff.; Galen, texts cited in R. Walzer, *Galen on Jews and Christians* (Oxford University Press, 1949), cf. R. L. Wilken, *The Christians as the Romans Saw Them* (New Haven, Yale University Press, 1984), ch. 4.

[41] Meeks, 1983, pp. 81–4; Stambaugh and Balch, 1986, pp. 142–5; Judge, 1960, 1961. Cf. K. Stendahl, *The School of St. Matthew* (Acta Sem. Neotest. Upsal. 20, Uppsala 1954); R. A. Culpepper, *The Johannine School* (SBLDS 26, Scholars Press, Missoula, 1975); and M. Hengel, *The Johannine Question* (SCM Press, London, 1990); Gerhardsson, 1961, pp. 329ff.). For Paul, cf. n. 29 above.

work for their discussion: what is the relationship between written text and oral teaching? When and why are texts written down? How do they achieve canonical status? What is the relationship between individual authorship and fidelity to tradition? How is tradition preserved and how is it updated? The body of literature which we have called the 'scientific tradition' might well provide just such a framework.

Appendix A

STRUCTURAL ANALYSIS OF LUKE 1.1–4
AND SELECTED SCIENTIFIC PREFACES

1. Luke 1. 1–4

1	Ἐπειδήπερ πολλοὶ ἐπεχείρησαν ἀνατάξασθαι διήγησιν περὶ τῶν πεπληροφορημένων ἐν ἡμῖν πραγμάτων,	Causal clause (*epei*): other writers.
2	καθὼς παρέδοσαν ἡμῖν οἱ ἀπ᾽ ἀρχῆς αὐτόπται καὶ ὑπηρέται γενόμενοι τοῦ λόγου,	Adverbial clause dependent on cl. 1: description of subject-matter.
3	ἔδοξε κἀμοὶ	Main verb: author's decision.
4	παρηκολουθηκότι ἄνωθεν πᾶσιν ἀκριβῶς	Participial clause dependent on ind. obj. of main vb.: author's qualifications.
5	καθεξῆς σοι γράψαι, κράτιστε Θεόφιλε,	Object clause: treatment of subject-matter. Address (rhetorical).
6	ἵνα ἐπιγνῷς περὶ ὧν κατηχήθης λόγων τὴν ασφάλειαν.	Final clause: results for dedicatee.

2. Diocles of Carystus, *Letter to Antigonus* (IV/III BC)

1	ΔΙΟΚΛΗΣ ᾽ΑΝΤΙΓΟΝΩΙ	Address: epistolary.
2	᾽Επειδή σοι συμβαίνει μουσικωτάτῳ πάντων βασιλέων γεγονέναι καὶ πλεῖστον χρόνον βεβιωκέναι φιλοσοφίας τε πάσης ἔμπειρον ὄντα τυγχάνειν καὶ τοῖς μαθηματικοῖς πρωταγωνιστήν,	Causal clause. Disposition of dedicatee (3-fold).

213

3 ὑπολαμβάνων βασιλικήν τε καὶ οἰκείαν [τὴν] φιλοσοφίαν τὴν περὶ τῶν ὑγιεινῶν ἀκοήν τε καὶ θεωρίαν	2nd causal clause (participial). Nature of subject-matter.
4 γέγραφά σοι	Main verb. Author's decision to write.
5 πόθεν αἱ νόσοι τοῖς ἀνθρώποις συνίστανται καὶ τίνων προγενομένων σημείων, καὶ πῶς ἄν τις αὐταῖς βοηθῶν ἐπιτυγχάνοι·	Object of main verb: indirect question. Contents of work.
6 οὔτε γὰρ χειμὼν < ἂν > ἐν τῷ οὐρανῷ συσταίη ποτὲ μὴ οὐχὶ σημείων τινῶν προγενομένων, οἷσπερ παρακολουθοῦσιν οἱ ναυτικοὶ καὶ οἱ πολύπειροι τῶν ἀνθρώπων, οὔτε πάθος ἐν ἀνθρώπου φύσει συσταίη ποτὲ μὴ οὐχὶ σημείου τινὸς προγενομένου.	Parenthesis: expansion of (5).
7 σὺ δὲ πεισθεὶς τοῖς ὑφ᾽ ἡμῶν λεγομένοις παρακολουθήσεις τῇ ἀκριβείᾳ τῇ περὶ αὐτῶν.	Additional sentence at end: results for dedicatee.

3. Demetrius, *Formae Epistolicae* (I BC)

1 Τῶν ἐπιστολικῶν τύπων, ὦ Ἡρακλείδη, ἐχόντων τὴν θεωρίαν τοῦ συνεστάναι μὲν ἀπὸ πλειόνων εἰδῶν, ἀναβάλλεσθαι δὲ ἐκ τῶν ἀεὶ πρὸς τὸ παρὸν ἁρμοζόντων, καὶ καθηκόντων μὲν ὡς τεχνικώτατα γράφεσθαι, γραφομένων δ᾽ ὡς ἔτυχεν ὑπὸ τῶν τὰς τοιαύτας τοῖς ἐπὶ πραγμάτων ταττομένοις ὑπουργίας ἀναδεχομένων,	Causal clause (genitive absolute). Nature of the subject-matter. Address: rhetorical, inserted after first few words. Causal cl. contd.: faults of practitioners.
2 θεωρῶν σε φιλοτίμως ἔχοντα πρός φιλομαθείαν	2nd causal clause: part. agreeing with subj. of main verb. Disposition of dedicatee.
3 ἐπραγματευσάμην	Main verb: author's decision.
4 διά τινων συστήσειν ἰδεῶν καὶ πόσας καὶ ἃς ἔχουσι διαφοράς,	Object of main vb.: indirect question. Contents of work.

5 καὶ καθάπερ δεῖγμα τῆς ἑκάστου γένους τάξεως ὑποδέδειχα	2nd vb.: method of composition.
6 προσεκθέμενος μερικῶς τὸν περὶ ἑκάστου λόγον,	Part. agreeing with subj. of main vb.: further details of composition.
7 ἅμα μὲν ὑπολαμβάνων καὶ σοὶ τοῦτο κεχαρισμένον ὑπάρχειν, εἴ τι τῶν ἄλλων περισσότερον εἰδήσεις τὸ λαμπρὸν τοῦ βίου τιθέμενος οὐκ ἐν τοῖς βρώμασιν, ἀλλ᾽ ἐν ταῖς ἐπιστήμαις,	2nd. participial cl. agreeing with subj. of main vb. Results for dedicatee.
8 ἅμα δὲ κἀμὲ νομίζων τοῦ προσήκοντος ἐπαίνου μεθέξειν.	3rd part. cl.: results for author.

Second long sentence of preface contains reflections of a general moral nature.

4. Hero of Alexandria, *Pneumatica* I (I AD)

1 Τῆς πνευματικῆς πραγματείας σπουδῆς ἠξιωμένης πρὸς τῶν παλαιῶν φιλοσόφων τε καὶ μηχανικῶν,	Causal clause (genitive absol.): nature of subject-matter/other writers.
2 τῶν μὲν λογικῶς τὴν δύναμιν αὐτῆς ἀποδεδωκότων, τῶν δὲ καὶ δι᾽ αὐτῆς τῆς τῶν αἰσθητῶν ἐνεργείας,	Participial cl. dependent on cl. 1: methodological classification of other writers.
3 ἀναγκαῖον ὑπάρχειν νομίζομεν καὶ αὐτοὶ	Main vb.: author's decision.
4 τὰ παραδοθέντα ὑπὸ τῶν ἀρχαίων εἰς τάξιν ἀγαγεῖν,	Object-clause: description of subject-matter.
5 καὶ ἃ ἡμεῖς δὲ προσευρήκαμεν εἰσθέσθαι·	2nd object-cl.: descr. contd.
οὕτως γὰρ τοὺς μετὰ ταῦτα ἐν τοῖς μαθήμασιν ἀναστρέφεσθαι βουλομένους ὠφελεῖσθαι συμβήσεται.	Additional main clause: results for readers.

Second sentence of pref. (same length) gives bibliographical details.

5. Galen of Pergamon, *De Typis* (II AD)

1 Πολλῶν πλατυτέρω ὑπὲρ τῆς
περὶ τύπων θεωρίας
πεπραγματευμένων,

Causal clause (genitive absol.):
other writers.

2 ἀναγκαῖον ἡγησάμην αὐτὸς

Main vb.: author's decision.

3 ὁριστικώτερον καὶ κατὰ
περιγραφὴν ἐπιδραμεῖν
ταῦτα,

Object clause: specifies
treatment of subject-matter.

4 οὕτως εὐκαταρίθμητον καὶ
εὐκαταμάθητον οἰόμενος τοῖς
νεωστὶ προσιοῦσι τῇ τέχνῃ τὸ
πρᾶγμα,

Participial cl. dep. on subj. of
main vb.: results for readers.

5 ὅν τε ἁπλοῦν καὶ μετὰ τὴν
ἁπλουστέραν κατάληψιν
εὐκολώτερον,
καὶ καθάπερ ἐξ ἑτοίμου τοῖς
πολλοῖς ἐντυγχάνον.

2 participial clauses dependent
on object of previous clause:
nature of subject-matter.

6 ἀρκτέον δ' ἐντεῦθεν.

Transitional formula.

Appendix B

BIBLIOGRAPHICAL NOTES ON SCIENTIFIC PREFACES

Note: This is not intended to be a complete bibliography on the authors cited. I have simply listed the editions and studies used in the text, together with translations where available and where known to me. The following general reference works on Greek science and technology (listed in the main bibliography) should also be consulted: Africa 1968; Burford 1972; Drachmann 1963; Fraser 1972; Fuhrmann 1960; Gille 1980; Heath 1921; Lloyd 1970, 1973; Neugebauer 1969; Oleson 1984.

1 Apollonius of Citium

Texts studied
Commentary on the De Articulis *of Hippocrates*, Bk. I (pref. and epilogue), Bk. II (pref. and epil.), Bk. III (pref. and epil.).

Edition
J. Kollesch and F. Kudlien, *Apollonios von Kitium, Kommentar zu Hippokrates Über das Einrenken der Gelenke* (*CMG* XI 1, 1). Berlin, Akademie-Verlag, 1965. (Greek text with German translation.)
   I use this as the most accessible text, while sharing the reservations expressed in his review by Alpers (*Gnomon* 39, 1967, pp. 26–33) about its value over against the earlier edition of Hermann Schöne (*Apollonius von Kitium illustrierter Kommentar zu der Hippokratischen Schrift περὶ ἄρθρων*, Leipzig 1896).

Date
Mid-first century BC (Schöne, 1896, p. xxiv). Schöne's historical introduction is still indispensable; but see also Deichgräber, 1930, pp. 206ff., 262–3, 321–2, 334; Fraser, 1972, I pp. 362–3, II pp. 536–7.

Textual note
The MS text in I 1, followed by Kollesch and Kudlien, should be emended: Cocchi's conjecture θεωρῶν for θεωρῶ is undoubtedly correct. The editors argue (Kollesch and Kudlien, 1961, p. 328) that Apollonius is quite capable of the asyndeton. This may well be true in general, but is surely least of all likely in his careful opening sentence; and the conjecture creates a structure

217

paralleled in many other scientific prefaces (cf. also Alpers, *Gnomon* 39 (1967) p. 31).

2 Apollonius of Perge

Tests studied

1 *Conica* Bk. I pref. (Heiberg vol. I pp. 2–4); Bk. II pref. (vol. I p. 192); Bk. IV pref. (vol. II pp. 2–4). Cited by volume, page and line of Heiberg's edition.

Edition

I. L. Heiberg, *Apollonii Pergaei Quae Graece Exstant* vols. I–II (Teubner, Leipzig 1891–93; repr. Stuttgart 1974).

Translation

Heiberg includes a German translation. ET on pp. lxviii-lxxv of T. L. Heath, *Apollonius of Perga: Treatise on Conic Sections* Cambridge University Press 1896), which includes a translation of the prefaces to Bks V–VII, which survive only in Arabic. See also Fraser, 1972, I pp. 415–22.

Date

Slightly later than Archimedes, i.e. in the latter part of the third century BC.: Fraser, 1972, I pp. 387, 415–18 (with notes); II p. 572 n. 148.

3 Archimedes

Texts studied

(Cited by short title with page and line of Heiberg):

De sphaera et cylindro I = *Sph.Cyl.* I pref. (Heiberg vol. I pp. 2–4); *Sph.Cyl.* II pref. (Heiberg vol. I pp. 168–70);
De conoidibus et sphaeroidibus pref. = *Con.Sph.* (Heiberg vol. I pp. 246–58);
De lineis spiralibus = *Spir.* (Heiberg vol. II pp. 2–12);
Psammites/Arenarius = *Aren.* pref. and epil. (Heiberg vol. II pp. 216, 258);
Quadratura Parabolae pref. = *Quadr.* (Heiberg vol. II pp. 262–6);
Stomachion pref. = *Stom.* (Heiberg vol. II p. 416);
De mechanicis propositionibus ad Eratosthenem methodus pref. = *Eratosth.* (Heiberg vol. II pp. 426–30).

Edition

I. L. Heiberg, *Archimedis Opera Omnis* vols. I–III (Leipzig, Teubner 1910–15). The reprint (ed. E. S. Stamatis: Stuttgart, Teubner 1972) adds nothing of significance.

Translation
German translation in Heiberg, ET in T. L. Heath, *The Works of Archimedes* (Cambridge University Press 1897), which also contains (pp. xv–xxxviii) a valuable account of Archimedes' life and works.

Date
287–212 BC. See further Fraser, 1972, I pp. 397ff., especially 399ff. on the prefaces. On Archimedes' work in general, and particularly on the MS tradition, see also E. J. Dijksterhuis, *Archimedes* (tr. C. Dikshoorn) (Princeton University Press, N.J. 1987), esp. chs. I and II and pp. 419–51.
  See further G. J. Toomer, *Diocles on Burning Mirrors* (Berlin/Heidelberg, Springer-Verlag 1976) for another example of the 'narrative' preface-type (surviving only in Arabic) in the work of a contemporary of Archimedes.

4 Artemidorus Daldianus

Texts studied
Oneirocritica (On the Interpretation of Dreams) Bk. I pref. and epil. (Pack pp. 1–3, 99); Bk. II pref. and epil. (Pack pp. 100, 202–3); Bk. III pref. and epil. (Pack pp. 204, 235); Bk. IV pref. and epil. (Pack pp. 236–8, 300); Bk. V pref. (Pack p. 301–2).

Edition
R. A. Pack, *Artemidorus Daldianus: Onirocriticon Libri V* (Leipzig, Teubner 1963).

Translation
French, with valuable introduction and notes: A.-J. Festugière, *Artémidore: La clef des songes* (Paris, Librairie Philosophique J. Vrin, 1975).
English: Robert J. White, *The Interpretation of Dreams* (New Jersey, Noyes Press, 1975).
German: F. S. Krauss and M. Kaiser, *Artemidor von Daldis: Traumbuch* (Basel/Stuttgart, Schwabe & Co., 1965).

Date
Latter part of the second century AD (cf. refs. to Hadrian and Antonius in I 26 and I 64). On Artemidorus see especially Th. Hopfner, *art.* 'Traumdeutung', *RE* VI A2 (1937) cols. 2233–45, esp. 2240–4; Claes Blum, 'Studies in the Dream-Book of Artemidorus', Uppsala, Diss. Inaug. 1936.

5 Bito

Texts studied
Kataskeuai pref. and epil. (Marsden pp. 66, 76). Reference numbers are to Wescher's pages, with Marsden's line numeration.

Edition
Text and English translation in Marsden II (1971) pp. 66–76. Marsden's text is based on the edition of A. Rehm and E. Schramm, *Abhandlungen der Bayrischen Akademie d. Wissenschaften, Phil.-hist. Abteilung*, NF II (1929).

Date
Second century BC. Marsden II (1971) p. 78 n. 1, and pp. vii, 5–6; L. Reinhardt, 'De Heronis Alexandrini dicendi genere', Münster, Diss. Inaug. 1930, Appendix I; Drachmann, 1963, p. 11.

6 [Pseudo]-Demetrius

Texts studied
Formae Epistolicae pref., Weichert pp. 1–2.

Edition
V. Weichert, *Demetrii et Libanii que ferunter τυποὶ ἐπιστολικοί et ἐπιστολιμαῖοι χαρακτῆρες* (Leipzig, Teubner, 1910), pp. 1–12. A slightly different recension, based on the Aldine text (*ed. princ.*) of 1499, is available in R. Hercher, *Epistolographi Graeci* (Paris, Didot, 1873), pp. 1–6.

Translation
Abraham J. Malherbe, 'Ancient Epistolary Theorists', *Ohio Journal of Religious Studies* 5 (1977); republished as SBLSBS 19 (Atlanta, Scholars Press, 1988).

Date
Datable elements suggest that the work first took shape in Egypt in the first century BC, but that it was progressively revised by users during the next four centuries: C. W. Keyes, 1935, pp. 28–44. For a study of the whole work in its literary context, see Koskenniemi, 1956, ch. 3; Stanley K. Stowers, *Letter-Writing in Greco-Roman Antiquity* (Philadelphia, Westminster Press, 1989) ch. 6.

7 Diocles of Carystus

Texts studied
Letter to Antigonus pref., Jaeger p. 75.

Edition
W. W. Jaeger, *Diokles von Karystos* (Berlin, de Gruyter, 1938).

Date
I follow Jaeger in placing the *Letter to Antigonus* roughly at the end of the

fourth century BC, but note the qualifications expressed by Edelstein in *OCD*² *art.* 'Diocles', note.

8 Dionysius Calliphontis Filius

Texts studied
Descriptio Graeciae pref., *GGM* pp. 238–9.

Edition
C. Müller, *Geographi Graeci Minores* I (Paris, Didot, 1855) pp. 238–43.

Date
Uncertain. Dionysius' sources are hellenistic or earlier (see Müller's introduction p. lxxx §120), and a date in the first century BC has been suggested (*KP* II (1967) col. 74, *art.* 'Dionysios, 32'). Müller argues (ibid.) that Dionysius must be later than Pausanias, since he refers in line 98 to the oracle at Lebadea as a thing of the past, whereas in Pausanias' day it was flourishing. But some oracles experienced a revival in the second century AD: Nock, 1933, p. 112.

9 Dioscorides Pedanius

Texts studied
(Cited by page and line of Wellmann):

De Materia Medica = *Mat.Med.* Bk. I pref. (Wellmann vol. I pp. 1–3); Bk. II pref. (Wellmann vol. I p. 121)
De Simplicibus = *Eup.* Bk. I pref. (Wellmann vol. III p. 151); Bk. II pref. and epil. (Wellmann vol. III pp. 242, 317).

Edition
M. Wellmann, *Dioscoridis Anazarbei De Materia Medica Libri V*, 3 vols., Berlin, Weidmann, 1907–14; repr. 1958). The *De Simplicibus* appears in vol. III.
John M. Riddle, *Dioscorides on Pharmacy and Medicine* (Austin, University of Texas Press, 1985) provides a valuable introduction, especially on the history and nature of the text.

Date
De Materia Medica: mid-first century AD: this text was probably being written around the same time as Pliny's *Natural History* (M. Wellmann, 'Sextius Niger, eine Quellenuntersuchung zu Dioscorides', *Hermes* 24 (1889) pp. 530–69). The Areius of the dedication is the Asclepiadean Laecanius Areius of Tarsus (*PIR*² (1970) V 1 n. 29), friend of C. Laecanius Bassus (*PIR*² V 1 n. 31), who was consul in AD 64 and is mentioned by Dioscorides at I pref. p. 3.1–2. Dioscorides himself was a Cilician from Anazarba.

De Simplicibus: Wellmann argued in his *RE* article (*RE* V 1 (1905), cols. 1131–42, *art*, 'Dioskurides, 12') col. 1140 that the *De Simplicibus* was a third/fourth-century AD forgery; but he later revised this view, arguing that the work was basically genuine, though interpolated (cf. esp. his *Die Schrift des Dioskorides περὶ ἁπλῶν φαρμάκων* (Berlin, Weidmann, 1914). Later scholars have tended to reject this argument: cf. Edelstein, *OCD²*, *art*. Dioscorides Pedanius. For the purposes of this study it does not greatly matter whether or not the work is genuine. Wellmann lists in some detail (1914, pp. 42–3) linguistic similarities between the prefaces of the two works: these do not necessarily prove identity of authorship, but they do amply illustrate general features of the preface-style of a non-Atticizing scientific writer, whether of the first or of the fourth century. It must be admitted, however, that there is a certain formality of tone and a rhetorical turn of expression in the *De Simplicibus* which are foreign to the author of the *Mat.Med.*

10 Erotian

Texts studied
Vocum Hippocraticarum Collectio pref. (Nachmanson pp. 3–9), epil. = frg. 60 (Nachmanson p. 116). Cited by page and line of Nachmanson.

Edition
E. Nachmanson, *Vocum Hippocraticarum Collectio* (Uppsala, Appelberg 1918).
Further information on the MS tradition in *idem. Erotianstudien* (Uppsala, A.-B. Akademiska Bokhandeln 1917).

Date
Around AD 60. The dedicatee Andromachus was Nero's court physician, or possibly his son: Nachmanson (1918) p. vii.

11 Galen

Texts studied
Cited by volume, page and (where necessary) line of Kühn). Prefaces to:

> *Ad Patrophilum* (K I p. 224);
> *De anatomicis administrationibus* VIII (K II pp. 651–2);
> *De venarum arteriarumque dissectione* (K II p. 779);
> *Quod animi mores corporis temperamenta sequuntur* (K IV p. 767);
> *De propriorum animi cuiusque affectum dignot. et curat.* (K V p. 1);
> *De Hipp. et Plat. decretis* (K V p. 587);
> *Utrum med. an gymnast. hygiene* (K V p.806 = SM III p. 33);
> *De parvae pilae exercitatione* (K V p. 899 = SM I p. 93);
> *De alimentorun facultatibus* I (K VI pp. 453–5); II (K VI pp. 554–5);
> *De probis parvisque alimentorum succis* (K VI p. 755);

De ptisana (K VI pp. 816–17);
De typis (K VII p. 463);
De tremore etc. (K VII pp. 584–5);
De methodo medendi I (K X p. 1); VII (K X pp. 456–8);
De comp.med.sec.loc. VI (K XII pp. 894–5);
De antidotis II (K XIV pp. 106–7);
De theriaca ad Pisonem (K XIV p. 210);
De remediis parabilibus II (K XIV p. 390).

Edition

The only complete edition is still that of C. G. Kühn, *Galeni Opera Omnia* (20 vols., Leipzig, Car. Cnobloch, 1821–33), which I have cited throughout for convenience of reference (= K), Newer editions, where available, normally give the Kühn pagination. A number of shorter works are available in the Teubner *Scripta Minora* (= SM), J. Marquardt, I. Müller and G. Helmreich (eds.) (3 vols. Leipzig 1884–93, repr. Hakkert, Amsterdam 1967).

Not all the texts printed by Kühn are genuine: the *De remediis parabilibus* is undoubtedly spurious (K I pp. cliv–clv), and the *De theriaca ad Pisonem* is probably so (K I p. clvi). In the latter case, Kühn's suspicions may be reinforced by observations on the difference in style between this preface and Galen's genuine dedications: here the tone is noticeably more formal and polite, and the vocabulary is uncharacteristically monotonous. However, Kühn suggests that the unknown author was roughly contemporary with Galen (cf. I pp. xxxvi–xxxviii). Whatever their provenance, these prefaces are included in the study because they display stylistic features characteristic of scientific prefaces in general.

Translation

Very partial coverage in English. Ch. Singer, *Galen on Anatomical Procedures* (Wellcome Historical Medical Museum, n.s.7: Oxford University Press, 1956) covers Books I–IX 5); cf. also W. L. H. Duckworth, *Galen on Anatomical Procedures: the Later Books*, M. C. Lyons and B. Towers, (eds.) (Cambridge University Press, 1962), which covers Books IX 6–XV.

Date

AD 129–c. 199. On Galen in general, see esp. G. Sarton, *Galen of Pergamon* (Clendening Lecture, Lawrence, University of Kansas Press, 1954); on his place in Roman society, Bowersock (1969) ch. 5; on his writings, J. Ilberg, *Über die Schriftstellerei des Klaudios Galenos* (Darmstadt, Wissenschaftliche Buchgesellschaft, 1974, repr. from a series of articles in *Rheinisches Museum* 1889–97). For bibliography, see O. Temkin, *Galenism: the Rise and Decline of a Medical Philosophy* (Ithaca, Cornell University Press, 1973), and L. Garcia Ballester, *Galeno en la Sociedad y en la Ciencia de su Tiempo* (Madrid, Edic. Guardarrama, 1972). Vivian Nutton (ed.), *Galen: Problems and Prospects* (Wellcome Institute for the History of Medicine, 1981) contains a number of important articles.

12 Hermogenes

Texts studied
(Cited by page and line of Rabe):

Περὶ τῶν στάσεων (= *Stat.*) pref., Rabe p. 28;
Περὶ εὑρέσεως (= *Inv.*) III pref. and ch. 4 (Rabe pp. 126, 133); IV
pref. (Rabe pp. 170–1);
Περὶ ἰδεῶν (= *Id.*) I pref. (Rabe pp. 213–14).

Edition
H. Rabe, *Hermogenis Opera* = *Rhetores Graeci* VI (Teubner, Leipzig, 1913,
repr. Stuttgart, 1969).

Date
Hermogenes of Tarsus (*PIR²* H 149) was a Sophist of the second century
AD: cf. Bowersock (1969), index s.v. for further details. But not all the texts
in the corpus which bears his name are necessarily by Hermogenes in
person: the corpus is a collection of 'technical writings, forming a complete
course in school rhetoric' (J. W. H. Adkins, *OCD²*, *art.* Hermogenes).

13 Hero of Alexandria

Texts studied
Cited by page and line of the Teubner edition:

> *Pneumatica* (= *Spir.*) I pref., vol. I p. 2;
> *De Automatis* (= *Aut.*) pref., vol. I pp. 338–42;
> *Mechanica* (= *Mech.*) III pref., vol. II pp. 200–1 (Arabic);
> *Catoptrica/De Speculis* (= *Catoptr.*) pref., vol. II pp. 316–20 (a
>   thirteenth century Latin version);
> *Metrica* (= *Metr.*) I pref., vol. III pp. 2–6;
> *Dioptra* (= *Dioptr.*) pref., vol. III p. 188;
> *Definitiones* (= *Def.*) pref., vol. IV p. 14.

Cited by Wescher's pagination with Marsden's line-numbers:
> *Belopoeica* (= *Bel.*) pref., Marsden II (1971) pp. 18–20.

Edition
All texts except the *Bel.* are found in W. Schmidt, L. Nix, H. Schöne, J. L.
Heiberg (eds) *Heronis Alexandrinus, Opera* (5 vols., Leipzig, Teubner,
1899–1914, repr. Stuttgart, 1976) with German translation.
Belopoeica: text and English translation in Marsden II (1971) pp. 18–20.
The earlier edition of H. Diels and E. Schramm (1918) is now available in a
separate reprint: *Herons Belopoiika, Philons Belopoiika* (Leipzig, Zentralan-
tiquariat der DDR, 1970).

Date
Second half of the first century AD: O. Neugebauer, 1969, p. 178; *idem*, 'Über eine Methode zur Distanzbestimmung Alexandria-Roms bei Heron', in *Kgl. Danske Vidensk. Selsk., hist.-filol. medd.* 26, 2 and 7 (Copenhagen 1938–9); Marsden II (1971) pp. 208–9. There is a full discussion of the problem of dating Hero in I. Hammer-Jensen, 'Die heronische Frage', *Hermes* 63 (1928) pp. 34–47. See further esp. A. L. Reinhardt, 'De Heronis Alexandrini dictione quaestiones selectae', Diss. Münster, 1930; Neugebauer, 1969, pp. 80, 146–8, 157–8, 178–80; M. Boas, 'Heron's *Pneumatica*: a study in its transmission and influence', in *Isis* 40 (1949) pp. 38–48.

14 Hipparchus

Texts studied
Commentary on the Phaenomena *of Aratus*, Bk. I pref. (Manitius pp. 2–8); Bk. II pref. and epil. (Manitius pp. 120–2, 216). Cited by page and line of Manitius.

Edition
C. Manitius, *Hipparchi in Arati et Eudoxi Phaenomena commentariorum libri III*, Greek text with German trans. (Leipzig, Teubner, 1894).

Date
Hipparchus' astronomical work can be dated between 161 and 127 BC, according to the dates of the observations cited by Ptolemy: Manitius pp. 282ff. Neugebauer, 1969, p. 69 suggests from the internal evidence of the preface that the *Commentary* is a youthful work. See further, D. R. Dicks, *The Geographical Fragments of Hipparchus* (University of London, Athlone Press, 1960), pp. 1–18 on Hipparchus' life and works.

15 Hypsicles

Texts studied
Preface to [Euclid], *Elements* Bk. XIV.

Edition
J. L. Heiberg, *Euclides V, 1 Elementa XIV, XV, Scholia in libros I–V* p. 2 (Leipzig, Teubner, 1888, repr. (ed. E. S. Stamatis), Leipzig, 1977).

Date
Mid-second century BC. Neugebauer (1969) p. 178 suggests c. 150 BC; Björnbo, *RE* IX 1 (1914), cols. 427–33, *art.* 'Hypsikles, 2' suggests c. 175 BC. The latter date rests entirely on the preface and its reference to Apollonius of Perge.

226   *Appendix B*

16 Philo of Byzantium

Note   Except for ch. 7, unqualified 'Philo' should be taken to refer to Philo of Byzantium, not to Philo Judaeus.

Texts studied

Belopoeica pref. (Marsden II pp. 106–8) and epilogue (Marsden II p. 154), cited by Thévenot's pagination with Marsden's line numeration.
Pneumatica pref. (Schmidt pp. 458–60), cited by page and line of Schmidt.

Edition

Belopoeica. Marsden II (1971) pp. 106–54, with English translation. The earlier edition of Diels and Schramm is now available in a reprint: see under Hero, above.
Pneumatica. No Greek text survives. A medieval Latin version is published in M. Schmidt, (ed.) *Heronis Opera* I (Leipzig, Teubner, 1899, repr. Stuttgart, 1976), pp. 458–89 (with German trans.). An Arabic text was published by Carra de Vaux in *Notices et extraits des manuscrits* 38 (ii) (Paris, 1906), pp. 41–121, with French translation and an invaluable discussion of the Arabic manuscript tradition. F. D. Prager, *Philo of Byzantium: Pneumatica* (Wiesbaden, Dr Ludwig Reichert Verlag, 1974) adds little to our knowledge of the preface, but the book contains a full and interesting account of the Latin and other western MSS. It is generally accepted that the extant Latin text is derived from an Arabic version, since it opens with standard Arabic formulae ('In nomine dei pii et misericordis . . . . Dixit:'), though Prager (pp. 45ff.) attempts to refute this. It is at least clear that the Latin version is independent of, and in many respects older than, the extant Arabic texts (Prager pp. 38–9, 54ff., 241).

Date

Around 200 BC: Marsden II (1971) pp. 6–8; Fraser II (1971) pp. 62–3 and n. 445; Tittel, *art.* 'Hydraulis', *RE* IX, 1 (1914) cols. 64–7. A detailed study of the language of the *Bel.* confirms this dating: M. Arnim, 'De Philonis Byzantii dicendi genere', Diss. Greifswald, 1912.

The *Belopoeica* and the *Pneumatica*, which have come down to us through widely different channels, are believed to have formed originally Books IV and V of a *Compilation of Mechanics* (*Mēchanikē Syntaxis*) in nine books. There are traces of the dedication to Ariston elsewhere in the tradition, but no other prefaces survive. Still fundamental is F. Haase, *art.* 'Philon' in S. Ersch und J. Grüber (eds.), *Allgemeine Enzyklopädie der Wissenschaften und Künste* (Leipzig, J. F. Gleditsch, 1818–89), vol. 23/III (1847), pp. 428–35.

17 Pseudo-Scymnus

Texts studied
Orbis Descriptio: the preface includes lines 1–139 of this didactic poem in iambic pentameters (*GGM* I pp. 196–9). Cited by line.

Edition
C. Müller, *Geographi Graeci Minores* I (Paris, Didot, 1855) pp. 196–237. Further fragments available in A. Diller, *The Tradition of the Minor Greek Geographers* (Philological monographs published by the American Philological Association no. 14, Lancaster, Pa., 1952), pp. 165ff.

Date
End of the second century BC: see F. Jacoby, *Apollodors Chronik: eine Sammlung der Fragmente* (Philologische Untersuchungen 16: Berlin, Weidmann, 1902), ch. 1. Lines 56–7 of the preface refer to Nicomedes II of Bithynia (reigned 149–27 BC), and the 'King Nicomedes' of the dedication is most probably his son, Nicomedes III (127–94 BC), or possibly Nicomedes IV (94–74 BC).

18 Serenus

Texts studied
Prefaces to *De Sectione Cylindri* (= *Sect.cyl.*), Heiberg p. 2; *De Sectione Coni* (= *Sect.Con.*): Heiberg pp. 120–2. Cited by page and line of Heiberg.

Edition
J. L. Heiberg (ed.), *Sereni Antinoensis opuscula* (Leipzig, Teubner, 1896), with Latin translation.

Date
Mathematically speaking, Serenus falls between Pappus (end of third century AD) and Theon of Alexandria (second half of fourth century AD). Linguistic observations tend to confirm this date: Orinsky, *art.* 'Serenus, 10' *RE* Reihe 2/II (1921) cols. 1677–8.

19 [Pseudo]-Thessalus

Texts studied
De Virtutibus Herbarum Bk. I pref. (Greek), Friedrich p. 45; Bk. II prefs. (Greek and Latin), Friedrich pp. 195–8.

Edition
H. von Friedrich, *Thessalos von Tralles* (Meisenheim am Glan, Verlag Anton

Hain, 1968). The text was published originally under the name of (Ps.-) Harpocration, but the correct form of the dedication was discovered in a Latin version and published by Franz Cumont in *Revue de Philologie* 42 (1918), pp. 85ff.; *Cod. Cat.Astrol.Gr.* VIII/4, 253ff.

Date

Cumont dates the text to the mid-first century AD, and identifies the author with Thessalus of Tralles, the founder of the Methodist school in medicine; if this is right, his dedicatee would be either Claudius or Nero, probably the former (*art. cit.* pp. 91–102). Not all scholars would agree with this identification: cf. F. Kudlien, *art.* 'Thessalos, 6', *KP* V (1975) cols 763–4 and the (anonymous) author of *art.* 'Thessalos, 6', *RE* Reihe 2/VI A1 (1937) cols. 180–2. But the text can scarcely be dated later than the end of the second century AD. It should be noted, however, that datable elements in the body of the text cannot necessarily be used to date the preface, which survives in a number of versions which cannot all be original: the Greek preface to Book I is the most interesting of these.

On the general character of the text, see Festugière, 1944–9, I pp. 143ff.; and, on the preface, the detailed commentary in Festugière, 'L'expérience religieuse du médecin Thessalos', *Revue Biblique* 48 (1939), pp. 45–77.

20 Vettius Valens

Texts studied

Anthologiae, Bk. II pref. (Kroll, p. 55); Bk. III pref. and epil. (Kroll pp. 132, 157); Bk. IV ch. 11 (Kroll p. 172.18–30); BK. VI ch. 9 (Kroll p. 260.26–43); Bk. IX pref. (part) (Kroll p. 331.4–14). Cited by page and line of Kroll.

Edition

W. Kroll (ed.), *Vettii Valentis Anthologiarum Libri* (Dublin/Zürich, Weidmann, 1908; repr. with same pagination, 1973). There is a new edition of Book I only by Joelle-Frédérique Bara, *Vettius Valens d'Antioche: Anthologies, Livre I* (Brill, Leiden, 1989) with French translation and commentary.

Date

The evidence of the horoscopes dates the book between c. AD 154 and 174, wiith perhaps a later addition around 184: O. Neugebauer and H. B. van Hoesen, *Greek Horoscopes* (Mem. American Philol. Soc. 48, 1959), pp. 176–7.

21 Vitruvius Pollio

Texts studied

De Architectura I 6.12 (Krohn p. 24.22–4); I 7.2 (Krohn p. 27.1–7); Bk. IV pref. 1 (Krohn p. 75.11–18); VI 6.7 (Krohn p. 138.3–6); VIII 3.27 (Krohn pp. 187.27–188.4); IX 1.16 (Krohn p. 206.27–31); IX 8.15 (Krohn pp. 222.25–223.3); X 8.1 (Krohn p. 240.9–11); X 8.6 (Krohn p. 242.7–12); X 11.2 (Krohn p. 247.24–27); X 13.8 (Krohn p. 253.11–13). Cited by book, chapter and verse, with page and line of Krohn where necessary.

Edition

F. Krohn (ed.), *Vitruvius De Architectura* (Leipzig, Teubner, 1912). English translation by M. H. Morgan, *Vitruvius: the Ten Books on Architecture* (Harvard University Press, 1914, repr. Dover Books, New York, 1960). The reprint contains a valuable introduction by H. L. Warren.

Date

The *De Architectura* is dedicated to Octavian, and can be dated with some precision to the beginning of his reign: Marsden II (1971) p. 3.

On the character of Vitruvius' work, see Fuhrmann, 1960, ch. 7; on the literary circle to which he is linked, see Rawson (1985) and F. Cichorius, *Römische Studien* (Leipzig/Berlin, Teubner, 1922), pp. 271–9; on the artillery side of his work, Marsden II (1971), *passim*. See further C. Watzinger, 'Vitruviusstudien', *Rheinisches Museum*, 64 (1909), pp. 202–23.

SELECT BIBLIOGRAPHY

For reasons of space, this bibliography does not contain all the works mentioned in the body of the text more than once, and should not be taken as either exhaustive or academically selective. A full list of secondary literature used may be obtained by consulting the Index of modern authors

Aberle, F. 1863. 'Exegetische Studien, Pt. 2: Über den Prolog des Lucasevangeliums', *Theologische Quartalschrift*, 45, pp. 98–120

Africa, Thomas W. 1968. *Science and the State in Greece and Rome*, John Wiley & Sons, New York

Aland, K. 1968. *Synopsis Quattuor Evangeliorum*, 5th edn

Alexander, L. C. A. 1978. 'Luke–Acts in its contemporary setting with special reference to the prefaces (Luke 1:1–4 and Acts 1:1)', D. Phil. thesis, Oxford

    1986. 'Luke's preface in the context of Greek preface-writing', *Novum Testamentum*, 1986, vol. 28 pp. 48–74

    1990. 'The living voice: scepticism towards the written word in early Christian and in Graeco-Roman texts', in *The Bible in Three Dimensions*, eds. D. J. A. Clines, S. E. Fowl and S. E. Porter, JSOT Supplements 87, Sheffield Academic Press, pp. 220–47

Aune, D. E. 1987. *The New Testament in its Literary Environment*, Westminster Press, USA; James Clarke & Co., Cambridge

Avenarius, G. 1956. *Lukians Schrift zur Geschichtsschreibung*, Verlag Anton Hain, Meisenheim am Glan

Bailey, C. 1949. *Lucretii De Rerum Natura I–III*, Geoffrey Cumberlege, London

Barrett, C. K. 1961. *Luke the Historian in Recent Study*, Epworth Press, London

Bauer, J. 1960. 'ΠΟΛΛΟΙ Luke i Γ', *Novum Testamentum*, 4 (1960), pp. 263–6

Birt, R. 1882. *Das antike Buchwesen in seinem Verhältnis zur Litteratur*, Herz, Berlin

Blum, C. 1936. 'Studies in the Dream-book of Artemidorus', Diss. Inaug. Uppsala

Boas, M. 1949. 'Heron's Pneumatica: a study in its transmission and influence', in *Isis*, 40 (1949), pp. 38–48

Bowersock, G. W. 1969. *Greek Sophists in the Roman Empire*, Clarendon Press, Oxford

230

Burford, A. 1972. *Craftsmen in Greek and Roman Society*, Cornell University Press, Ithaca, New York; Aspects of Greek and Roman Life, Thames & Hudson, London

Cadbury, H. J. 1920a. 'The style and literary method of Luke', *Harvard Theological Studies*, 6, Cambridge, Mass.

1920b. 'Luke – translator or author?' *American Journal of Theology*, 24 pp. 436ff.

1921. 'The purpose expressed in Luke's preface', *The Expositor* (June 1921), pp. 431–41

1922a. *The Beginnings of Christianity*, vol. II, inc. Commentary on the preface of Luke, Appendix C, pp. 489–510

1922b. 'The knowledge claimed in Luke's preface', *The Expositor* (December 1922), pp. 401–20

1927. *The Making of Luke–Acts*, 1st edn 1927, rep. 1958, Macmillan & Co., London

1956. '"We" and "I" passages in Luke–Acts', *NTS* 3 (1956/7), pp. 128ff.

Colson, F. H. 1913. 'τάξει in Papias (the gospels and the rhetorical schools)', *JTS*, 14 (1913), pp. 62–9

Conzelmann, H. 1966. 'The address of Paul on the Areopagus', in *Studies*, Keck and Martyn, pp. 217–30

1987. *The Acts of the Apostles*, Hermeneia, Fortress Press, Philadelphia. Tr. J. Limbury, A. Thomas Kraabel, and D. H. Juel from *Die Apostelgeschichte (2)*, 1972, Hdbuch NT, KCB Mohr (Paul Siebeck), Tübingen

Corssen, P. 1899. Review of F. Blass, *The Philology of the Gospels* (1898), *GGA* 1899, pp. 305ff.

Curtius, E. R. 1953. *European Literature and the Latin Middle Ages*, ET W. R. Trask from 2nd German edn. Routledge, London, 1953; 3rd German edn 1961

Dahlmann, H. 1953. *Varros Schrift 'De poematis' und die hellenistisch-römische Poetik*, Mainz Akad. der Wiss. u. der Lit. Abhandlungen der Geistes- und Sozialwissenschaftl.- Klasse, 1953/3

Deichgräber, K. 1930. *Die griechische Empirikerschule: Sammlung der Fragmente und Darstellung*, Berlin

Dibelius, M. 1951/1956. *Aufsätze zur Apostelgeschichte*, ed. H. Greeven, Göttingen. ET *Studies in the Acts of the Apostles*, trs. M. Ling and P. Schubert, SCM, London

1966. *Die Formgeschichte des Evangeliums*, 5th edn, JCB Mohr, Tübingen

Dodds, E. R. 1965. *Pagan and Christian in an Age of Anxiety*, Cambridge University Press

Drachmann, A. G. 1963. *The Mechanical Technology of Greek and Roman Antiquity: a Study of the Literary Sources*, Acta Historica Scientiarum Naturalium et Medicinalium 17. Munksgaard, Copenhagen & Hafner, London

Duckworth, W. L. H. 1962. *Galen on Anatomical Procedures: the Later Books*, ed. M. C. Lyons & B. Towers, Cambridge University Press

Earl, D. 1972. 'Prologue-form in ancient historiography', *ANRW*, ed. H. Temporini I/2 (1972), pp. 842–56

Engel, G. 1910. 'De antiquorum epicorum didacticorum historicorum pro-oemiis', Diss. Inaug. Marburg

Fehling, D. 1975. 'Zur Funktion und Formgeschichte des Proömiums in der älteren griechischen Prosa', in *ΔΩPHMA: Festschrift Hans Diller zum 70 Geburtstag*, Athens

Festugière, A. J. 1939. L'Expérience réligieuse du médecin Thessalos. *Revue Biblique*, 48 (1939), pp. 45–77. Repr. in A. J. Festugière, *Hermétisme et Mystique Païenne* (Aubier-Montaigne, Paris, 1967), pp. 141–80

1944. *La Révélation d'Hermes Trismégiste I: l'astrologie et les sciences occultes* (1st edn), Librairie Lecoffre, Paris

Fraenkel, E. 1961. 'Eine Anfangsformel attischer Reden', *Glotta*, 29 (1961), pp. 1ff

Fraser, P. M. 1970. 'Aristophanes of Byzantium and Zoilus Homeromastix in Vitruvius', *Eranos*, 68 (1970), pp. 115–22

1972. *Ptolemaic Alexandria I–III*, Clarendon Press, Oxford

Friedländer, P. 1958. *Plato: an Introduction*, ET rev., Bollingen Foundation LLX, New York

Friedrich, H. von 1968. *Thessalos von Tralles*, Beiträge zur Klassischen Philologie, Hft. 28. Verlag Anton Hain, Meisenheim am Glan

Fuhrmann, M. 1960. *Das Systematische Lehrbuch: ein Beitrag zur Geschichte der Wissenschaften in der Antike*, Vandenhoeck & Ruprecht, Göttingen

Gager, J. G. 1972. 'Religion and social class in the early Roman empire', in *Early Church History*, ed. S. Benko and J. J. O'Rourke, Oliphants, London, pp. 99–120

Gärtner, B. 1955. *The Areopagus Speech and Natural Revelation*, Acta Sem. Neotest., Upsal. 21 (1955), Lund

Gerhardsson, B. 1961. *Memory and Manuscript – Oral Transmission and Written Transmission in Rabbinic Judaism and Early Christianity*, Acta Sem. Neotest., Upsal. 22 (1961), C. W. K. Gleerup, Lund

Gille, B. 1980. *Les Mécaniciens grecs: la naissance de la technologie*, Éd. du Seuil, Paris

Glockmann, G. 1968. *Homer in der frühchristlichen Literatur bis Justinus*, Texte u. Untersuchungen 105, Akademie-Verlag, Berlin

Gold, B. K. 1987. *Literary Patronage in Greece and Rome*, University of North Carolina Press, Chapel Hill and London

Goodspeed, E. J. 1954. 'Was Theophilus Luke's publisher?', *JBL*, 73 (1954), p. 84

Graefenhain, R. 1892. 'De more libros dedicandi apud scriptores Graecos et Romanos obvio', diss. Inaug., Marburg

Grimm, W. 1871. 'Das Proömium des Lucas-evangeliums', *Jahrbücher für deutsche Theologie*, 16 (1871), pp. 33–78

Groningen, B. Van 1963. 'ἔκδοσις' *Mnemosyne* 4/16 (1963), pp. 6–17

Grundmann, W. 1961. *Das Evangelium nach Lukas* (second edn), Theologi-scher Handkommentar zum NT, 3; Evangelische Verlagsanstalt, Berlin

Haenchen, E. 1971. *The Acts of the Apostles*, Blackwell, Oxford. ET (rev.) of *Die Apostelgeschichte*, Meyer Kommentar, Göttingen, 1961

Harris, W. V. 1989. *Ancient Literacy*, Harvard; Oxford University Press, London

Heath, Sir T. L. 1896. *Apollonius of Perga: Treatise on Conic Sections*, Cambridge University Press
　　1921. *A History of Greek Mathematics*, 2 vols. Clarendon Press, Oxford
Hengel, M. 1974. *Property and Riches in the Early Church*, SCM Press, London
　　1985. *Studies in the Gospel of Mark*, SCM Press, London
　　1990. *The Johannine Question*. SCM Press, London
Herkommer, E. 1968. 'Die Topoi in der Proömien der römischen Geschichtswerke', Diss., Tübingen
Hobart, W. K. 1882. *The Medical Language of St. Luke*, Hodges, Figis & Co., Dublin, reprint Baker Book House, Grand Rapids, Michigan, 1954
Hock, R. F. 1980. *The Social Context of Paul's Ministry: Tentmaking and Apostleship*, Fortress Press, Philadelphia
Horsley, G. H. R. 1987. *New Documents Illustrating Early Christianity, vol. 4, a review of the Greek inscriptions and papyri published in 1979*, Australian Ancient History Documentary Research Centre, Macquarie University
Jacoby, F. 1902 *Apollodors Chronik: eine Sammlung der Fragmente*, Philologische Untersuchungen, 16, Weidmann, Berlin
　　1923–1958. *Die Fragmente der griechischen Historiker, I–III*, Brill, Leiden & Weidmann, Berlin
Jaeger, W. W. 1938. *Diokles von Karystos*, de Gruyter, Berlin
　　1948. *Aristotle: Fundamentals of the History of his Development*, 2nd edn, ET, Clarendon Press, Oxford
　　1954. *Paideia: the Ideals of Greek Culture*, vols. I–III, 4th edn, Basil Blackwell, Oxford
Janson, T. 1964. *Latin Prose Prefaces: Studies in Literary Conventions*. Acta Universitatis Stockholmiensis: Studia Latina Stockholmiensia 13, Almqvist & Wiksell, Stockholm
Jervell, J. 1962. 'The problems of traditions in Acts', *Studia Theologica*, 16 (1962), pp. 25–41, rep. as pp. 19–39 of Jervell, *Luke and the People of God: a New Look at Luke–Acts*, Augsburg, Minneapolis, Minnesota
Jewett, R. 1986. *The Thessalonian Correspondence: Pauline Rhetoric and Millenarian Piety*, Fortress Press, Philadelphia
Judge, E. A. 1960. *The Social Pattern of the Christian Groups in the First Century*, Tyndale Press, London
　　1960/1961. 'The early Christians as a scholastic community', *Journal of Religious History*, I (1960–1), pp. 4–15, II (1961–2), pp. 125–37
Keck, L. E. and Martyn, J. L. (eds.) 1966. *Studies in Luke–Acts*, Festschrift P. Schubert, Abingdon Press, Nashville
Kenyon, F. G. 1951. *Books and Readers in Greece and Rome*, 2nd edn, Clarendon Press, Oxford
Keyes, C. W. 1935. 'The Greek letter of introduction', *American Journal of Philology*, 56 (1935), pp. 28–44
Kim, C. H. 1972. 'Form and structure of the Greek letter of introduction', SBLDS, 4 (1972)
Klein, G. 1964. 'Lukas 1:1–4 als theologisches Programm', in *Zeit und Geschichte*, Dankesgabe R. Bultmann, zum 80 Geburtstag, Tübingen

234   Select bibliography

Klostermann, E. 1929. *Das Lukasevangelium*, Handbuch zum NT, 2nd edn, Tübingen

Kollesch, J. and Kudlien, F. 1961. 'Bemerkungen zum ΠΕΡΙ ΑΡΘΡΩΝ – Kommentar des Apollonios von Kition', *Hermes* 89 (1961), pp. 322–32

1965. *Apollonios von Kitium, Kommentar zu Hippokrates Über das Einrenken der Gelenke* (*CMG* XI 1,1), Akademie-Verlag, Berlin

Koskenniemi, H. 1956. *Studien zur Idee und Phraselogie des griechischen Briefes bis 400 n. Chr.*, Suomalaisen Tiedeakatemian toimituksia, Helsinki

Kreissig, H. 1967. 'Zur sozialen Zusammensetzung der frühchristlichen Gemeinden im ersten Jahrhunderten u.Z', *Eirene* 6, (1967), pp. 91–100

Kümmel, W. G. 1966. *Introduction to the New Testament*, ET P. Feine from the 14th German edn SCM, London

Lagarde, Paul de 1874. *Psalterium iuxta Hebraeos Hieronymi*, Lipsiae

Lane Fox, R. 1986. *Pagans and Christians*, Harmondsworth, Viking Penguin

Laqueur, R. 1911. 'Ephoros: 1, Die Proömien', in *Hermes*, 46 (1911), pp. 161–206

Lausberg, H. 1960. *Handbuch der literarischen Rhetorik: eine Grundlegung der Literaturwissenschaft*, 2 vols. Hueber, Munich

Lieberich, H. 1899. 'Studien zu den Proömien in der griechischen und byzantinischen Geschichtsschreibung I–II', Diss. Inaug. München, 1899–1900

Liebermann, S. 1962. *Hellenism in Jewish Palestine* 2nd edn, Jewish Theological Society of America, New York, Texts and Studies, vol. XVIII 'The publication of the Mishnah', pp. 83–99

Lightfoot, R. H. 1962. *The Gospel Message of St. Mark*, Clarendon Press, Oxford

Lloyd, G. E. R. 1970. *Early Greek Science: Thales to Aristotle*, Chatto & Windus, London

1973. *Greek Science after Aristotle*, Chatto & Windus, London

Malherbe, A. J. 1983. *Social Aspects of Early Christianity*, 2nd edn enlarged, Fortress Press, Philadelphia. 1st edn chs. 1–3 only, Louisiana State University Press, 1977

Marrou, H. I. 1949. 'Le Technique de l'édition à l'époque patristique', *Vigiliae Christianae*, 3 (1949), pp. 208ff.

1964. *A History of Education in Antiquity*, ET G. Lamb from the 3rd French edn (*De la connaissance historique*, Éditions du Seuil, Paris, 1959), New American Library, New York

Marsden, E. W. 1969/71. *Greek and Roman Artillery*, vols. I–II, Clarendon Press, Oxford

Marshall, I. Howard 1970. *Luke, Historian and Theologian*, Paternoster, Exeter

Meeks, W. 1983. *The First Urban Christians*, Yale University Press, London & New Haven

Meyer, E. 1921–3. *Ursprung und Anfänge des Christentums*, vols. I–III, J. G. Cotta, Stuttgart

Millar, F. G. B. 1964. *A Study of Cassius Dio*, Clarendon Press, Oxford

Momigliano, A. 1969. *Studies in Historiography*, Weidenfeld & Nicholson, London

Neugebauer, O. 1969. *The Exact Sciences in Antiquity*, 2nd edn, Harper & Row, New York

Neugebauer O. and van Hoesen H. B. 1969. *Greek Horoscopes*, Memoirs of the American Philological Society 48

Nineham, D. E. 1958a. 'Eyewitness testimony and the gospel tradition (I)', *JTS*, 9 (1958), pp. 13–25

  1958b. 'Eyewitness testimony and the gospel tradition (II)', *JTS*, 9 (1958), pp. 242–52

  1960. 'Eyewitness testimony and the gospel tradition (III)', *JTS*, 11 (1960), pp. 252–64

Nock, A. D. 1933. *Conversion*, Oxford University Press, London

  1953. Review of Dibelius, 1951, *Gnomon*, 25 (1953), pp. 497–506. Repr. in Nock, 1972, vol. II pp. 821–32

  1972. *Essays on Religion and the Ancient World*, vols. I–II, Clarendon Press, Oxford

Norden, E. 1909. *Die antike Kunstprosa vom VI Jahrhundert v. Chr. bis in die Zeit der Renaissance*, vols I–II, 2nd edn, Leipzig

  1913. *Agnostos Theos, Untersuchungen zur Formengeschichte religiöser Rede*, Leipzig and Berlin

Nutton, V. 1981. (ed.) *Galen: Problems and Prospects*, Wellcome Institute for the History of Medicine

Oleson, J. P. 1984. *Greek and Roman Mechanical Water-lifting Devices. The History of a Technology*, Phoenix Supplement XVI, University of Toronto Press

Overbeck, F. 1919. *Christentum und Kultur*, Basel

Paassen, C. van 1957. *The Classical Tradition of Geography*, Groningen, Djakarta

Palm. J. 1955. 'Über Sprache und Stil des Diodoros von Sizilien: ein Beitrag zur Beleuchtung der hellenistischen Prosa', Diss. Lund

Pelletier, A. 1962. *Flavius Josèphe, adaptateur de la lettre d'Aristée: une réaction atticisante contre la koinè*, Études et Commentaires 45,*1962*, Paris

Pervo, R. I. 1987. *Profit with Delight: the Literary Genre of the Acts of the Apostles*, Fortress Press, Philadelphia

du Plessis, I. I. 1974. 'Once more: the purpose of Luke's prologue (Lk I 1–4)', *Novum Testamentum* 16 (1974), pp. 259–71

Plümacher, E. 1972. *Lukas als hellenistischer Schriftsteller*. Vandenhoeck & Ruprecht, Göttingen

Plummer, A. 1922. *St. Luke*, International Critical Commentary, 5th edn, T. & T. Clark, Edinburgh

Rabe, H. 1907. 'Aus Rhetoren-Handschriften', *Rheinisches Museum*, 62 (1907), pp. 247–64, 559–90

  1913. *Rhetores Graeci III*, rep. 1969, Teubner, Leipzig

  1931. *Prolegomenon Sylloge*, Teubner, Leipzig

Rajak, T. 1973. 'Justus of Tiberias', *CQ*, 23 (1973), pp. 345ff.

  1983. *Josephus. The Historian and his Society*, Duckworth, London

Rawson, E. 1985. *Intellectual Life in the Late Roman Republic*, Duckworth, London

Reinhardt 1930. 'De Heronis alexandrini Dictione Quaestiones Selectae', Diss. Inaug. Münster (Borna)

Rengstorf, K. H. 1962. *Das Evangelium nach Lukas* (Das NT Deutsch 3), 9th edn Vandenhoeck & Ruprecht, Göttingen
Roberts, C. H. 1977. *Manuscript, Society and Belief in Early Christian Egypt*, Schweich Lectures 1977, Oxford University Press for the British Academy, London
Roberts, C. H. & Skeat, T. C. 1987. *The Birth of the Codex*. Oxford University Press for the British Academy, London
Robertson, A. T. 1923–4. 'The implications of Luke's preface', *Expository Times*, 345 (1923–4), pp. 319–21
Ropes, J. H. 1923–4. 'St Luke's preface; ἀσφάλεια and παρακολουθεῖν', *JTS*, 25 (1923–4), pp. 67–71
Rose, H. J. 1921. 'The Greek of Cicero', *JHS*, 41 (1921), pp. 91–116
Ruch, M. 1958. *Le Prooemium philosophique chez Cicéron*, Paris
Ruppert, J. 1911. 'Quaestiones ad historiam dedicationis librorum pertinentes', Diss. Inaug. Lipsiae
Rydbeck, L. 1967. *Fachprosa, vermeintliche Volkssprache und neues Testament*, Acta University Upsal., Studia Graeca Upsal. 5, 1967, Uppsala
Samain, E. 1973. 'La notion de ARCHE dans l'oeuvre lucanienne', in *L'évangile de Luc: problèmes littéraires et théologiques; Mémorial Lucien Cerfaux*, Bibliotheca Ephemeridum Theologicarum Lovaniensium, ed. F. Neirynck, Gembloux, Ducolot, pp. 299–328
Schlatter, A. von 1931. *Das Evangelium nach Lukas*, Calwer Vereinsbuchhandlung, Stuttgart
Schmid, J. 1955. *Das Evangelium nach Lukas*, Regensburger NT III, 3rd edn, Pustet, Regensburg
Schmidt, K. L. 1918. 'Der geschichtlicher Wert des lukanischen Aufrisses der Geschichte Jesu (Tradition und Komposition im Lukasevangelium)' *Theologische Studien und Kritiken*, 91 (1918), pp. 277–92
Schürmann, H. 1962. 'Evangelienschrift und kirchliche Unterweisung – Die repräsentative Funktion der Schrift nach Lk. 1:1–4', *Miscellanea Erfordiana*, Erfurter Theologische Studien, 12, Leipzig
Simpson, E. K. 1930. 'Vettius Valens and the Greek NT', *Evangelical Quarterly*, 2 (1930), pp. 389–400
Singer, C. 1956. *Galen on Anatomical Procedures*, Wellcome Historical Medical Museum, n.s. 7: Oxford University Press
Sparks, H. F. D. 1943. 'The semitisms of St. Luke's gospel', *JTS* 44 (1943), pp. 129ff.
Spoerri, W. 1959. *Späthellenistische Berichte über Welt, Kultur und Götter: Untersuchungen zu Diodor von Sizilien*, Basel
Stambaugh, J. and Balch, D. 1986. *The Social World of the First Christians*, SPCK, London
Steinmetz, P. 1964. *Die Physik des Theophrastos von Erestos*, Palingenesia I, 1964, M. Gehlen, Bad Homburg
Swete, H. B. 1902. *Introduction to the OT in Greek*, rev. R. R. Ottley, 1914, Cambridge University Press
Temkin, O. 1953. 'Greek medicine as science and craft', *Isis*, 44 (1953), pp. 213–25
  1973. *Galenism, the Rise and Decline of a Medical Philosophy*, Cornell University Press, Ithaca, NY

Thomas, R. 1989. *Oral Tradition and Written Record in Classical Athens*, Cambridge University Press

Toomer, G. J. 1976. *Diocles on Burning Mirrors*, Springer-Verlag, Berlin/ Heidelberg

Toynbee, A. J. 1924. *Greek Historial Thought from Homer to the Age of Heraclius*, J. M. Dent & Sons, London and Toronto

Trilling, L. 1970. *The Liberal Imagination*, Harmondsworth, Penguin Books

Trocmé, E. 1957. *Le 'Livre des actes' et l'histoire*, Presses Universitaires de France, Paris

Turner, E. G. 1968. *Greek Papyri: an Introduction*, Clarendon Press, Oxford

Turner, N. 1963/1976. *J. H. Moulton, Grammar of NT Greek*, vol. III Syntax (1963), vol. IV Style (1976), T. & T. Clark, Edinburgh

Unnik, W. C. van 1955. 'Opmerkingen over het Doel van Lucas' Geschied-werk', *Nederlands Theologisch Tijdscrift*, 9 (1955), pp. 323–31. Repr. in van Unnik, *Sparsa Collecta*, I, Supplements to Novum Testamentum XXIX, E. J. Brill, Leiden, 1973, vol. I, pp. 1–15 as *Remarks on the Purpose of Luke's Historical Writing, Luke i 1–4*

1963. 'Once more St. Luke's prologue', *Neotestamentica*, 7 (1963), pp. 7–26

Valk, M. van der 1957. 'On the edition of books in antiquity', *Vigiliae Christianae*, 11 (1957), pp. 1ff

Verdin, H. 1970. 'Notes sur l'attitude des historiens grecs à l'égard de la tradition locale', *Ancient Society*, 1 (1970), pp. 183–200

Vogel, F. 1933. 'Zu Luk. I 4', *Neue Kirchliche Zeitschrift*, 44 (1933), pp. 203–305

Völkel, M. 1973. 'Exegetische Erwägungen zum Verständnis des Begriffs kathexēs im lukanischen Prolog', *NTS*, 20 (1973–4), pp. 289–99

Volkmann, R. 1963. *Die Rhetorik der Griechen und Römer in systematischer Übersicht* (repr. of 2nd edn, Leipzig, 1885). Olms, Hildesheim, 1963

Walbank, F. W. 1972. *Polybius*, University of California Press, Berkeley, London

Walzer, R. 1944. *Galen on Medical Experience*, Oxford University Press, London

1949. *Galen on Jews and Christians*, Oxford University Press, London

Warren, H. L. 1960. Introduction to M. H. Morgan, *Vitruvius: the Ten Books on Architecture* (repr. from Harvard edn of 1914), Dover, New York

Weichert, V. 1910. *Demetrii et Libanii qui feruntur* τυποὶ ἐπιστολικοί *et* ἐπιστολιμαῖοι χαρακτῆρες, Teubner, Leipzig

Wellmann, M. 1901. *Die Fragmente der Sikelischen Aertze Akon, Philiston und des Diokles von Karystos*, Frag.-Sammlung der Griechischen Aertze Bd. I, Berlin

Wengst, K. 1987. *Pax Romana and the Peace of Jesus Christ*, ET J. Bowden, SCM Press, London of *Pax Romana* (1986), Christian Kaiser Verlag, München

Whitaker, G. H. 1920–1. 'The philology of Luke's preface', *The Expositor*, Oct. 1920, pp. 262ff.; Nov. 1920, pp. 380ff.; Mar. 1921, pp. 239ff.

Wifstrand, A. 1940. 'Lukas och Klassicismen', *Svensk Exegetisk Årsbok*, 5 (1940), pp. 131–51

Wilamowitz-Moellendorf, U. von 1889. *Commentariolum Grammaticum*, Index Scholarum Gottingae, Per Semestre Aestivum

Winter, B. 1988. 'Paul and Philo among the sophists: a hellenistic Jewish and a Christian response', Ph.D. Diss., School of History, Philosophy and Politics, Macquarie University

INDEX OF SCIENTIFIC AUTHORS

Apollonius of Citium 47, 48, 56, 59, 65, 68, 69, 70, 71, 72, 73, 74, 75, 79, 82, 83, 84, 85, 86, 90, 91, 92, 93, 94, 95, 96, 97, 98, 99, 100, 101, 107, 110, 111, 116, 117, 123, 126, 128, 134, 137, 143, 144, 184, 196, 205, 217–18

Apollonius of Perge 47, 50, 51, 56, 67, 71–2, 73, 74, 76, 79, 88, 92, 97, 98, 100, 144, 156, 189, 199, 218

Archimedes 47, 49–50, 50–1, 52, 56, 58, 60, 67, 70, 71, 72, 73, 74, 75, 76, 78, 79, 88, 90, 92, 96, 97, 98, 99, 100, 107, 110, 120, 144, 156, 185, 189, 192, 203, 218–19

Artemidorus Daldianus 49, 58, 60, 62, 66, 71, 72, 73, 74, 75, 76, 79, 80, 81, 86, 90, 92, 93, 94, 95, 96, 97, 98, 99, 100, 104, 107, 109, 120, 125, 126, 130, 132, 134, 137, 144, 145, 147, 189, 190, 219

Bito 47, 51, 56, 58, 65, 67, 70, 71, 74, 75, 88, 132, 189, 219–20

Demetrius 48, 57, 64, 65, 67, 70, 71, 72, 73, 75, 79, 91, 92, 97, 98, 100, 101, 103, 104, 107, 109, 116, 126, 145, 190, 214–15, 220

Diocles of Carystus 46–47, 50, 55, 56, 64, 65, 70, 71, 72, 73, 74, 75, 78, 79, 88, 92, 95, 97, 107, 126, 128, 131, 132, 189, 213–14, 220–1

Dionysius Calliphontis 48, 57, 70, 71, 74,75, 79, 88, 94, 96, 98, 100, 140, 145, 221

Dioscorides 10, 35, 36, 37, 40, 48, 54, 57, 59, 61, 67, 70, 71, 72, 73, 75, 76, 77, 79, 81, 82, 86, 90, 91, 92, 93, 95, 96, 97, 98, 99, 101, 107, 109, 110, 114, 115, 121, 122, 125, 126, 128, 132, 133, 134, 143f, 144, 166, 173, 182, 205, 221–2

Erotian 48, 57, 61, 67, 70, 71, 72, 73, 76, 77, 78, 90, 91, 92, 93, 95, 96, 97, 98, 107, 114, 115, 131, 132, 147, 189, 205, 222

Galen 10, 34, 36, 40, 48–9, 57, 59, 61, 63, 66, 70, 71, 72, 73, 74, 75, 76, 77, 78, 81, 83, 84, 85, 86, 88, 90, 92, 93, 94, 95, 96, 97, 98, 99, 100, 103, 104, 106, 107, 108, 109, 110, 111, 114, 115, 120, 121, 125, 126, 127, 128, 130, 131, 132, 133, 134, 135, 136, 137, 144, 145, 164, 182, 183, 184, 185, 190, 192–3, 194, 197, 198, 199, 209, 211, 216, 222–3

Hermogenes of Tarsus 49, 57, 61, 63, 70, 71, 73, 76, 79, 85, 90, 92, 94, 97, 98, 99, 104, 106, 107, 109, 114, 120, 125, 127, 132, 137, 144, 164, 174, 175, 205, 224

Hero 21, 48, 57, 61, 67, 68, 70, 71, 72, 73, 75, 76, 77, 78, 80, 85, 86, 88, 89, 92, 93, 94, 95, 96, 97, 98, 99, 101, 103, 106, 107, 109, 114, 115, 116, 117, 119, 120, 125, 126, 128, 132, 134, 135, 136, 143, 147, 154, 190, 202, 205, 208, 215, 224–5

Hipparchus 47, 51, 56–7, 58, 59, 60, 65, 68, 70, 71, 73, 74, 75, 76, 78, 79, 91, 92, 94, 95, 96, 97, 98, 100, 101, 114, 128, 131, 132, 143, 145, 225

Hypsicles 47, 51, 60, 64, 70, 72, 73, 76, 79, 88, 93, 99, 104, 145, 225–6

Philo of Byzantium 47–8, 52, 57, 59, 65, 67, 68, 70, 71, 73, 74, 75, 76, 78, 79, 80, 82, 83, 84, 85, 86, 88, 89, 92, 93, 94, 95, 97, 98, 99, 100, 104, 106, 107, 117, 118, 119, 120, 134, 137, 143, 144, 185, 190, 205, 208, 226

INDEX OF ANCIENT AUTHORS AND NAMES

242   Index of ancient authors and names

Ctesias 33, 37
Ctesibius 54, 80, 83, 89, 119
Cyrus (addressee) 49, 61

Dead Sea Scrolls 15
Demetrius, *De Elocutione* 15
Demetrius the Cynic 195
Democritus 89
Demonicus 55
Demosthenes 10, 64, 108, 121, 130, 131, 172
Diades 85
Didache 185
Dinarchus 35
Diocles, *On Burning Mirrors* 47, 51, 56, 76, 79
Diodorus Siculus 24, 25, 27, 29, 30, 31, 32, 33, 34, 37, 96, 109, 110, 156
Diogenes Laertius 28, 52, 53, 96, 203
Diogenianus 61
Dionysius (addressee) 49, 61
Dionysius of Halicarnassus 24, 25, 27, 28, 29, 30, 32, 33, 34, 37, 109, 110, 112, 139
Dionysius Thrax 46
Diophantus 49
Dositheus 51

Ecclesiastes 110
Ecclesiasticus 10, 15, 109, 111, 127, 148, 151–4, 157, 165, 166, 167
Eleazar 156
Empedocles 45
Ep.Jer. 15
Epaphroditus 27, 161
Ephorus 24, 32, 33, 64
Epigenes 61
Erasistratus 84
Eratosthenes 39, 54, 150
Esther 154
Euclid 42, 43, 44, 47
Eudoxou technē 60
Eugenianus 61, 63, 192
Eunapius 140
Eusebius 10, 25, 28, 118, 181, 186

Fabius Pictor, Q. 185

Galatians 138, 139
Gelon 47, 51, 60
Gorgias 32

Haggai 15
Hebrews 8, 15, 105, 109
Hecateus 26

Hephaestion 46
Heraclides (addressee) 48
Heraclides of Tarentum 47
Hermippus 108
Hermodorus 49
Herodian 30, 31, 32, 33, 110
Herodotus 20, 23, 24, 25, 26, 28, 29, 30, 32, 33, 37, 38, 39, 54, 112, 121, 144, 161, 166
Hesiod 45, 46, 82
Hippocrates 10, 42, 43, 44, 45, 47, 48, 82, 84, 101, 109, 111, 139, 166, 184, 203, 209
Hippocrates of Chios 203
Homer 82, 172, 176, 184, 194
Horace 149

Iamblichus 122
IG Rom. 131
Irenaeus 110
Isocrates 18, 19, 32, 53, 55–6, 64, 96, 132

Jason of Cyrene 148, 149
Jerome 115, 128, 183
Jesus 4, 201, 204, 205, 206, 207
Job 14
John, Epistles of 15
John, Gospel of 15, 201, 211
Joseph and Aseneth 154
Josephus 1, 4, 10, 15, 24, 25, 27, 28, 29, 30, 31, 32, 33, 35, 38–9, 96, 104, 108, 109, 110, 111, 112, 120, 121, 127, 128, 130, 138, 148, 160–4, 165, 166, 167, 173, 175, 181, 209, 211
Joshua 15
Judges 14
Judith 201
Julius Marcus 49, 61
Junia Theodora 191
Justin 112, 123, 206

bar Kochba letters 109, 140

Leviticus 14
Libanius 133
Livy 1
Lucian 23, 24, 26, 29, 30, 31, 32, 34, 35, 36, 102, 111
Lucretius 89
Luke–Acts 15, 145–6, 183, 203, 204, 206, 207
Lydia 191

II Maccabees 10, 15, 30, 109, 111, 112,

INDEX OF MODERN AUTHORS

245

INDEX OF SUBJECTS